Using Quattro Pro 2.0/3.0

Lisa Rosner & James Shuman

Mitchell **McGRAW-HILL**

New York St. Louis San Francisco Auckland Bogotá Caracas
Lisbon London Madrid Mexico Milan Montreal New Delhi Paris
San Juan Singapore Sydney Tokyo Toronto Watsonville

Mitchell **McGraw-Hill**
Watsonville, CA 95076

Using Quattro Pro 2.0/3.0

I 2 3 4 5 6 7 8 9 0 SEM SEM 9 0 9 8 7 6 5 4 3

ISBN 0-07-057588-6

Sponsoring editor: Roger Howell
Editorial assistant: Laurie Boudreau
Director of production: Jane Somers
Production assistant: Richard De Vitto
Project manager: Gary Palmatier, Ideas to Images
Interior designer: Gary Palmatier
Cover designer: Michael Rogondino
Copy editor: Anna Huff
Proofreader: Elizabeth von Radics
Composition and illustration: Ideas to Images
Printer and binder: Semline

Library of Congress Catalog Card Number 91-66877

Contents

Preface

The rapid rise of electronic spreadsheet programs has been extraordinary, even for the personal computer field which has itself grown remarkably over the past ten years. Whatever their chosen field, students will, almost certainly, work with a personal computer; the odds are very good that their work will involve using electronic spreadsheets. ***Using Quattro Pro 2.0/3.0*** provides a practical, hands-on guide to developing expertise in one of the fastest, most powerful—and most popular—electronic spreadsheet programs: Quattro Pro, versions 2.0 and 3.0.

Using Quattro Pro 2.0/3.0 teaches commands and features specific to Quattro Pro, but at the same time emphasizes the underlying concepts and uses of electronic spreadsheets in general, e.g., how a spreadsheet is used in data analysis, problem solving, forecasting, and report development. Students acquire skills in spreadsheet design, including how to plan a spreadsheet and how to avoid common pitfalls. The examples, applications, and exercises used in the text are drawn from management, marketing, accounting, finance, and personal budgeting.

This text assumes no prerequisites. It is designed to be used as a stand-alone textbook in a spreadsheet course using Quattro Pro 2.0 or 3.0, as a lab supplement in an introductory computer course, or by anyone who wishes to master spreadsheet programs to increase their own productivity.

FEATURES AND BENEFITS

As you review the chapters, please note these features and benefits:

- **Either version 2.0 or 3.0** of Quattro Pro can be used with this text. Those features not available in version 2.0, such as the WYSIWYG option, are clearly labeled.

- **Students gain an understanding** of electronic spreadsheets and graphs beyond the specific program taught. The concepts and skills learned are easily transferred to other software programs.

- **Step-by-step instructions** allow students to progress at their own pace from basic commands to more advanced concepts. Word lists, questions, and challenge exercises guide students through the material covered in each chapter.

- **Extensive use of screen displays** allows students to check what is shown on their monitor against screen displays provided in the text.

- **Students are guided** by a series of interactive steps that ask them to carry out an Action (keystrokes) and observe the Result (screen display). This reinforces learning and keeps students on track.
- **The data disk** packaged with the Instructor's Manual has 34 files, including practical exercises, comprehensive applications, spreadsheet templates, report setups, and challenge exercises. The data disk enables students to work with larger and more complex worksheets by conserving data entry.

TEXT ORGANIZATION

Using Quattro Pro 2.0/3.0 is presented as a self-paced tutorial. Each chapter begins with an overview of the material to be covered and introduces commands by developing specific applications. In each chapter the student works through several examples so new commands can be practiced as they are presented. We recommend that applications be assigned in the order they appear in the book. However, many of the chapter sections can stand alone and can be assigned to illustrate material an instructor has covered in class.

Chapter One: Introduction to the IBM PC Students develop skills necessary to operate an IBM PC or compatible and practice the most common DOS commands. They also learn about the components of a personal computer and how to use data disks to store and retrieve information.

Chapter Two: Electronic Spreadsheets Includes a description of spreadsheets and is designed to teach the most commonly used functions. It assumes no prior knowledge of spreadsheets.

Chapter Three: Worksheet Planning and Decision Making Discusses the planning process and includes step-by-step instructions for the development of practical applications.

Chapter Four: Putting Quattro Pro to Work Teaches students how to design presentation-quality spreadsheets and reports, develop graphs, and utilize the worksheet as a database. Upon completing this chapter students will have acquired the basic skills for using electronic spreadsheets in business and personal decision making.

Chapter Five: Advanced Features Includes creating a data entry form, writing macros, determining a frequency distribution, using the Solve For option, annotating graphs, working with more than one spreadsheet, and using Quattro Pro with other programs.

Chapter Six: Customizing Quattro Pro Students learn how to change default values, alter the menu structure, and undo mistakes they have made. They also learn how to take advantage of special hardware they may have as well as how to debug their macros.

Appendix Lists cell selector movement keys, shortcut keys, function keys, macro commands, and error messages.

By the time they complete this text, students should have a broad range of spreadsheet skills that will stand them in good stead as they prepare to develop their own applications. Of course, the ultimate test of any textbook comes when students are ready to move beyond it. We hope that ***Using Quattro Pro 2.0/3.0*** passes that test with flying colors.

Lisa Rosner
Pomona, NJ

James Shuman
Bellevue, WA

1 Introduction to the IBM PC

GETTING STARTED WITH THE IBM PC

This chapter helps you develop the skills necessary to operate an IBM PC or IBM-compatible microcomputer. You will learn about components of a microcomputer system, the programs used to operate the system, and how to store information using data disks. This chapter should be mastered before you continue with the rest of the book.

To complete this text you will need:

- An IBM PC (or compatible) computer with 640 kilobytes (640K) of memory, a hard disk drive, at least one floppy disk drive, and a graphics card.
- The Disk Operating System (DOS) version 2.0 or later. Version 3.1 is used here for most of the examples, but a brief discussion of the Microsoft Disk Operating System (MS-DOS) version 5.0 is included at the end of the chapter.
- A blank disk.
- The data disk provided by your instructor. The disk contains several files (documents such as budgets, sales reports, and financial statements) that utilize the Quattro Pro program taught in this text. You will use these files throughout the text and will also use the data disk to store your own work.
- For the following chapters, you will need Quattro Pro version 2.0 or 3.0.

The most common configuration for an IBM PC consists of a keyboard, system unit with hard disk drive and one or two floppy disk drives, a monitor, and possibly a mouse. Figure 1-1 illustrates this configuration.

Overcoming Computer Anxiety

If this is your first experience with a computer, you might feel anxious. A computer can seem very mysterious because it is able to do so much so quickly, and computer jargon can make even simple tasks sound very complicated. Don't worry: Developing expertise in computers is similar to learning any new skill. Follow the instructions, learn the basics, and practice, practice, practice. Soon even the jargon will seem crystal clear, and you will be able to help your friends get over their own computer anxiety.

As you prepare to use the computer, remember that it is simply a tool. You cannot do anything that will damage the computer, and, of course, it will not damage you. Other than typing at the keyboard, the only mechanical operations necessary are opening and closing disk drive doors, inserting and removing disks, and turning the computer and monitor on and off. Of course, a computer, like a stereo or a videocassette recorder (VCR), is an expensive electronic device, and you should treat it as gently as you would a stereo or VCR. Don't spill food or drinks on it, and if you ever have to carry it, do so carefully. Don't drop disks on the ground or in the pool or use them for Frisbee practice, unless you are sure you *never* want to use them again. Before long, using a computer will seem as easy as using a typewriter or calculator, and you will wonder how you ever got along without it.

Using a Microcomputer

The following example is used throughout this chapter to help explain the process of using a computer.

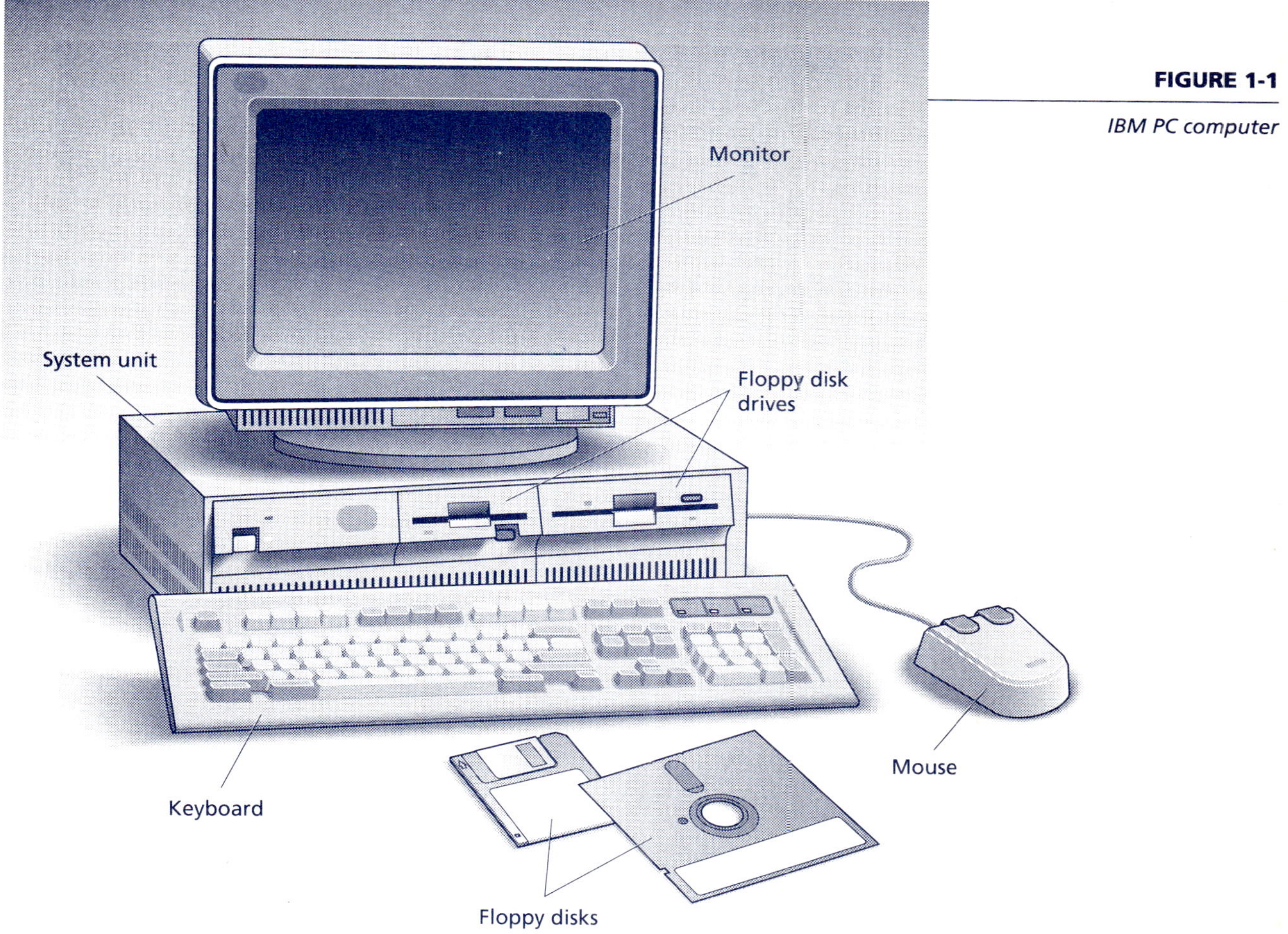

FIGURE 1-1

IBM PC computer

Susan, a college instructor, is interested in computerizing her grading system. Currently, she manually enters student names and scores in a gradebook and uses a calculator to add the scores and determine percentages for every student. Each time she enters new scores, she has to recalculate the totals. If she computerizes her grading system, totals and percentages will be automatically recalculated each time she records a new assignment or test, saving her a great deal of time. To move from the manual system to the computerized system, Susan will need:

- computer components (the **hardware**)
- instructions that control the operations of the computer and perform necessary calculations (the **software** or **program**)
- student names and scores (the **data**)
- knowledge of the **procedures** necessary to use the hardware and software (acquired through reading books like this one)
- a person to work with the above equipment (a **user**—in this case, Susan herself)

These elements work together through the steps used in processing data: input, processing, and output. **Input** involves entering program instructions and data into the computer. **Processing** is what happens to data after it is entered; for example, it is calculated, compared, edited, and so on. Once data is processed, it may be displayed, printed, or stored: This is the **output**. Figure 1-2 illustrates these data processing steps and shows the hardware component related to each step.

FIGURE 1-2

Hardware components associated with input, processing, and output

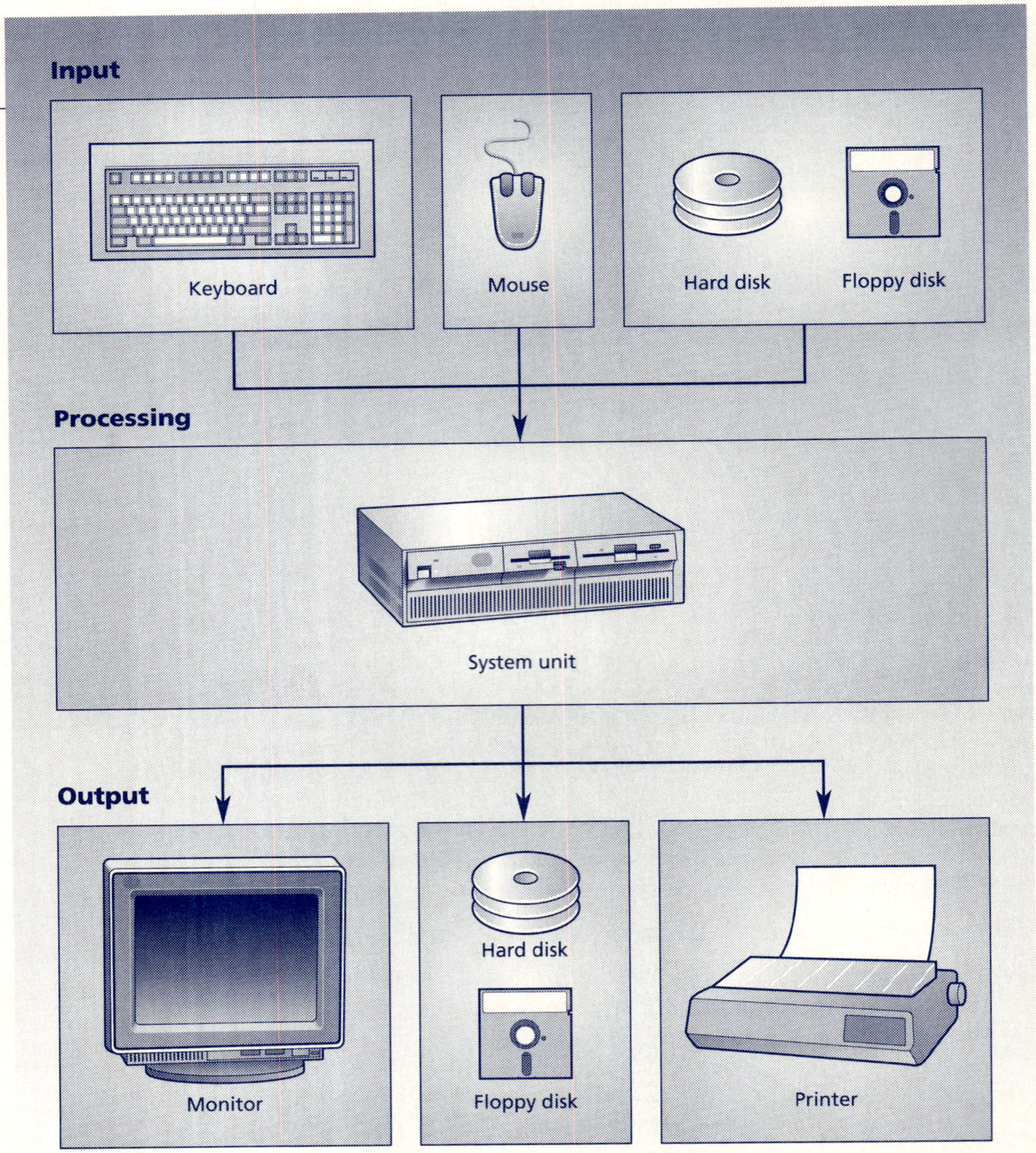

Input To computerize the grade report, Susan's first step is to load the program into the computer. She has decided to use an electronic spreadsheet program that contains the instructions for calculating rows and columns of numbers—ideal for working with a grade sheet. An electronic spreadsheet comes on one or more **disks** (see Figure 1-3), a medium used to store instructions and data used by the computer. To load the program from the disk into the computer, you use a disk drive, which copies the instructions from the disk into the memory of the computer. Once loaded, the program will present Susan with a framework for typing in the data (student names and scores) or entering it using both the keyboard and a mouse.

Processing As data for a student is typed in, the computer carries out the instructions to perform calculations, such as adding the scores and determining percentages.

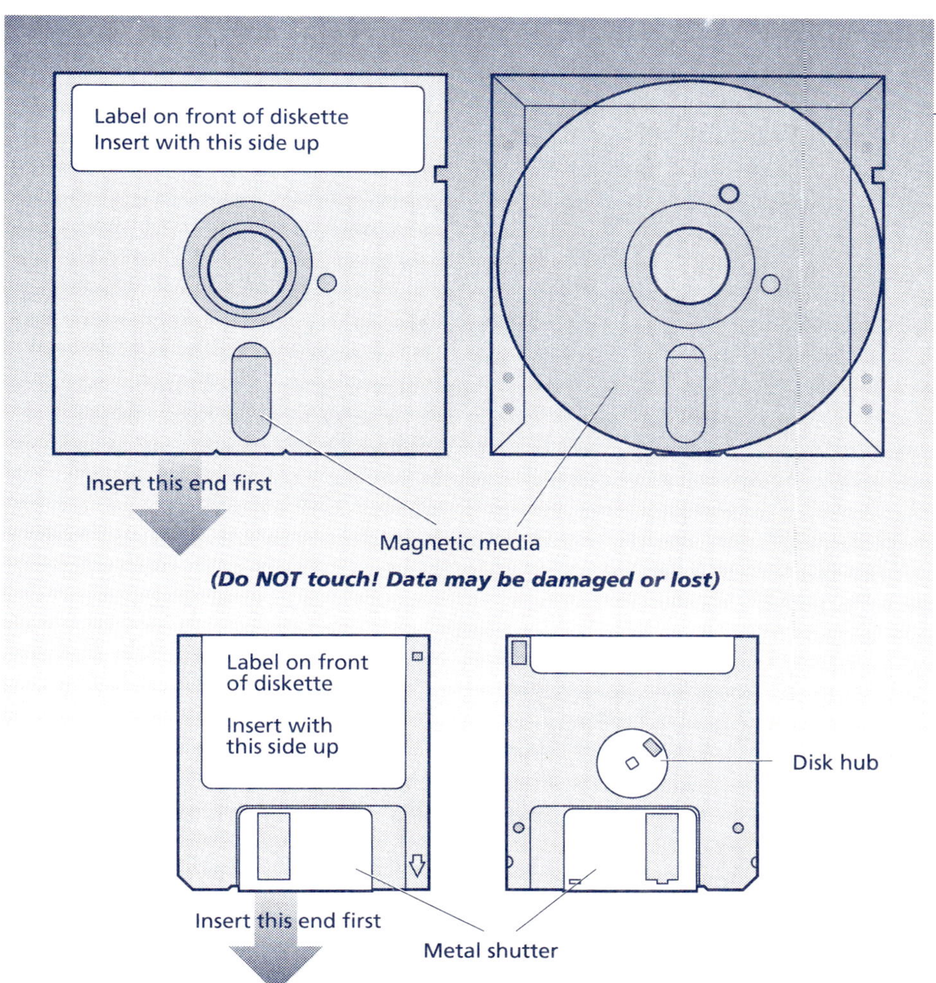

FIGURE 1-3

Floppy disks. At top is a 5¼-inch disk with a cutaway view of the magnetic media inside the jacket; below are front and back views of a 3½-inch disk.

Output Output can be obtained in three primary ways when using a microcomputer: through the monitor, a disk drive, or a printer. As Susan enters the student names, scores, and other data, it is displayed on the monitor. She also can save the grade report by using a disk drive to record the information onto a **data disk**, the main storage medium for data developed on a computer. Unlike the disks containing a program, data disks are blank when purchased. Disks come in two sizes, 5.25" and 3.5", and two types, double density and high density. 3.5" disks, developed more recently, can hold more data, but some older computers require 5.25" disks. Disks containing software such as electronic spreadsheets can cost anywhere between $50 and $2,000, depending on the software. Blank disks, though, cost between $1 and $3. The third way for Susan to store the grade report is on paper, by printing it on a printer attached to the computer. This is called a **printout** or **hard copy**.

The following sections explain each of the hardware components that make up a microcomputer, the programs that provide the instructions for the computer, and the procedures needed to operate the computer.

HARDWARE COMPONENTS

Keyboard

Figure 1-4 shows the IBM PC keyboard. It is made up of standard typewriter keys, function keys, special keys, and ten-key numeric pad/cursor movement keys. Learning how to use the function keys and the special keys is important, because software programs often use these as "shortcut keys" to carry out certain tasks. The keys used will vary from software program to software program. For instance, the F2 function key may be used in a word processing program to save your work, whereas in a spreadsheet program it may be used to edit your data. Instructions that come with the program, called **manuals** or **documentation**, explain the use of these keys.

Refer to Figure 1-4 as you read the following description of the keyboard. Please note, though, that computers are manufactured by many different companies, and keyboard design can vary. Function keys, for example, may appear in two columns on the left side of the keyboard or in a row across the top. Locate the function and special keys on the keyboard you will be using.

Key	Operation
Standard Typewriter Keys	
Tab	Press to move the **cursor**, the blinking indicator of the screen position where the next keystroke will be placed, to the next tab position to the right.
⇧ Shift	Hold down and press another key for an uppercase letter or for the second (upper) character on a key.
Letters, numbers, special characters	Similar to a typewriter keyboard.
CapsLock	Press to lock keyboard into uppercase. (***NOTE:*** Only the *letters* are locked into uppercase, not the numbers and other keys.

FIGURE 1-4

The IBM PC keyboard. At top is the AT-style keyboard, below it the enhanced 101 keyboard.

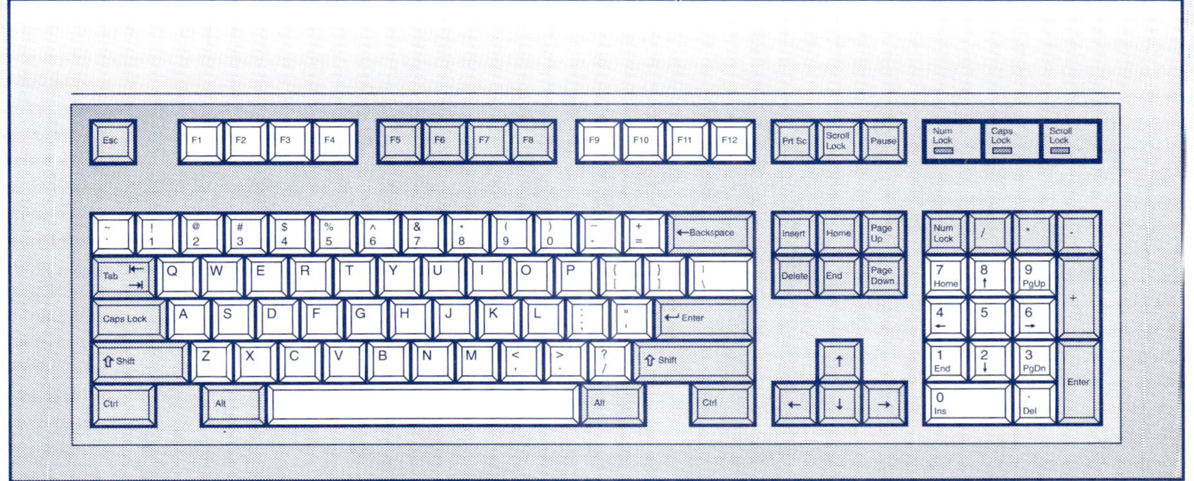

For example, to type a $, you must still hold down the Shift key while typing 4, even if you have pressed (CAPS LOCK).) Press again to return to lowercase. On some keyboards, a small light goes on when (CAPS LOCK) is in the "on" position.

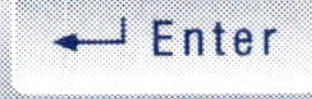

Used as a Return key, similar to a return on a typewriter, to move the cursor to the beginning of the next line. Also used to (ENTER) as specified by the program in operation.

The Backspace key, usually found on the top right corner of the standard typewriter keyboard, should not be confused with the left-arrow key on the numeric keypad. It is similar to a typewriter backspace key and can be used to edit data as it is being typed. If you make a mistake while typing, press (BACKSPACE) and the cursor will move back and erase one character at a time.

Function Keys

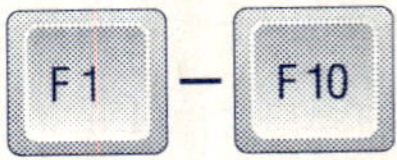

Perform specific functions that depend on the program being used.

Special Keys

Perform specific functions that depend on the program being used.

Numeric Keypad/Cursor Movement Keys

Used for entering numbers and performing calculations when (NUM LOCK) is on. When the (NUM LOCK) key is off, the keys within the numeric keypad act as cursor movement keys.

Press once to change the numeric keypad from cursor movement mode to numeric mode. Press again to return to cursor movement mode. On some keyboards, a small light indicates when (NUM LOCK) is on.

Remember, the function keys and special keys vary in meaning depending on the program being used. In Chapter 2, you learn how these keys work with Quattro Pro.

Mouse

In addition to a keyboard, the computer may use a **mouse** or **trackball** as an input device (see Figure 1-5). In many programs, as you move the mouse on a special **mouse pad**, an arrow or pointer moves on the monitor screen. By positioning the arrow properly on the screen and pressing the mouse button

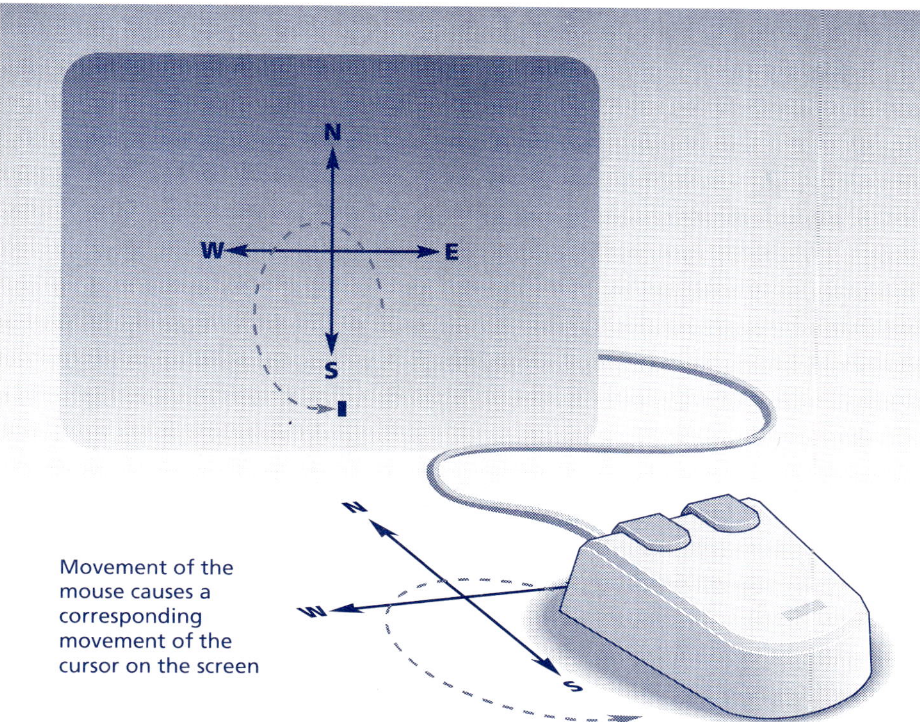

FIGURE 1-5

Mouse

either once (called a **click**) or twice (a **double click**), you can choose features of many programs. See Chapter 6 to find out how to use a mouse with Quattro Pro.

System Unit

Figure 1-6 shows the system unit. There are several components within the system unit; the most important are the main memory, the central processing unit (CPU), and the disk drives.

Main Memory When program instructions and data are entered into the computer, they are stored in the system unit's **main memory**. This storage area is temporary, and the data entered is lost when the computer is turned off. For that reason, data is usually permanently stored on a disk. In the grade report example, Susan would start off by entering the electronic spreadsheet program into the main memory of the computer and then typing in the student scores.

Central Processing Unit (CPU) The **CPU** is the "brains" of the computer. Calculations (such as adding scores and determining percentages) and logical comparisons (such as who has the highest score in the class) are carried out in this part of the system unit. In addition, the CPU supervises the operations of the computer by specifying the order in which various functions are carried out.

Disk Drives **Disk drives** are storage devices that allow the user to (1) load instructions into the computer from program disks and (2) save and retrieve

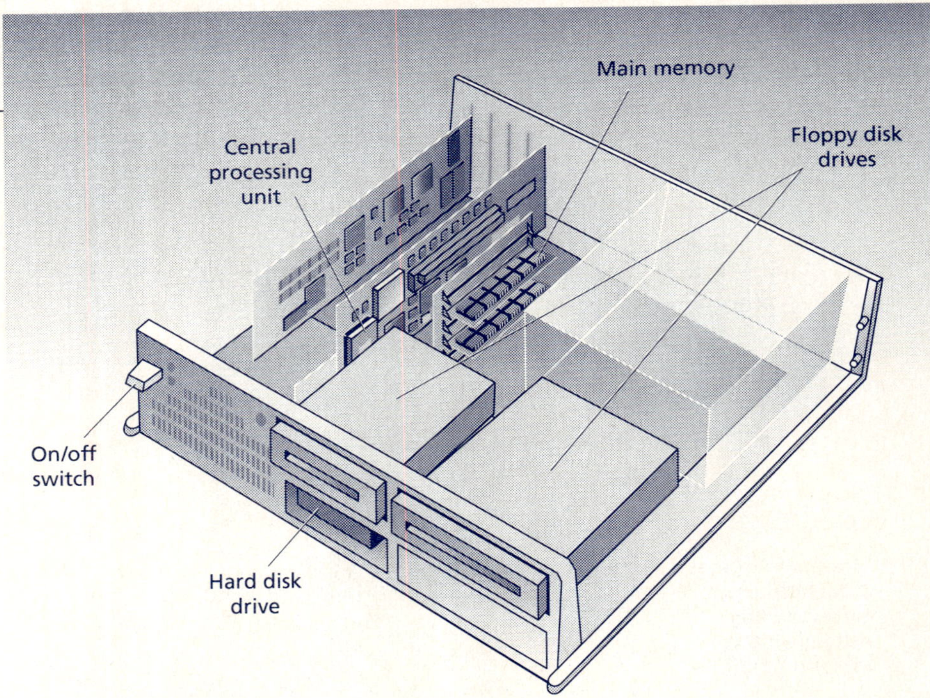

FIGURE 1-6

System unit

data using data disks. Disk drives "read" disks just as tape players and VCRs "read" tapes and videos. Drives come in two sizes, 5.25" and 3.5", to match the two sizes of disks.

The on/off switch for the system unit is located either on the rear of the right side or on the front.

Monitor

The monitor, as pictured in Figure 1-7, provides a "window" into the main memory of the computer. As Susan enters the students' scores, the data is displayed on the monitor. The monitor also displays information helpful to the person operating the program. For instance, Susan could follow displayed messages, called **prompts**, that lead her through the steps necessary to print a copy of the grade report. Software used for business applications typically provides one screen area in which data is entered and another area where messages are displayed. ***NOTE:*** It is important to watch the monitor for any instructions, prompts, and other messages from the software program in use.

Disk Drives and Disks

Computers generally have one or more disk drives that read the removable disks, often called **floppy disks.** Some disk drives are shown in Figure 1-8. A computer may also have a **hard disk drive** that reads a **hard disk**, which is built into the system unit and cannot be removed (see Figure 1-6). Older computers tend to have two floppy disk drives, but the more usual arrangement for recently built computers is one hard disk drive and one floppy disk drive. Disk drives and disks, whether floppy or hard, work in a manner similar to a tape

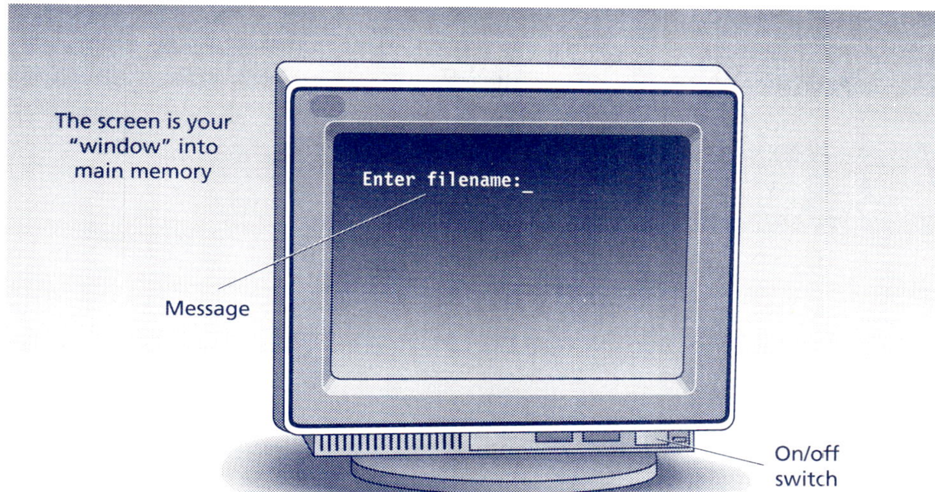

FIGURE 1-7

Monitor

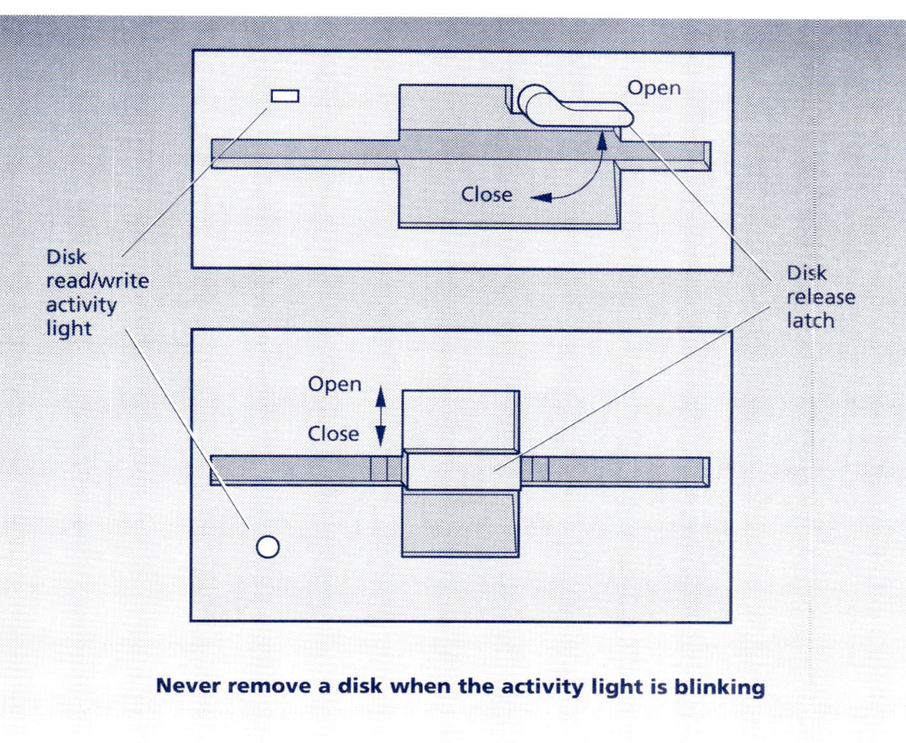

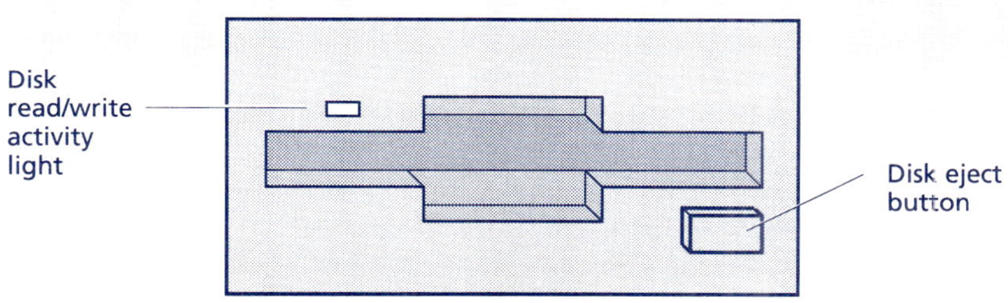

FIGURE 1-8

Floppy disk drives. At top are two types of drives for 5¼-inch disks; below is a drive for 3½-inch disks.

recorder and tape. A tape recorder moves a tape to record or play sounds on the tape. Similarly, a disk drive rotates a disk to save or retrieve data on the disk.

Always handle floppy disks with care to avoid losing program instructions or data. To insert a disk into a disk drive, place your thumb on the label and, with the label side up and toward you, slide the disk into the drive. If the drive has a door or latch, close it. Each disk drive has a light located on the front of the drive (see Figure 1-8). When this light is on, the motor in the drive is in operation. Do not insert or remove a disk when the in-use light is on. To do so could damage the disk.

When working with disk drives, you should distinguish between them in the same way a computer does. If there is only one floppy disk drive, it is referred to as **drive A**; if there are two, they are referred to as **drive A** and **drive B**. If the drives are positioned side by side, drive A is usually to the left (see Figure 1-6). If they are stacked one above the other, drive A is usually on the top. If there is a hard disk, it is referred to as **drive C**. Even if there is only one floppy disk drive, the hard drive is still referred to as drive C, not drive B.

Hard Disk Drives A hard disk drive, like a floppy disk drive, has an in-use light on the front so you can tell when it is in operation. Hard disks operate more quickly and have more storage capacity than floppy disks. A 5.25" double-density floppy disk can hold approximately 360,000 characters of data (this book can be put on two 5.25" floppy disks). A 3.5" double-density floppy disk can hold approximately twice that many characters, so this book would fit on only one. A 5.25" high-density disk can hold approximately 1,200,000 characters, and a 3.5" high-density disk can hold approximately 1,440,000 characters. Hard disks, in comparison, can hold from 20 to 200 million characters of data. With such a large storage capacity, an individual file—a chapter of this book, for example—could easily get lost among many other files. For that reason, hard disks are usually organized into sections.

Directories and Subdirectories A hard drive can be divided into sections and subsections, called **directories** and **subdirectories**, each with its own set of program instructions or data. In our example, Susan, without a hard disk drive, would use several floppy disks to store her work. She would keep the disks with instructions and data for her electronic spreadsheet separate from the disks with instructions and data for her word processor. With a hard disk, she could still keep the instructions and data separate, by placing them in separate sections, or directories, of her hard disk. She might keep the instructions and data for Quattro Pro in a directory called QPRO and the instructions and data for her word processor in a directory called PCWORD. She might also have a separate directory for other work done for her classes, called COURSES. If she wanted to keep the scores for different classes separate, she could create subdirectories of her QPRO directory, each of which would store data for a different class.

This structure is often called a **tree** structure (see Figure 1-9). At the bottom is the **root** directory. Above it are, in this example, Susan's three main directories, QPRO, PCWORD, and COURSES. Branching out from COURSES are the subdirectories for Susan's three courses, MGMT101A, MGMT101B, and MGMT101C. You cannot really see the tree structure on the hard disk. But you can use software to command the computer to go from one directory to another.

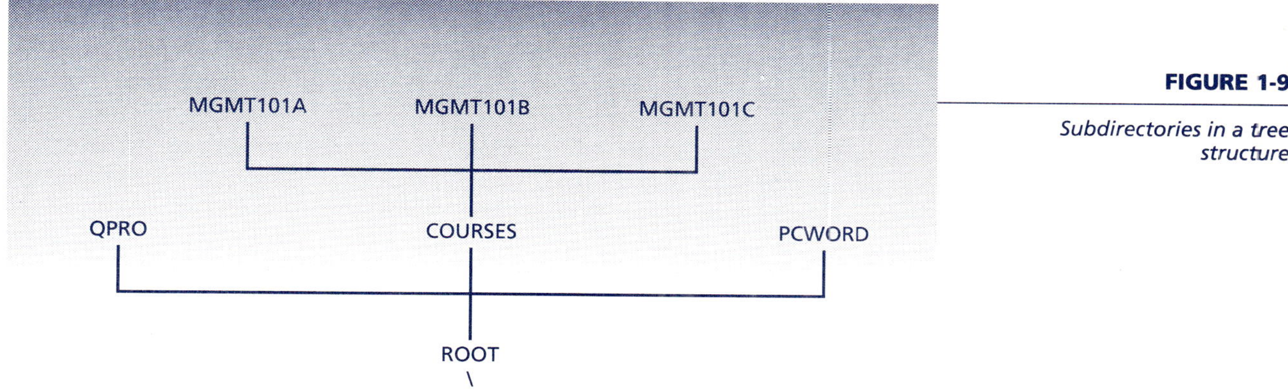

FIGURE 1-9

Subdirectories in a tree structure

SOFTWARE (PROGRAM INSTRUCTIONS)

For the hardware components of a computer to operate, there must be a set of program instructions for the computer to follow. Two types of programs, the **applications software** and the **systems software**, are needed. Applications software is the name given to programs designed to be applied to specific tasks, such as word processing or electronic spreadsheets. Quattro Pro is an example of applications software.

The rest of this chapter describes systems software, DOS, that contains the instructions that control computer input and output. Systems software is the link among the system unit, disk drives, hard disk, monitor, and printer. Systems software must be loaded into the computer's main memory before any application software. It can be loaded from a floppy disk drive, but most computers with hard disks load DOS automatically when the computer is turned on.

DISK OPERATING SYSTEM (DOS)

The systems software for the IBM PC and compatibles is called DOS. DOS stands for **Disk Operating System**. Before you use any applications software, DOS must be loaded into the main memory of the computer.

NOTE: In any sequence of activities, carefully follow all instructions.

Loading DOS

Computers with a Hard Disk Drive If the computer you are using has a hard disk drive, DOS is installed on it. When you turn on the computer, DOS is loaded from the hard drive into the memory of the computer. Make sure drive A is empty and the drive A door is open, and then turn on the monitor and the system unit.

The first thing you will hear is the fan inside the computer that helps keep it cool. Nothing visible happens for a few moments while the computer is executing a built-in diagnostic program that makes sure the components are in working order and determines the memory capacity of the computer. Next you will notice a blinking cursor in the upper left of the screen, and the drive C in-use light will come on. You will hear a whirring noise as the disk drive rotates the disk and loads the DOS instructions into main memory.

Menus If you are using a computer in a college computing lab, it probably has been set up so that the first thing you see on the monitor is a **menu**, or a list of choices. To complete this chapter, you will need to choose an item called "DOS Utilities" or "DOS Commands" or "Exit to C> Prompt." Follow the instructions on the screen to choose that menu item, or ask your instructor or lab assistant for help.

Date and Time If you do not see a menu when you turn on the computer, you may see a message prompting you to enter the current date and time into the memory of the computer. It is wise to always specify the date and time, because when you save your work, the date and time are saved with it, which will allow you to list a directory of your work later and see when each file was created or updated. The message will read:

```
Current date is Wed 1-01-1992
Enter new date (mm-dd-yy):_
```

(***NOTE:*** The actual date may vary.)

At this point you have two choices:

1. If the date is incorrect, type in the date in the following format: mm-dd-yy (e.g., January 1, 1992, would be entered as 01-01-92). Press ↵.
2. If the displayed date is correct, press ↵. This loads the displayed date.

Then the prompt for the time appears:

```
Current time is 0:03:05.15
Enter new time:_
```

(***NOTE:*** The actual time may vary.)

Again, you have two choices:

1. If the time is incorrect, type in the time in the following format: hh:mm:ss (e.g., 2:30 P.M. would be entered as 14:30:00). Press ↵.
2. If the displayed time is correct, press ↵. This loads the displayed time.

The next thing to appear is the C> prompt, as shown in Figure 1-10.

Some computers keep track of the date and time automatically, and do not prompt you to enter them. In that case, the first thing you will see when you turn on the computer is the C> prompt. To check that the computer has loaded the correct date:

Type DATE (***NOTE:*** You can use upper- or lowercase letters.)

Press ↵

You will be prompted for the date, as previously described.

To check that the computer has loaded the correct time:

Type TIME

Press ↵

You will be prompted for the time.

The C> prompt signifies that DOS has been loaded into the memory of the computer, the computer is working with drive C, and it is waiting for

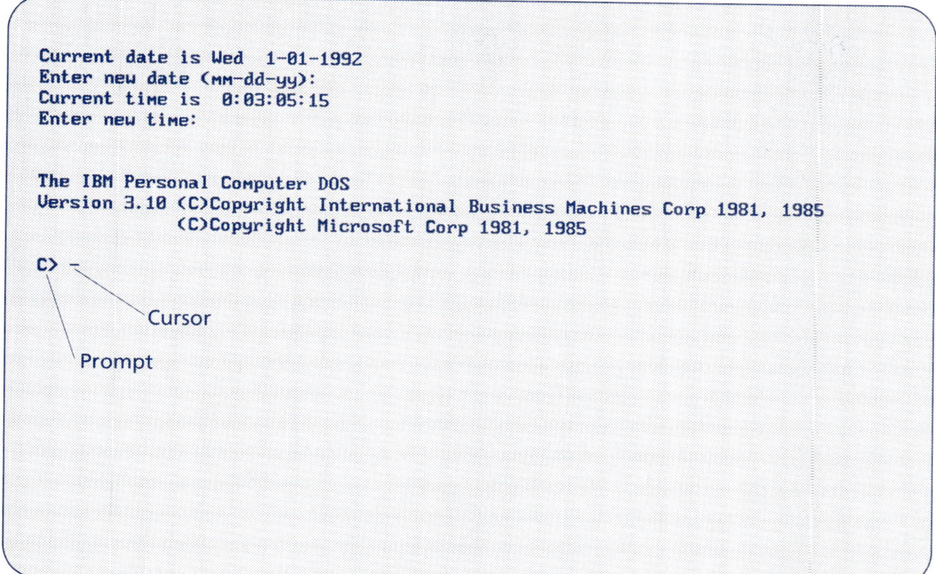

FIGURE 1-10

Loading DOS

further instructions from the user (you). At this point you could execute a DOS command as explained in the following section or load an applications program such as Quattro Pro (as explained in Chapter 2).

DOS Commands

In addition to controlling the input/output process for the computer, DOS allows you to carry out some useful functions. You can:

- Change the date and time within the main memory of the computer, as described above.
- Obtain a **directory**, or listing, of all the **files** you have saved. A **file** is a piece of work, such as a letter, grade report, or other document, that you have developed and saved on your data disk.
- Format a blank or used disk so it works with the IBM PC to store data.
- Copy a file, or many files, from one disk to another.
- Copy the entire contents of your data disk onto another disk. This is called **backing up** your disk and prevents the loss of your work should something happen to the original disk.
- Delete a file from your data disk.
- Move between different directories on your hard disk.
- Display a prompt to let you know what directory the computer is working in.

Let's work with these commands. The DATE and TIME commands were explained earlier. The DIR (directory) command obtains a listing of the files on the student data disk or any other disk; the FORMAT command formats your blank disk; the COPY command copies a file, or a set of files, from one disk to another; the DISKCOPY command creates a backup copy of an entire disk; the DEL command deletes a file from a disk; the CD command moves between directories on your hard disk; and the PROMPT PG command tells you what directory the computer is working in. The FORMAT, COPY, DISKCOPY, and DEL commands require the use of your blank disk, which will serve as a backup to the data disk distributed by your instructor.

Error Messages As you type these commands in the sections that follow, you may make an occasional typing mistake. If you do, you will get the following error message.

```
Bad command or file name
```

This does not mean you have done anything really "bad"—to DOS, any command it cannot understand is a "bad command." If, for example, you typed DATW instead of DATE, DOS would tell you it was a bad command or file name (see Figure 1-11). If you get this error message, first look carefully at what you typed to see where the mistake is. Then, retype the command correctly and press ↵.

Obtaining a Directory (DIR) As mentioned earlier, the student data disk distributed by your instructor contains several files—documents such as budgets, sales reports, and financial statements. These files were developed using the Quattro Pro program and then saved onto the data disk. You will use each of these files as you complete the following chapters. To get a listing of the names of these files, use the DOS command DIR (directory). With the data disk in drive A and the C> prompt displayed, complete the following steps.

Type DIR A:

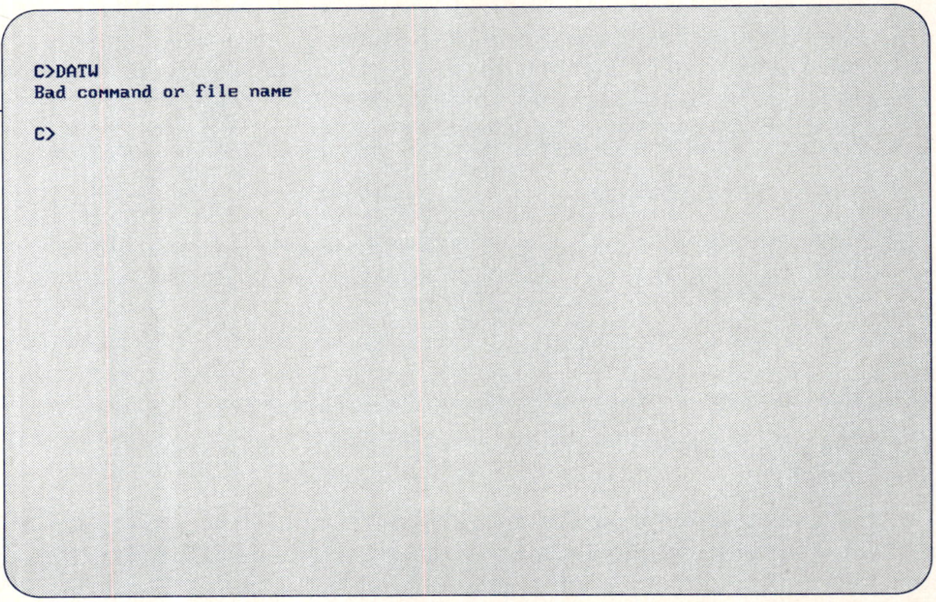

FIGURE 1-11

"Bad command" error message

```
C>DATW
Bad command or file name

C>
```

DIR is the DOS command to obtain a directory, and A: signifies that the directory is to be found on the data disk in drive A (see Figure 1-12a). ***NOTE:*** There is no distinction between uppercase and lowercase letters when using DOS commands. This command could have been entered dir a:.

Press ↵

The screen displays a list of the files on the data disk in drive A (see Figure 1-12b). These are the files you will use as you work through the chapters

```
C>DATE
Current date is Tue  1-01-1980
Enter new date (mm-dd-yy):

C>DIR A:
```

FIGURE 1-12a

DIR (directory) command

```
AUTOMAC  WQ1      3309 07-31-91   3:05p
REPORT   WQ1      6892 09-28-91  11:12a
SALES    WQ1      1895 07-31-91   3:31p
SALESRPT WQ1      3858 07-31-91   3:31p
SCORES   WQ1      2067 07-31-91   3:32p
CIRCREF  WQ1      1643 07-31-91   3:07p
CUSTOMER WQ1      3111 07-31-91   3:07p
DOWJONES WQ1      2082 07-31-91   3:08p
EMPLOYEE WQ1      2054 07-31-91   3:08p
SICKLEVE WQ1      1840 07-31-91   3:32p
FORECAST WQ1      4137 07-31-91   3:21p
FORECST2 WQ1      4137 07-31-91   3:22p
GRADERPT WQ1      2674 07-31-91   3:11p
GRADES   WQ1      2723 07-31-91   3:12p
INVOICE  WQ1      2449 09-28-91   6:19p
INVOICE2 WQ1      2482 07-31-91   3:14p
LABBUDGT WQ1      6135 07-31-91   3:15p
STORE1   WQ1      2402 07-31-91   3:33p
STORE2   WQ1      2432 07-31-91   3:34p
STORE3   WQ1      2450 07-31-91   3:34p
TESTING  WQ1      3039 07-31-91   3:35p
       32 File(s)     245760 bytes free

C:\->
```

FIGURE 1-12b

Directory of data disk

FIGURE 1-12c

DIR /P command (pause)

```
SALESFIG WQ1     3298   8-08-91   4:13p
LINKSALE WQ1     2906   8-08-91   6:39p
CARPAYMT WQ1     2309   8-08-91   3:22p
LEASE    WQ1     2727   7-31-91   3:23p
LOANPAY  WQ1     8562   7-31-91   3:24p
MEMBERS  WQ1     2371   7-31-91   3:24p
MO_SALES WQ1     1922   7-31-91   3:25p
MO_SALS2 WQ1     3816   7-31-91   3:25p
PASSFAIL WQ1     3484   7-31-91   3:27p
PRODSALE WQ1     3052   8-06-91   3:34p
AUTOMAC  WQ1     3309   7-31-91   3:05p
REPORT   WQ1     6918   7-31-91   3:29p
SALES    WQ1     1895   7-31-91   3:31p
SALESRPT WQ1     3858   7-31-91   3:31p
SCORES   WQ1     2067   7-31-91   3:32p
CIRCREF  WQ1     1643   7-31-91   3:07p
CUSTOMER WQ1     3111   7-31-91   3:07p
DOWJONES WQ1     2082   7-31-91   3:08p
EMPLOYEE WQ1     2054   7-31-91   3:08p
SICKLEVE WQ1     1840   7-31-91   3:32p
FORECAST WQ1     4137   7-31-91   3:21p
FORECST2 WQ1     4137   7-31-91   3:22p
GRADERPT WQ1     2674   7-31-91   3:11p
Strike a key when ready . . .
```

that follow. Along with each file is listed the amount of disk space that file occupies in number of characters (called **bytes**) and the date and time the file was last saved.

As the file names were being listed on the screen, you may have noticed them move (**scroll**) up. This happens because the screen can display only 23 file names at a time. If there are more than 23, the computer keeps listing them until the last name is displayed. There are two other ways to display a list of file names. The DIR /P command pauses after one screenful of file names (23) has been displayed. Then you would be prompted to press a key to display the next 23 names, and so forth, until the end of the list (Figure 1-12c). The DIR /W command displays the file names across the width of the screen as well as down it. This allows you to view more names at once (Figure 1-12d). Practice these commands:

Type DIR A:/P

Press ↵

The first 23 file names on the disk are displayed, and the following message appears at the bottom of the screen.

`Strike a key when ready...`

Press ↵

The remaining names are displayed and the C> prompt appears.

Type DIR A:/W

Press ↵

All the files are displayed across the screen. However, the date and time each file was last saved is omitted with this command.

```
C:\->DIR A:/W

 Volume in drive A has no label
 Directory of A:\

PRODSALE.WQ1     CARPAYMT.WQ1     SALESFIG.WQ1     LEASE.WQ1        LINKSALE.WQ1
!BLANK.WQ1       LOANPAY.WQ1      MEMBERS.WQ1      MO_SALES.WQ1     MO_SALS2.WQ1
PASSFAIL.WQ1     AUTOMAC.WQ1      REPORT.WQ1       SALES.WQ1        SALESRPT.WQ1
SCORES.WQ1       CIRCREF.WQ1      CUSTOMER.WQ1     DOWJONES.WQ1     EMPLOYEE.WQ1
SICKLEVE.WQ1     FORECAST.WQ1     FORECST2.WQ1     GRADERPT.WQ1     GRADES.WQ1
INVOICE.WQ1      INVOICE2.WQ1     LABBUDGT.WQ1     STORE1.WQ1       STORE2.WQ1
STORE3.WQ1       TESTING.WQ1
       32 File(s)      247808 bytes free

C:\->
```

FIGURE 1-12d

DIR /W command (wide)

Formatting a Blank Disk (FORMAT) A blank data disk must be **formatted** in order to be used. When you format a disk, you are preparing it for use with a particular type of computer and operating system. The disk is divided into sections, called **tracks** and **sectors**, to make it easier for the computer to store and find data. (You won't be able to see the tracks and sectors on the disk, but the computer will recognize them.)

Complete the steps below to format a blank disk. The C> prompt should be showing on the monitor and you should have a brand-new blank disk ready to use. Drive A should be empty, so remove the data disk from drive A if you have not already done so. (See Figure 1-13.)

Type FORMAT A:

NOTE: Depending on the type of disk drive you are using, you may need to type FORMAT A:/4. Check with your instructor or lab assistant.

Press ↵

The following message will be displayed.

```
Insert new diskette for drive A: and strike ENTER when ready
```

Place the blank disk in drive A and close the drive door, if necessary.

CAUTION: When you format a disk, all of the information on the disk is destroyed. Therefore, be sure that the disk is blank or that there is no data on it that you wish to save. If you are not sure whether there is data on the disk, use the DIR A: command to find out. It is a good idea to format only brand-new disks until you become familiar with computers.

Press ↵

FIGURE 1-13

FORMAT command

```
C>FORMAT A:
Insert new diskette for drive A:
and strike ENTER when ready

Formatting...Format complete

    362496 bytes total disk space
    362496 bytes available on disk

Format another (Y/N)?N
C>
```

The in-use light will come on for drive A as the disk is being formatted. The process takes a few moments; depending on the computer, it may tell you how the formatting is progressing. When the DOS program is finished formatting the blank disk, a message appears on the screen telling you the amount of total disk space and the amount available on the disk. If you have formatted a 5.25" disk, the message will read either:

```
362496 bytes total disk space
362496 bytes available on disk
```

or:

```
1213952 bytes total disk space
1213952 bytes available on disk
```

If you have formatted a 3.5" disk, the message will read either:

```
730112 bytes total disk space
730112 bytes available on disk
```

or:

```
1457664 bytes total disk space
1457664 bytes available on disk
```

This indicates how many characters (bytes) can be saved on the disk. Near the bottom of the screen is the message:

```
Format another (Y/N)?
```

Type N (for no—"Y" would mean yes)

You will be prompted for the volume label. For now, just press ↵.

The C> prompt will appear, and you are ready to proceed with another DOS command. Before continuing you need to label your newly created data disk. Remove the disk from drive A. Use the label that came with the disk and write the following information. (***CAUTION:*** If the label is already affixed to the disk, do not use a hard-point pen or pencil, as it may damage the disk. Use a soft-tip pen, such as a felt pen.)

NAME:

DATE:

BACKUP DATA DISK

Affix the label to the disk. See Figure 1-3 for the usual location. You now have two data disks ready to be used. One is the data disk provided by your instructor, and the other is your newly formatted backup disk.

Copying a File (COPY) To make sure that you don't lose any of your work, you need to make backup copies of your files. In addition, as you save more and more files on a single disk, you may find it useful to copy a file from one data disk to another. In the example we have been using, Susan may wish to separate her grade reports by course level at the end of the term. Thus, she would copy all of the freshman classes to one disk, the sophomore classes to another disk, and so forth. The DOS COPY command can be used to copy a file between any two disks, even if they are of different sizes or one is a floppy and the other is a hard disk. To illustrate this, you will copy a file called GRADES.WQ1 from the data disk to the backup disk you have just formatted (Figure 1-14).

If you have two floppy disk drives: To duplicate a file from your data disk, perform the following (make sure the C> prompt is showing).

Place the data disk in drive A

Place the newly formatted backup disk in drive B

NOTE: If the floppy disks are different sizes, you will have to place them in the drives that fit each size. Check with your instructor on how to proceed.

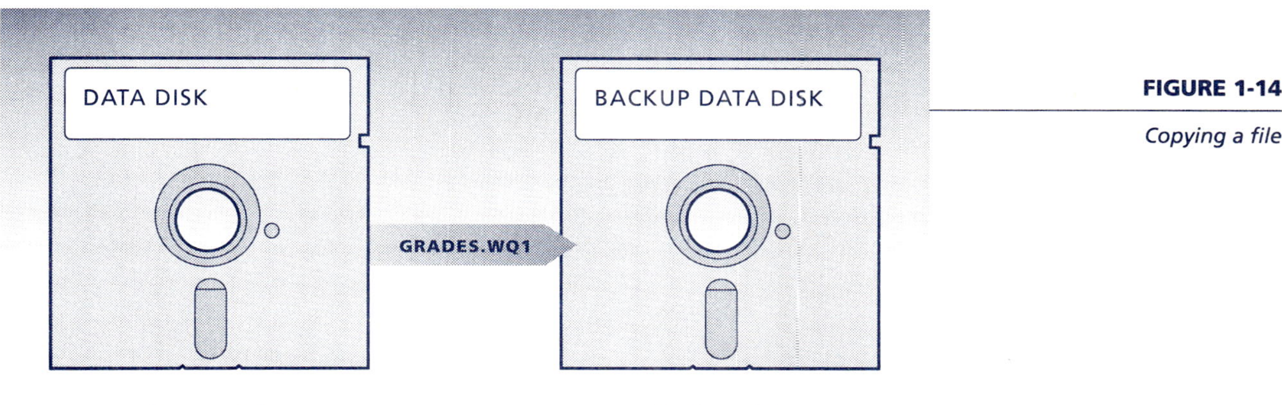

FIGURE 1-14

Copying a file

FIGURE 1-15

COPY command

```
C>COPY A:GRADES.WQ1 B:
        1 File(s) copied

C>DIR B:

 Volume in drive B has no label
 Directory of  B:\

GRADES   WQ1      2723   7-31-91    3:12p
        1 File(s)     359424 bytes free

C>
```

Type COPY A:GRADES.WQ1 B:

The in-use light comes on for drive A as the GRADES.WQ1 file is read into the memory of the computer. Then the in-use light comes on for drive B as GRADES.WQ1 is copied to the disk in drive B. The following message appears.

1 File(s) copied

You now have a copy of the file named GRADES.WQ1 on each of the data disks. Use the DIR command to obtain a directory of the newly formatted disk. (See Figure 1-15.)

Type DIR B:

 GRADES.WQ1 is displayed as the only file on the disk

If you have only one floppy disk drive: What if you have only one floppy disk drive? How can you copy a file from one disk to another?

You can copy the file by taking advantage of the way that the computer recognizes disk drives. As you already know, if the computer has two floppy disk drives, one is drive A and the other is drive B. But if the computer has only one floppy disk drive, it will recognize that drive as drive A *and* drive B, depending on how you refer to it. You can therefore use the COPY command as though you had two disk drives, so long as you follow the directions the computer gives you to switch disks at the proper time.

To illustrate this, perform the following (make sure the C> prompt is showing).

Place the data disk in drive A

```
C>COPY A:GRADES.WQ1 B:

Insert diskette for drive B: and strike
any key when ready

        1 File(s) copied

C>DIR B:

 Volume in drive B has no label
 Directory of  B:\

GRADES   WQ1      2723   7-31-91   3:12p
        1 File(s)    359424 bytes free

C>
```

FIGURE 1-16a

COPY with only one floppy disk drive

Type COPY A:GRADES.WQ1 B:

↵

The in-use light comes on for the drive as the GRADES.WQ1 file is read into the memory of the computer. Then, the following message appears.

```
Insert diskette for drive B: and strike
any key when ready
```

This is your signal that the computer, having read the file into memory, is now considering the floppy disk drive to be drive B and is looking for the disk to copy the file to.

Replace the data disk in the floppy disk drive with the backup disk

↵

The in-use light comes on as GRADES.WQ1 is copied to the disk in the floppy disk drive, now recognized by the computer as drive B. The following message appears.

```
1 File(s) copied
```

You now have a copy of the file named GRADES.WQ1 on each of the data disks. Use the DIR command to obtain a directory of the newly formatted disk.

Type DIR B:

↵ GRADES.WQ1 is displayed as the only file on the disk (see Figure 1-16a)

FIGURE 1-16b

COPY with one floppy disk drive, continued

```
any key when ready

        1 File(s) copied

C>DIR B:

 Volume in drive B has no label
 Directory of  B:\

GRADES    WQ1      2723   7-31-91    3:12p
        1 File(s)     359424 bytes free

C>DIR A:

Insert diskette for drive A: and strike
any key when ready

 Volume in drive A has no label
 Directory of  A:\

GRADES    WQ1      2723   7-31-91    3:12p
        1 File(s)     359424 bytes free

C>
```

At this point, the computer still recognizes the floppy disk drive as drive B. To have it recognize the disk drive as drive A again:

Type DIR A:

The following message appears:

`Insert diskette for drive A: and strike`
`any key when ready`

This is your signal that the computer recognizes the disk drive as drive A. To confirm this:

GRADES.WQ1 is displayed as the only file on the disk, as before, but this time the message tells you this directory is for drive A (see Figure 1-16b).

A variation of the COPY command is COPY A:*.* B:. This copies all the files from one disk to another disk. Do not use this command now.

Creating a Backup of an Entire Disk (DISKCOPY) Copying each file to a backup disk individually can be time-consuming, so much so that you may neglect doing it, even though you know your work would be lost if the disk were damaged. If Susan lost or damaged her data disk, the entire grade report would have to be redone. Thus, it is very important to periodically copy your entire data disk to a **backup data disk**. This section leads you through the steps necessary to make a backup copy of a data disk (Figure 1-17). The DOS command for this is DISKCOPY. ***NOTE:*** When you use the DISKCOPY command, all the data already on the backup data disk is removed. Therefore, you should use

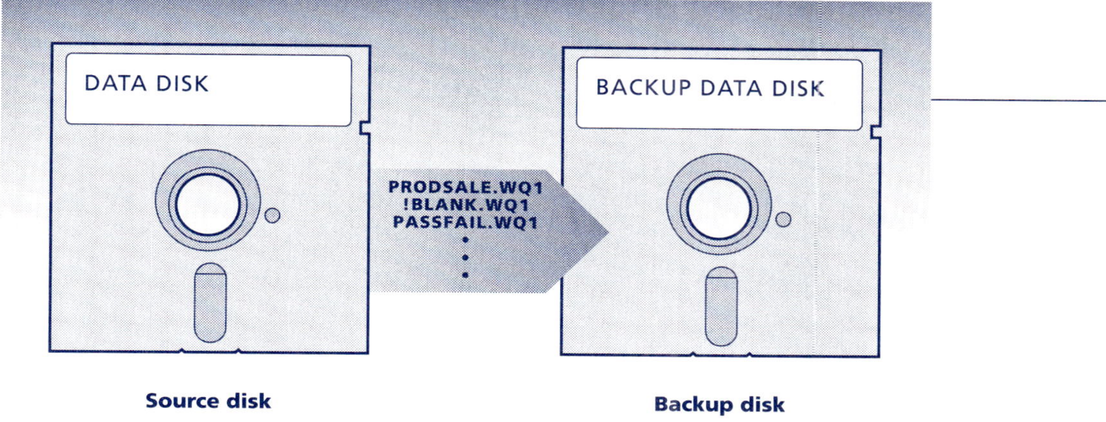

FIGURE 1-17

Copying all files

only a disk that is blank or that has no data you wish to save. If you are unsure, use a brand-new disk.

Make sure the C> prompt is showing on the monitor.

If you have two floppy disk drives:

Type DISKCOPY A: B:

The following appears on the screen:

```
Insert SOURCE diskette in drive A:
Insert TARGET diskette in drive B:
Press any key when ready...
```

The **source** disk is the one you will copy *from*. The **target** disk is the one you will copy *to*. Therefore, you should:

Place the data disk in drive A and the newly formatted backup disk in drive B

Notice how the in-use lights go on and off as the files on the disk in drive A are copied to the disk in drive B. In a few moments, the process is complete. You now have an original and a backup copy of your files.

The following prompt appears on your screen.

```
Copy another diskette (Y/N)?
```

Type N

Now use the DOS directory (DIR) command to show how all the files have been copied to the backup disk.

Type DIR B:

The files on the backup disk are listed on the screen.

If you have only one floppy disk drive: You can still use DISKCOPY if you have only one floppy disk drive. The computer will prompt you to switch disks in the drive, as it did with the COPY command. It is especially important that you keep track of the two disks: the original data disk that came with this text is always the **source** disk, and the newly formatted backup disk is always the **target** disk. You may find it helpful to write SOURCE and TARGET on the disk labels. To use DISKCOPY with one floppy drive, make sure that the C> prompt appears on the monitor.

Type DISKCOPY A: A:

The following appears on the screen (Figure 1-18):

Insert SOURCE diskette in drive A:
Press any key when ready...

Again, the **source** disk is the one you will copy *from;* the **target** disk is the one you will copy *to*. Therefore, you should:

Place the data disk in drive A

The in-use light comes on as the computer reads the contents of the disk into memory. You then see the following message:

Insert TARGET diskette in drive A:
Press any key when ready...

Remove the data disk from drive A,
and insert the backup disk

FIGURE 1-18

DISKCOPY command

```
C>DISKCOPY A: A:

Insert SOURCE diskette in drive A:

Press any key when ready . . .

Copying 40 tracks
9 Sectors/Track, 2 Side(s)

Insert TARGET diskette in drive A:

Press any key when ready . . .


Copy another diskette (Y/N)?N


C>
```

In a few moments, the process is complete. You now have an original and a backup copy of your files. The following prompt appears on your screen.

Copy another diskette (Y/N)?

Type N

Now use the DOS directory (DIR) command to show how all the files have been copied to the backup disk.

Type DIR A:

The files on the backup disk are listed on the screen.

Deleting a File (DEL) The DOS command DEL (delete) can be used to delete a file from your data disk, to make room for new work, or to remove any obsolete files. Delete the GRADES.WQ1 file from your backup disk as follows.

Place the backup disk in drive A if it is not there already, and make sure the C> prompt is on the monitor

Type DEL A:GRADES.WQ1

When the delete process is completed, the C> prompt reappears (see Figure 1-19). Now use the DIR command to show that GRADES.WQ1 is no longer on the backup disk.

Type DIR A:/W

As Figure 1-19 illustrates, all files except GRADES.WQ1 are on your backup disk.

```
C:\->DEL A:GRADES.WQ1

C:\->DIR A:/W

 Volume in drive A has no label
 Directory of A:\

PRODSALE.WQ1    CARPAYMT.WQ1    SALESFIG.WQ1    LEASE.WQ1       LINKSALE.WQ1
!BLANK.WQ1      LOANPAY.WQ1     MEMBERS.WQ1     MO_SALES.WQ1    MO_SALS2.WQ1
PASSFAIL.WQ1    AUTOMAC.WQ1     REPORT.WQ1      SALES.WQ1       SALESRPT.WQ1
SCORES.WQ1      CIRCREF.WQ1     CUSTOMER.WQ1    DOWJONES.WQ1    EMPLOYEE.WQ1
SICKLEVE.WQ1    FORECAST.WQ1    FORECST2.WQ1    GRADERPT.WQ1    INVOICE.WQ1
INVOICE2.WQ1    LABBUDGT.WQ1    STORE1.WQ1      STORE2.WQ1      STORE3.WQ1
TESTING.WQ1
       31 File(s)     248832 bytes free

C:\->
```

FIGURE 1-19

DEL command

If, in the future, you wish to remove all files from a disk in drive A, you can use the following command: DEL A:*.* This erases *all* the data on the disk, so be very careful with this command.

Moving around a Hard Disk (CD) CD stands for "**change directory**." As mentioned earlier, hard disks are usually divided into directories and subdirectories; they can be imagined as organized into a **directory tree** (see Figure 1-9). Usually, when you turn on the computer you start off in the root directory, or the base of the tree. To get to other directories or subdirectories, to locate files or start applications software, the computer must follow a specific route, or **path**. To understand paths, you may find it helpful to imagine a squirrel starting at the trunk (root) of a tree and climbing up one of the branches. From the trunk, it can climb to any branch, but unless it is a flying squirrel, it cannot leap from one of the outermost branches to another branch.

A computer moves around a hard disk like an ordinary, rather than a flying, squirrel. This can be illustrated by using the example of Susan's hard disk, as shown in Figure 1-9. When Susan turns on her computer, she is automatically positioned in her root directory. If she wishes to move into her QPRO directory to start Quattro Pro, she needs to change directories. She would do this by typing *CD\QPRO* and pressing ↵. This would place her in the directory with Quattro Pro, and she could start the program.

If, however, she then wished to move into her MGMT101A directory to work on her class materials, she could not type *CD\MGMT101A,* because that would involve "flying" from one branch to another. Instead, she would have to follow the path that leads from the root directory, through COURSES, to MGMT101A. One way to do this would be to type *CD\COURSES\MGMT101A* and press ↵. To return to the root directory, Susan would type *CD* and press ↵.

Displaying the Current Hard Disk Directory (PROMPT PG) When you move around directories in your hard disk, you may find it difficult to keep track of which directory you are in. For that reason, DOS provides a command to have the C> prompt keep you informed of which directory or subdirectory you are in. With the C> prompt on the monitor:

Type PROMPT PG

NOTE: Don't worry at this point if you don't understand what this command means. The important thing is that the computer will understand it.

You should notice a change in the C> prompt. If you are in the root directory, it will now say C:\>. The \ (backslash) is the symbol for the root directory. The prompt will change as you change directories. For example, if Susan were to use the CD\QPRO command to change to her QPRO directory, the prompt would change to read C:\QPRO>. If she moved to her MGMT101A subdirectory, the prompt would read C:\COURSES\MGMT101A>. This makes it much easier for her to keep track of what directory or subdirectory she is working with.

MS-DOS Version 5.0

DOS was invented many years ago and has been reissued several times with improvements. These improvements are called **versions**, or **upgrades**, and are given numbers. The latest version is 5.0. Microsoft is the company that manufactures DOS, so the program is referred to as MS- (for Microsoft) DOS. Though all of the commands discussed in this chapter will work with MS-DOS 5.0, you may encounter changes from earlier versions of DOS. Three changes you may need to be aware of are the MS-DOS shell, the DOSKEY program, and the UNDELETE command.

Startup Menu (MS-DOS Shell) If the computer you are using has DOS version 5.0 as its system software, the first thing you may see when you turn it on is a menu with the title MS-DOS SHELL. Press ALT-F4 (while holding down the ALT key, tap the F4 key, then release the ALT key) and the C> prompt will appear on the screen. Once you are familiar with DOS commands, you may wish to use the shell menu.

Retrieving Previously Entered Commands (DOSKEY) This program allows DOS to keep track of commands you type in so you don't have to completely retype them if you make a mistake. With the C> prompt on the screen:

Type DOSKEY

You will not notice any immediate difference: The C> prompt will still be on the screen. From that point, though, DOS will remember commands that you type. If you get a "Bad command or file name" message because you made a typing mistake, you can retrieve the command you typed and correct only the incorrect letters, instead of having to retype the entire command. To retrieve the previously typed command:

Press ↑

Your previously typed command appears on the monitor at the command line. Pressing ↑ once retrieves the most recently typed command, pressing ↑ twice retrieves the second most recently typed command, and so on. Use the arrow keys, backspace, and typewriter keys to correct your mistake, and press ↵.

Retrieving a Deleted File (UNDELETE) With DOS 5.0, you can change your mind and retrieve a file you have deleted. This is called **undeleting** a file. ***NOTE:*** UNDELETE works best if you undelete a file that you have only just deleted. If you wait until after you have worked on other files, UNDELETE may not recover the file properly. To undelete a file you have previously deleted, such as GRADES.WQ1 from the backup disk, follow these instructions:

Make sure the C> prompt is on the monitor and the backup disk is in drive A

Type UNDELETE A:GRADES.WQ1

The message on the monitor tells you that the file has been undeleted. Use DIR A: to check that the file has been restored to the backup disk.

ENDING THE SESSION

When you have finished working with the computer:

Remove the disks from the drives and put them in their holders

Turn off the monitor

Turn off the system unit

SUMMARY

Having completed this chapter, you should be able to identify the hardware components of the IBM PC and distinguish between applications software and systems software. You also should be able to perform the DATE, TIME, DIR, FORMAT, COPY, DISKCOPY, DEL, CD, and PROMPT PG commands. Finally, you have the knowledge to handle disks properly and to use data disks to store information, and you are now prepared to work through the applications software chapters that follow.

WORD LIST

applications software
backup data disk
central processing unit (CPU)
data disk
directory
disk
disk drive
disk operating system (DOS)
file
hard disk drive
IBM PC
main memory
program disk
systems software
system unit

DOS COMMANDS

CD
COPY
DATE
DEL
DIR
DISKCOPY
FORMAT
PROMPT PG
TIME

QUESTIONS

1. What three hardware components make up the standard configuration for the IBM PC?
2. Specify any computer anxiety you may feel.
3. How can this class help you overcome computer anxiety?
4. What five things are needed to move from a manual system for processing data to a computerized system?
5. List and describe the three steps in processing data.
6. List and describe the major components of the system unit.
7. What does the following mean: "The monitor provides a 'window' into the main memory of the computer."
8. Describe how a disk drive and a disk are similar to a tape player and a tape.
9. What are some advantages of a hard disk?
10. Describe how a hard disk is organized. What are the advantages of this form of organization?
11. Distinguish between applications software and systems software.
12. What is the purpose of DOS?
13. If you see the message "Bad command or file name" on the monitor, what is the most likely explanation?
14. Describe the function of each of these DOS commands: DATE, TIME, DIR, FORMAT, COPY, DISKCOPY, DEL, CD, and PROMPT PG.

2 Electronic Spreadsheets

In this chapter you learn how to use the electronic spreadsheet called Quattro Pro, version 2.0 or 3.0. The chapter includes a description of electronic spreadsheets and step-by-step instructions for the development of practical applications. The two applications in this chapter lead you from very simple to more involved spreadsheet operations. The chapter is designed to teach the most commonly used commands and assumes no prior knowledge of spreadsheets. When you complete this chapter, you will be able to use an electronic spreadsheet for business and personal applications. Exercises throughout the chapter will help you to practice the skills you have learned.

WHAT IS AN ELECTRONIC SPREADSHEET?

An **electronic spreadsheet** is a computer program used in business to analyze company operations and provide information for effective decision making. It can be used as a management tool to measure past and current activities and as an aid in planning company strategy. The program is particularly useful for evaluating alternative, "what-if" courses of action.

Let's assume you are the marketing manager for a company that sells five different products in four territories. You need to develop a sales forecast for the coming year. You could start by analyzing last year's sales (Figure 2-1). If you project a 5 percent increase in sales for next year, you would recalculate all the sales figures, totals, and percentages. But you are not sure whether 5 percent is an appropriate estimate. What would happen to the company's forecasted income if sales were increased by 10 percent or 20 percent? Or what if the West region increased twice as much as the Northeast region? To study each of these alternatives requires a recalculation of the sales forecast figures and a rewriting of the report. If the reports are produced manually, the tools you use would be a pencil, paper, and calculator. Any corrections, additions, or deletions would involve erasing, recalculating, and rewriting. This would be a tedious, time-consuming process.

An electronic spreadsheet computerizes this manual operation. It is a computer program that allows you to enter data, perform calculations, and print out reports. Because it replaces the pencil, paper, and calculator as tools, the use of an electronic spreadsheet to analyze company operations and provide information for decision making saves time and increases productivity.

Study Figure 2-1 and you will notice that this report:

- Utilizes numbers with calculations, such as totals and percentages.
- Is formatted in columns and rows. For example, each territory is a column and each product is a row.

The link between developing this report manually and developing it with an electronic spreadsheet is the layout of the report. Figure 2-2 illustrates the same report using an electronic spreadsheet. The spreadsheet is laid out in a grid of rows and columns. You enter the numbers into specific locations, called **cells**, within the spreadsheet, just as you would write the numbers out manually on a sheet of paper. You can also enter formulas that perform mathematical calculations, such as totaling a column of numbers. These formulas create relationships between values in different cells. When a change is made in the value in one cell, the formulas automatically update the values in other cells. In

	Northeast	South	Midwest	West	Total	Percent
Product 1	$2,241	1,557	1,833	3,298	8,929	18.18
Product 2	2,843	1,832	1,449	3,722	9,846	20.05
Product 3	1,782	1,274	965	2,286	6,307	12.84
Product 4	4,822	3,844	2,743	7,213	18,622	37.92
Product 5	841	372	1,529	2,666	5,408	11.01
Total	12,529	8,879	8,519	19,185	49,112	100.00

FIGURE 2-1

Sales analysis

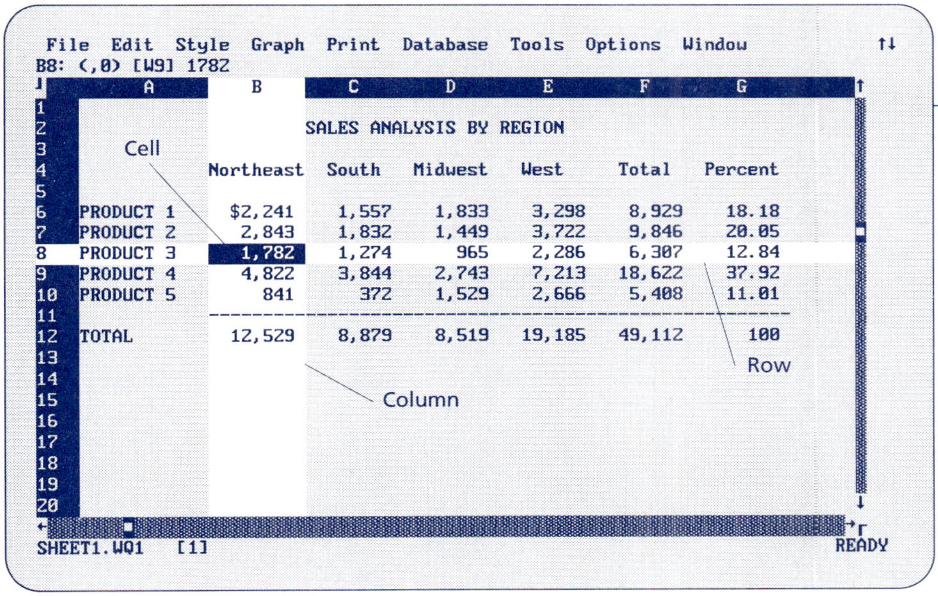

FIGURE 2-2

Sales analysis using an electronic spreadsheet

our example, whenever a new sales value is entered, the totals are automatically recalculated. To utilize an electronic spreadsheet, you organize the data in columns and rows and enter the data and formulas.

Typical business applications for electronic spreadsheets include sales forecasting (Figure 2-2), financial statement analysis (Figure 2-3), and budget development (Figure 2-4). As shown in Figure 2-4, by projecting anticipated revenues and anticipated costs, a company can calculate its cash flow requirements. Then the company can determine the effect of a change in any number of different conditions. For instance, how would the cash flow be affected by a rise in the interest rates, an increase in raw materials' cost, or a slowdown in collection of accounts receivables? All of these "what-if" situations could be inserted into the spreadsheet for quick answers.

FIGURE 2-3

Financial statement analysis

INCOME STATEMENT

BJS Enterprises

July 31, 1992

Sales	$ 42,500	
Less returns	1,200	
Net Sales		$ 41,300
Merchandise, Aug. 1	13,500	
Purchases	8,200	
Merchandise available	21,700	
Merchandise, July 31	11,600	
Cost of goods sold		10,100
Gross profit		31,200
Operating expenses		18,200
Net income		$ 13,000

COMPARATIVE BALANCE SHEET

Jerdon Corporation

(in thousands)

	1991	**1992**	**Change**	**% Change**
Assets				
Current	$ 12,000	$ 13,000	$ 1,000	8.3
Plant	6,000	6,900	900	15.0
Total	18,000	19,900	1,900	10.6
Liabilities				
Current	6,000	5,000	(1,000)	(16.7)
Long-term	7,000	8,500	1,500	21.4
Total	13,000	13,500	500	3.8
Equity	5,000	6,400	1,400	28.0
Total liabilities and equity	$ 18,000	$ 19,900	$ 1,900	10.6

The use of electronic spreadsheets is not limited to business applications. Any application in which there are rows and columns of numbers with calculations is a candidate for the use of an electronic spreadsheet. In education, an instructor may wish to computerize his or her gradebook, which is essentially rows of students' names and columns of scores. The gradebook includes total

FIGURE 2-4

Budget development

RGS ENTERPRISES			CASH FLOW ANALYSIS				1992
CASH RECEIPTS	JAN	FEB	MAR	APR	MAY	JUN	JUL
BEGINNING CASH BAL	22,500	24,535	23,470	20,690	20,055	2,290	4,070
CASH SALES	11,700	11,450	15,330	16,280	23,300	19,300	19,800
COLLECTIONS	11,300	7,900	7,655	10,200	10,900	9,320	19,020
LOAN						5,000	
TOTAL RECEIPTS	45,500	43,885	46,455	47,170	54,255	35,910	42,890
CASH DISBURSEMENTS							
OPERATING EXPENSE	3,200	3,250	3,300	3,350	3,400	3,375	3,550
ADMIN EXPENSE	850	850	850	850	850	850	850
INTEREST EXPENSE	165	165	165	165	165	165	165
PURCHASES	16,440	15,800	21,100	22,400	32,200	27,100	26,600
OTHER EXPENSES	350	350	350	350	350	350	350
CAPITAL OUTLAY					15,000		
TOTAL EXPENSE	20,965	20,415	25,765	27,115	51,965	31,840	31,515
CASH BALANCE	24,535	23,470	20,690	20,055	2,290	4,070	11,375

points for each student and his or her grade percentages. If the instructor uses an electronic spreadsheet, the totals and percentages are automatically updated each time new scores are entered.

Another nonbusiness application would be a student's college budget. A student developing a projected budget for college would list anticipated income and subtract anticipated expenses, as shown in Figure 2-5. This simple example would not take much time to do by hand, but if the student wanted to break down the budget by month, the process would take longer. And if he or she wished to see the effect on the budget of a tuition increase, a pay raise, or a semester of summer school, the process would take longer still. All these what-if situations, so time-consuming to examine manually, can be easily handled with the aid of a computer.

FIGURE 2-5

Student budget

	STUDENT BUDGET		
	FALL SEMESTER		
Income			
Loan	$ 1,200		
Part-time job	1,600		
			$ 2,800
Expenses			
Tuition	750		
Books/supplies	200		
Housing/Food	1,200		
Transportation	180		
Entertainment	400		
			2,730
Contingency		$	70

Electronic spreadsheets are available from several vendors. They all allow you to enter data, perform calculations, and study alternatives. Some are more sophisticated than others and have special enhancements, such as word processing and database management features. Although this chapter helps you to develop expertise in Quattro Pro, you can also use the skills you learn in other spreadsheet programs.

GETTING STARTED WITH QUATTRO PRO

This section describes the steps (including keystrokes) necessary to load Quattro Pro. If you are unfamiliar with the IBM PC or DOS, refer to Chapter 1 before continuing. To complete this chapter you need:

- An IBM PC (or compatible) with 640K memory, a hard disk drive, and at least one floppy drive.
- DOS version 2.0 or later (version 3.1 is used here).
- Quattro Pro, version 2.0 or 3.0, available on the hard disk. The examples given in the text assume that Quattro Pro is installed on drive C in directory C:\QPRO.
- The data disk provided by your instructor.

Using the Keyboard

You need to be familiar with the keyboard to use Quattro Pro effectively. Certain keys are explained as you work through this chapter. To get started, you must know how to use the following keys.

Key	**Location**	**Function**
ESC	Upper right side or upper left side	Escape. Used to exit from a command and return to the worksheet or to cancel a prompt from Quattro Pro.
↵	Right side	Enter. Used to enter data that has been typed and also to execute a command.
↑ ← → ↓	Right side	Cell selector (highlight) movement keys. Used to move the cell selector up and down the rows or left and right across the columns. The cell selector indicates your location on the spreadsheet.

For most keystrokes, you press the key for the count of 1, as you would on a typewriter. For some Quattro Pro features, though, you need to hold down one key and tap another simultaneously. In this text, these keystrokes are indicated by one key followed by a hyphen and then another key. For example, if you see CTRL-←, you should hold down the CTRL key while tapping the ←. Then, release the CTRL key.

If You Have a Mouse

If you have a mouse, a **pointer** will appear on the screen when you start Quattro Pro. The pointer appears as either a highlighted rectangle or an arrow, depending on how your computer is set up. You position the pointer on the screen by moving the mouse on the mousepad. You will also see the **mouse palette**, the column on the right side of the screen. You can use the mouse with the mouse palette to carry out certain tasks more quickly than you could with the keyboard. For more information, see "Using a Mouse" in Chapter 6.

Loading Quattro Pro

If you are using a computer in a college computer lab, Quattro Pro will probably appear as a menu item when you turn on the computer. Follow the instructions on the computer screen to choose Quattro Pro, or ask your instructor or lab assistant for help.

If, when you turn on the computer, you see the C> prompt, you will probably need to move to the directory with Quattro Pro to start the program. Assuming it is located in the C:\QPRO directory, you would:

ACTION	*RESULT*
Type CD\QPRO ↵	Moves to the directory
Type Q ↵	Starts the program

The computer you are using may be set up differently, so check with your instructor or lab assistant if you are not sure how to proceed. Once Quattro Pro is loaded, your screen should look like Figure 2-6.

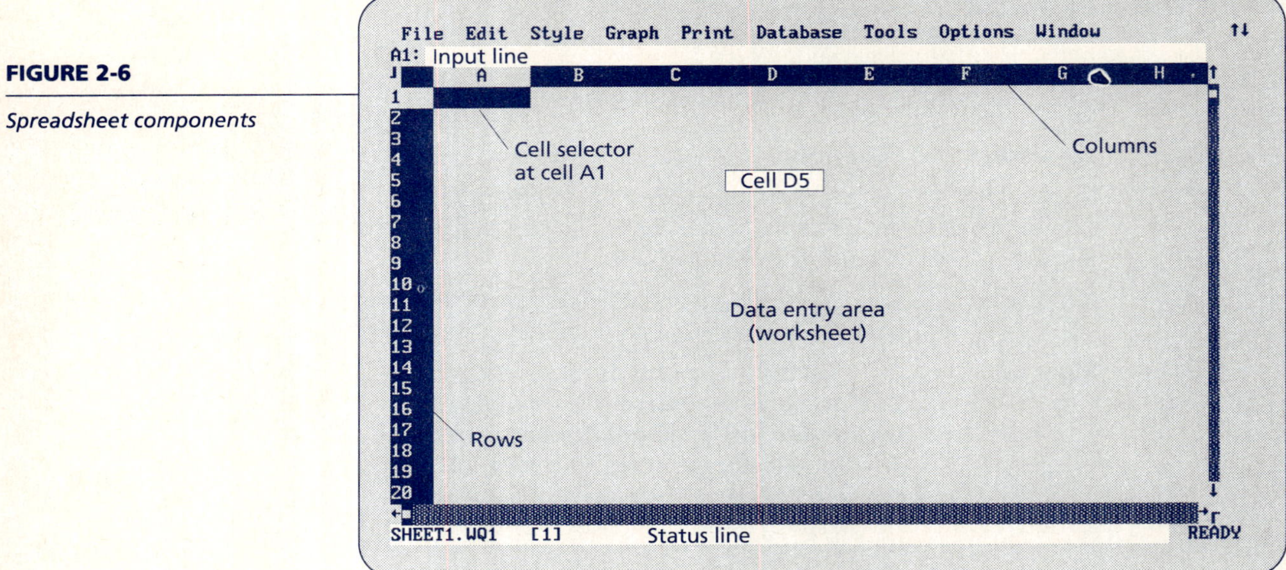

FIGURE 2-6

Spreadsheet components

ORGANIZATION OF THE SPREADSHEET

This screen may look like one continuous surface, but it is actually made up of two parts, the **spreadsheet** and the **command menu**. When you start Quattro Pro, the screen is set up for you to begin typing into a blank spreadsheet. The spreadsheet is organized in columns and rows (see Figure 2-6). The columns are identified by letters across the top, and the rows are identified by numbers down the left side. A **cell** is formed by the intersection of a row and a column. Each cell has a name, called an **address**: A1 is the address of the cell where column A and row 1 come together, D5 is the address of the cell where column D and row 5 come together, and so on. To enter data into the spreadsheet, you locate the **cell selector** (highlight) on the desired cell, type in the data, and press V. When you load the program, the cell selector will be on A1 and the spreadsheet will be empty. As you can see from Figure 2-6, the spreadsheet has the following components.

- Data entry area: This is called the **worksheet** and will contain the data you type in.
- Column headings (A, B, C,...).
- Row headings (1, 2, 3,...).
- Cells: locations in the worksheet where columns and rows intersect.
- Cell selector: the highlight that is moved to a cell so that data can be entered.
- Input line: The top line is used to enter and edit data. It usually displays information about the cell where the cell selector is located, such as the cell address and cell contents. It can also display messages that help lead you through the use of the program.

FIGURE 2-7a

Screen view of worksheet

- Status line: The bottom line displays the current status of the program, including mode and status indicators and the name of the worksheet you are in. When you start Quattro Pro, you are always placed in a blank worksheet called SHEET1.WQ1. If you later change the name of the worksheet, the status line will reflect the change.

Data Entry Area

The data entry area, called the worksheet, is defined by the column and row headings. Across the top are the column headings A through H. Down the left side are the row headings 1 through 20. What you can see is a window (Figure 2-7a) into a much larger spreadsheet. In fact, the Quattro Pro worksheet has 256 columns across and 8,192 rows down. Where the rows and columns intersect defines a cell name, such as A1, A2, A20, B1, B2, F8, or H12. Data is entered into these cells. The cells are set to display 9 characters, but it is possible to type a data item up to 253 characters into a cell.

The Cell Selector

Before you can type in data, the cell selector must be located at the cell where you wish to enter data. The following keys are most commonly used to position the cell selector.

(↑) (←) (→) (↓)	On the right side of the keyboard are the arrow keys, which move the pointer up or down one row at a time and left or right one column at a time. Thus, if the pointer is located at cell B8, pressing (↓) once moves the pointer to B9. Then pressing (→) once moves the pointer to cell C9.
(HOME)	Moves the cell selector to cell A1.
(CTRL)-(←) or (SHIFT)-(TAB)	Moves the cell selector left one screen.
(CTRL)-(→) or (TAB)	Moves the cell selector right one screen.
(PGUP) and (PGDN)	These two keys move the cell selector up or down one screen (20 rows).
(F5)	This function key allows you to go to any cell in the worksheet. When you press (F5) a prompt appears at the top of the screen asking you to specify a cell address. When you type a cell address and press (↵), the cell selector quickly moves to that cell. This is referred to as the GoTo prompt.

The following instructions illustrate the use of the cell selector movement keys and give you a feel for the size of the worksheet. The cell selector is now at A1. Watch the screen as you complete the following. (***NOTE:*** As you work through this text, you will see a series of "Action/Result" sections. Carry out the action and notice the result. The actual heading "Action/Result" is not used in all cases.)

ACTION	*RESULT*
When you press:	Cell selector moves to:
(→)	B1
(→)	C1
(↓)	C2
(←)	B2
(PGDN)	B22 (down 20 rows)
(PGUP)	B2 (up 20 rows)
(HOME)	A1
(→) **9 times**	J1

You will notice that once the pointer moves past the H column, the I column appears at the right of the screen. As the I column appears, the A column disappears from the left of the screen. You are scrolling the screen across the worksheet (Figure 2-7b). You can also scroll down the worksheet. Take a moment to practice using these keys. Then use the (HOME) key to return to A1.

FIGURE 2-7b

Scrolling the screen across the worksheet

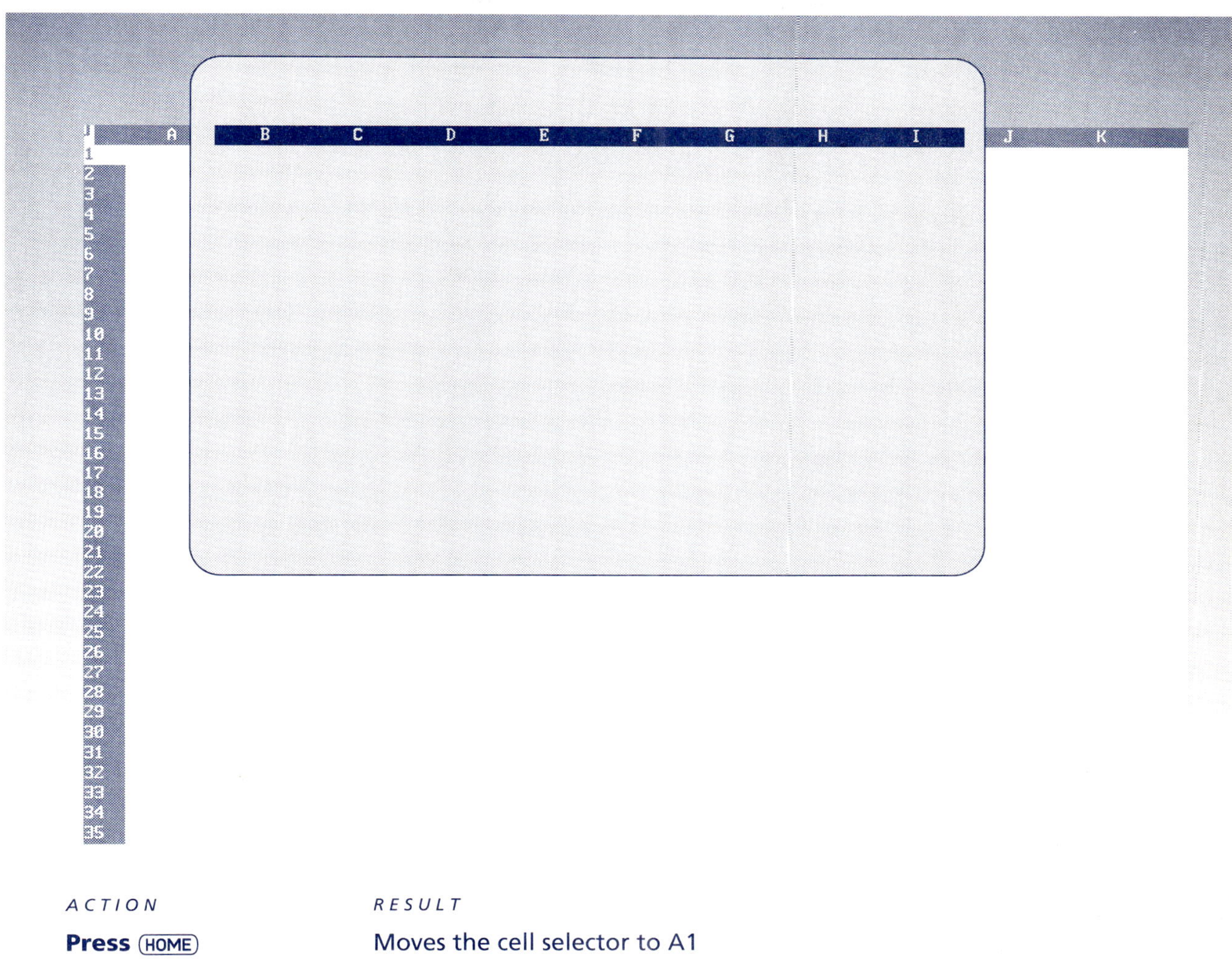

ACTION	*RESULT*
Press (HOME)	Moves the cell selector to A1

How Data Is Entered

Now that you can move around the worksheet, you are ready to learn how to enter data. Remember that data is entered in a cell location. Move the cell selector first, type the data, and then press (↵). Virtually anything can be entered into a cell. The computer, however, must be able to distinguish between different types of data. You can enter data into a worksheet as **values** (numeric data) or **text** (nonnumeric data). You can also enter **formulas** and **functions** that perform calculations and other operations on numeric data. The differences between these types of data are explained in the following sections.

Values Values are numbers. If the first character typed into a cell is a digit (0, 1, 2, 3, 4, 5, 6, 7, 8, 9), a decimal point (.), a plus sign (+), or a minus sign (–), the computer considers the entry a value. Characters such as a dollar sign ($) or a comma (,) cannot be used when typing a value. However, the contents of a cell can be formatted to display dollar signs and commas, as you will see later in this chapter.

Formulas A formula is a mathematical statement that uses one or more cell locations and/or values. The following are examples of formula entries and their meanings.

Formula Entry	Meaning
+C5+C6+C7	Add the values in cells C5, C6, and C7.
+F12–F13+99	Subtract the value in cell F13 from the value in cell F12 and add 99.
+T17*.08	Multiply the value in cell T17 by .08.
+A15/A12	Divide the value in cell A15 by the value in cell A12.
+K2–K1*L4	Multiply the value in cell K1 by the value in cell L4, and subtract the result from the value in cell K2.
+B14^2	Square the value in cell B14.
(L43+L4)*12	Add the values in cells L43 and L4 and multiply the result by 12.

Each example contains at least one arithmetic operator (+ – * / ^). These operators indicate to the program that the entry is a formula. An operator is needed between each cell location and/or value in a formula. If more than one arithmetic operator is specified in a formula, the following is the order in which the operations are performed.

1. Exponentiation (^) first.
2. Multiplication and division next (left to right).
3. Addition and subtraction last (left to right).

For example, if the formula +A1*B1+B2/B3 was entered into a cell, first the values in cells A1 and B1 would be multiplied together; then the value in cell B2 would be divided by the value in cell B3; and, finally, the results of the first two operations would be added together. This order of operation can be altered by using parentheses. Any arithmetic operation enclosed in parentheses is completed first. If the formula above was changed to +A1*(B1+B2)/B3, then the values in cells B1 and B2 would be added together first, and the result would be multiplied by the value in cell A1 and then divided by the value in cell B3.

Functions These are statements that perform specific operations using data in a cell or cells. A list of the functions most frequently used in Quattro Pro can be found in the appendix. Examples are:

- @SUM: adds the values in a group of cells.
- @AVG: calculates the average of the values in a group of cells.
- @MAX: determines the highest value in a group of cells.
- @MIN: determines the lowest value in a group of cells.
- @NPV: computes the net present value.

Text Any data can be entered as text (also called **labels**). Usually text consists of words typed in as headings and titles. However, numbers can be entered as text instead of values. To do this, you type an apostrophe (') before the first digit. The program then treats the number entered as text. This may be useful if, for example, you wanted to enter a zip code that began with 0, such as 08002. If you entered this zip code without the apostrophe, Quattro Pro would consider it a number and remove the first zero, so that it would become 8002. Entering the apostrophe first lets Quattro Pro know that it should keep all the numbers precisely as you enter them. Note that the apostrophe is an indicator only: It will appear on the input line, but not in the cell. You can also type a space before the number, instead of an apostrophe, and the number will be treated as text. Once a number is entered as text, it cannot be used for calculations.

When entering values, you need to be concerned with the width of a cell. If the cell is nine characters wide, then a value larger than eight characters is displayed in scientific notation (one character is used for a space so that numbers do not run together on the screen). If, however, a text entry is longer than the width of the cell, the data is completely displayed unless the cell immediately to the right contains data. In that case, the screen displays only the part of the text entry that fits within the cell.

Another distinction between values and text is that they are aligned differently within a cell. Figure 2-8 shows a simple worksheet. Notice that the text entries are aligned along the left side of column A and the values (numbers) are aligned along the right side of column B. This is useful when you are designing reports that include columns of numbers, because the numbers will line up on the decimal points and make the report easier to read.

You can determine whether a particular cell contains a value, formula, function, or text by locating the cell selector at the cell and looking at the input line at the top of the worksheet. If there is an apostrophe at the beginning of the entry, then the entry is considered text.

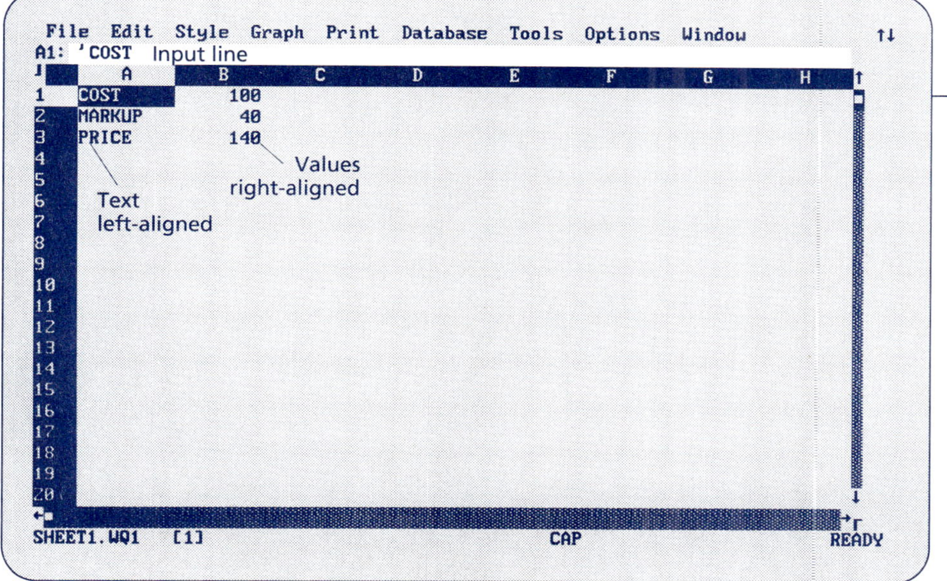

FIGURE 2-8

Alignment of values and text within cells

Input Line

The **input line** near the top of the worksheet displays the location of the cell selector (A1 in Figure 2-8) and the data, if any, entered into the cell (value, text, function, or formula). It also shows information about the format of the cell. For example, if the cell is formatted to display two decimal places, the input line shows (F2). The F stands for fixed and the 2 stands for two decimal places. This means that when a number is entered, it is displayed with two decimal places.

In Figure 2-8, the cell selector is located at cell A1 and the input line shows A1: 'COST. This means that the cell selector is located at cell A1 and the entry is COST, which is text (indicated by the apostrophe). Figure 2-9a illustrates the changes in the input line after the pointer is moved to B1. The input line shows that the pointer is at B1 and the entry, 100, is a value (no apostrophe).

The input line also displays messages that help lead you through the various operations of the program. For instance, when you want to change the width of a column, a message appears on the input line telling you the column's current width and prompting you to enter a number from 1 to 254 for the new width, as discussed below. It is very important to watch the input line for help in using Quattro Pro.

Status Line

At the bottom of the screen is the **status line**, which displays the name of the current worksheet as well as two indicators: mode and status. The three most common modes are (1) READY, indicating you can enter data into a cell; (2) EDIT, indicating you are editing the contents of a cell; and (3) MENU, indicating you are in the process of selecting a command from the menu bar. The status indicator displays such things as CAP when the CAPS LOCK key is on. Figure 2-9a

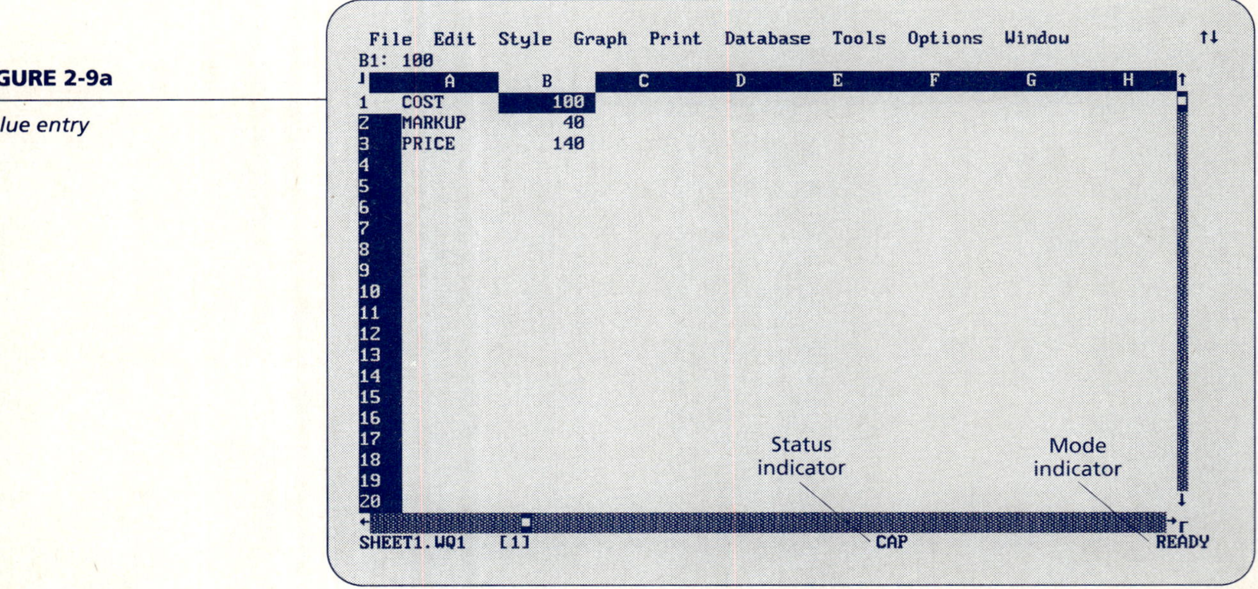

FIGURE 2-9a

Value entry

shows the mode indicator displaying READY and the status indicator displaying CAP. The status line also gives a brief description of each command from the menu bar as it is highlighted (see below, "Command Menu Bar").

Error Messages

If you do something Quattro Pro cannot understand, such as entering data incorrectly or leaving off a parentheses in a function, you will see a box with an error message in the middle of the worksheet. If you do not understand the error message, press (F1) for help. If you do understand it and know how to correct the mistake, press (ESC) to remove the message from the worksheet. The appendix includes a list of the most common error messages.

APPLICATION 1

Now that you understand how a spreadsheet is organized, you are ready to complete the first application, which will give you practice moving around the spreadsheet and entering data. In this example, you will add cost and markup figures together to obtain the selling price. Then you will change the markup and see the effect on the selling price. You will develop the worksheet shown in Figure 2-9a.

Entering Data

To complete this first application, you will move the cell selector to the desired cell, type the data or formula, and then press (↵). If you make a mistake while typing, use the (BACKSPACE) key to move back and then retype the entry. To start, the cell selector should be at cell A1.

ACTION	RESULT
Press (CAPS LOCK)	Locks the keyboard (letters only) into uppercase
Type COST (↵)	Enters COST into cell A1
(→)	Moves cell selector to B1
Type 100 (↵)	Enters 100 into cell B1
(↓) (←)	Moves cell selector to A2
Type MARKUP (↵)	Enters MARKUP into cell A2
(→)	Moves cell selector to B2
Type 40 (↵)	Enters 40 into cell B2
(↓) (←)	Moves cell selector to A3
Type PRICE (↵)	Enters PRICE into cell A3
(→)	Moves cell selector to B3
Type +B1+B2 (↵)	Adds contents of cells B1 and B2 and enters the sum (140) into cell B3

Now you are ready to experience one of the most powerful aspects of a spreadsheet program. Change the markup amount in cell B2 to 44 and watch the effect on the price in cell B3.

(↑)	Moves the cell selector to B2
Type 44 (↵)	Enters 44 into cell B2

The price in cell B3 is automatically recalculated to 144. Although this is a very simple example, it illustrates the ease with which data can be entered and the speed with which calculations and recalculations can be performed.

Using the same example, change the fixed dollar markup (44) to a percentage of the cost (60%). To do this, enter the following formula into cell B2: +B1*.60.

Type +B1*.60 (↵)	Enters the formula into B2 and recalculates the price

The price is again recalculated based on the markup percentage. Now move the pointer to cell B1 and enter a different cost amount.

(↑)	Moves the cell selector to B1
Type 200 (↵)	Enters 200 into B1

The markup and price amounts are recalculated. As you can see, once you set up the basic worksheet and specify the relationships among the various cells using formulas, you can make any number of changes and quickly determine the results.

Making Changes and Corrections

When you make a mistake in entering data, or when you want to change the contents of a particular cell, you can edit the contents of a cell in one of three ways. First, if you notice a mistake while typing, use the (BACKSPACE) key to move back and then retype the entry. Try this method by following the steps below. (***NOTE:*** The (BACKSPACE) key is usually located above the (↵) key.)

Press (F5)	Brings up the GoTo prompt
Type D3 (↵)	Moves the cell selector to D3
Type TOTTAL	TOTTAL appears on the input line at the top of the spreadsheet
Press (BACKSPACE) **3 times**	Moves the cursor back three spaces
Type AL	Corrects the spelling of TOTAL
(↵)	Enters corrected spelling into D3

You can use the second method of editing a cell if you want to change data already entered in a cell. First, locate the cell selector at that cell and enter the new data. This replaces the original entry with the new entry. Replace the word COST with OUR COST, using the following steps.

Press (HOME)	Moves the cell selector to A1
Type OUR COST (↵)	Replaces COST with OUR COST

A third way to change the cell is to use the Edit mode to change the contents of a cell without retyping the entire entry. Use the Edit mode to change MARKUP to MARKUP %.

(↓)	Moves cell selector to A2
(F2)	Enters Edit mode and displays a cursor on the input line at the top of the screen

Notice that the status line displays the word EDIT (Figure 2-9b).

Press the spacebar and type %	Enters a space and a % sign
(↵)	Enters the change into A2

If you change your mind about wanting to replace the original entry before you have pressed (↵), you could preserve the original entry by pressing (ESC). In the above examples, if you decided after typing OUR COST that you really preferred that the entry remain COST or after adding the % sign that you preferred to leave it out, you could press (ESC) to undo the change. However, pressing (ESC) only works if you do it *before* you press (↵) to enter your changes.

You may also wish to remove the data currently in the cell and leave the cell blank. You can do this by locating the cell selector at the cell and pressing (DEL). Complete the following steps to remove the word TOTAL.

Press (→) **3 times and then press** (↓)	Moves cell selector to D3
Press (DEL)	Deletes the word TOTAL from the cell and leaves the cell empty

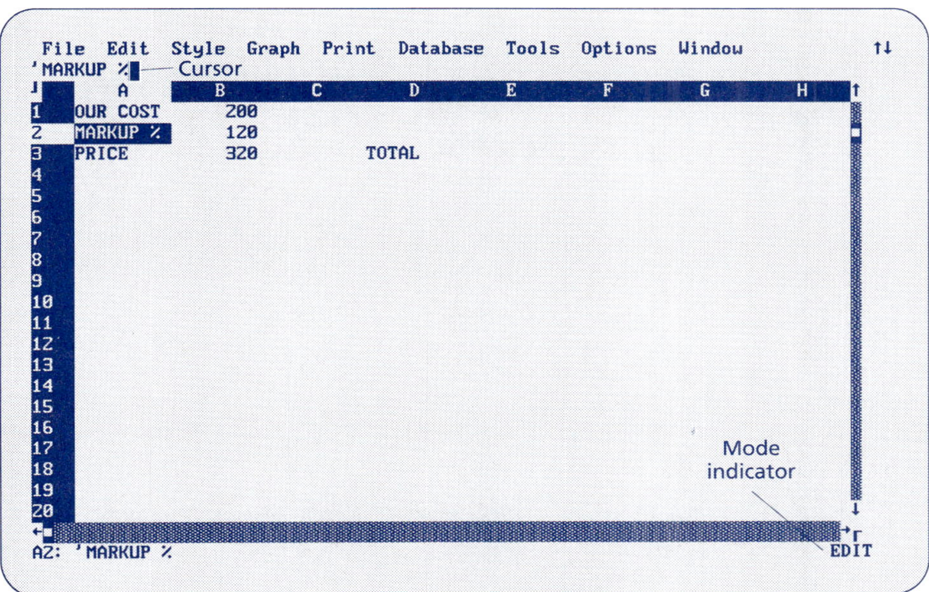

FIGURE 2-9b

Editing an entry

Command Menu Bar

Across the top of the screen is the **menu bar**, through which you choose Quattro Pro commands. The commands are organized into the categories you see in a line across the screen: File, Edit, Style, Graph, Print, Database, Tools, Options, and Window (Figure 2-10a). To choose a command, you have to "jump" out of the spreadsheet to the menu. You cannot do this by pressing ↑ or PGUP. Instead, you activate the menu by pressing the slash (/) key. Once you press /, you will notice that the word File in the menu is highlighted, and the word MENU appears on the status line. On the left side of the status line you will see the words File Operations, which lets you know that this part of the menu contains commands for managing files, such as opening or saving a new worksheet or a previously created worksheet. This kind of menu is called a **pull-down menu**, because you have to "pull" the list of choices "down" from the main heading on the menu bar. After pressing /, you can pull down the list of commands in two ways:

- Use → and ← to move around the menu until the category you want is highlighted, and then press ↵; or
- Press the highlighted letter of the choice you want.

For example, to pull down the File Operations menu, you could either make sure the word File is highlighted and press ↵, or just press F. Either way, the File Operations menu is pulled down (see Figure 2-10b). Try this now by activating the menu bar and pulling down the File menu.

Press /	Activates the menu bar
Press F	Pulls down the File menu

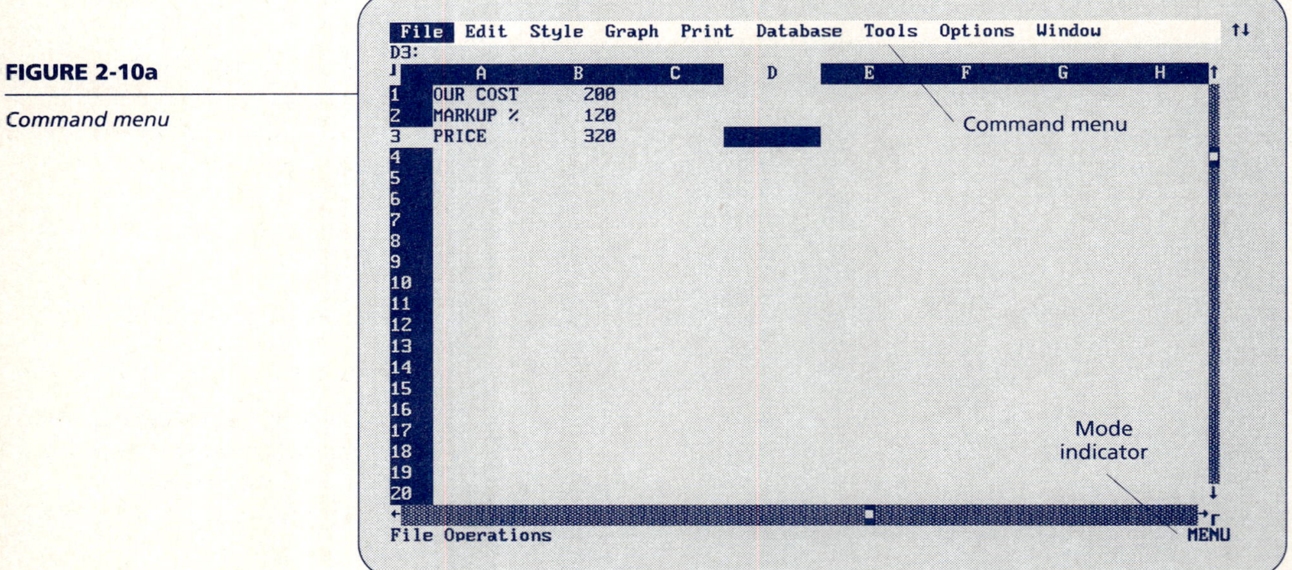

FIGURE 2-10a

Command menu

To move up and down the menu, use ↑ and ↓. If you press → or ← from a pulled-down menu, the menu you move to will be automatically pulled down.

To "close up" any menu you have pulled down, press ESC. Once all menus are closed, pressing ESC lets you "jump" back to the worksheet. You should become very familiar with using / and ESC to move back and forth between the worksheet and the menu in Quattro Pro. Take some time to move around the command menu, pulling down menus in each category and reading their descriptions on the status line along with the following descriptions. After studying the File menu, press → to display the Edit menu. Read the Edit menu descriptions, and then press → to display the Style menu, and so forth.

The menus, with their most important commands, are:

File Used to open, retrieve, save, close, and erase files and to exit Quattro Pro. You can also access DOS from this menu.

Edit Used to edit data in the worksheet. You can copy, move, and erase individual cells and groups of cells. You can also insert and delete columns and rows.

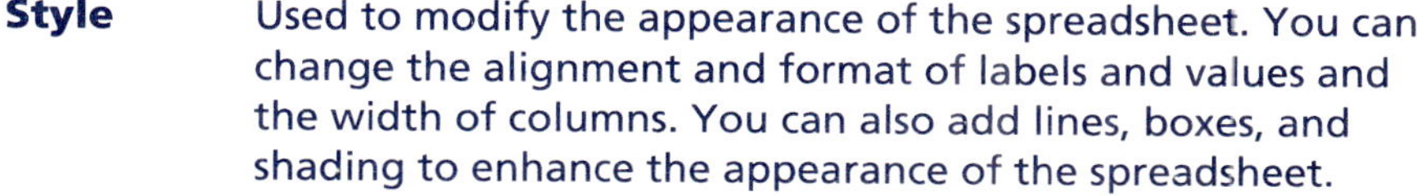

Style Used to modify the appearance of the spreadsheet. You can change the alignment and format of labels and values and the width of columns. You can also add lines, boxes, and shading to enhance the appearance of the spreadsheet.

Graph Used to create and annotate graphs.

Print Used to print spreadsheets and graphs.

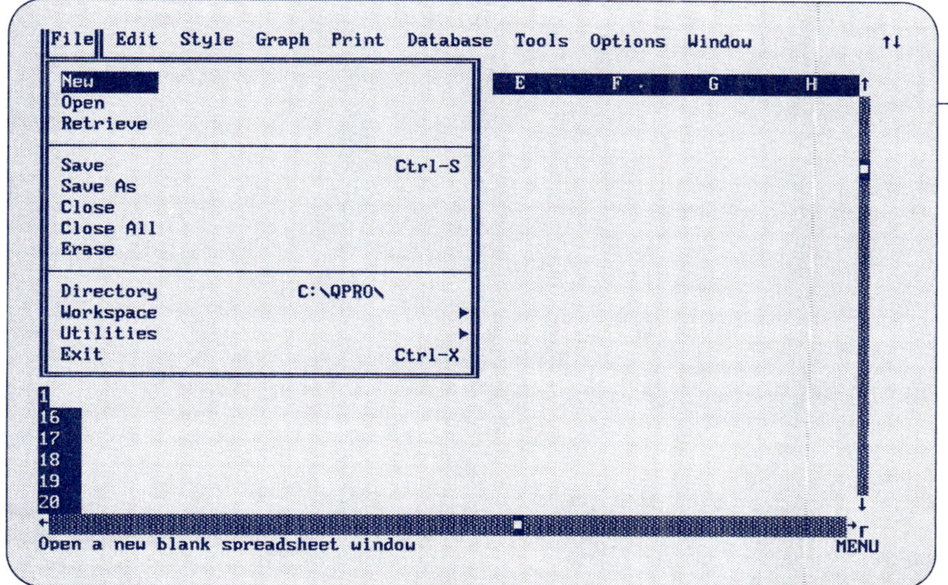

FIGURE 2-10b

Pull-down menu

Database Used to organize data into a database consisting of records and fields. It is especially useful for sorting data and searching for data that fits specific criteria.

Tools Contains advanced commands for creating macros, importing files from other programs, and performing advanced math calculations.

Options Used to customize spreadsheet settings.

Window Used to divide the screen into separate "windows," to view or edit two or more spreadsheets simultaneously.

After displaying the Window menu,

Press (ESC)	Returns to the worksheet

Erasing a Spreadsheet The first command you will work with is the Erase command on the File menu. The Erase command clears the contents of the spreadsheet and resets the spreadsheet formats to the default settings. A default setting is one that is built in to the program. For example, the default setting for the column width is 9.

To activate the command menu if none of the choices on the menu bar are highlighted:

Press /	Highlights File
Press (↵) **or** F	Pulls down the menu

To choose Erase, either use (↓) to move the highlight to Erase and then press (↵), or press E to choose Erase. A box appears with the prompt:

`Lose your changes? No Yes`

This box is called a **pop-up menu**, because it only "pops up" when it is needed. You select items from it as you would from the menu bar: either by using (↑) and (↓) to highlight the choices and then pressing (↵), or by pressing the highlighted letter of the choice you want. In this case, you don't care whether you lose your changes, so:

Press Y	Erases the worksheet

If you change your mind during this or any other command, you can exit from it by pressing (ESC).

Menu Terminology

Throughout this text, when you are to choose a command from the menu, it will be written as

`/(menu bar choice)¦(pull-down menu choice)`

For example, the Erase command just used would be written:

`/File¦Erase`

You have now completed Application 1. You have learned some basics of electronic spreadsheets, including how to move around a spreadsheet, how to enter and edit data, and how to perform calculations. You have also learned how to activate the menu and use commands. In the next application, a more detailed example, you will learn additional features of an electronic spreadsheet. If your practice time is up and you wish to quit and return later to complete this chapter, follow the instructions below.

Exiting Quattro Pro

The command for exiting Quattro Pro is also on the File menu, so choosing it is similar to choosing /File¦Erase. Choose /File¦Exit. That is:

Press /	Activates the command menu
Press F	Chooses the File menu
Press X	Exits Quattro Pro

NOTE: The letter used to choose a menu item is not always the first letter! In the case of Exit, you must press X, not E, because E chooses Erase. Always press the **highlighted** letter to choose a menu item. Or, use the arrow keys to move the highlight to the desired menu item, Exit in this case, and press ↵.

After choosing /File¦Exit, you leave Quattro Pro and return either to the initial menu or to the C> prompt. At that point you may turn off the computer.

QUESTIONS

1. What is an electronic spreadsheet?
2. Which types of business reports would be most appropriate to develop with an electronic spreadsheet?
3. Explain the following: "Electronic spreadsheets are useful when working with what-if situations."
4. Describe the components of a spreadsheet.
5. List the steps involved in loading Quattro Pro.
6. How many columns are there in Quattro Pro?
7. How many rows are there in Quattro Pro?
8. Explain what each of the cell selector movement keys does.
9. Distinguish among values, formulas, and text.
10. What is the purpose of typing an apostrophe (') as the first character in an entry?
11. Describe three ways to edit data within a cell. Which do you think is most useful, and why?
12. What keystroke is needed to activate the menu bar? What keystroke is needed to get back to the spreadsheet?
13. What are the two ways to choose an item from a menu?

14. If you forget what a menu command does, where on the screen should you look to find out?
15. What does /File¦Erase do?

CHALLENGE EXERCISES

1. Enter the following data and formulas into a worksheet.

	A	B	C
1		DEPART 1	
2	SALES	800	
3	EXPENSES	600	
4	PROFIT	+B2-B3	

2. Using the same worksheet as in exercise 1, add the following:

	A	B	C	D	E
1		DEPART 1	DEPART 2	TOTALS	PERCENT OF SALES
2	SALES	800	400	+B2+C2	+D2/D2*100
3	EXPENSES	600	300	+B3+C3	+D3/D2*100
4	PROFIT	+B2-B3	+C2-C3	+D2-D3	+D4/D2*100

3. Use the Erase command to clear the previous worksheet and then create a new one, using the data that follows. In a ski race in which each contestant has two runs, the times were:

NAME	RUN #1	RUN #2
MAYER	45	44
KELLIE	47	45
JOHNSTONE	44	44

Enter the data into a worksheet and include columns for total time and average time for each racer. Use formulas in these columns. When done, clear the worksheet with the Erase command.

APPLICATION 2

This section leads you step by step through a second application. When you finish it, you will be able to enter cell addresses into formulas and functions without having to type them out. You will also know how to use the Sum function to add the values in a series of cells, and you will know the shortcut keys for highlighting groups of cells. Finally, you will learn the commands, and their shortcuts, used to save, retrieve, and print worksheets.

This application uses the example of a college student budget, as shown in Figure 2-11. Before you start, study Figure 2-11. At the top of the worksheet, the input line indicates that the cell selector is at A1 and the cell is empty. As you move the cell selector and type in data, notice how the input line changes. If you have not already done so, press the CAPS LOCK key so that all your text

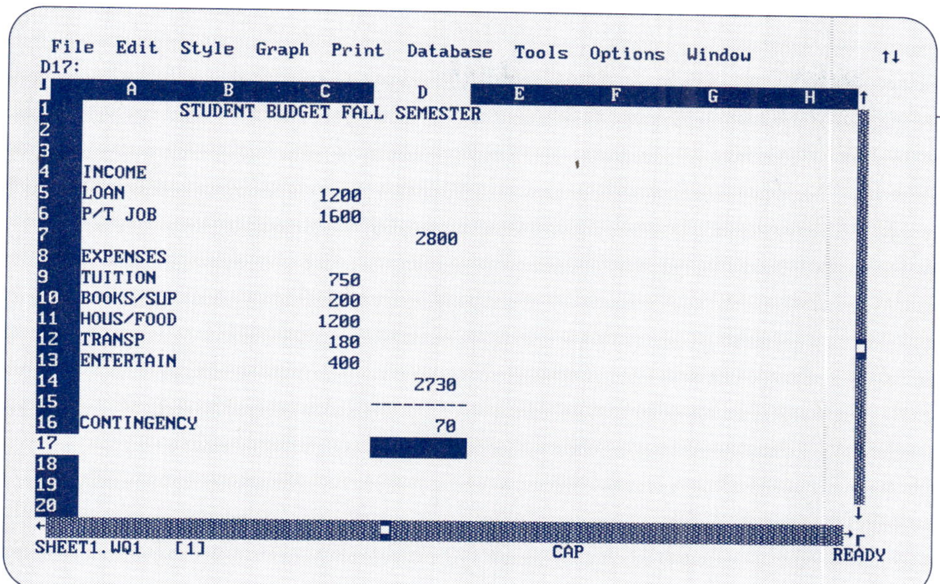

FIGURE 2-11

Application 2: Student budget

entries are in uppercase. Complete the following instruction. If the cell selector is not at A1, press (HOME) to move it there.

(→)	Moves cell selector to B1
Type STUDENT BUDGET FALL SEMESTER	

Notice that the text entry is longer than nine characters. You can enter text that is longer than the cell width. The entire entry is displayed unless the adjacent cell to the right contains an entry. If the adjacent cell contains data, only the first nine characters of this entry are displayed.

(↵)	Enters the title STUDENT BUDGET FALL SEMESTER
Press (↓) **3 times and then press** (←)	Moves cell selector to A4
Type INCOME (↵)	Enters INCOME into A4
(↓)	Moves cell selector to A5
Type LOAN (↵)	Enters LOAN into A5
Press (→) **twice**	Moves cell selector to C5
Type 1200 (↵)	Enters 1200 into C5
(↓) (←) (←)	Moves cell selector to A6
Type P/T JOB (↵)	Enters P/T JOB into A6
(→) (→)	Moves cell selector to C6
Type 1600 (↵)	Enters 1600 into C6
(↓) (→)	Moves cell selector to D7

You are now ready to enter a formula, +C5+C6. You already know how to enter formulas by typing them in. But to reduce the likelihood of typing mistakes, Quattro Pro provides you with a way of entering formulas by highlighting cells, instead of by typing cell addresses. To do this, once the cell selector is located in the cell you wish to contain the formula (D7 in this case), you must:

Type +	Indicates that you are beginning a formula

Note that + appears on the input line.

Press ← **and press** ↑ **twice**	Moves the cell selector to the first cell in the formula, in this case C5

Note that the input line changes as you move the cell selector to reflect whatever cell is currently highlighted. When the cell selector is positioned at C5:

Type +	Continues the formula

The cell selector should be back at the starting point, D7.

Press ← ↑	Moves the cell selector to the second cell in the formula, in this case C6

Again, note that the input line changes as you move the cell selector to reflect whatever cell is currently highlighted.

Press ↵	Completes the formula entry

The complete formula, +C5+C6, appears on the input line, and the cell selector is back at your starting point, D7, which now contains the result of the calculation, 2800.

Until now you have used ↵ to enter the data after it is typed; then you have used an arrow key to move the cell selector. Note that the arrow keys can be used to enter data without ↵, thus saving a keystroke.

Press ↓ **and then** ← **3 times**	Moves cell selector to A8
Type EXPENSES ↓	Enters EXPENSES into A8 and moves cell selector to A9
Type TUITION → →	Enters TUITION into A9 and moves cell selector to C9
Type 750 ↓ ← ←	Enters 750 into C9 and moves cell selector to A10
Type BOOKS/SUP → →	Enters BOOKS/SUP into A10 and moves cell selector to C10
Type 200 ↓ ← ←	Enters 200 into C10 and moves cell selector to A11
Type HOUS/FOOD → →	Enters HOUS/FOOD into A11 and moves cell selector to C11
Type 1200 ↓ ← ←	Enters 1200 into C11 and moves cell selector to A12

Type TRANSP (→) (→)	Enters TRANSP into A12 and moves cell selector to C12
Type 180 (↓) (←) (←)	Enters 180 into C12 and moves cell selector to A13
Type ENTERTAIN (→) (→)	Enters ENTERTAIN into A13 and moves cell selector to C13
Type 400 (↓) (→)	Enters 400 into C13 and moves cell selector to D14

Using the Sum Function

At D14 you need to enter a formula that will add the expenses. You can do this in two ways. The first is similar to the method you used in D7, which would involve entering +C9+C10+C11+C12+C13 and pressing (↵). But there is an easier way to add a column of cells: You can use an arithmetic function called Sum.

Quattro Pro provides a variety of functions, and the Sum function is one of the most useful. An arithmetic function is arranged in the format @function(block):

- the @ symbol tells Quattro Pro to expect a function.
- function is the name of the function, Sum in this case.
- block is the set of cells to be used in the function. We discuss blocks in more detail later in this section.

One way to indicate a block is by typing the first cell location, a period, and then the last cell location. Thus, to use the Sum function to add the expense amounts, you would enter the following into cell D14:

```
@SUM(C9.C13)
```

This formula adds the values in cells C9 through C13 and enters the sum in the cell where the cell selector is located (Figure 2-12). If you look at the input line, you will see that after the function is entered, the program adds a second period, so that the function reads (C9..C13). This makes the cell addresses easier to read.

Type @SUM(C9.C13) (↵)	Enters result of calculation into D14
Press (↓)	Moves cell selector to D15
Type '--------- (9 minus signs) (↵)	Enters a dashed line in D15

To create a dashed line, use the minus sign (–). However, in order to enter a minus sign that the program will not consider a formula, you must type an apostrophe (') before the first minus sign. Remember, an apostrophe indicates text.

Press (↓) **and then** (←) **3 times**	Moves the cell selector to A16
Type CONTINGENCY **and then** (→) **3 times**	Enters CONTINGENCY into A16 and moves cell selector to D16

FIGURE 2-12

Sum function

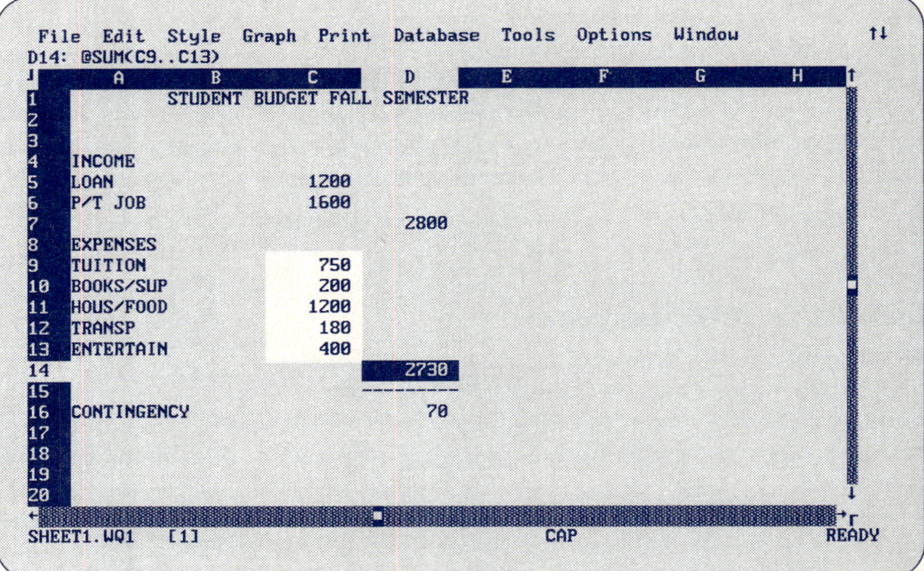

Type +D7–D14 ⏎	Subtracts the contents of D14 (expenses) from D7 (income) and enters the result (70) into D16

To enter this formula without typing cell addresses, you would:

Type +	Lets Quattro Pro know you are starting a formula
Press ↑ **9 times**	Moves cell selector to D7
Type –	Next part of the formula. Enters D7 into the formula and returns the cell selector to D16
Press ↑ **twice**	Moves cell selector to D14
⏎	Enters D14 into the formula, returns the cell selector to D16, and calculates the result, 70

Congratulations! You have completed entering the data for this worksheet. Now you can make a simple change and see how readily the program updates the numbers. Assume that the student changes jobs and that earnings increase from $1,600 to $1,850. When you enter 1850 into C6 and press ⏎, the total in D7 is recalculated. Remember the formula (+C5+C6) you entered in D7? With this formula, any change in either C5 or C6 is automatically reflected in D7. Try making this change:

Press F5	Brings up the GoTo prompt
Type C6 ⏎	Moves the cell selector to C6
Type 1850 ⏎	Enters 1850 into C6 and recalculates D7

The contingency amount in cell D16 also has been recalculated, to 320. This is the result of the formula entered in the cell, +D7-D14.

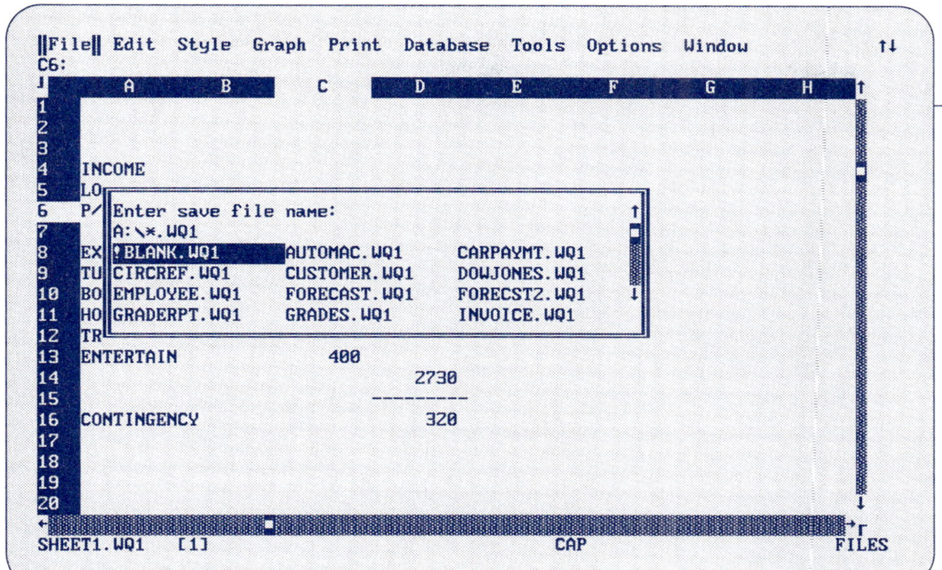

FIGURE 2-13a

Saving a file on the data disk

What if the student decides to buy used books instead of new ones or to live in an apartment instead of a dorm? Using the electronic spreadsheet, he or she can make any amount of changes and the values will be quickly updated.

Saving a Worksheet

You are now ready to save the worksheet you have just created. The worksheet is in a temporary storage area, the **memory**, of the computer. If you turn the computer off, you will lose the worksheet. To store the worksheet for future retrieval, you must save it to a disk. When you save a worksheet to a disk you create a **file**. You can use the data disk provided by your instructor. Make sure your data disk is in drive A. The command to save your spreadsheet is /File¦Save.

Follow these steps to save your worksheet:

Type /	Activates the menu bar
Press F	Chooses the File menu
Press S	Chooses the Save command

A pop-up menu appears on the screen (see Figure 2-13a) with the following prompt.

Enter save file name:

The program is asking you to enter a file name.

Depending on how Quattro Pro has been set up, the file name will begin with either C:\ or A:\. If the name of the file in the prompt begins with C:\, Quattro Pro expects to save the file on drive C. Follow these steps to save your file to drive A:

Press (ESC) **twice**	Clears the C:\ prompt

Type A:BUDGET ↵ — Saves the worksheet as BUDGET onto the A disk

Quattro Pro automatically adds the suffix .WQ1, so the worksheet is saved on the A disk as BUDGET.WQ1.

If the name of the file in the prompt begins with A:\, Quattro Pro is already set up to save the file on drive A. Follow these steps to save the file to drive A.

Type BUDGET ↵ — Saves the worksheet as BUDGET onto the A disk

As in the previous example, Quattro Pro automatically adds the suffix .WQ1, so the worksheet is saved on the A disk as BUDGET.WQ1.

You may notice the disk drive light coming on as the worksheet is saved to your data disk. It takes a few seconds to save the worksheet onto the disk. When the Save command is completed, you will have two copies of the worksheet: one in the memory of the computer and the other on your data disk. The Save As command from the File menu is used to give a new name to an already created file. So, if you wanted to save the BUDGET worksheet with a different name you would use the Save As command.

Before continuing to the next section to learn how to retrieve a worksheet, you need to clear the current worksheet from the memory of the computer. Do this with the /File¦Erase command. The /File¦Erase command will not affect the copy of the worksheet that has been saved to a data disk. ***NOTE:*** If you try to erase a worksheet before you have saved it, Quattro Pro displays a "Lose your changes?" prompt.

Press / F E — Erases the worksheet from the screen

With a blank worksheet, you can retrieve A:BUDGET.

Retrieving a Worksheet

The Retrieve command is used to get a copy of a file from a disk into the memory of the computer. As you might expect, this command, too, is on the File menu: /File¦Retrieve.

Press / F R — Selects the Retrieve command

This may bring up a box with the following prompt.

```
Enter name of file to retrieve:
```

Depending on how Quattro Pro has been set up, the name of the file will begin with either C:\ or A:\. If it begins with C:\, follow these steps:

Press ESC **twice** — Clears the C:\ prompt

Type A: ↵ — Specifies drive A and brings up a list of files on that disk

Move the highlight to BUDGET and press ↵ — Retrieves BUDGET

Another way to retrieve a file is to type the drive and file name without bringing up a list on the screen. Thus, you could have typed *A:BUDGET* ↵ after pressing the ESC key twice.

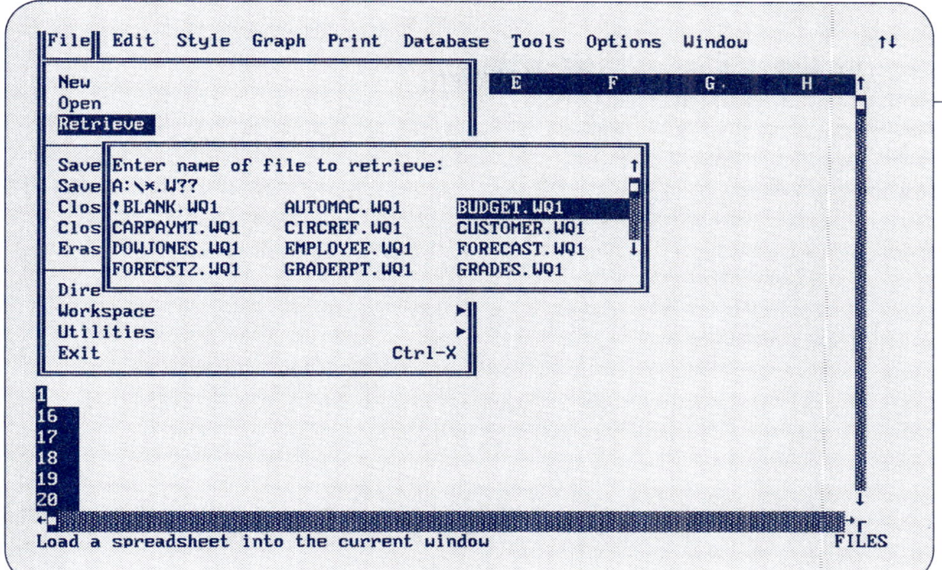

FIGURE 2-13b

Retrieving a file from the data disk

If the name of the file in the prompt begins with A:\, all the files on drive A, including BUDGET, will be displayed (see Figure 2-13b).

Move the highlight to BUDGET and press ↵ Retrieves BUDGET

Printing a Worksheet

In this section you learn how to print your worksheet using the /Print|Block command. If no printer is available, you may skip this section. If your computer does not have a printer attached, move to one that does, and then load Quattro Pro and retrieve the BUDGET worksheet.

When you print a worksheet, you are given the option of printing what is shown on the screen or creating a report including headings, page numbers, current date, margins, and so on. You will learn how to create a report in Chapter 4. For now, you will print the worksheet by activating the Print menu, indicating the block of the worksheet to print, and selecting Spreadsheet Print.

When printing a worksheet, you print from the data in the memory of the computer. Because the screen is only a window into the computer's memory, you can print out more than is displayed on the screen. You need to specify what part of the worksheet to print. Make sure your printer is turned on and ready to receive output from your computer, and follow these steps to print the entire worksheet.

Press / P Selects the Print menu

Figure 2-14 shows the Print options, which allow you to print the worksheet as it is or to set up a report design. When printing a worksheet, you must indicate the block to print. The first step is to select the Block option and specify the group of cells to print.

Press B Selects Block option

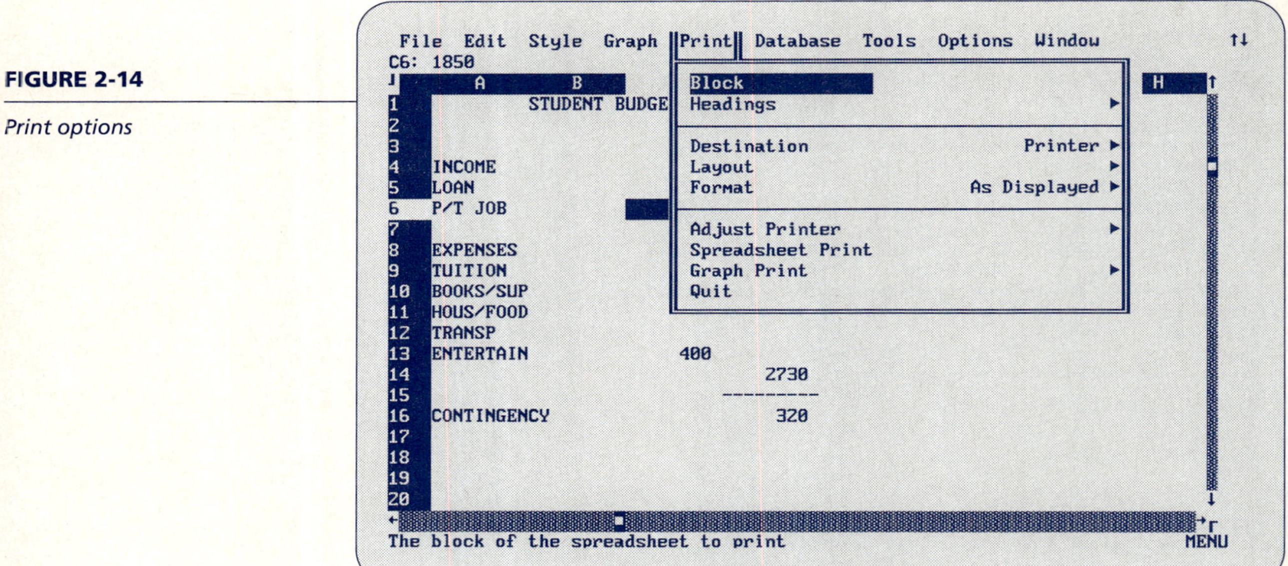

FIGURE 2-14

Print options

The prompt at the input line is:

The block of the spreadsheet to print : C6

You want to print the entire worksheet, so you will specify A1.E16 (you need to specify the E column because the word SEMESTER overlaps into this column).

Type A1.E16 ↵	Specifies the block to print
Press S	Selects Spreadsheet Print

If all has gone well, you now have a "hard copy" of the worksheet. (***NOTE:*** If the paper is not ejected from the printer, use the Form Feed option from the Adjust Printer menu. First, press A for Adjust Printer and F for Form Feed. Then press ESC to return to the Print menu.)

Press Q or ESC	Exits from the Print menu

Formatting the Contents of a Cell

Quattro Pro is set up so that as values are entered, no commas are displayed. In fact, if you try to enter a number with a comma, an error message is displayed. Also, if you type a number with zeros as decimal places (e.g., 100.00), the zeros are not displayed. You can, however, use the /Style¦Numeric Format command to have commas, decimal places, and even dollar signs displayed within a cell.

Change the student budget so it resembles Figure 2-15a.

Press / S	Selects the Style menu
Press N	Selects Numeric Format

As Figure 2-15b shows, there are several ways you can format a cell, including specifying a certain number of decimal places (Fixed x.xx); a comma

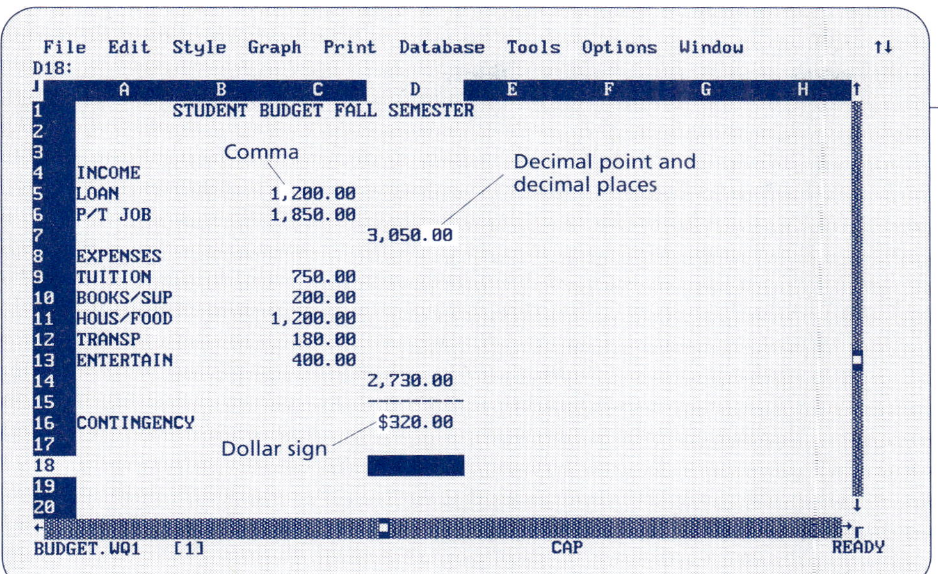

FIGURE 2-15a

Formatting the contents of a cell

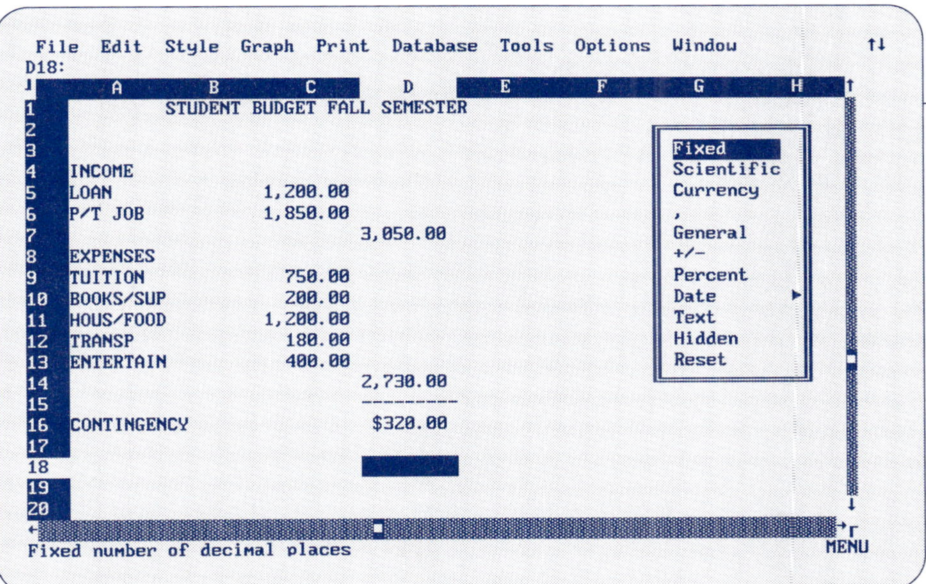

FIGURE 2-15b

Pop-up format menu

and decimal places (the Comma option, referred to as Financial x,xxx.xx); or a dollar sign, comma, and decimal places (Currency $x,xxx.xx).

Press F Selects fixed number of decimal places

The prompt at the pop-up box is:

`Enter Number of decimal places [0..15]:`

Quattro Pro assumes you want two decimal places, but it is possible to enter any number from 0 to 15.

Press ↵	Accepts two decimal places

The prompt on the input line is:

```
Block to be modified : C6..C6
```

At this point, you need to indicate the block (group of cells) that you want formatted. You specify a block by typing the cell in the upper left corner of the block, a period, and the cell in the lower right corner. As you want all the values to be two decimal places, the block will be A1 through D16.

Type A1.D16 ↵	Specifies the block to format

All values are changed to two decimal places. Now change the format to include commas (Financial).

Press / S N	Selects the Numeric Format command
Press ,	Selects the Comma option, also known as Financial format
Press ↵	Indicates two decimal places
Type A1.D16 ↵	Specifies the block to format

Finally, you will format cell D16 to display a dollar sign.

Press F5	Brings up the GoTo prompt
Type D16 ↵	Moves the cell selector to D16
Press / S N C	Selects the Currency format
Press ↵	Indicates two decimal places
Press ↵	Indicates D16 as the cell to format

Remember, you cannot type a dollar sign or comma when entering a number. You can only display them by using /Style¦Numeric Format to format a cell.

Using Blocks

When you performed the Print and Numeric Format commands or added a column of numbers with the Sum function, you had to specify a block that included one or more cells. Many Quattro Pro commands require you to specify a block, so we need to take a closer look at blocks in general.

A block can consist of one cell or several cells. When you are working with more than one cell in a block, the following rules apply.

- The cells either must be in a straight line (row or column) or they must make a rectangle.
- The cells must be connected.

In other words, a block cannot be made up of cells that run diagonally or are separated. Figure 2-16 illustrates acceptable cell blocks.

To specify a block, type the cell address for the first cell in the block, followed by a period, followed by the address for the last cell in the block. For a

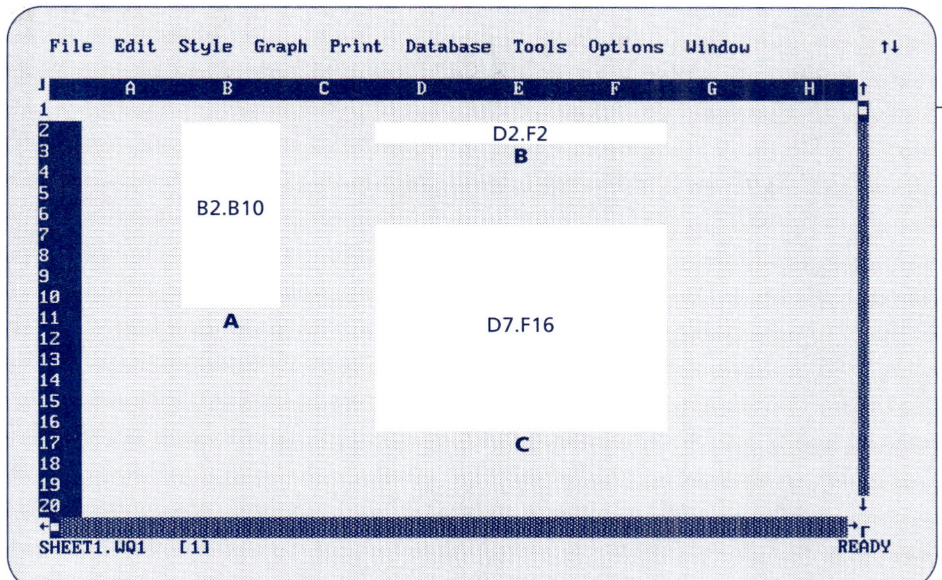

FIGURE 2-16

Example of acceptable cell blocks

rectangle, enter the upper left cell and the lower right cell, separated by a period. Using this method, you would type the following to specify the various blocks in Figure 2-16. (***NOTE:*** Quattro Pro adds a second period between the cell addresses.)

Block	Cell locations that specify the block
A	B2.B10
B	D2.F2
C	D7.F16

Typing cell addresses is one method. There are, however, two other ways to indicate a group of cells: using cell selector keys to highlight a block and naming a block.

Highlighting a Block To highlight a block, use the cell selector movement keys to locate one cell, type a period, and then use the cell selector movement keys to locate the other cell. Try this now by highlighting the block used in the Sum function to add the student's expenses.

Press (F5) **and type** D14 (↵)	Moves the cell selector to D14
Type @SUM(	Begins the Sum function

At this point you need to specify a block. Use the cell selector movement keys to locate the first cell in the block.

Press (←) **and then** (↑) **5 times**	Moves the cell selector to C9
Type a period	Specifies C9 as the beginning of the block

Press ↓ **4 times**	Moves the cell selector to C13 and highlights the block
Type)	Ends the Sum function
Press ↵	Executes the Sum function

Notice that highlighting is useful because you can see exactly the cells that are included in the block.

You can use this method to specify a block with any command that prompts you for a block. For example, when prompted for a block during the /Print¦Block command discussed above, you would:

- Move the cell selector to A1
- Type a period
- Move the cell selector to E16
- Press ↵

Specifying Block Names Quattro Pro allows you to give a name to a block of cells. This helps you remember which cells are included in the block. For example, it is easier to remember that the block EXPENSES contains the expense amounts than to remember the cells C9.C13. In the student budget example, the block of cells C9.C13 could be named EXPENSES. Then, to add the block you could type SUM(EXPENSES). The process is to select the /Edit¦Names¦Create command and enter the block name and cells. Try this now by specifying a block name for the expense amounts. With the cell selector at D14:

Press / E	Brings up the Edit menu
Press N	Selects the Names option
Press C	Selects the Create command

The prompt is:

```
Enter Name to create/modify:
```

Type EXPENSES ↵	Enters the block name

The prompt is:

```
Enter block: D14..D14
```

Type C9.C13 ↵	Enters the cell coordinates

Notice on the input line that the Sum function has been changed to indicate the new block name. Any function or command that uses a cell block, such as Sum or Print, can use a block name.

Shortcuts

Quattro Pro provides shortcuts to make entering and modifying data easier. The three most important are CTRL keys for commands, ALT-F3 to bring up the function menu, and SHIFT-F7 to enter the Extended mode to highlight blocks.

Control Keys Quattro Pro provides shortcuts you can use for frequently chosen commands such as Save. These involve pressing CTRL together with a letter key. For example, instead of pressing / to activate the menu bar, F for the File menu, and S for Save, you could press CTRL-S (while holding down the CTRL key, tap the S key, and then release the CTRL key). This gives you precisely the same pop-up menu as pressing / F S. Similarly, to exit Quattro Pro you could press CTRL-X instead of pressing / F X. The shortcut keys are listed on the pull-down menus next to their commands. Shortcut keys for the commands already discussed are:

CTRL-X	E**x**it
CTRL-S	**S**ave
CTRL-F	Numeric **F**ormat

Practice using the CTRL key by displaying the Numeric Format menu.

Press CTRL-F	Displays the Numeric Format pop-up menu
Press ESC	Returns to spreadsheet

Use / and arrow keys to look for other shortcut keys listed on the command menu. A complete list is given in the appendix.

Function Menu Instead of typing out the name of a function, such as @SUM, you can enter it in a cell by choosing it from the function menu, which is a list of all functions available in Quattro Pro. The function menu is a pop-up menu: Press ALT-F3 (while holding down the ALT key, tap F3, then release the ALT key) to see it on the screen and ESC to close it. Within the menu, you can use the ↑ and ↓ keys to move to the function you wish to insert and then press ↵ to insert it into the cell. For example, to insert the Sum function in D14, first place the cell selector on D14. Then:

Press ALT-F3	Brings up the function menu, listing the functions in alphabetical order

Use the PGDN and ↓ keys until Sum is highlighted. As you move through the functions, each appears on the input line. When you reach Sum:

Press ↵	Enters the function on the input line

Note that the input line now says @SUM(. At this point, you may enter the cell addresses for the block in any of the ways already discussed: typing the cell addresses, using the arrow keys and the period to anchor and move through the block, or specifying the name. In this case, because you have already named the block, you can:

Type EXPENSES) ↵	EXPENSES is the name of the block, and the final parenthesis is needed to complete the function

NOTE: Quattro Pro always requires a close parenthesis at the end of a function. If you forget to type it, you will see an error message. To remove the error message, press ESC. Then type the parenthesis and press ↵.

Extended Mode As you know, many Quattro Pro commands require you to specify a block to work with. You can always choose the command and let Quattro Pro prompt you for the block. But it can be quicker and more intuitive to first specify the block and then choose the command. For example, instead of choosing the /Print¦Block command from the menu and then typing cell addresses or highlighting a block, you could first highlight the block and then press / P B. Instead of prompting you for the block, Quattro Pro would use the already highlighted block. You could then press S to print the spreadsheet.

To specify a block, move to the first cell in the block and press SHIFT-F7. You will see EXT (for Extended mode) in the lower right of the status line. Then move through the cells you wish to include in the block. All the cells will be highlighted. When the entire block is highlighted, choose a command, either from the command menu or by using CTRL keys. Quattro Pro carries out the command on the specified block.

Practice using EXT to print out only the INCOME part of the worksheet.

Press HOME	Returns to A1
Press SHIFT-F7	Enters Extended mode and begins highlighting the block

Notice EXT on the status line.

Move the cell selector to E7	The worksheet area should be highlighted
Press / P B	The Print menu is displayed

Notice that the block is specified.

Press S	Prints the specified block
Press ESC	Exits the Print menu

During Application 2, you used the Sum function to add a series of numbers and you saved, retrieved, and printed a worksheet. You learned how to format cells and work with blocks. You also learned some shortcuts to save time and prevent typing mistakes. You now have the skills to develop a more involved spreadsheet. You can pause now and return later to complete this chapter, or you can continue with the next application. If you decide to continue, use the /File¦Erase command to clear the worksheet. If you wish to take a break, use the Quit command to exit Quattro Pro. Try this using the shortcut keys:

Press CTRL-X	Selects the Exit command

The prompt is:

```
Lose your changes? No Yes
```

Type Y

SUMMARY

Having completed this chapter, you should understand how electronic spreadsheets can be used for common business and personal applications. You have acquired skills in the popular spreadsheet program Quattro Pro. With this program, you can develop, save, retrieve, and print worksheets. The challenge exercises that follow will help you practice the skills you have just learned. You are now prepared to learn the more involved decision-making features of Quattro Pro presented in Chapter 3.

WORD LIST

↵ key
block
cell
cell selector
cell selector movement keys
command menu
commands
data
default setting
electronic spreadsheet
file
file name
formulas
functions
highlight
input line
label
menu
pop-up menu
pull-down menu
status line
text
values
worksheet

QUESTIONS

1. What does the following formula do: @SUM(B5.B10)?
2. Describe the process for saving a worksheet.
3. What is a file?
4. What are the rules for naming a worksheet when you save it?
5. List the steps used in printing a worksheet.
6. List three ways a cell can be formatted.
7. What is a cell block, and what rules must be kept in mind when using a cell block?
8. List and describe three ways to specify a block.
9. What is Extended mode? How do you enter it?

CHALLENGE EXERCISES

The following exercises provide practice in using the functions and commands presented in Application 2. Use the techniques discussed in the application to highlight a block without typing the cell addresses.

1. Prepare a grade report, as follows:
   a. If necessary, use the /File|Erase command to clear the worksheet.
   b. Retrieve the worksheet called GRADERPT from your data disk.
   c. Use the Sum function to enter a total of each student's points. (***NOTE:*** You will sum across each row.)

   d. Use the Save As command from the File menu to save the revised worksheet as GRADEREV. Be sure to specify drive A.

   e. Print the revised worksheet.

2. Prepare a sales report: On your data disk is a worksheet called SALES. Retrieve this worksheet and use the Style menu to format the values with commas and two decimal places. Then format the grand total with a dollar sign and two decimal places. Save the worksheet as SALESFMT.

3 Worksheet Planning and Decision Making

Thus far we have emphasized the mechanics involved in using an electronic spreadsheet, moving the cell selector, and entering data and formulas. Remember, though, that an electronic spreadsheet is a tool used to analyze data for decision making and problem solving. Although you will be learning new functions and commands, keep in mind that the mechanics used in developing a worksheet are a means to an end.

APPLICATION 1

The problem presented in this application is typical of both business and nonbusiness budgeting: Which of several loan options is the best? The electronic spreadsheet allows you to study the loan options and determine the best one. Carefully follow this section step by step. New commands are presented in a structured way, so resist the temptation to skip ahead.

How to Plan a Worksheet

As this is a more involved spreadsheet, the first step is planning the development of the worksheet. In Chapter 2, both Applications 1 and 2 were simple worksheets that did not require planning. However, planning larger and more complex worksheets aids in data entry and provides ways of checking the accuracy of calculations.

A worksheet can be quickly sketched out on a preprinted form. Two such forms are presented in Figure 3-1. One is a standard accounting columnar pad. The other is a sheet of paper with grid lines. If you use a preprinted form, the planning process involves the following steps.

1. Determine column widths for values. Quattro Pro begins with a column width of nine characters. However, this width can be changed using the /Style¦Column Width command. The column width is especially important for values. When you enter a value, a space is added at the end of the number so that numbers in adjacent cells do not run together. Thus, a column width of 9 will accommodate a number with eight digits. If a cell has been formatted to display decimal places, commas, or dollar signs, these are included in the length of the number. Therefore, the number 10000 entered into a cell formatted with commas and two decimal places would be displayed as 10,000.00 and would need a cell width of 10 (one space at the end). If a cell has been formatted for a dollar sign, a comma, or decimal places and the number is too long to fit in the cell width, the cell will fill with asterisks (*). If you see a cell displaying asterisks you will need to increase the width of the column.

If a cell has not been formatted and the number is too long, the number is displayed in scientific notation. Thus, the entry 1000000 in a cell with a width of six would be displayed as 1E+06. Scientific notation uses 10 raised to a power, so that this number is read 1 times 10 to the power of 6. This type of notation is useful for very large or very small numbers, although it is used more often in scientific, rather than business, applications.

Figure 3-2 shows four value entries in column B. In each case, the cell width is 6. The table below it shows the format and explains the problem, if any, with each entry.

FIGURE 3-1

Preprinted forms

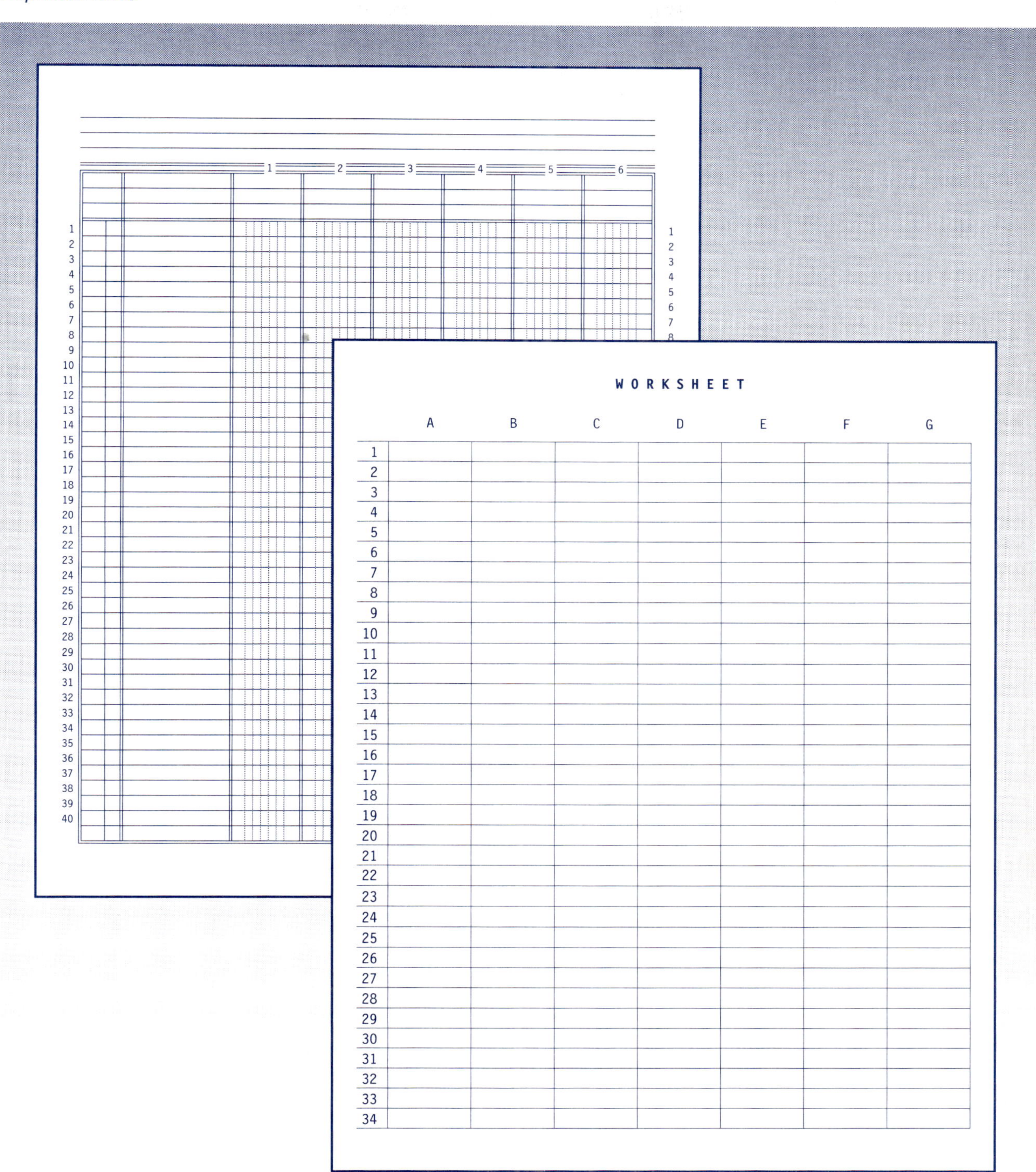

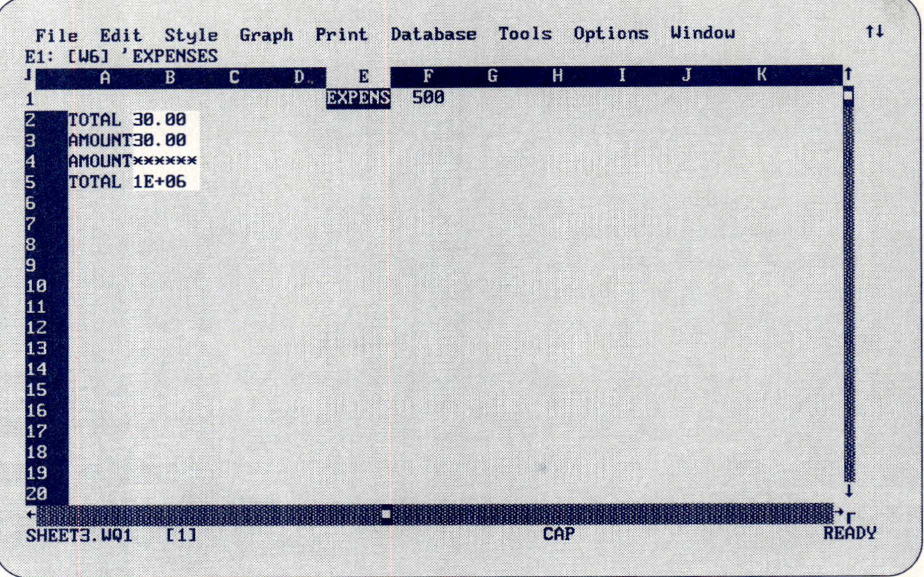

FIGURE 3-2

Examples of value entries

Cell	Entry	Problem	Format fixed with:
B2	30.00	None	Two decimal places
B3	30.00	Runs together with adjacent cell	Two decimal places
B4	7000.00	Number too long— ****** displayed	Two decimal places
B5	1000000	Displayed in scientific notation	No decimal places

The rule of thumb is to determine the longest possible value entry (including dollar signs, commas, and decimal places where appropriate) and add 1 for a space. This would be the minimum column width. In the example above, the entries in cells B4 and B5 would need a cell width of 8.

2. Determine column widths for text. Cell width for text, such as titles, is not as crucial as it is for values. If text data that is longer than the cell width is entered, the data overflows into the adjacent cell. However, if the adjacent cell to the right already contains data, then the entire entry is not displayed on the screen and does not print out. Figure 3-2 shows the text entry EXPENSES in E1 (note the input line). But only part (EXPENS) of the entry is displayed, because F1 contains an entry (500) and the cell width is only 6. It would be necessary to either widen column E or abbreviate the entry.

3. Determine the formulas needed. Specifying the formulas in the planning process reduces the chance of making an error when developing the worksheet. In addition, formulas can be developed to check the accuracy of calculations within the worksheet. A common technique to verify the accuracy of calculations is **crossfooting**.

Crossfooting is useful for rows and columns of numbers that are added together to obtain a grand total. Figure 3-3 illustrates this concept. Columns B,

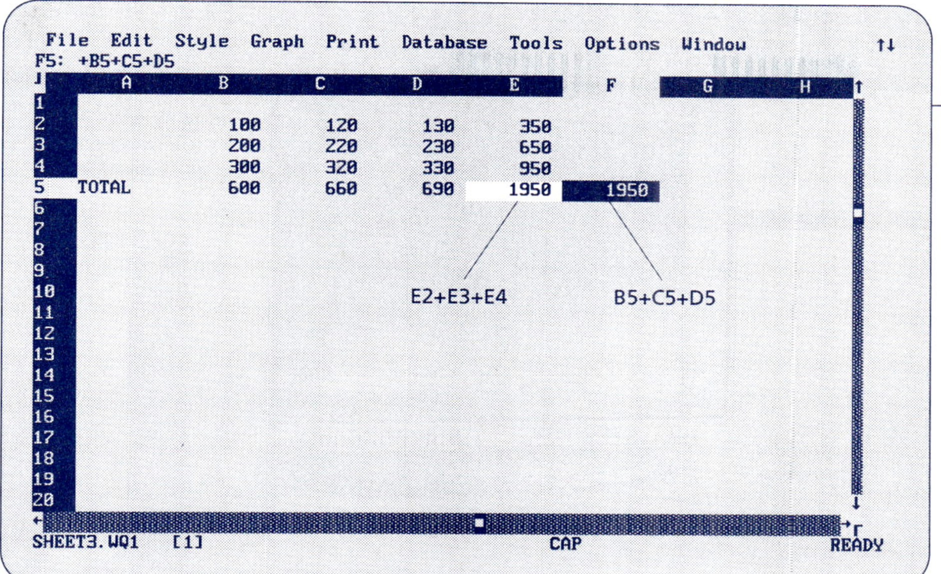

FIGURE 3-3

Crossfooting

WORKSHEET

	A	B	C	D	E	F	G	H
1	STUDENT	BUDGET	ANALYSIS					
2								
3		SEP	OCT	NOV	DEC	JAN	FEB	MAR
4								
5	P/T JOB							
6								
7	TUITION							
8	BKS/SUP							
9	HOUS/FD							
10	TRANSP							
11	SAV ACC							
12	ENTERTAIN							
13	TOTAL EXP	SUM(B7-B12)	→	→	→	→	→	
14								
15	INC-EXP	B5-B13	→	→	→	→	→	
16								
17								
18								

FIGURE 3-4

Preplanned worksheet

C, and D are added across to obtain totals in column E. They also are added down to obtain totals in row 5. Cell E5 contains the total of all cells, which is calculated by adding E2+E3+E4. As a check on the accuracy of the number in E5, a formula can be entered into F6 to add B5+C5+D5. If the numbers are different, there is an error in the worksheet.

Figure 3-4 shows the layout of the worksheet for Application 1. Note that the column widths are left at 9 (the default value), the titles include abbreviations, and the formulas have been determined. With this planning completed, you are ready to create the worksheet. But before beginning, you need to review the situation.

Reviewing the Situation

A student wishes to develop a budget for the first year of college. The budget will include projected expenses and anticipated income for the months of September through May. Because tuition must be paid at the beginning of each semester, expenses in September and January are higher than in other months. A part-time job will pay for monthly expenses, but the student needs a loan to cover the cost of tuition, books, and supplies. Thus, a loan payment will become part of the monthly expenses. As the student lives in a dorm, housing and food costs are constant and transportation costs are minimal.

In approaching several banks for a loan, the student was told to develop a budget. After obtaining loan information, the student decides to develop a spreadsheet to analyze the alternatives and make a decision on the best loan option. The following section contains the budget information to be included in the worksheet.

Income

Part-time job: $450 per month

Expenses

Tuition: $750 per semester

Books and supplies: $200 per semester

Housing and food: $300 per month

Transportation: $50 per month

Savings account: $30 per month
(needed for gifts in December and vacation in May)

Entertainment: $50 per month

Figure 3-5 shows part of the completed worksheet, except for the loan and loan payment amounts. Notice that when expenses are subtracted from income,

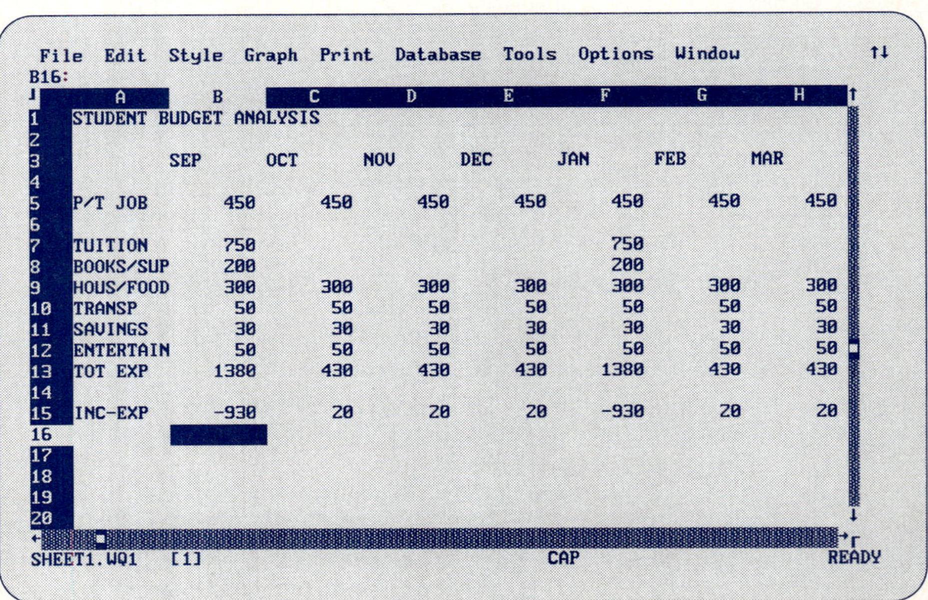
File Edit Style Graph Print Database Tools Options Window
B16:

	A	B	C	D	E	F	G	H
1	STUDENT BUDGET ANALYSIS							
2								
3		SEP	OCT	NOV	DEC	JAN	FEB	MAR
4								
5	P/T JOB	450	450	450	450	450	450	450
6								
7	TUITION	750				750		
8	BOOKS/SUP	200				200		
9	HOUS/FOOD	300	300	300	300	300	300	300
10	TRANSP	50	50	50	50	50	50	50
11	SAVINGS	30	30	30	30	30	30	30
12	ENTERTAIN	50	50	50	50	50	50	50
13	TOT EXP	1380	430	430	430	1380	430	430
14								
15	INC-EXP	-930	20	20	20	-930	20	20
16								
17								
18								
19								
20								

SHEET1.WQ1 [1] CAP READY

FIGURE 3-5

Application 1: Loan Payment worksheet

there is a substantial shortfall in September and January, when tuition must be paid and books and supplies must be purchased. You will first develop this worksheet and then insert the various loan options to determine which option is the best.

Before you start entering data, study the worksheet in Figure 3-5. The screen is 80 characters wide, so only the amounts through March are visible. Because the columns are nine characters wide, only eight columns (A–H) will fit on the screen (later you will reduce the column widths so that you can view more). To develop the worksheet, your first step is to enter STUDENT BUDGET ANALYSIS into cell A1. (***NOTE:*** If you cannot complete this application in one session, use the /File¦Save command ((CTRL)-S) before quitting. Then use the /File¦Retrieve command to load your worksheet at a later time.)

ACTION	RESULT
Type STUDENT BUDGET ANALYSIS (↵)	
	Enters STUDENT BUDGET ANALYSIS into A1
(↓) (↓) (→)	Moves cell selector to B3
Type SEP (→)	Enter SEP into B3 and moves cell selector to C3
Type OCT (→)	Enters OCT into C3 and moves cell selector to D3
Type NOV (→)	Enter NOV into D3 and moves cell selector to E3
Type DEC (→)	Enters DEC into E3 and moves cell selector to F3
Type JAN (→)	Enters JAN into F3 and moves cell selector to G3
Type FEB (→)	Enters FEB into G3 and moves cell selector to H3
Type MAR (→)	Enters MAR into H3 and moves cell selector to I3

Figure 3-6 shows how the screen has scrolled past column A, which is no longer visible.

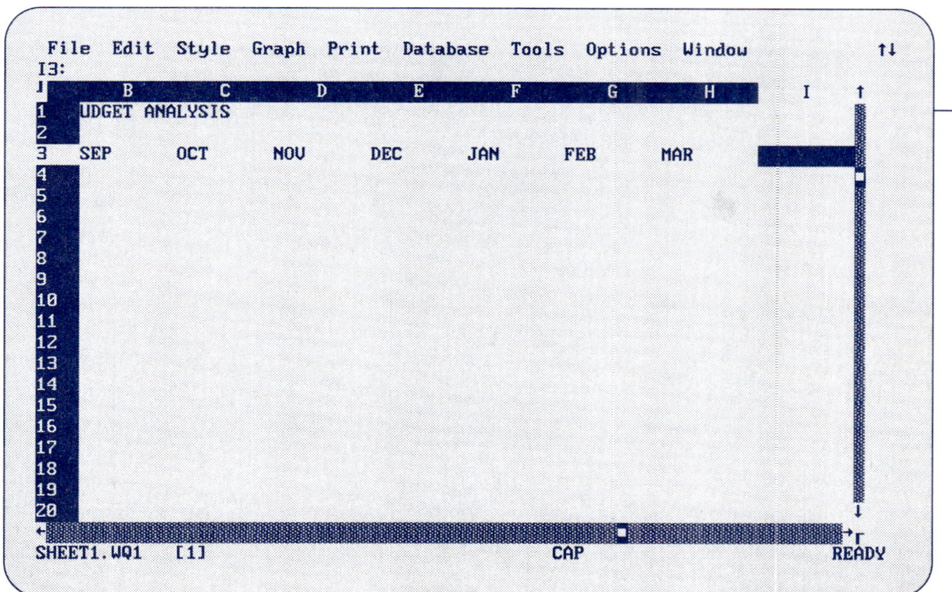

FIGURE 3-6

Scrolling the screen left to right

ACTION	RESULT
Type APR [→]	Enters APR into I3 and moves cell selector to J3
Type MAY [↓] [↓]	Enters MAY into J3
Press [CTRL]-[←]	Moves cell selector to A5
Type P/T JOB [→]	Enters P/T JOB into A5 and moves cell selector to B5
Type 450 [→]	Enters 450 into B5 and moves cell selector to C5
Type 450 [→]	Enters 450 into C5 and moves cell selector to D5
Type 450 [→]	Enters 450 into D5 and moves cell selector to E5
Type 450 [→]	Enters 450 into E5 and moves cell selector to F5
Type 450 [→]	Enters 450 into F5 and moves cell selector to G5
Type 450 [→]	Enters 450 into G5 and moves cell selector to H5
Type 450 [→]	Enters 450 into H5 and moves cell selector to I5
Type 450 [→]	Enters 450 into I5 and moves cell selector to J5
Type 450 [↓] [↓]	Enters 450 into J5
Press [CTRL]-[←]	Moves cell selector to A7
Type TUITION [→]	Enters TUITION into A7 and moves cell selector to B7
Type 750 **and press** [→] **4 times**	Enters 750 into B7 and moves cell selector to F7
Type 750 [↓]	Enters 750 into F7
Press [←] **5 times**	Moves cell selector to A8
Type BOOKS/SUP [→]	Enters BOOKS/SUP into A8 and moves cell selector to B8
Type 200 [→] **4 times**	Enters 200 into B8 and moves cell selector to F8
Type 200 [↓]	Enters 200 into F8
Press [←] **5 times**	Moves cell selector to A9
Type HOUS/FOOD [→]	Enters HOUS/FOOD into A9 and moves cell selector to B9
Type 300 [↵]	Enters 300 into B9

Copying Data

At this point 300 must be entered eight more times, for the months October through May. This is a time-consuming, redundant process. To speed things up, you can copy the value in cell B9 (300) into cells C9 through J9. This is done with the /Edit¦Copy command. The shortcut for Copy is [CTRL]-C. The procedure is to specify the cell (B9) that the data is to be copied from and then to specify the block of cells that the data is to be copied to. As you complete these steps, refer to Figures 3-7 and 3-8, and notice how the

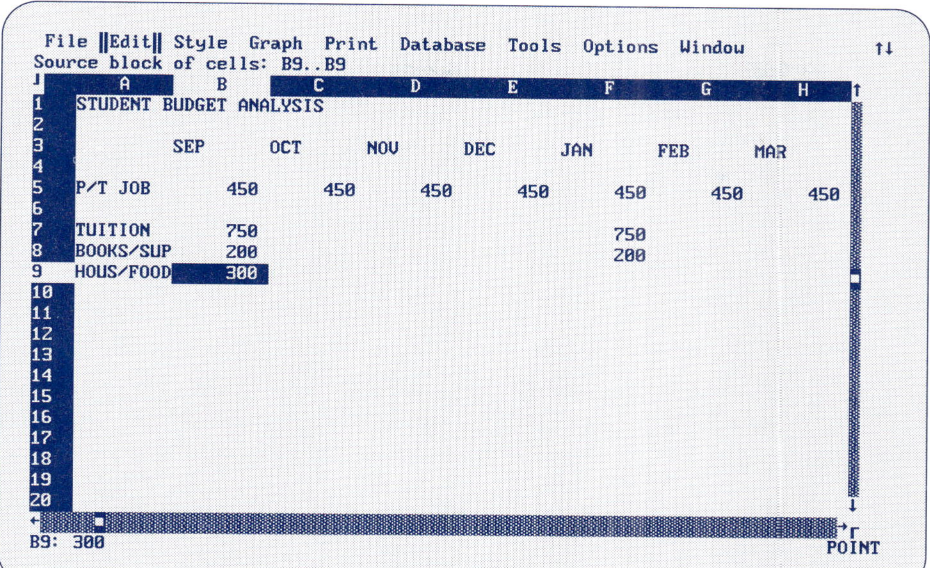

FIGURE 3-7

Copy: source block

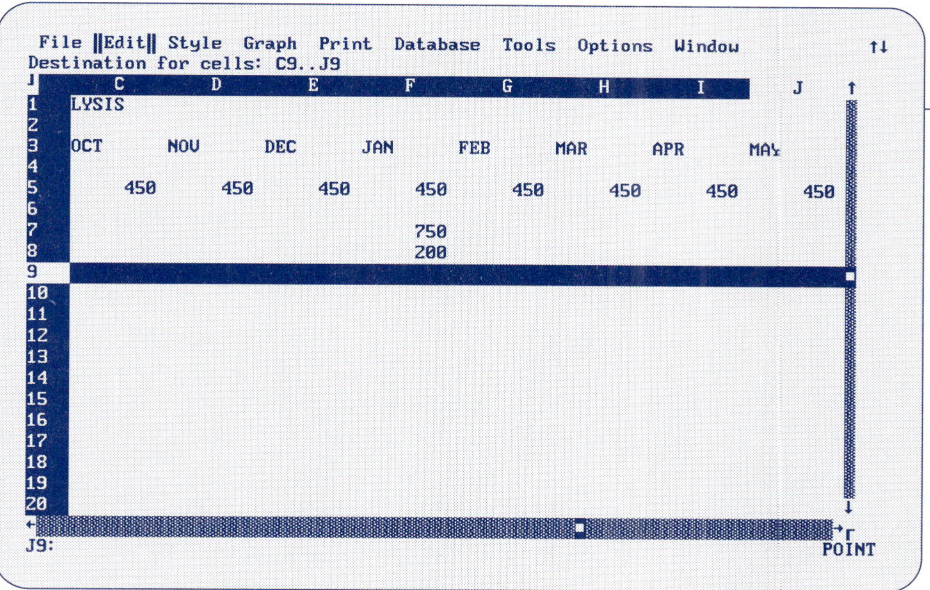

FIGURE 3-8

Copy: destination block

/Edit|Copy command is executed. With the cell selector at B9, watch the screen as you follow these steps:

Press / E	Brings up the Edit menu
Type C	Selects the Copy command

(***NOTE:*** You could have pressed CTRL-C to get the same result.)

The following prompt appears on the input line.

Source block of cells: B9..B9

When you use the /Edit¦Copy command, you must indicate the source block: the cell or cells you wish to copy *from*. In this case you want to copy the contents of cell B9 (source). (See Figure 3-7.) As the cell selector is already on B9:

Press (↵)	Enters B9 as the cell to copy from

If you had wished to copy a different cell, you would have typed in the cell address. The following prompt appears.

Destination for cells: B9

You must now specify the destination: the block of cells you wish to copy *to*. This would be cells C9 through J9. To indicate the block to copy to, move the cell selector to the first cell, type a period to indicate the start of the block, move the cell selector to the last cell, and press (↵). The contents of cell B9 will be copied into cells C9, D9, E9, F9, G9, H9, I9, and J9. Assuming that the cell selector is still on B9:

Press (→)	Moves cell selector to C9
Type a period	Indicates the start of a block
Press (→) **7 times**	Extends block from (highlights) cells C9 through J9

This specifies the destination block for the Copy command (Figure 3-8). The input line should display:

Destination for cells: C9..J9

Press (↵)	Enters 300 into the destination block and returns the cell selector to B9
(↓) (←)	Moves cell selector to A10
Type TRANSP (↓)	Enters TRANSP into A10 and moves cell selector to A11
Type SAVINGS (↓)	Enters SAVINGS into A11 and moves cell selector to A12
Type ENTERTAIN (→)	Enters ENTERTAIN into A12 and moves cell selector to B12
Type 50 (↑)	Enters 50 into B12 and moves cell selector to B11
Type 30 (↑)	Enters 30 into B11 and moves cell selector to B10
Type 50 (↵)	Enters 50 into B10

As transportation, savings, and entertainment amounts are the same for all nine months, you can use /Edit¦Copy to fill in these values. However, instead of performing three copy procedures, one for each row, you can do one copy for all three rows. This is similar to the copy performed earlier, except that you need to specify a block of cells to copy *from* instead of specifying a single

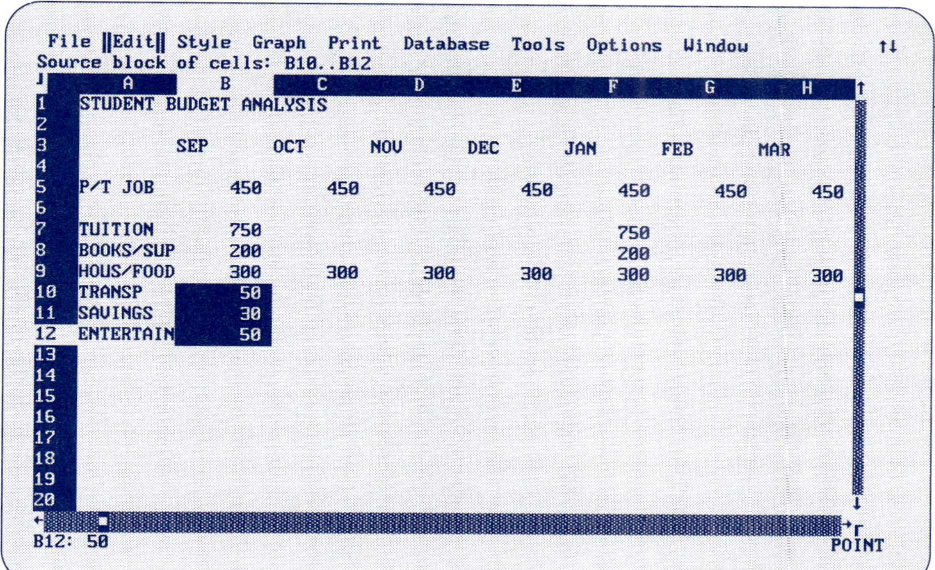

FIGURE 3-9

Copy: source block

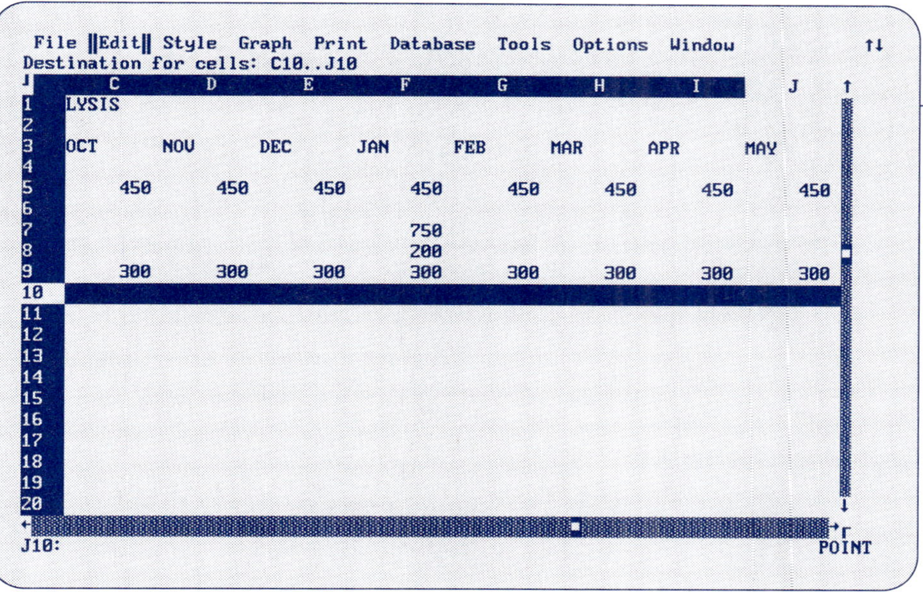

FIGURE 3-10

Copy: destination block

source cell. Figures 3-9 and 3-10 show how this /Edit|Copy command works. Move the cell selector to B10 if it is not there already.

Press / E C (or CTRL-C)	Brings up the Copy command and prompts you for the source block
↓ ↓	Extends source block (highlights) cells B10 through B12

↵	Enters the source block and returns the cell selector to B10

This brings up the next prompt:

```
Destination for cells: B10
```

→	Moves the cell selector to C10
Type a period	Specifies the beginning cell of the destination block as C10
Press → 7 times	Extends destination block from cells C10 through J10

NOTE: When copying to a block you need to specify only the top row of the destination block; the program will fill in the entire block (Figure 3-10).

↵	Copies the contents of the source block into the destination block and returns the cell selector to B10
Press ↓ 3 times and then ←	Moves the cell selector to A13
Type TOT EXP →	Enters TOT EXP into A13 and moves cell selector to B13
ALT-F3	Brings up function menu
Press PGDN **8 times and ↓ 8 times**	Positions highlight on the Sum function
↵	Enters @SUM(into the input line
↑	Moves cell selector to cell B12
Type a period	Indicates the first cell of the block for the Sum function
Press ↑ 5 times	Extends block to include cells B12 through B7
Type)↵	Ends the Sum function and enters the result (1380) of the calculation into B13

Copying Formulas

The next step is to copy the formula in B13 into columns for the other months. This is also done with /Edit¦Copy. With the cell selector located on cell B13, the cell to be copied:

Press / E C (or CTRL-C)	Brings up Copy command
↵	Specifies the source block
→	Moves the cell selector to C13
Type a period	Specifies the beginning cell of the destination block
Press → 7 times	Extends destination block from cells C13 through J13

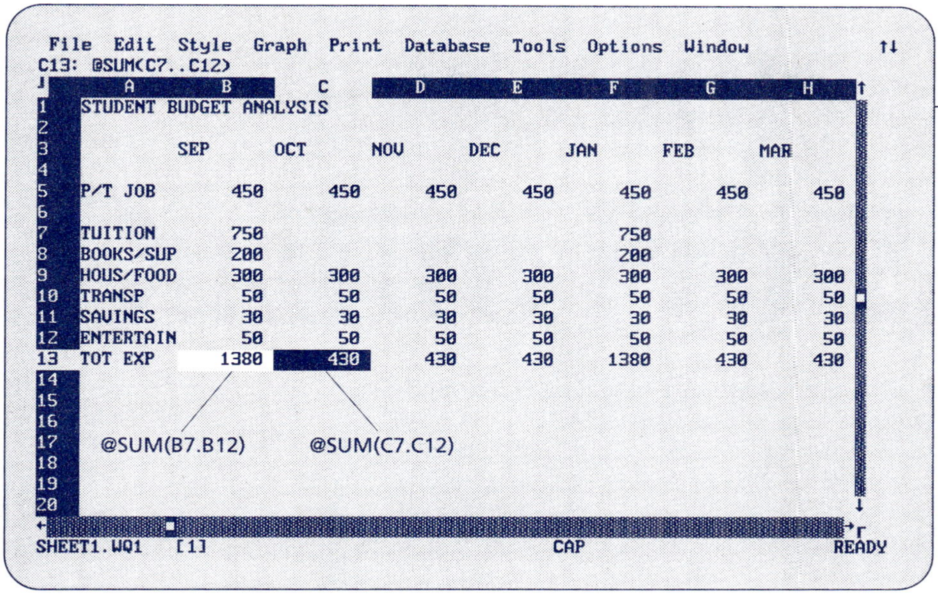

```
 File  Edit  Style  Graph  Print  Database  Tools  Options  Window              ↑↓
C13: @SUM(C7..C12)
      A          B          C          D          E          F          G          H
1  STUDENT BUDGET ANALYSIS
2
3             SEP        OCT        NOV        DEC        JAN        FEB        MAR
4
5  P/T JOB        450        450        450        450        450        450        450
6
7  TUITION        750                                      750
8  BOOKS/SUP      200                                      200
9  HOUS/FOOD      300        300        300        300        300        300        300
10 TRANSP          50         50         50         50         50         50         50
11 SAVINGS         30         30         30         30         30         30         30
12 ENTERTAIN       50         50         50         50         50         50         50
13 TOT EXP       1380        430        430        430       1380        430        430
14
15
16
17   @SUM(B7.B12)        @SUM(C7.C12)
18
19
20
SHEET1.WQ1   [1]                         CAP                                 READY
```

FIGURE 3-11

Copying a formula

↵	Copies the formula and returns the cell selector to B13

It is important to understand that when you copy a formula from one column to another the formula needs to change as the column changes. The formula as you first typed it for column B contains the block B7.B12. When this formula is copied into column C, the block needs to be changed to C7.C12. Quattro Pro does this automatically. As you copy the formula from the B column to the C, D, and E columns (and so on), the block referenced in the formula changes from B7.B12 to C7.C12, D7.D12, E7.E12, and so on. This is called a **relative cell reference**, because B7.B12 relates to the B column, C7.C12 relates to the C column, and so on (Figure 3-11).

Finish the worksheet by entering the last row, which is INC-EXP.

↓ ↓ ←	Moves cell selector to A15
Type INC-EXP →	Enters INC-EXP into A15 and moves cell selector to B15

Now you need to enter a formula to subtract total expenses (TOT EXP) from income (P/T JOB). As the value for P/T JOB is in B5 and the value for TOT EXP is in B13, you will use these cell locations in the formula.

Type +	Begins formula
Press ↑ **10 times**	Moves cell selector to B5
Type –	Continues formula, enters B5 into formula, and returns cell selector to B15
↑ ↑ ↵	Enters B13 into formula and enters result of calculation (income minus expense) into B15

Type / E C (or CTRL-C)	Brings up Copy command
↵	Specifies B15 as the source block
→	Moves the cell selector to C15
Type a period	Specifies the beginning cell of the destination block as C15
Press → 7 times	Extends destination block from cells C15 through J15
↵	Copies the contents of the source block into the destination block and returns the cell selector to B15

Congratulations! You have entered the basic worksheet for the student budget. As you have seen, /Edit¦Copy is a useful way to quickly enter repetitive data into a worksheet.

Now you will be able to see how an electronic spreadsheet is used as an aid in decision making. As you can see from the "bottom line" of your worksheet, the student is in trouble. Although income exceeds expenses in seven out of the nine months, in the other two months, September and January, the student comes up short. Moreover, the total of the surpluses in the positive months does not come close to covering the shortfalls in the negative months. This is due to the once-per-semester expenses for tuition, books, and supplies. The problem for the student is how to cover these expenses. Alternatives are asking parents, working more, reducing other expenses, or getting a loan. Let us assume that the bank loan emerges as the only possibility. As tuition, books, and supplies total $1,900 for the year, the student would need a loan of at least this amount. The student contacts several banks and identifies the options listed below.

Option	Amount	Rate (%)	Time (months)	Monthly payment
1	$2,000	10	24	92.00
2	2,200	12	36	73.00
3	2,500	14	36	85.00

Option 1 looks appealing because it can be paid off in only two years and the interest rate is the lowest available; the overall cost of the loan (principal + interest) will be less than with the other options. Option 2 also looks good because the monthly payments are the lowest. Option 3, with the high interest rate, seems the least attractive. By inserting the loan amount (as income) and the monthly payments (as expenses) into the worksheet, the student can analyze which is the best alternative.

Inserting a Row

When you return to the worksheet, you will see that more rows are needed for these two items (loan and loan payment). The /Edit¦Insert command can be used to insert blank rows anywhere on the worksheet. The shortcut for this command is CTRL-I. To make room for an inserted row, all the rows move down from where the new row is inserted. For example, if you insert a row at row 5

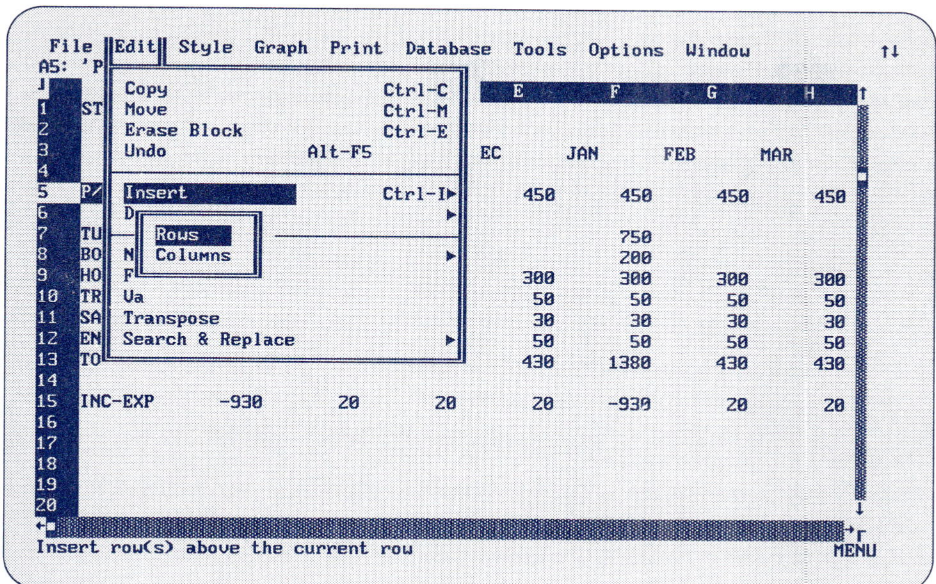

FIGURE 3-12

Inserting a row

(making row 5 blank), all the data currently in row 5 moves down to row 6, all the data in row 6 moves down to row 7, and so forth. The process is to select the Edit menu from the menu bar, choose the Insert command, choose Row, and specify the location of the row to be inserted.

You need to insert three rows. The first is at row 5, for the loan amount. Move the cell selector to A5 (or you could place it on any cell in row 5).

Press / E I (or CTRL-I) Chooses the Insert command from the Edit menu

You will see a menu that asks whether you wish to insert rows or columns (Figure 3-12). Because you want to insert rows:

Press ↵ Specifies Rows

The prompt on the input line is:

Enter row insert block: A5..A5

If you wanted to insert more than one row, you could specify a block. Pressing ↵ inserts the row at row 5.

Press ↵ Inserts a blank row at row 5

All the data on row 5 moves to row 6, and a blank row appears at row 5.

As you perform the Insert command the formulas change to reflect the re-alignment of rows. For instance, before the row was inserted, cell B13 contained the formula @SUM(B7.B12). After the row is inserted, the formula in cell B14 automatically changes to @SUM(B8.B13). The bottom of Figure 3-13 shows the new formula. This is another powerful feature of an electronic spreadsheet: As it carries out various commands, such as Copy, Insert, or Delete, the formulas using a block are automatically updated to reflect these changes. The /Edit¦Delete command works the same way as the /Edit¦Insert

FIGURE 3-13

Formula change due to row insertion

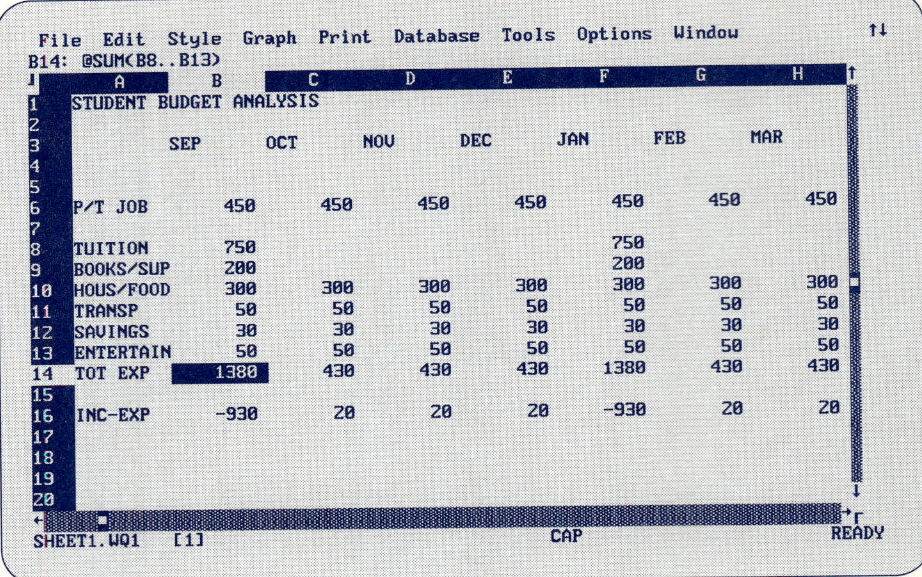

command; both rows and columns can be inserted or deleted. There is no shortcut for the Delete command, however.

With the cell selector at A5, you can enter the headings for the loan and the loan payment amounts. The assumption is that the student will need $1,000 in September and $1,000 in January to pay for tuition, books, and supplies for each semester.

Type LOAN (→)	Enters LOAN into A5 and moves cell selector to B5
Type 1000 **and press** (→) **4 times**	Enters 1000 into B5 and moves cell selector to F5
Type 1000 (↵)	Enters 1000 into F5

Now that there are two categories for income (part-time job and loan), they need to be totaled. Insert a row at row 7 and type in a formula to add the loan and part-time job amounts together.

Press (F5) **and type** A7 (↵)	Moves cell selector to A7
Press / E I (or (CTRL)-I)	Brings up the Insert command
(↵)	Chooses Insert Rows
(↵)	Inserts a blank row at row 7
Type TOT INC (→)	Enters TOT INC into A7 and moves cell selector to B7
Type + (↑) (↑)	Begins formula and moves cell selector to B5
Type +	Enters B5+ into formula and returns cell selector to B7

Keystroke	Result
[↑]	Moves cell selector to B6
[↵]	Enters B6 into formula and enters result of calculation into B7
Type / E C (or [CTRL]-C)	Brings up Copy command
[↵]	Specifies B7 as the source block
[→]	Moves the cell selector to C7
Type a period	Specifies the beginning cell of the destination block as C7
Press [→] **7 times**	Extends destination block from cells C7 through J7
[↵]	Copies the contents of the source block into the destination block and returns the cell selector to B7

Continue by inserting another row for the loan payments and entering the amounts for option 1. The loan payment amounts will be placed in row 14.

Keystroke	Result
Press [F5] **and type** A14 [↵]	Moves cell selector to A14
Press / E I (or [CTRL]-I)	Brings up the Insert command
[↵]	Chooses Insert Rows
[↵]	Inserts a blank row at row 14
Type LOANPAYMT [→]	Enters LOANPAYMT into A14 and moves cell selector to B14
Type 92 [↵]	Enters 92 into B14
Type / E C (or [CTRL]-C)	Brings up Copy command
[↵]	Specifies B14 as the source block
[→]	Moves the cell selector to C14
Type a period	Specifies the beginning cell of the destination block as C14
Press [→] **7 times**	Extends destination block from cells C14 through J14
[↵]	Copies the contents of the source block into the destination block and returns the cell selector to B14

The last action necessary to evaluate option 1 is to enter a formula to subtract the total expenses from the total income. Although this was done earlier, the formula is now incorrect because the new total income row was added to the spreadsheet.

Keystroke	Result
Press [↓] **4 times**	Moves cell selector to B18
Type + **and press** [↑] **11 times**	Begins formula and moves cell selector to B7
Type –	Enters B7– into formula and returns cell selector to B18

↑ ↑	Moves cell selector to B16
↵	Enters B16 into formula and enters result of calculation into B18
Type / E C (or CTRL-C)	Brings up Copy command
↵	Specifies B18 as the source block
→	Moves the cell selector to C18
Type a period	Specifies the beginning cell of the destination block as C18
Press → 7 times	Extends destination block from cells C18 through J18
↵	Copies the contents of the source block into the destination block and returns the cell selector to B18

"What-If" Analysis

You have calculated the bottom line. Figure 3-14 shows that the student is not able to cover total expenses in any of the months with option 1. Now move on to what-if option 2. As you recall, both the amount of the loan ($2,200) and the interest rate (12%) are higher than for option 1. Fortunately, the payments can be spread over three years, so they are only $73 per month. Locate the cell selector at the LOAN row and enter the loan amounts (1100) for September and January. Then move the cell selector to the LOANPAYMT row and enter the monthly payments for option 2.

Press F5 **and type** B5 ↵	Brings up the GoTo prompt, and moves cell selector to B5

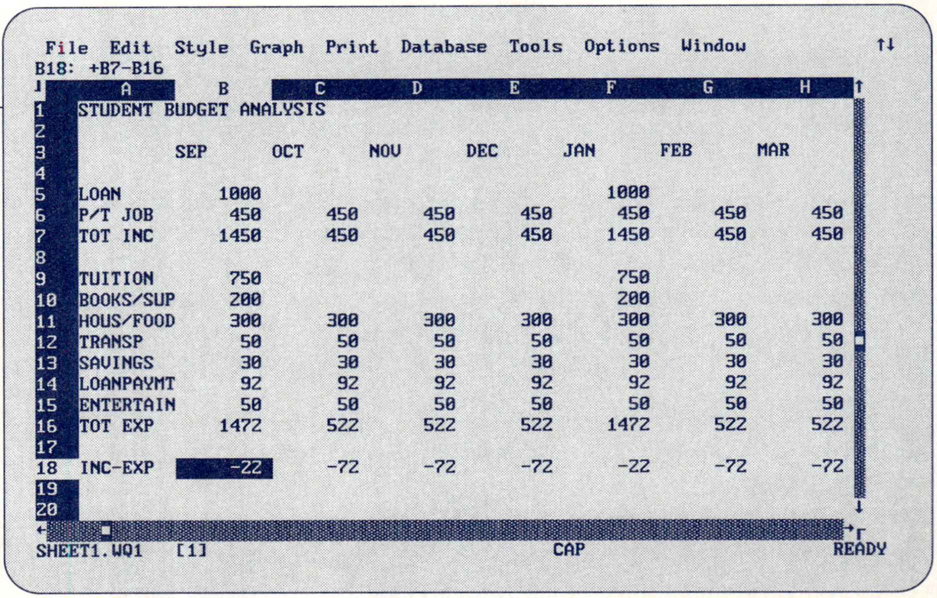

FIGURE 3-14

Loan option 1

```
 File  Edit  Style  Graph  Print  Database  Tools  Options  Window
B18: +B7-B16
      A            B         C         D         E         F         G         H
1  STUDENT BUDGET ANALYSIS
2
3              SEP       OCT       NOV       DEC       JAN       FEB       MAR
4
5  LOAN        1000                                    1000
6  P/T JOB      450       450       450       450       450       450       450
7  TOT INC     1450       450       450       450      1450       450       450
8
9  TUITION      750                                     750
10 BOOKS/SUP    200                                     200
11 HOUS/FOOD    300       300       300       300       300       300       300
12 TRANSP        50        50        50        50        50        50        50
13 SAVINGS       30        30        30        30        30        30        30
14 LOANPAYMT     92        92        92        92        92        92        92
15 ENTERTAIN     50        50        50        50        50        50        50
16 TOT EXP     1472       522       522       522      1472       522       522
17
18 INC-EXP      -22       -72       -72       -72       -22       -72       -72
19
20
SHEET1.WQ1   [1]                          CAP                           READY
```

Type 1100 **and press** (→) **4 times**	Enters 1100 into B5 and moves cell selector to F5
Type 1100 (↵)	Enters 1100 into F5
Press (F5) **and type** B14 (↵)	Brings up the GoTo prompt and moves cell selector to B14
Type 73 (↵)	Enters 73 into B14
Type / E C (or (CTRL)-C)	Brings up Copy command
(↵)	Specifies B14 as the source block
(→)	Moves the cell selector to C14
Type a period	Specifies the beginning cell of the destination block as C14
Press (→) **7 times**	Extends destination block from cells C14 through J14
(↵)	Copies the contents of the source block into the destination block and returns the cell selector to B14

With a few keystrokes you have created a new bottom line that reflects the payments for option 2. Figure 3-15 shows that things look a little better. Two months, September and January, have a positive balance, though the others still have a negative balance. To see whether the surpluses in those two months are enough to cover the shortages in the other months, you need to create a "cash balance" line. This will reflect the carryover of the balance in one month to the succeeding month. The cash balance line can be placed in a row at the bottom of the worksheet.

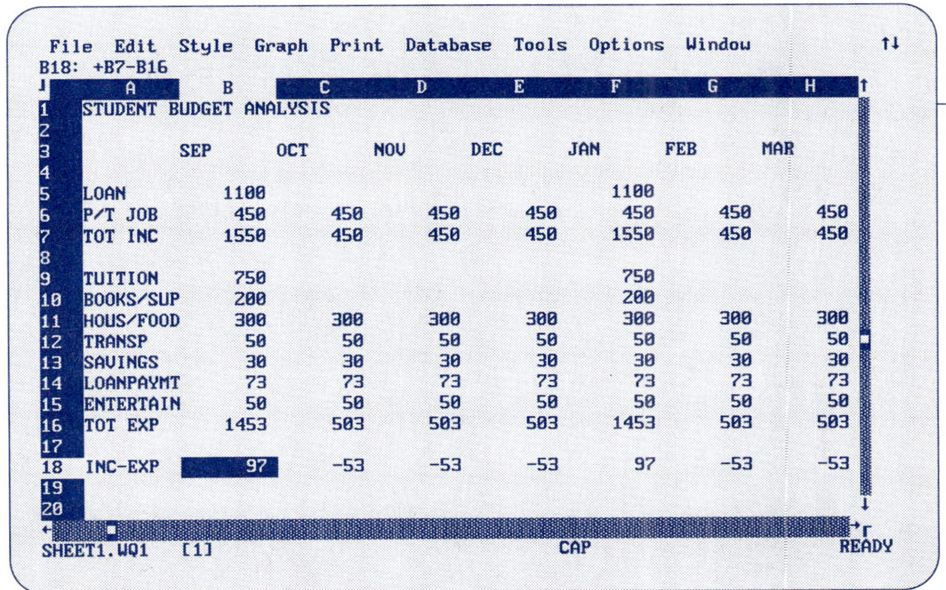

File Edit Style Graph Print Database Tools Options Window

B18: +B7-B16

	A	B	C	D	E	F	G	H
1	STUDENT BUDGET ANALYSIS							
2								
3		SEP	OCT	NOV	DEC	JAN	FEB	MAR
4								
5	LOAN	1100				1100		
6	P/T JOB	450	450	450	450	450	450	450
7	TOT INC	1550	450	450	450	1550	450	450
8								
9	TUITION	750				750		
10	BOOKS/SUP	200				200		
11	HOUS/FOOD	300	300	300	300	300	300	300
12	TRANSP	50	50	50	50	50	50	50
13	SAVINGS	30	30	30	30	30	30	30
14	LOANPAYMT	73	73	73	73	73	73	73
15	ENTERTAIN	50	50	50	50	50	50	50
16	TOT EXP	1453	503	503	503	1453	503	503
17								
18	INC-EXP	97	-53	-53	-53	97	-53	-53
19								
20								

SHEET1.WQ1 [1] CAP READY

FIGURE 3-15

Loan option 2

Press (F5) **and type** A19 (↵)	Brings up the GoTo prompt and moves cell selector to A19
Type CASH BAL (→)	Enters CASH BAL into A19 and moves cell selector to B19

In the first month, September, the cash balance is the same as the income minus expenses amount. A simple formula can be placed in B19 to reflect the amount in B18.

Type +B18 (↵)	Enters the value in B18 into B19

Note that with this formula, any change in B18 is reflected in B19.

(→)	Moves cell selector to C19

The next step is to enter a formula that will add the cash balance amount for September (B19) to the balance (income minus expenses) for October (C18), to determine the cash balance for October. Figure 3-16 shows how the cash balance of $97 (September) is added to the income minus expenses of $–53 (October). The result is a $44 cash balance amount (October); this is carried over to the next month, November. Once the formula is entered, it can be copied to the other months. The formula is +B19+C18.

Type + (←)	Begins formula and moves cell selector to B19
Type +	Enters B19+ into formula and returns cell selector to C19
(↑)	Moves cell selector to C18
(↵)	Enters C18 into formula and enters result of calculation into C19

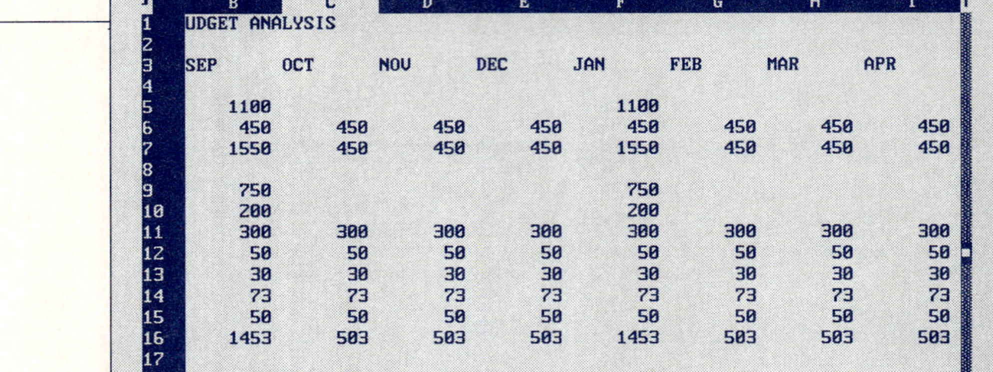

File Edit Style Graph Print Database Tools Options Window

C19: +B19+C18

	B	C	D	E	F	G	H	I
1	UDGET ANALYSIS							
2								
3	SEP	OCT	NOV	DEC	JAN	FEB	MAR	APR
4								
5	1100				1100			
6	450	450	450	450	450	450	450	450
7	1550	450	450	450	1550	450	450	450
8								
9	750				750			
10	200				200			
11	300	300	300	300	300	300	300	300
12	50	50	50	50	50	50	50	50
13	30	30	30	30	30	30	30	30
14	73	73	73	73	73	73	73	73
15	50	50	50	50	50	50	50	50
16	1453	503	503	503	1453	503	503	503
17								
18	97	-53	-53	-53	97	-53	-53	-53
19	97	44						
20								

SHEET1.WQ1 [1] CAP READY

FIGURE 3-16

Cash balance calculation

Type / E C (or [CTRL]-C)	Brings up Copy command
[↵]	Specifies C19 as the source block
[→]	Moves the cell selector to D19
Type a period	Specifies the beginning cell of the destination block as D19
Press [→] **6 times**	Extends destination block from cells D19 through J19
[↵]	Copies the contents of the source block into the destination block and returns the cell selector to C19

Well, perhaps option 2 is not quite so good after all. As Figure 3-17 illustrates, the student is getting deeper and deeper into debt. That leaves option 3. Option 3 provides a larger principal ($2,500), but the interest rate (14%) is quite a bit higher than option 1 or 2. The principal can be divided by allocating $1,250 for each semester. Enter this amount for September and January and then enter the monthly payments of $85.

Press [F5] **and type** B5 [↵]	Brings up the GoTo prompt and moves cell selector to B5
Type 1250 **and press** [→] **4 times**	Enters 1250 into B5 and moves cell selector to F5
Type 1250 [↵]	Enters 1250 into F5
Press [F5] **and type** B14 [↵]	Brings up the GoTo prompt and moves cell selector to B14
Type 85 [↵]	Enters 85 into B14

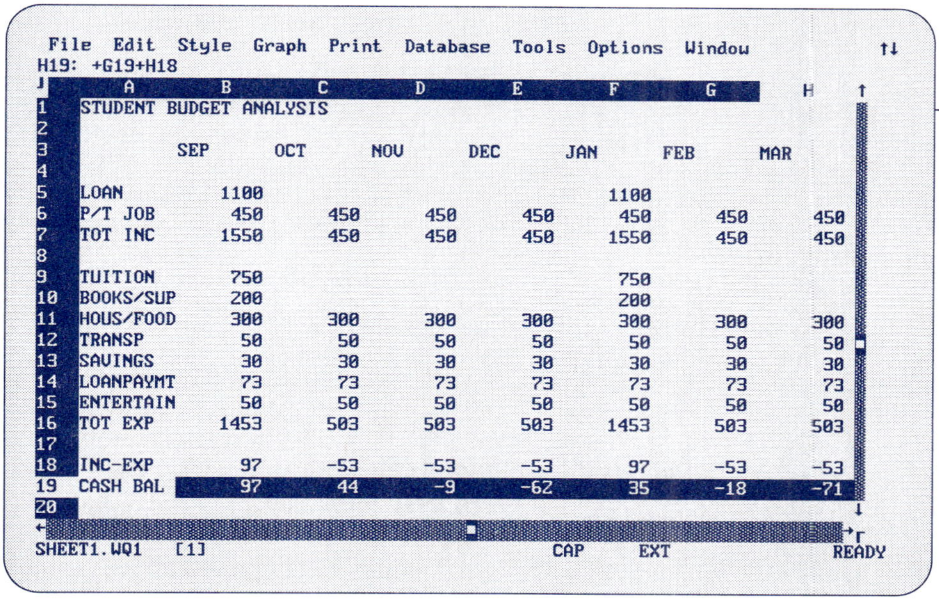

File Edit Style Graph Print Database Tools Options Window
H19: +G19+H18

	A	B	C	D	E	F	G	H
1	STUDENT BUDGET ANALYSIS							
2								
3		SEP	OCT	NOV	DEC	JAN	FEB	MAR
4								
5	LOAN	1100				1100		
6	P/T JOB	450	450	450	450	450	450	450
7	TOT INC	1550	450	450	450	1550	450	450
8								
9	TUITION	750				750		
10	BOOKS/SUP	200				200		
11	HOUS/FOOD	300	300	300	300	300	300	300
12	TRANSP	50	50	50	50	50	50	50
13	SAVINGS	30	30	30	30	30	30	30
14	LOANPAYMT	73	73	73	73	73	73	73
15	ENTERTAIN	50	50	50	50	50	50	50
16	TOT EXP	1453	503	503	503	1453	503	503
17								
18	INC-EXP	97	-53	-53	-53	97	-53	-53
19	CASH BAL	97	44	-9	-62	35	-18	-71
20								

SHEET1.WQ1 [1] CAP EXT READY

FIGURE 3-17

Cash balance, loan option 2

FIGURE 3-18

Cash balance, loan option 3

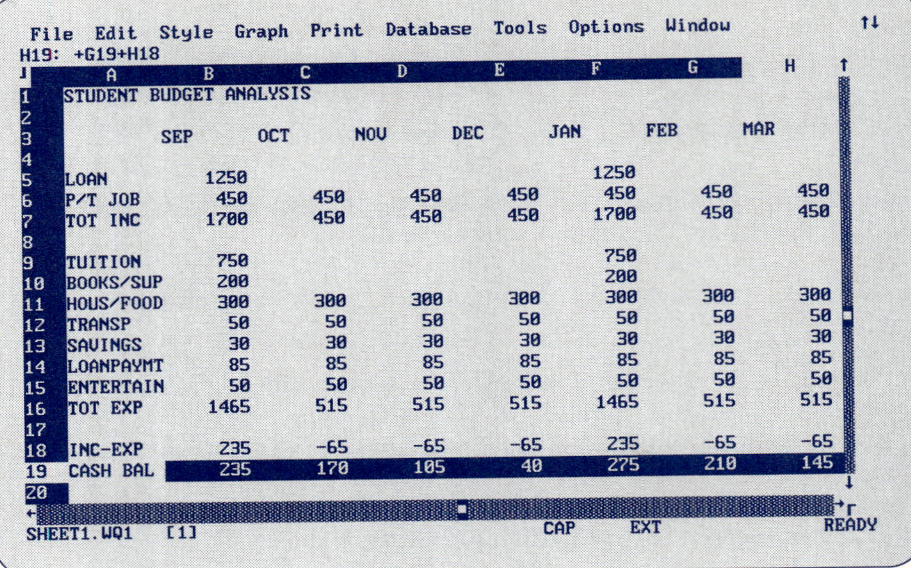

File Edit Style Graph Print Database Tools Options Window

H19: +G19+H18

	A	B	C	D	E	F	G	H
1	STUDENT BUDGET ANALYSIS							
2								
3		SEP	OCT	NOV	DEC	JAN	FEB	MAR
4								
5	LOAN	1250				1250		
6	P/T JOB	450	450	450	450	450	450	450
7	TOT INC	1700	450	450	450	1700	450	450
8								
9	TUITION	750				750		
10	BOOKS/SUP	200				200		
11	HOUS/FOOD	300	300	300	300	300	300	300
12	TRANSP	50	50	50	50	50	50	50
13	SAVINGS	30	30	30	30	30	30	30
14	LOANPAYMT	85	85	85	85	85	85	85
15	ENTERTAIN	50	50	50	50	50	50	50
16	TOT EXP	1465	515	515	515	1465	515	515
17								
18	INC-EXP	235	-65	-65	-65	235	-65	-65
19	CASH BAL	235	170	105	40	275	210	145
20								

SHEET1.WQ1 [1] CAP EXT READY

Type / E C (or CTRL-C)	Brings up Copy command
↵	Specifies B14 as the source block
→	Moves the cell selector to C14
Type a period	Specifies the beginning cell of the destination block as C14
Press → 7 times	Extends destination block from cells C14 through J14
↵	Copies the contents of the source block into the destination block and returns the cell selector to B14

Figure 3-18 shows that option 3 might get the student through the year, even though some of the months have a negative balance (INC-EXP). The carryover from each previous month may be enough to cover the shortfalls. You can now move the cell selector to see the final balance in May. This amount is located in cell J19.

Press ↓ 5 times and → 8 times	Moves cell selector to J19

Figure 3-19 illustrates that the cash balance is just enough to make it through May, with an ending balance of $15. Before you continue, move the cell selector to A1.

HOME	Moves the cell selector to A1

Worksheet Enhancements

The worksheet is complete in the sense that it has answered the what-if questions concerning the best loan option. However, the format is a little

```
 File  Edit  Style  Graph  Print  Database  Tools  Options  Window      ↑↓
J19: +I19+J18
       C        D        E        F        G        H        I        J
1  LYSIS
2
3  OCT      NOV      DEC      JAN      FEB      MAR      APR      MAY
4
5                             1250
6       450      450      450      450      450      450      450      450
7       450      450      450     1700      450      450      450      450
8
9                              750
10                             200
11      300      300      300      300      300      300      300      300
12       50       50       50       50       50       50       50       50
13       30       30       30       30       30       30       30       30
14       85       85       85       85       85       85       85       85
15       50       50       50       50       50       50       50       50
16      515      515      515     1465      515      515      515      515
17
18      -65      -65      -65      235      -65      -65      -65      -65
19      170      105       40      275      210      145       80       15
20
SHEET1.WQ1    [1]                         CAP                        READY
```

FIGURE 3-19

Final balance, loan option 3

```
 File  Edit  Style  Graph  Print  Database  Tools  Options  Window      ↑↓
A1: [W10]
       A        B    C    D    E    F    G    H    I    J    K     L
1                          STUDENT BUDGET ANALYSIS
2                                                   Moved to center
3                SEP  OCT  NOV  DEC  JAN  FEB  MAR  APR  MAY TOTAL  PERCT
4  -----------------------------------------------------------------------
5  LOAN         1250                1250                     2500  38.2%
6  P/T JOB       450  450  450  450  450  450  450  450  450 4050  61.8%
7    TOT INC    1700  450  450  450 1700  450  450  450  450 6550 100.0%
8
9  TUITION       750  Indented       750  Right-aligned      1500  23.0%
10 BOOKS/SUP     200                 200                      400   6.1%
11 HOUS/FOOD     300  300  300  300  300  300  300  300  300 2700  41.3%
12 TRANSP         50   50   50   50   50   50   50   50   50  450   6.9%
13 SAVINGS        30   30   30   30   30   30   30   30   30  270   4.1%
14 LOANPAYMT      85   85   85   85   85   85   85   85   85  765  11.7%
15 ENTERTAIN      50   50   50   50   50   50   50   50   50  450   6.9%
16   TOT EXP    1465  515  515  515 1465  515  515  515  515 6535 100.0%
17 -----------------------------------------------------------------------
18 INC-EXP       235  -65  -65  -65  235  -65  -65  -65  -65
19 CASH BAL      235  170  105   40  275  210  145   80   15
20
SHEET1.WQ1    [1]                         CAP                        READY
```

FIGURE 3-20

Worksheet enhancements

awkward and not as easy to read as it might be. In this section of the chapter you will learn how to enhance the look of a worksheet and how to change the format (appearance) of various cells. Figure 3-20 shows some changes that make the worksheet more presentable (perhaps to a loan officer). Compared to Figure 3-18, Figure 3-20 has the following advantages.

- The entire worksheet can be viewed on the screen.
- The column headings, SEP, OCT, NOV, and so on, are moved over to the right side of the cells so they line up more evenly with the numbers.

- A TOTAL column (K) shows the totals for each category.
- A PERCENT column (L) shows the percentage of the total for each category.
- The TOT INC and TOT EXP headings are indented to set them apart from the items they represent.
- Horizontal lines separate the categories to make them easier to read.
- The worksheet heading STUDENT BUDGET ANALYSIS is moved so it appears centered.

Column Width First you will shrink the worksheet so it fits on the screen. The column widths now are nine characters each. This can be changed to any width from 0 to 254 characters. As there are 12 columns (A–L, with K [TOTAL] and L [PERCENT] to be created later), six characters is the widest that each cell could be and still have the entire worksheet fit on the screen. Column widths can be changed for individual columns or for a specified block, which may include the entire worksheet. Because column A has the titles—TUITION, BOOKS/SUP, and so on—which are longer than six characters, you will change only columns B through L. To illustrate the Column Width command, you will first change an individual column, column B. You will then change the widths of columns C through L.

The command to use to change individual column widths is /Style¦Column Width; its shortcut key is CTRL-W. To change the width of column B from the default of 9 to 6, first position the cell selector anywhere in column B. Assuming you are at A1:

Press →	Moves the cell selector to B1
Press / S C (or CTRL-W)	Brings up the Column Width command

The prompt on the input line is:

Alter the width of the current column [1..254]: 9

Type 6 ↵	Makes column B six characters wide

You could follow the same procedure for each column from C to L, but that would be time-consuming. Instead, you will change the width of columns C through L by specifying them in a block. The command for this is also on the Style menu: /Style¦Block Widths¦Set Width. You can either bring up the command and then specify the block, or specify the block first and then invoke the command. In this case, use Extended mode to specify the block first.

Press →	Moves the cell selector to C1
Press SHIFT-F7	Enters Extended mode, so that moving the cell selector movement keys automatically extends the block
Press → **10 times**	Extends the block from C1 through L1

NOTE: It is only necessary to include one row in the block if you wish to change column widths.

Press / S B	Brings up the Block Widths command

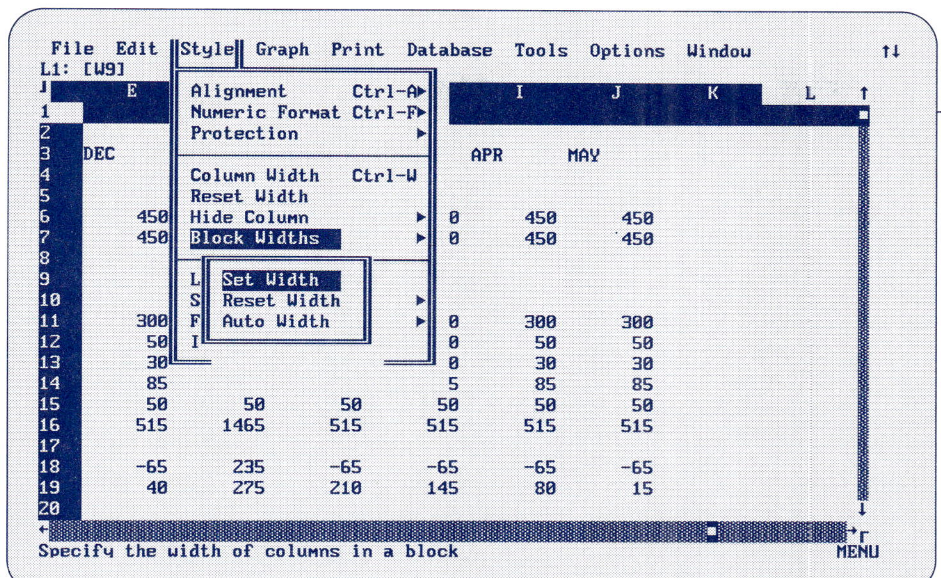

FIGURE 3-21

/Style¦Block Widths command

A pop-up menu appears with the following choices (Figure 3-21).

Set Width
Reset Width
Auto Width

Press ↵ **(or type** S)	Selects Set Width and displays a prompt for the new width
Type 6 ↵	Changes columns C through L to a width of six characters
Press HOME	Moves cell selector to A1

The entire worksheet now fits on the screen, with two blank columns, K and L.

Aligning Data with a Cell When you enter text it is left-aligned within the cell. Values are right-aligned (Figure 3-22). You can make the worksheet even more readable by moving the column headings (SEP, OCT, NOV, and so on) to the right side of the cells using the /Style¦Alignment command. The shortcut for this command is CTRL-A. You will use the same procedure as you did with the /Style¦Block Widths command, first specifying the block and then invoking the command. You also could first invoke the command and wait for Quattro Pro to prompt you for the block. The block to be modified is B3 through L3.

Press F5 **and type** B3 ↵	Brings up the GoTo prompt and moves the cell selector to B3
Press SHIFT-F7	Enters Extended mode, so that moving the cell selector movement keys automatically extends the block
Press → **10 times**	Extends the block from B3 through L3

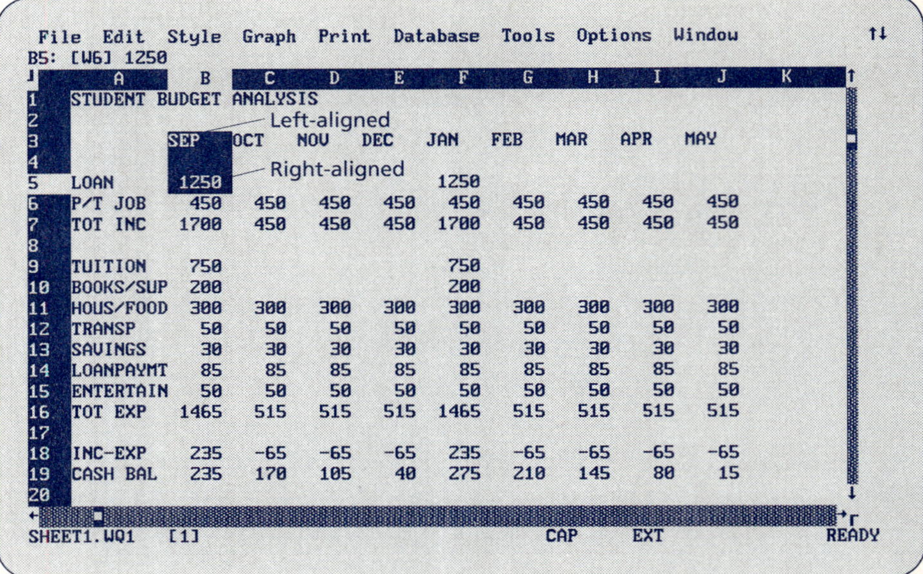

FIGURE 3-22

Data alignment within a cell

Press / S A (or CTRL-A)	Brings up the /Style¦Alignment command

A pop-up menu appears with the following choices.

General
Left
Right
Center

Type R	Selects right-alignment for the block of cells B3 through L3

The next step to enhance the worksheet is to add total and percent columns. These provide a total and a percentage of each income and expense category for the entire school year. Column K will be used for the total amounts and column L will be used for the percentages.

Press F5 **and type** K3 ↵	Brings up the GoTo prompt and moves the cell selector to K3
Type TOTAL ↓ ↓	Enters TOTAL into K3 and moves cell selector to K5

Note that TOTAL is right-aligned, because K3 is formatted for right-alignment.

ALT-F3	Brings up the function menu
Press PGDN **8 times and** ↓ **8 times**	Positions highlight on the Sum function
↵	Enters @SUM(into the input line
←	Moves cell selector to J5

Type a period	Indicates the first cell of the block for the Sum function
Press ← **8 times**	Extends block to include cells J5 through B5
Type) ↵	Ends the Sum function and enters the result (2500) of the calculation into K5

You can now copy the formula in K5 down the TOTAL column. Until now you have used the /Edit¦Copy command only to copy across a row. The /Edit¦Copy command can also be used to copy down a column, as illustrated below.

Type / E C (or CTRL-C)	Brings up Copy command
↵	Specifies K5 as the source block
↓	Moves the cell selector to K6
Type a period	Specifies the beginning cell of the destination block as K6
Press ↓ **10 times**	Extends destination block from cells K6 through K16
↵	Copies the contents of the source block into the destination block and returns the cell selector to K5

The percent column (L) shows the percent that each income and each expense category is of the total income and total expenses, respectively. The total income, located in cell K7, is $6,550. This amount is divided into each of the income categories, loan and part-time job, to determine the percentages.

Press ↑ ↑ →	Moves cell selector to L3
Type PERCT ↓ ↓	Enters PERCT into L3 and moves cell selector to L5

Begin the formula to divide total income (K7) into total loan amount (K5):

Type + ←	Begins formula and moves cell selector to K5
Type /	Enters K5/ into formula and returns cell selector to L5
← ↓ ↓	Moves cell selector to K7
↵	Enters K7 into formula and enters result of calculation into L5
↓	Moves cell selector to L6

Begin the formula to divide total income (K7) into total part-time job amount (K6):

Type + ←	Begins formula and moves cell selector to K6
Type /	Enters K6/ into formula and returns cell selector to L6
← ↓	Moves cell selector to K7

(↵)	Enters K7 into formula and enters result of calculation into L6
(↓)	Moves cell selector to L7

Finally, enter the formula for the total income (K7) divided by itself:

Type + (←)	Begins formula
Type / (←)	Enters K7/ into formula
(↵)	Enters K7 into formula and enters result of calculation into K7

This takes care of the proportion of total income attributed to each different category. The next step is to move on to expenses. To facilitate this, you will learn how to incorporate into a formula an **absolute cell address,** which is a cell address that does not change when the formula is copied. Study Figure 3-23. This figure shows the formulas that will be created when you carry out the /Edit¦Copy command. Notice that the TOT EXP cell (K16) does not change as the formula is copied: K16 is fixed, not relative. To specify a fixed (or absolute) cell reference, you need to type a $ before the row and column. Thus, $K$16 means that this cell reference, when used in a formula, does not change if the formula is copied. Because entering absolute cell addresses is a common task, Quattro Pro provides a shortcut, so you need not type the $ yourself. Instead, press (F4). To see how this works, first enter the formula +K9/$K$16 into L9.

Press (↓) **twice**	Moves cell selector to L9
Type + (←)	Begins formula and moves cell selector to K9
Type /	Enters K9/ into formula and returns cell selector to L9

FIGURE 3-23

Copying a formula with an absolute cell reference

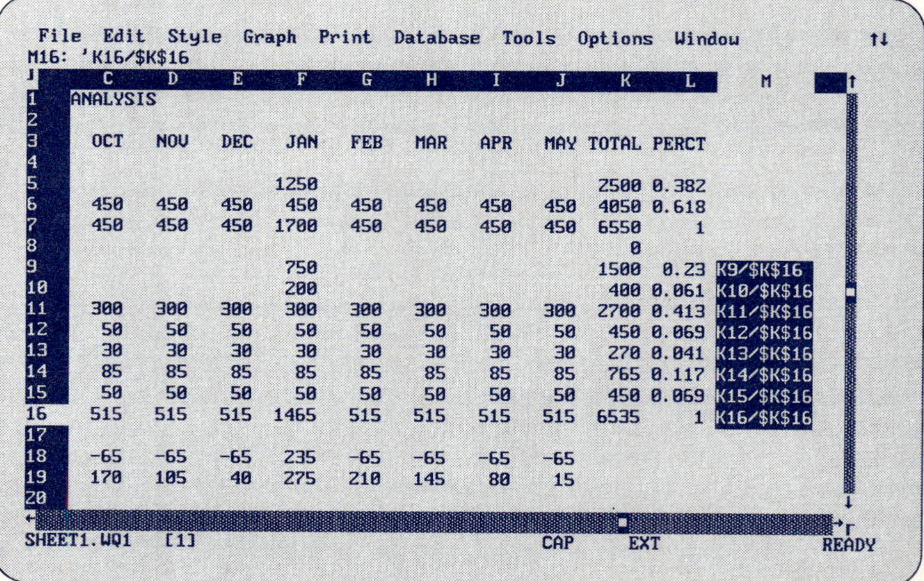

Press (←) **and then** (↓) **7 times**	Moves cell selector to K16 and +K9/K16 appears on the input line
Press (F4)	Automatically inserts dollar signs and +K9/$K$16 appears on the input line
(↵)	Enters K16 into formula and enters result of calculation into L9

Next, copy the formula into cells L10 through L16.

Type / E C (or (CTRL)-C)	Brings up Copy command
(↵)	Specifies L9 as the source block
(↓)	Moves the cell selector to L10
Type a period	Specifies the beginning cell of the destination block as L10
Press (↓) **6 times**	Extends destination block from cells L10 through L16
(↵)	Copies the contents of the source block into the destination block and returns the cell selector to L9

Note that though the first cell address in the formula changed as the formula was copied, $K$16 remained unchanged.

Using the Percent Format Notice that the numbers in column L are expressed in decimal form and not in percentages. Use the /Style¦Numeric Format¦Percent command to format the values as percentages. When you format a value as a percentage, the number is multiplied by 100 and a percent sign is displayed.

Press (F5) **and type** L5 (↵)	Brings up the GoTo prompt and moves the cell selector to L5
Press (SHIFT)-(F7)	Enters Extended mode, so that moving the cell selector movement keys automatically extends the block
Press (↓) **11 times**	Extends the block from L5 through L16
Press / S N (or (CTRL)-F)	Selects Numeric Format command
Press P	Selects Percent format
Type 1 (↵)	Specifies one decimal place. Percent signs are displayed and numbers are aligned

Erasing the Contents of a Cell Now you have the TOTAL and PERCT columns, but there is a superfluous zero. Cell K8 has a zero because you copied a formula into it to sum the contents of row 8, but row 8 is blank. Though there are several ways to remove the contents of a cell, this time you will use the /Edit¦Erase Block command. Earlier you used the /File¦Erase command to erase an entire worksheet. With the /Edit¦Erase Block command you can erase only the contents of a cell or block of cells. The shortcut key for /Edit¦Erase Block is (CTRL)-E.

Press (F5) **and** **type** K8 (↵)	Brings up the GoTo prompt and moves cell selector to K8
Press / E E (or (CTRL)-E)	Brings up the Erase Block command

The prompt is:

```
Block to be modified: K8..K8
```

Press (↵)	Clears the contents of cell K8

Editing the Contents of a Cell The next step to make the worksheet more readable is to indent the TOT INC and TOT EXP headings. There are two ways to indent text that has previously been entered. You can retype the entry, placing one or more spaces before the word, or you can use the Edit mode by pressing (F2). The following steps demonstrate both methods.

Press (F5) **and** **type** A7 (↵)	Brings up the GoTo prompt and moves the cell selector to A7
Press the spacebar twice	Enters two spaces
Type TOT INC (↵)	Enters TOT INC preceded by two spaces into A7

Edit mode allows you to change the contents of a cell without retyping the entire entry. The process is to locate the cell selector on the cell to be edited, press the Edit key ((F2)), and then use a combination of (←), (→), (BACKSPACE), (HOME), and (DEL) to edit the cell contents.

Press (F5) **and** **type** A16 (↵)	Brings up the GoTo prompt and moves the cell selector to A16
Press (F2)	Enters Edit mode

Figure 3-24 shows the screen as it appears in Edit mode. At the input line, the cell contents appear as well as a blinking cursor located at the end of the entry. Because you want to insert two spaces in front of TOT EXP, you first move the cursor to the beginning of the entry.

Press (HOME) (→)	Moves cursor to beginning of entry
Press the spacebar twice	Inserts two spaces before the "T" in TOT EXP
Press (↵)	Enters the edited entry

This may seem to take longer than retyping the entry. However, the process is very useful for long or complicated entries such as formulas.

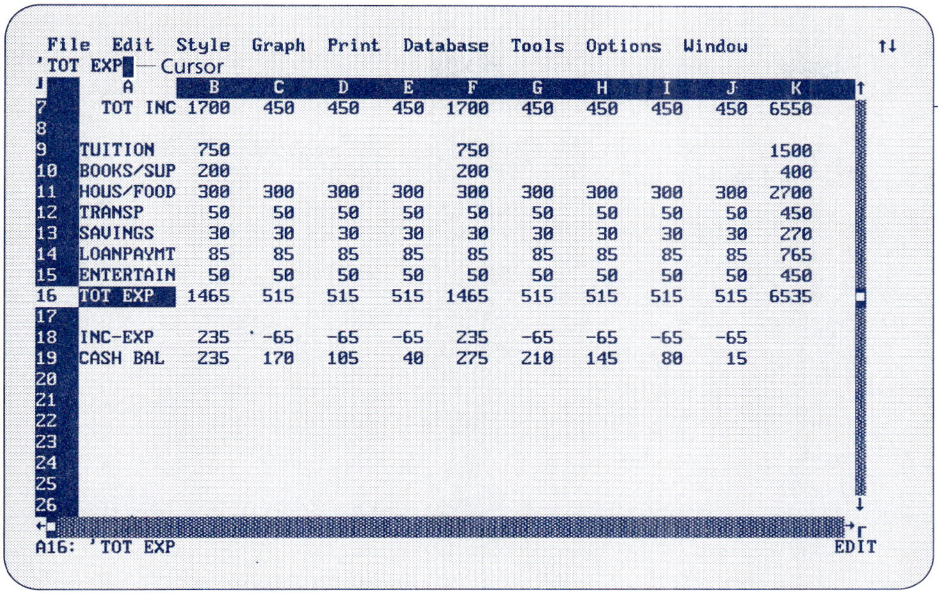

```
 File  Edit  Style  Graph  Print  Database  Tools  Options  Window        ↑↓
'TOT EXP█— Cursor
       A        B      C      D      E      F      G      H      I      J      K
7    TOT INC  1700    450    450    450   1700    450    450    450    450   6550
8
9  TUITION     750                         750                              1500
10 BOOKS/SUP   200                         200                               400
11 HOUS/FOOD   300    300    300    300    300    300    300    300    300   2700
12 TRANSP       50     50     50     50     50     50     50     50     50    450
13 SAVINGS      30     30     30     30     30     30     30     30     30    270
14 LOANPAYMT    85     85     85     85     85     85     85     85     85    765
15 ENTERTAIN    50     50     50     50     50     50     50     50     50    450
16 TOT EXP    1465    515    515    515   1465    515    515    515    515   6535
17
18 INC-EXP     235    -65    -65    -65    235    -65    -65    -65    -65
19 CASH BAL    235    170    105     40    275    210    145     80     15
20
21
22
23
24
25
26
A16: 'TOT EXP                                                              EDIT
```

FIGURE 3-24

Editing cell contents

Adding Lines The next step is to add horizontal lines to the spreadsheet to separate titles at the top and totals at the bottom. One way to do this is to insert dashed lines (–). This is done by typing hyphens into one cell and then copying them into a block of cells. Whenever you fill a cell with the same character, you can use the repeating Label feature. When you type a backslash (\) and then a character, the character automatically repeats to fill the cell, as demonstrated below.

Press (F5) **and type** A4 (↵)	Brings up the GoTo prompt and moves the cell selector to A4
Type \ – (↵)	Fills in the cell with dashes
(→)	Moves the pointer to B4
Type \ – (↵)	Fills in the cell with dashes
Press / E C (or (CTRL)-C)	Brings up the Copy command
Press (↵)	Specifies B4 as the source block
Press (→)	Positions cell selector at C4
Type a period	Specifies the beginning cell of the destination block as C4
Press (→) **9 times**	Extends destination block from C4 through L4
Press (↵)	Enters a dashed line across the worksheet

To create the other dashed line, you can either locate the cell selector at the desired row and repeat the steps above or you can copy the line just created. The following steps copy the line.

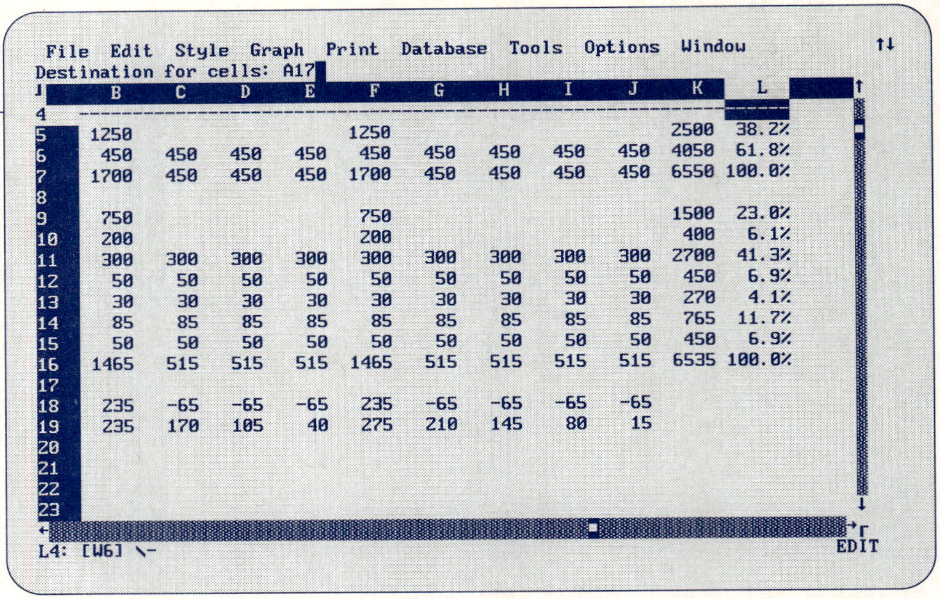

```
 File  Edit  Style  Graph  Print  Database  Tools  Options  Window              ↑↓
Destination for cells: A17
 B       C       D       E       F       G       H       I       J       K       L
4  ---------------------------------------------------------------------------------
5   1250                           1250                                   2500  38.2%
6    450     450     450     450    450     450     450     450     450   4050  61.8%
7   1700     450     450     450   1700     450     450     450     450   6550 100.0%
8
9    750                            750                                   1500  23.0%
10   200                            200                                    400   6.1%
11   300     300     300     300    300     300     300     300     300   2700  41.3%
12    50      50      50      50     50      50      50      50      50    450   6.9%
13    30      30      30      30     30      30      30      30      30    270   4.1%
14    85      85      85      85     85      85      85      85      85    765  11.7%
15    50      50      50      50     50      50      50      50      50    450   6.9%
16  1465     515     515     515   1465     515     515     515     515   6535 100.0%
17
18   235     -65     -65     -65    235     -65     -65     -65     -65
19   235     170     105      40    275     210     145      80      15
20
21
22
23
L4: [W6] \-                                                                    EDIT
```

FIGURE 3-25

Copying a dashed line

Press (F5) **and type** A4 (↵)	Brings up GoTo prompt and moves cell selector to A4
Press (SHIFT)-(F7)	Enters Extended mode
Press (→) **11 times**	Extends the block from A4 through L4
Press / E C (or (CTRL)-C)	Brings up the Copy command
Type A17	Specifies A17 as the start of the destination block (Figure 3-25)

Note: If a row or column is being copied, you do not have to indicate the entire destination block, only the upper left cell.

Press (↵)	Copies dashed line to row 17

Moving Data

The last enhancement you will make to the worksheet is to move the heading STUDENT BUDGET ANALYSIS so that it appears more centered on the worksheet. The /Edit¦Move command is used to do this; the shortcut is (CTRL)-M.

Press (HOME)	Moves the cell selector to A1
Press / E M (or (CTRL)-M)	Brings up the Move command
Press (↵)	Specifies A1 as the cell to move from (source)
Press (→) **4 times, then** (↵)	Specifies E1 as the cell to move to (destination)

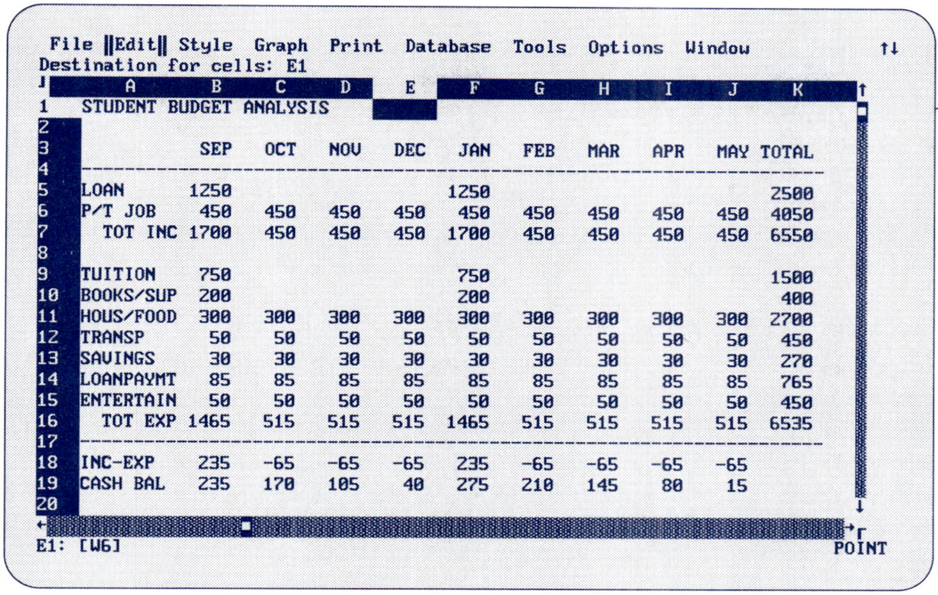

```
 File ||Edit|| Style  Graph  Print  Database  Tools  Options  Window        ↑↓
Destination for cells: E1
       A         B      C      D      E      F      G      H      I      J      K
1   STUDENT BUDGET ANALYSIS
2
3                SEP    OCT    NOV    DEC    JAN    FEB    MAR    APR    MAY  TOTAL
4   ------------------------------------------------------------------------------
5   LOAN        1250                         1250                              2500
6   P/T JOB      450    450    450    450     450    450    450    450    450  4050
7     TOT INC   1700    450    450    450    1700    450    450    450    450  6550
8
9   TUITION      750                          750                              1500
10  BOOKS/SUP    200                          200                               400
11  HOUS/FOOD    300    300    300    300     300    300    300    300    300  2700
12  TRANSP        50     50     50     50      50     50     50     50     50   450
13  SAVINGS       30     30     30     30      30     30     30     30     30   270
14  LOANPAYMT     85     85     85     85      85     85     85     85     85   765
15  ENTERTAIN     50     50     50     50      50     50     50     50     50   450
16    TOT EXP   1465    515    515    515    1465    515    515    515    515  6535
17  ------------------------------------------------------------------------------
18  INC-EXP      235    -65    -65    -65     235    -65    -65    -65    -65
19  CASH BAL     235    170    105     40     275    210    145     80     15
20
E1: [W6]                                                                    POINT
```

FIGURE 3-26

Move command

Figure 3-26 illustrates the move process. Cell A1 contains the entire entry: STUDENT BUDGET ANALYSIS.

Press ↵	Moves STUDENT BUDGET ANALYSIS from A1 to E1

Your worksheet is now complete, and you can save it. You may want to refer back to the section of Chapter 2 that presents the process used to save a worksheet. Make sure your data disk is in drive A and save the worksheet as A:STUBUDGT.

QUESTIONS

1. How can planning a worksheet be useful?
2. Explain the difference between a relative cell reference and a fixed (absolute) cell reference when used in a formula.
3. What is the process for changing (a) the width of a cell, (b) the format of a cell, and (c) the alignment of a cell?
4. Explain how you would use Edit mode to change the entry SALES FORCAST to SALES FORECAST.
5. Distinguish between the /File¦Erase command and the /Edit¦Erase Block command.
6. Explain the process for using Extended mode to specify blocks before invoking a command, and give examples of how it can be used.

APPLICATION 2

In this section you will use the worksheet from Application 1 to learn three new techniques. First, you will learn to speed up the entry of data by using manual recalculation. Next, you will learn how to lock column and row titles within the worksheet. Finally, you will divide the screen to get two views of the worksheet. ***NOTE:*** From this point on, the text assumes you understand the various possible ways to enter formulas, functions, and blocks. Instead of specifying each keystroke for each formula, therefore, the text simply says **Enter** followed by the formula and block as it would appear on the input line.

Recalculating the Spreadsheet

As you worked on Application 1, you may have noticed that the time involved in entering data increased as the worksheet grew in size. This is because each time an entry is made, the entire worksheet is automatically recalculated. To speed up data entry, you can turn off the automatic recalculation. Then, no matter how many entries you make, the worksheet will not recalculate until you press (F9). Changing from automatic to manual recalculation is done with the /Options¦Recalculation command. Activate the menu bar, select the Options menu, and choose the Recalculation command. Then specify Mode and manual recalculation. This can be demonstrated using the STUBUDGT file. If this file is still on your screen, proceed with the steps below. If not, retrieve the file first.

Press (F5) **and type** B6 (↵)	Brings up the GoTo prompt and moves cell selector to B6
Type 400 (↵)	Enters 400 into B6 and recalculates the totals
Press / O	Brings up the Options menu
Press R	Specifies Recalculation command

The window shown in Figure 3-27 lists the options. You need to select the Mode option and indicate Manual.

Press M	Selects Mode menu
Press M	Specifies manual recalculation
Press Q **twice**	Returns to the worksheet
Type 600 (↵)	Enters 600 into B6

No recalculation occurs after this entry; instead, the word CALC appears on the status line at the bottom of the screen. With automatic recalculation turned off, you can make entries more quickly.

Type 300 (↵)	Enters 300, with no recalculation
Type 450 (↵)	Enters 450, with no recalculation

When you see the word CALC on the status line, you know you need to press (F9) to recalculate the values.

Press (F9)	Recalculates the worksheet

Manual recalculation remains in effect until you change it with the Recalculation command or you quit the program. Before continuing, turn automatic recalculation back on.

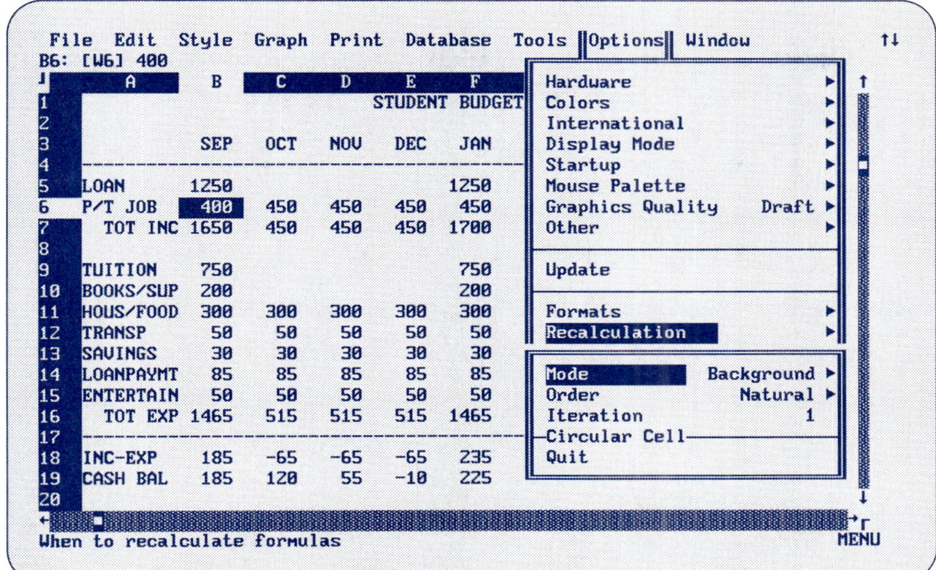

FIGURE 3-27

Choosing manual recalculation

Press / O R — Brings up Recalculation command

Press M — Selects Mode menu

Press A — Specifies automatic recalculation

Press Q **twice** — Returns to the worksheet

Fixing Titles in Place

Another useful command when you're working with large spreadsheets is /Window¦Options¦Locked Titles. This function allows you to fix titles in place while you scroll the rest of the worksheet. Study Figure 3-25. In column L it is difficult to determine which percentage applies to which category. For instance, is 4.1% the percentage for transportation or savings? You need a way to move the percent column to be adjacent to the category titles. This can be done with the Locked Titles command from the /Window¦Options menu.

The process for locking a column of titles into place is to locate the cell selector one column to the right and execute the Locked Titles command. The effect is to fix all columns to the left of the cell selector so that they always stay in view. With the cell selector at column B:

Press / W — Selects the Window menu

Press O — Selects the Options menu

Press L — Selects the Locked Titles option

The message is:

```
Horizontal
Vertical
Both
Clear
```

You need to choose one of these options. If you choose:

- Horizontal: the titles above the row where the cell selector is located are fixed into position.
- Vertical: the titles to the left of the column where the cell selector is located are fixed into position.
- Both: both of the above occur.
- Clear: all titles previously locked are cleared.

Choose Vertical to lock the titles in column A.

Press V	Specifies Vertical and locks titles in column A

Now you can scroll the screen without losing sight of the budget categories.

Press (→) **16 times**	Scrolls the percent column until it is adjacent to column A

Your screen should resemble Figure 3-28, in which the percentages are right next to the titles. You can use the same command to fix the months (row 3 and above) into place. First, bring the complete worksheet back into view and clear the column titles.

Press (HOME)	Brings entire worksheet into view
Press (F5) **and type** B4 (↵)	Moves the cell selector to B4
Press / W O L C	Clears all Locked Titles settings
Press / W O L H	Brings up the Locked Titles command and specifies Horizontal, which fixes the rows above row 4

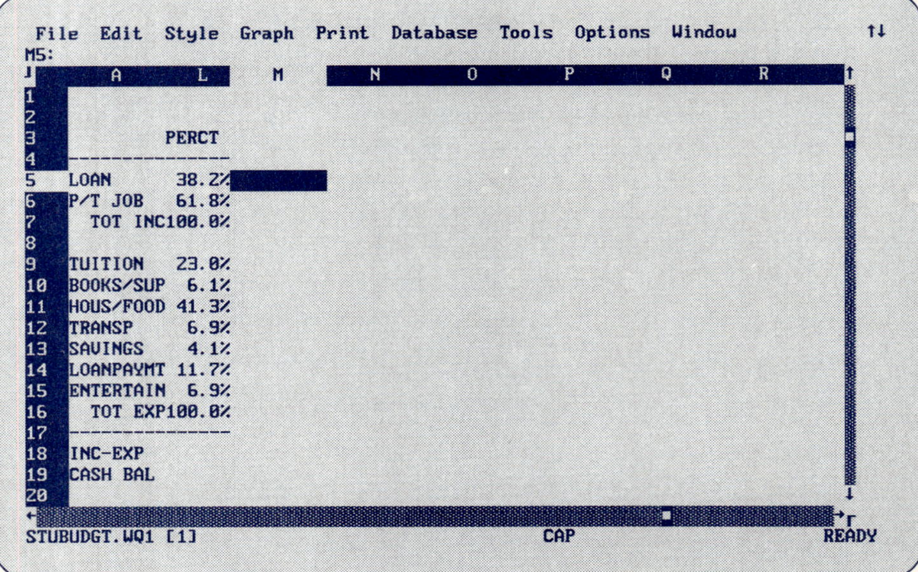

FIGURE 3-28

Freezing columns

With rows 1, 2, and 3 fixed into place, you can scroll the worksheet up.

Press ⓓ **29 times** — Scrolls the screen up so that the INC-EXP line is below the months (Figure 3-29)

Press / W O L C — Clears all Locked Titles settings

As you can see, the Locked Titles command is useful when you have a large worksheet and wish to scroll through the data with row or column headings fixed.

Splitting the Screen to Create Two Windows

The /Window¦Options command splits the screen into two horizontal or vertical windows, thereby creating two separate views of the spreadsheet. This is useful if you have a large worksheet and want to see the effect of a change in one area of the worksheet on another area that is off the screen. Figure 3-30 shows the screen split into two windows. Notice that each window has its own row and column designations. The window on the right side of the screen shows columns E–J. The left side of the screen shows columns A–D. You can move the cell selector in either window and any changes are reflected in both windows.

To create two windows, position the cell selector on the row or column where you want to split the screen. Then complete the /Window¦Options command.

Press (HOME) **and then** (→) **4 times** — Moves cell selector to E1

Press / W O — Selects /Window¦Options menu

The options on the top part of the menu are:

- Horizontal: splits screen with top and bottom windows.

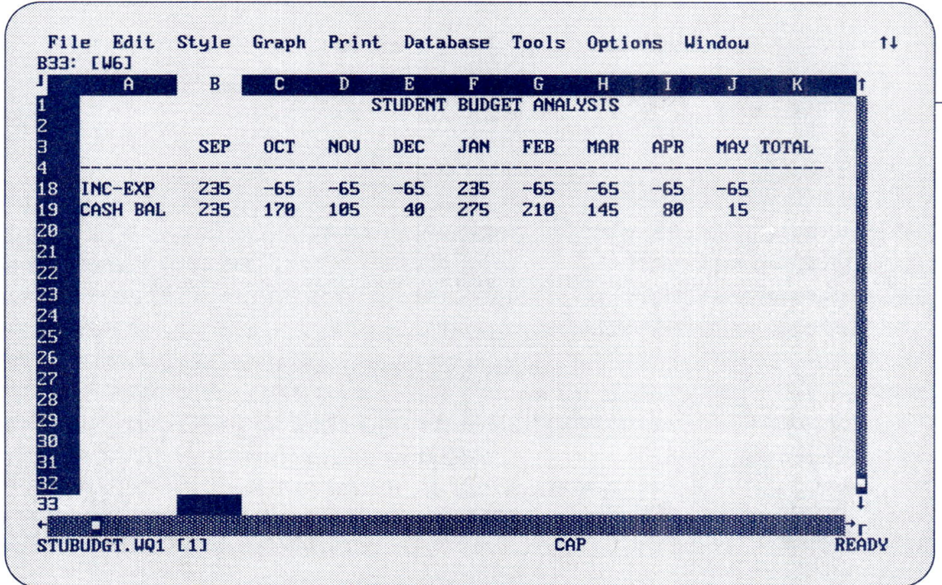

FIGURE 3-29

Freezing rows

FIGURE 3-30

A screen split into two windows

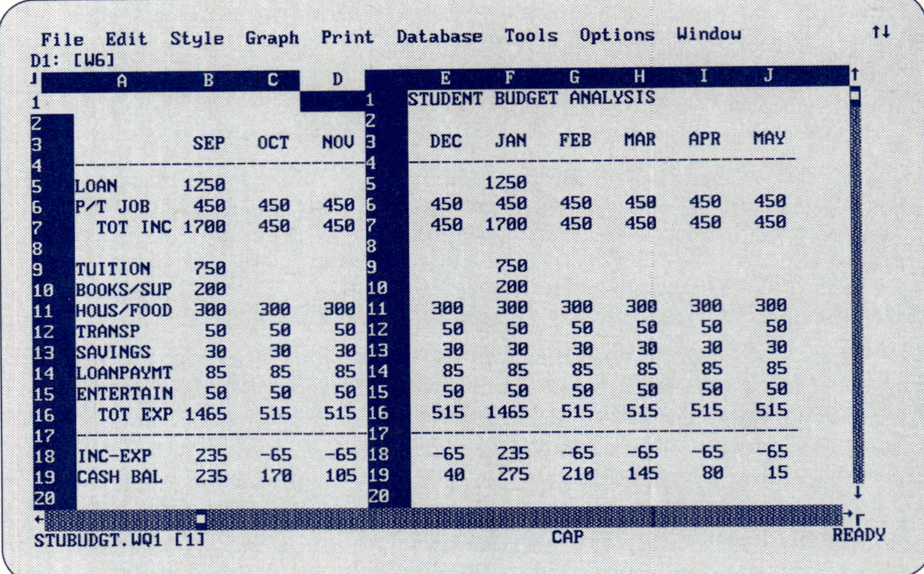

- Vertical: splits screen with side-by-side windows.
- Sync: synchronizes the scrolling of the two windows.
- Unsync: the windows scroll independently.
- Clear: returns to one window.

Press V — Splits the screen vertically

After you split the screen, the cell selector will be located in one of the windows. To move the cell selector to the other window, use the (F6) key. Now you can experiment by changing figures in the left window and seeing the effects in the right window (TOTAL column). Change the BOOKS/SUP value to 250 in September and see the effect on the totals.

Press (F5) **and type** B10 (↵) — Moves cell selector to B10

Type 250 (↵) — Recalculates the worksheet

Notice that even though the entry was made in the left window the right window is recalculated also. This is because you have two views of the same spreadsheet (similar to having two monitors displaying the same spreadsheet). Take a few moments to move around each window and make changes in the entries. Then return to one window.

Press / W O C — Returns to one window

Use /File¦Erase to erase the worksheet without saving it.

Mathematical Functions

Because worksheets deal primarily with the manipulation of numbers, several mathematical functions are provided in an electronic spreadsheet. You have

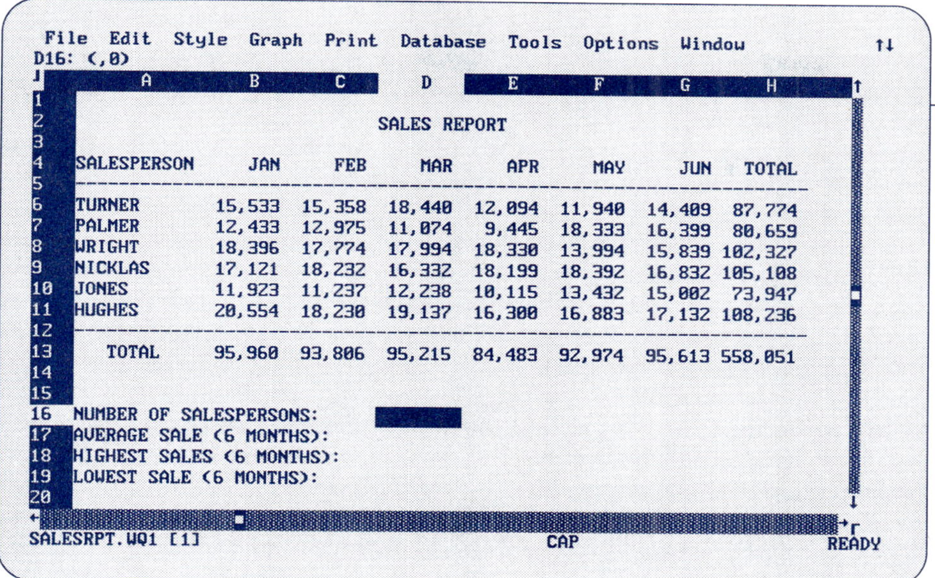

FIGURE 3-31

SALESRPT worksheet

already used one of these, the Sum function. These functions save you the time and effort of entering complex formulas. A list of the functions covered in this section and a brief description of each are presented below.

Function	**Description**
@SUM	Calculates the sum of a block of cells.
@COUNT	Determines the number of cells that contain values (including zeros) in a block.
@AVG	Calculates the average of a block of cells.
@MAX	Determines the highest number in a block.
@MIN	Determines the lowest number in a block.

The same process is used to enter any of these functions: Locate the cell selector on the desired cell and enter the function followed by a block enclosed in parentheses. The format is @function(block), for example @AVG(B5.B10). This would calculate the average of the numbers within the cells B5 through B10 and enter the average in the cell where the cell selector is located. You can either type the function name or enter it from the function menu, which is accessed by pressing (ALT)-(F3).

To illustrate each of these functions you will use a worksheet named SALESRPT located on your data disk. This worksheet lists the sales per month for each salesperson (see Figure 3-31). You will determine the following:

- Number of salespeople
- Average sales amount per person for the entire six months
- Individual with the highest sales amount for the six months
- Individual with the lowest sales amount for the six months

Retrieve the file called SALESRPT. (The cell selector should be at D16.)

Enter @COUNT(A6.A11) (↓)	Determines the number of cells with values in the block, enters the number into D16, and moves cell selector to D17
Enter @AVG(B6.G11) (↓)	Calculates the average amount for the block, enters it into D17, and moves cell selector to D18
Enter @MAX(B6.G11) (↓)	Determines the highest number within the block, enters it into D18, and moves cell selector to D19
Enter @MIN(B6.G11) (↵)	Determines the lowest number within the block and enters it into D19

Using the If Function

In addition to the mathematical functions presented earlier, Quattro Pro provides an If function. The If function allows you to set up a relation and check the validity of the relation. If the relation is true, one condition occurs; if the relation is false, another condition occurs. The SALESRPT worksheet can be used to illustrate the If function.

Notice the BONUS column at the right of the worksheet (Figure 3-32). This column indicates the bonus paid to any salesperson who qualifies. A bonus of 1 percent of total sales is paid to any salesperson whose total sales exceed $100,000. If a salesperson's total sales for six months is over $100,000, he or she is paid a bonus of 1 percent. If a salesperson's total sales is not over

FIGURE 3-32

If function

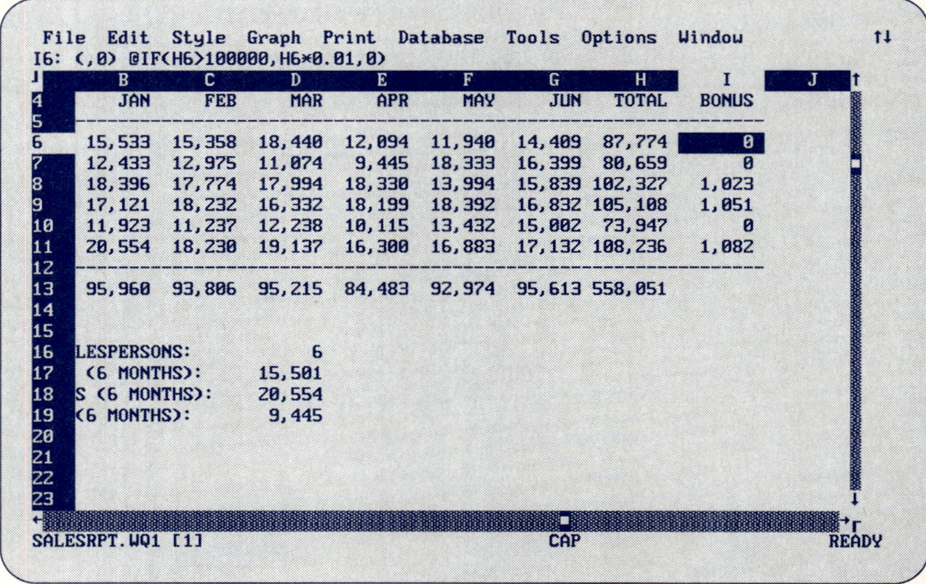

$100,000, no bonus is given. The relation is "sales greater than 100,000." If the relation is true, the salesperson receives a bonus of 1 percent of the sales. If the relation is false, the salesperson receives no bonus. The format for the If function is:

```
@IF(relation,condition1,condition2)
```

Thus, to determine Turner's bonus, the following If statement would be needed.

```
@IF(H6>100000,H6*.01,0)
```

This says that if the amount in H6, Turner's total sales, is greater than 100,000, then the amount is multiplied by .01 and the result is entered at the cell selector location. If the amount in H6 is not over 100,000, then 0 is entered (Figure 3-32). H6 is the cell location of total sales for the first salesperson. After you have entered the function once, it can be copied for the other salespersons. The following steps lead you through the use of the If function. Remember that If, like other functions, can be entered from the function menu, which is invoked by pressing (ALT)-(F3).

Press (F5) **and type** I6 (↵)	Moves cell selector to I6
Enter @IF(H6>100000,H6*.01,0)	Specifies the If function
(↵)	Executes the If function
Press / E C (or (CTRL)-C)	Brings up the /Edit¦Copy command
(↵)	Specifies I6 as the source block
Enter I7.I11 (↵)	Specifies the destination block and enters the results of the calculations

You can now finish the SALESRPT worksheet by entering a formula to calculate total bonuses.

Press (F5) **and type** I13 (↵)	Moves cell selector to I13
Enter @SUM(I6.I11) (↵)	Enters result of calculation

A common application of the If function is to cause a text entry to be displayed in a cell. An example would be a class that is graded pass/fail. Using an electronic spreadsheet to determine the grades, the instructor could calculate each student's grade percentage. Then the If function would be used to compare each student's percentage to the minimum needed to pass the course. In addition, the appropriate comment (pass or fail) could be entered next to the student's percentage. To illustrate this, you will retrieve a worksheet called PASSFAIL (Figure 3-33) and type in the If function. The completed worksheet is shown in Figure 3-34. Assume that 70 percent or better is needed to pass the course. Use the /File¦Erase command to clear the SALESRPT worksheet and the /File¦Retrieve command to load the PASSFAIL worksheet. The cell selector should be at H8.

Enter @IF(G8>=70,"PASS","FAIL")	Specifies that if the value in G8 is greater than or equal to 70, enter the word PASS; if not, enter FAIL

FIGURE 3-33

PASSFAIL worksheet

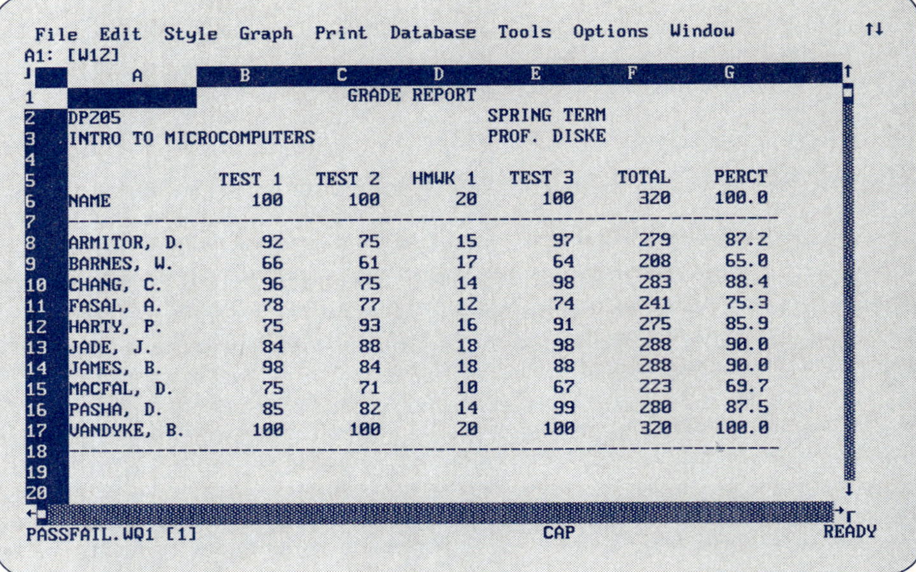

File Edit Style Graph Print Database Tools Options Window

A1: [W12]

	A	B	C	D	E	F	G
1			GRADE REPORT				
2	DP205				SPRING TERM		
3	INTRO TO MICROCOMPUTERS				PROF. DISKE		
4							
5		TEST 1	TEST 2	HMWK 1	TEST 3	TOTAL	PERCT
6	NAME	100	100	20	100	320	100.0
7	----------	----------	----------	----------	----------	----------	----------
8	ARMITOR, D.	92	75	15	97	279	87.2
9	BARNES, W.	66	61	17	64	208	65.0
10	CHANG, C.	96	75	14	98	283	88.4
11	FASAL, A.	78	77	12	74	241	75.3
12	HARTY, P.	75	93	16	91	275	85.9
13	JADE, J.	84	88	18	98	288	90.0
14	JAMES, B.	98	84	18	88	288	90.0
15	MACFAL, D.	75	71	10	67	223	69.7
16	PASHA, D.	85	82	14	99	280	87.5
17	VANDYKE, B.	100	100	20	100	320	100.0
18	----------	----------	----------	----------	----------	----------	----------
19							
20							

PASSFAIL.WQ1 [1] CAP READY

FIGURE 3-34

PASSFAIL worksheet, completed

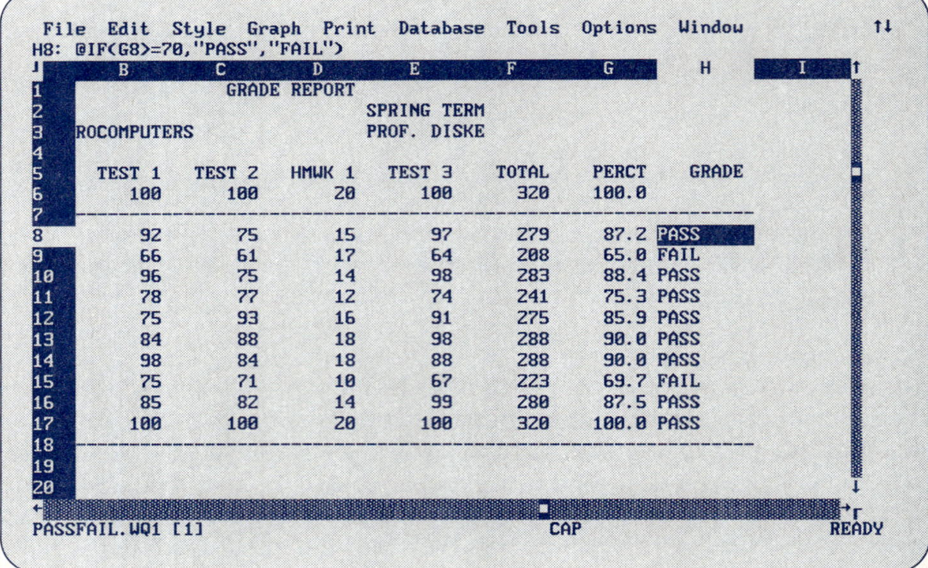

File Edit Style Graph Print Database Tools Options Window

H8: @IF(G8>=70,"PASS","FAIL")

	B	C	D	E	F	G	H
1		GRADE REPORT					
2				SPRING TERM			
3	ROCOMPUTERS			PROF. DISKE			
4							
5	TEST 1	TEST 2	HMWK 1	TEST 3	TOTAL	PERCT	GRADE
6	100	100	20	100	320	100.0	
7	----------	----------	----------	----------	----------	----------	----------
8	92	75	15	97	279	87.2	PASS
9	66	61	17	64	208	65.0	FAIL
10	96	75	14	98	283	88.4	PASS
11	78	77	12	74	241	75.3	PASS
12	75	93	16	91	275	85.9	PASS
13	84	88	18	98	288	90.0	PASS
14	98	84	18	88	288	90.0	PASS
15	75	71	10	67	223	69.7	FAIL
16	85	82	14	99	280	87.5	PASS
17	100	100	20	100	320	100.0	PASS
18	----------	----------	----------	----------	----------	----------	----------
19							
20							

PASSFAIL.WQ1 [1] CAP READY

↵	Enters the appropriate comment
Press / E C (or CTRL-C)	Brings up the /Edit¦Copy command
↵	Specifies H8 as the source block
Enter H9.H17 ↵	Specifies the destination block and copies the If statement

Now each student has been graded and the PASSFAIL worksheet is complete.

The If function is a powerful tool for analyzing relationships within a worksheet. Below is a list of the relations, their meaning, and an example of each.

Relation	Meaning	Example
=	Equal to	B5=100
<>	Not equal to	H9<>25
>	Greater than	A1>99
<	Less than	C12<C9
>=	Greater than or equal to	85>=F8
<=	Less than or equal to	A5*.08<=300

When specifying conditions, you can use values, formulas, text, or cell addresses. You can also have nested If statements by using parentheses, and you can create complex relations by using #AND#, #OR#, and #NOT# (e.g., @IF(D8>18 #AND# C8>90,"VERY GOOD","OK").

CHALLENGE EXERCISES

1. Your data disk contains a worksheet with the file name GRADES.

- **a.** Retrieve the worksheet.
- **b.** Insert a column for test 4 and record the following scores: Armitor 88, Barnes 82, Chang 80, Fasal 78, Harty 83, Jade 91, James 91, MacFal 66, Pasha 75, VanDyke 100.
- **c.** Insert a row for another student named K. Sampson and enter the following scores: 77, 79, 16, 84, 75.
- **d.** Complete the total and percent columns. (**Hint:** Multiply the percent formula by 100.)
- **e.** Align the headings (TEST 1 and so on) on the right side.
- **f.** Save the worksheet as GRADES2.

2. Create a payroll worksheet for 10 employees of the Microhard Manufacturing Company. The worksheet should include automatic calculations for gross pay (including overtime and regular time), net pay, taxes, and other deductions. The worksheet should include:

Employee name

Regular hours worked (weekly)

Hourly rate of pay for regular hours (up through 40)

Overtime hours worked

Overtime rate of pay (time-and-a-half)

Gross salary (before taxes and deductions)

Federal and state income taxes (fixed rate of 22%)

Other deductions (e.g., insurance, parking, dues)

Net salary (gross salary less taxes and other deductions)

Develop the worksheet with titles and appropriate totals. The data for the worksheet is presented below in the following order: name, regular hours, regular pay rate, overtime hours, and other deductions.

Kerns, K., 40, 8.50, 5, 18.50

Adams, F., 40, 7.30, 0, 15.32

Yu, S., 36, 8.50, 0, 17.88

Faral, A., 40, 6.40, 4, 14.88

Collins, B., 32, 7.30, 0, 14.48

Arneld, J., 30, 5.00, 0, 16.00

Caras, T., 40, 8.50, 8, 28.40

Sommers, B., 32, 5.00, 0, 14.20

Links, D., 40, 6.40, 8, 18.80

Dune, F., 35, 5.00, 0, 13.80

Save the worksheet.

3. Using the GRADES worksheet, enter the following mathematical functions (place these in rows below the grades).

   - the average class grade for each test and assignment
   - the highest and lowest individual grades for each test and assignment
   - the number of students

   Then use the If function to display the word EXCELLENT, in column I, if a student received over 300 total points, and the word FAIR if not.

COMMON PITFALLS IN USING SPREADSHEETS

This is a good time to discuss some of the pitfalls that commonly occur when using spreadsheets. The most crucial involve erroneous calculations. No matter how beautifully presented a worksheet is, if the calculations contain errors, the worksheet is worthless. The following section covers the more common problems that can affect the accuracy of a worksheet.

Inserting Rows and Columns

Figures 3-35 and 3-36 demonstrate how the insertion of a row can lead to an inaccurate total. In Figure 3-35, cells B6 through B10 were added to obtain the total located in B11. The formula used was @SUM(B6.B10). Then a row was inserted at B11 (Figure 3-36). The row with the total moved down to line 12. However, the formula stayed the same because the block (B6.B10) was not affected. Thus, any number entered into B12 will not be included in the total. To avoid this situation, check all formulas after inserting rows or columns.

Circular Reference in a Formula

Figure 3-37 illustrates a problem in which a formula refers to its own cell. In Figure 3-37 the formula in cell B7 is @SUM(B3.B7). This formula says, "calculate

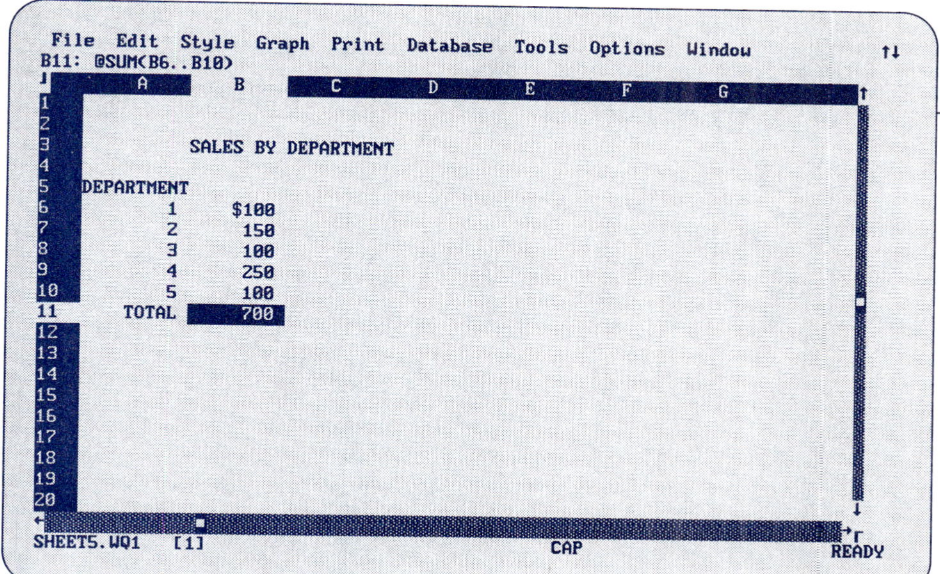

FIGURE 3-35

Correct sum, before inserting a row

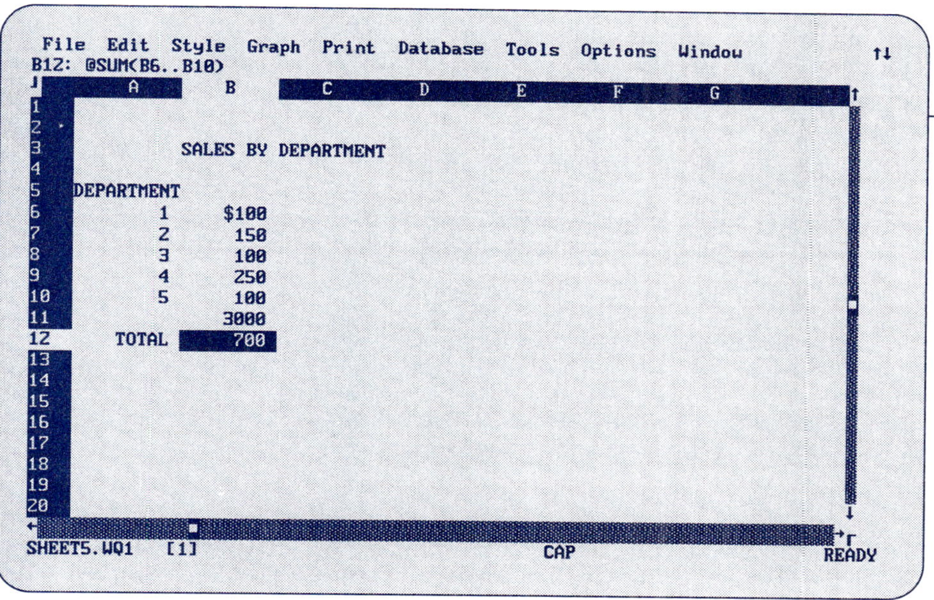

FIGURE 3-36

Error due to inserting a row

the sum of the values in cells B3 through B7," and the result of that calculation will be entered into B7. If the formula is recalculated, the result (210) will be incorrect, because the spreadsheet is including B7 in the calculation. The correct formula is @SUM(B3.B6), and the correct amount is 105. Quattro Pro displays the word CIRC at the bottom of the screen when it encounters a circular reference. To illustrate this you will retrieve a worksheet called CIRCREF and enter a formula that causes a circular reference.

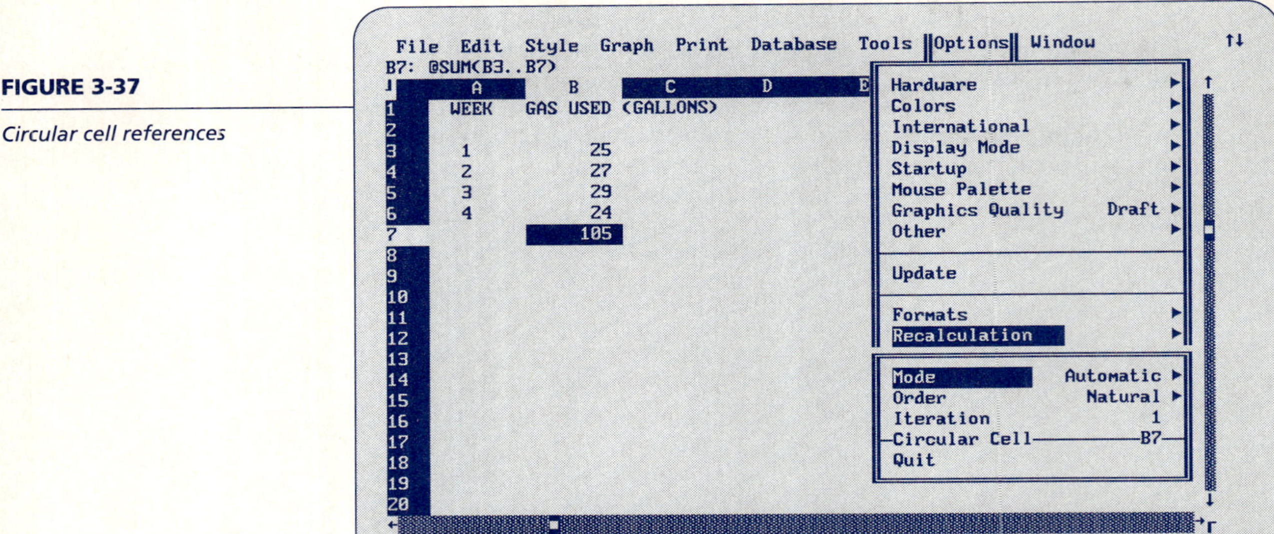

FIGURE 3-37

Circular cell references

Use the /File¦Erase command to clear the current worksheet and the /File¦Retrieve command to load CIRCREF. With the cell selector at B7:

Enter @SUM(B3.B7) ↵ — Enters the formula

The word CIRC appears on the status line to indicate a circular reference. The sum (105) is correct. But if you recalculate the spreadsheet, the sum changes.

Press F9 — Recalculates the worksheet and changes the sum to 210

To correct the error, you need only change the formula. You could do this by positioning the cell selector on B7 and pressing F2 to edit the formula.

In this case, you can easily see where the problem is. In some cases, though, the circular reference can be harder to find. For that reason, Quattro Pro provides the /Options¦Recalculation¦Circular Cell command. This command lists the address of the first cell in a formula with a circular reference.

Press / O R — Brings up the Recalculation menu

To the right of the Circular Cell line is the address of the first cell reference in a circular formula, in this case B7 (see Figure 3-37).

Press Q — Removes the Recalculation menu

Press Q — Removes the Options menu

Move to B7 if you are not there already, and enter the correct formula, @SUM(B3.B6). The CIRC message on the status line will disappear.

If you have many circular references, CIRC continues to be displayed on the status line until they are all corrected. Because /Options¦Recalculation¦Circular Cell lists one circular reference at a time, it allows you to check your spreadsheet thoroughly. You can think of it as a "spell checker" for spreadsheets. It will only find circular references, not other kinds of calculation errors. ***NOTE:*** If you have chosen manual recalculation, CIRC may not appear.

Testing a Worksheet

The pitfalls presented in the preceding section illustrate the need to test your worksheet for errors. Once a worksheet has been developed, you can test it by:

- Checking for the CIRC message at the bottom of the screen and using /Options¦Recalculation¦Circular Cell to locate any circular references.
- Using crossfooting (as presented earlier in this chapter) to check the accuracy of calculations.
- Manually calculating some or all of the parts of the worksheet.
- Inserting simple values into the worksheet to test the accuracy of formulas.

CHALLENGE EXERCISE

In this exercise you practice testing a worksheet for errors and then correcting them. On your data disk is a file called TESTING. You will retrieve this worksheet and find and correct the errors. First, clear the current worksheet and retrieve TESTING. Then use the techniques mentioned above to find and correct the errors.

APPLICATION 3

This section presents some common business application worksheets. The basic worksheet with headings and formulas (called a "template") has already been developed. You just enter the desired data and note the results. Templates are useful when generating periodic reports or performing periodic analysis in which the data changes but the format remains the same. The following templates are located on your data disk.

Template	Filename
Loan repayment schedule	LOANPAY
Lease analysis	LEASE
Financial statement analysis	FORECAST

Loan Repayment Schedule

The Rainier Ski School wants to purchase a copy machine. The company is trying to determine the monthly payments for various loan plans. Figure 3-38 shows the worksheet template for a loan repayment schedule. When the purchase price, down-payment percent, interest rate, and loan term in months are entered, the worksheet lays out the payments per month and breaks down the amounts paid on the interest and principal. In addition, the worksheet gives the principal balance after each month and the total paid to date. The purchase

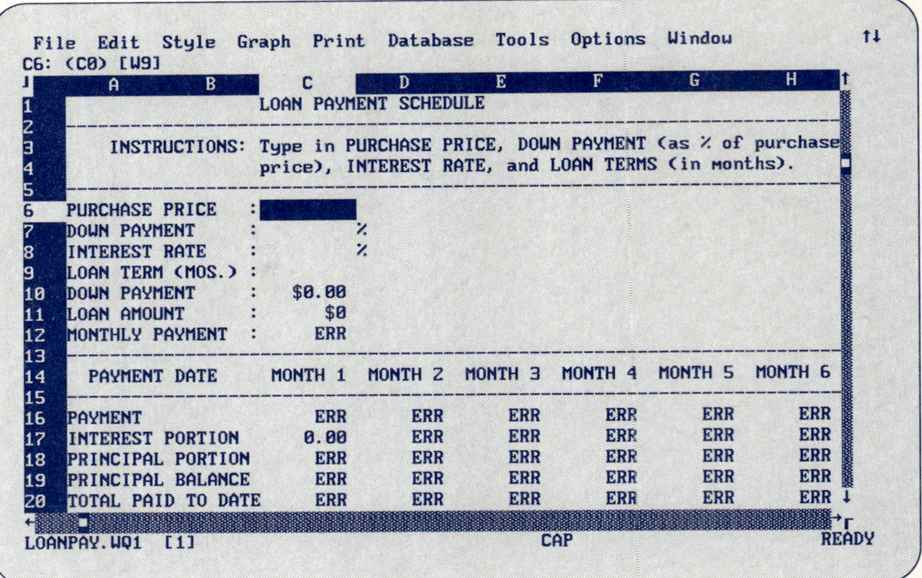

FIGURE 3-38

LOANPAY template

price for the copier is $3,800. The company wants to compare the monthly payments for the following loans.

	Loan A	**Loan B**
Purchase price	$3,800	$3,800
Down payment (%)	10	20
Interest rate (%)	12	10
Terms (months)	24	24

The LOANPAY template was developed using the Quattro Pro payment function (@PMT). Retrieve LOANPAY and enter the data as specified below. After loading the worksheet notice that ERR (error) appears throughout the worksheet (Figure 3-38). This is because the loan data has not yet been entered. Make sure the cell selector is at C6.

Type 3800 ⓓ	Enters 3800 into C6 and moves the cell selector to C7
Type 10 ⓓ	Enters 10 into C7 and moves the cell selector to C8
Type 12 ⓓ	Enters 12 into C8 and moves the cell selector to C9
Type 24 ↵	Enters 24 into C9

As Figure 3-39 shows, the payments would be $160.99 per month. Now enter the data for loan B and find the monthly payments. As shown on your screen, the higher down payment and lower interest rate reduce the monthly payments to $140.28.

Using this template, monthly payments can be quickly calculated for any combination of purchase price, down-payment requirement, interest rate, and monthly terms. This particular template can accommodate loans of up to two years (24 months), and it can easily be expanded to accommodate longer terms.

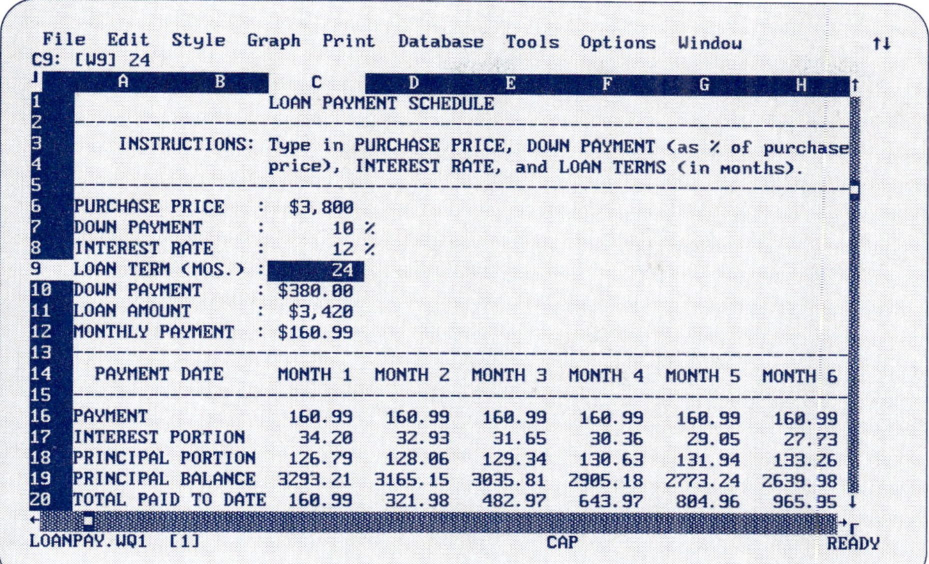

FIGURE 3-39

Completed loan payment schedule

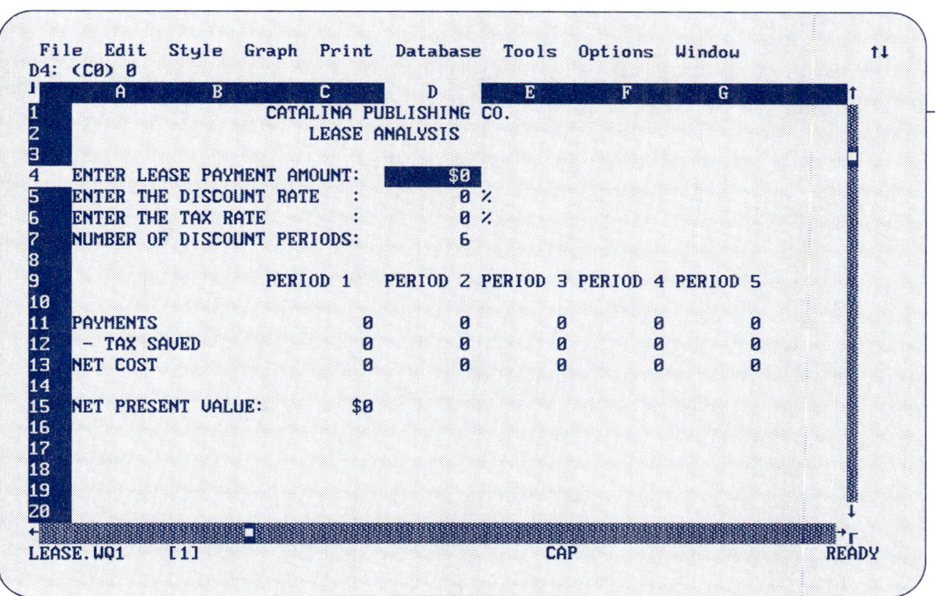

FIGURE 3-40

LEASE template

Lease Analysis

The Catalina Publishing Company needs to acquire a new printing press. The financial management personnel want to calculate the net present value to lease the printing press for six years. They have decide to use Quattro Pro, which provides a mathematical function called Net Present Value (@NPV), for the analysis. This function determines the current value of a series of payments given a specific discount rate. Using the worksheet template called LEASE (Figure 3-40), you can enter the payments, discount rate, and tax rate to determine the NPV. The payments are $25,000, the discount rate is 14 percent, and the tax rate is 48 percent. Retrieve the LEASE worksheet. The cell selector should be at D4.

Type 25000 ⓥ	Enters 25000 into D4 and moves the cell selector to D5
Type 14 ⓥ	Enters 14 into D5 and moves the cell selector to D6
Type 48 ⏎	Enters 48 into D6

As shown on your screen, the net present value is $50,553. That is, if the company currently has $50,553 it would be able to cover the payments for the term of the lease. This template can be used to determine the net present value for any combination of payments, discount rate, and tax rate.

Financial Statement Forecast

Cascade Medical, Inc., manufactures a pressure gauge used to diagnose glaucoma. The company is considering a merger and needs, among other things, a forecast of its income statement. Figure 3-41a shows the actual (1991) breakdown of income and expenses and the projection with a sales growth rate of zero for the next three years. The company is interested in comparing a conservative sales growth rate (4%) with a more ambitious one (12%). Retrieve the worksheet (FORECAST) and enter these rates. After you load the file the cell selector should be at A1.

Press (F5) **and type** F2 ⏎	Moves the cell selector to F2
Type 12 ⏎	Enters 12 into F2

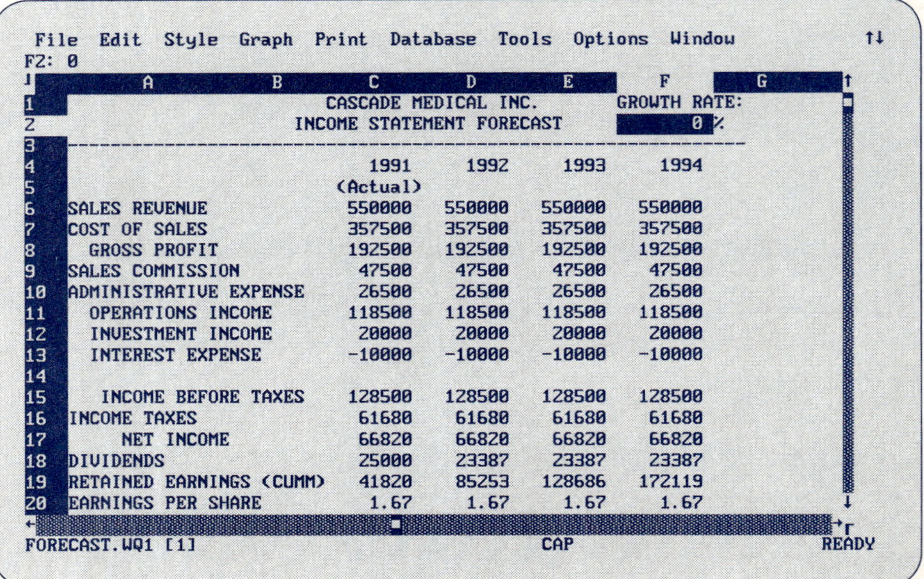

File Edit Style Graph Print Database Tools Options Window

F2: 0

CASCADE MEDICAL INC. — GROWTH RATE: 0%

INCOME STATEMENT FORECAST

	1991 (Actual)	1992	1993	1994
SALES REVENUE	550000	550000	550000	550000
COST OF SALES	357500	357500	357500	357500
GROSS PROFIT	192500	192500	192500	192500
SALES COMMISSION	47500	47500	47500	47500
ADMINISTRATIVE EXPENSE	26500	26500	26500	26500
OPERATIONS INCOME	118500	118500	118500	118500
INVESTMENT INCOME	20000	20000	20000	20000
INTEREST EXPENSE	-10000	-10000	-10000	-10000
INCOME BEFORE TAXES	128500	128500	128500	128500
INCOME TAXES	61680	61680	61680	61680
NET INCOME	66820	66820	66820	66820
DIVIDENDS	25000	23387	23387	23387
RETAINED EARNINGS (CUMM)	41820	85253	128686	172119
EARNINGS PER SHARE	1.67	1.67	1.67	1.67

FORECAST.WQ1 [1] CAP READY

FIGURE 3-41a

FORECAST template

With a growth rate of 12 percent, sales revenue would be forecast at $772,710 and retained earnings would be $211,236 for 1994 (Figure 3-41b). Now enter the lower growth rate of 4 percent.

Type 4 (↵)	Enters 4 into F2

With a 4 percent growth rate, the 1994 forecast is $618,675 for sales and $184,490 for retained earnings.

Spreadsheet templates that are used to model actual business conditions are useful in helping to analyze company operations, make forecasts, and provide information for decision making. But remember, spreadsheet templates are only as good as their built-in assumptions: Care should be exercised in using them.

Getting Help

When you need assistance in working through Quattro Pro, you can press the Help key, (F1). Information is then displayed on the screen which leads you through the program. If you are working on a particular command, such as Print, and press (F1), the screen provides information on this command. If you are entering data, the screen displays a menu of topics. To select a topic, move the highlight and press (↵). To return to the worksheet, press (ESC). Help screens that vary depending on what part of the program you are using are called **context-sensitive help**.

Try the Help key now. With the financial statement template in view:

Press (F1)	Brings up the Help Topics screen (Figure 3-42)
Press (→) **5 times**	Moves the highlight to Menu Commands

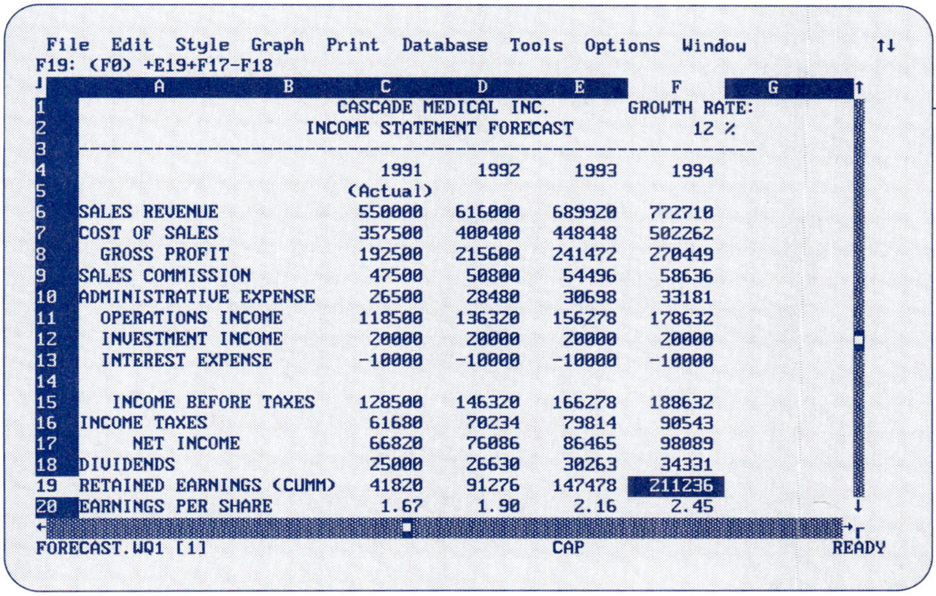

```
 File  Edit  Style  Graph  Print  Database  Tools  Options  Window          ↑↓
F19: (F0) +E19+F17-F18
     A              B         C         D         E         F          G
1                     CASCADE MEDICAL INC.            GROWTH RATE:
2                  INCOME STATEMENT FORECAST                 12 %
3   ---------------------------------------------------------------
4                              1991      1992      1993      1994
5                            (Actual)
6  SALES REVENUE             550000    616000    689920    772710
7  COST OF SALES             357500    400400    448448    502262
8    GROSS PROFIT            192500    215600    241472    270449
9  SALES COMMISSION           47500     50800     54496     58636
10 ADMINISTRATIVE EXPENSE     26500     28480     30698     33181
11   OPERATIONS INCOME       118500    136320    156278    178632
12   INVESTMENT INCOME        20000     20000     20000     20000
13   INTEREST EXPENSE        -10000    -10000    -10000    -10000
14
15     INCOME BEFORE TAXES   128500    146320    166278    188632
16 INCOME TAXES               61680     70234     79814     90543
17       NET INCOME           66820     76086     86465     98089
18 DIVIDENDS                  25000     26630     30263     34331
19 RETAINED EARNINGS (CUMM)   41820     91276    147478    211236
20 EARNINGS PER SHARE          1.67      1.90      2.16      2.45
FORECAST.WQ1 [1]                         CAP                        READY
```

FIGURE 3-41b

Forecast—12 percent growth rate

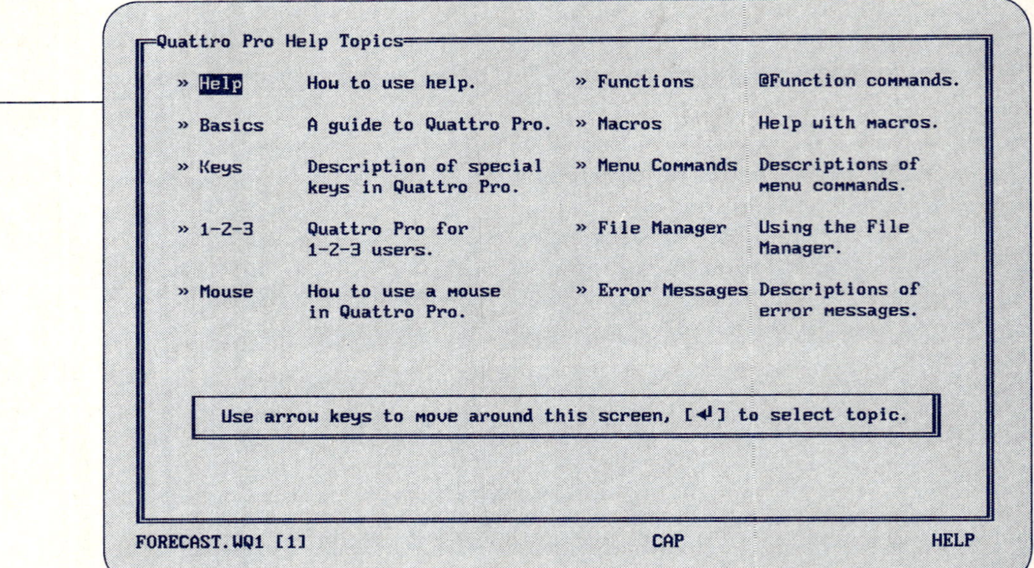

FIGURE 3-42

Help feature

↵	Menu Commands screen appears
ESC	Returns to worksheet

Now try the Help key while carrying out a command.

Press / P	Selects the Print command
Press F1	Help screen appears with information about specifying a block to print
ESC	Returns to print process

Take a few moments to explore the Help function. When you are finished, use ESC to return to the worksheet.

Accessing DOS

Quattro Pro allows you to execute a DOS command without having to quit the spreadsheet program. The command for this is on the File menu, /File¦Utilities¦DOS Shell. The spreadsheet disappears and the DOS prompt appears. Then you can issue a DOS command or run another program if your computer has enough memory. When you are finished, type EXIT and press ↵ to return to Quattro Pro. Try this now by looking at a directory of the data disk in drive A.

Press / F	Brings up the File menu
Press U	Brings up the Utilities menu
Press D	Selects DOS Shell and the DOS prompt appears
Type DIR A: ↵	Lists the files on the disk in drive A
Type EXIT ↵	Returns to Quattro Pro

SUMMARY

Having completed this chapter, you should understand how to plan worksheets and make decisions using electronic spreadsheets. You should also understand one of the most powerful features of electronic spreadsheets: quick recalculation of numbers for evaluation of alternative (what-if) scenarios.

With Quattro Pro, you should be able to make worksheet enhancements, use functions and formulas, test worksheets for errors, and create and use templates. The challenge exercises that follow will help you practice the skills you have learned. You are now prepared for the additional features of Quattro Pro presented in Chapter 4.

WORD LIST

absolute cell reference
circular reference
context-sensitive help
crossfooting
DOS shell
Help key
locking titles
relative cell reference
templates
titles
what-if analysis
windows

QUESTIONS

1. What is the benefit of using manual recalculation?
2. Distinguish between the /Window¦Options¦Locked Titles command and the /Window¦Options¦Vertical command.
3. What would the following mathematical function do: @AVG(C12.C25)?
4. Explain the meaning of the following function: @IF(K40<5000,B12+B13,B12).
5. What is a circular reference?
6. List four ways to test a worksheet for errors.
7. What are worksheet templates and what are the advantages of using them?
8. What is context-sensitive help?

CHALLENGE EXERCISES

1. Develop, save, and print a worksheet using the data in Figure 2-1.
2. Develop a worksheet using the data for the income statement in Figure 2-3.
   a. Insert a row and divide the operating expenses into the cost of goods sold (10,100) and other expenses (8,100).
   b. Add a percent (of sales) column to the right of the subtotal and total amounts.
   c. Save and print the worksheet.

3. Develop a worksheet using the data for the balance sheet in Figure 2-3.
   a. Format the last row with a dollar sign and no decimal places.
   b. Change the Current Liabilities from 5,000 to 5,500.
   c. Save and print the worksheet.

4. Below is an expense voucher form with one week's worth of expenses for a salesperson. Develop a worksheet using this data. Fill in the Total column and row using the Sum function and the Copy command. Use crossfooting to check the accuracy of the grand total. Also, enhance the worksheet by using horizontal lines where appropriate.

EXPENSE VOUCHER

EXPENSE	**MON**	**TUE**	**WED**	**THUR**	**FRI**	**TOTAL**
TRANSP	12.00	10.50	11.30	15.20	10.50	
PARK/TOLL	3.00	3.00	3.00	3.00	3.00	
BREAKFAST	4.01	4.75	4.30	4.75	5.15	
LUNCH	5.25	5.20	6.15	5.75	9.32	
DINNER	18.33	16.90	8.02	7.30	15.20	
MISC	15.21	21.00	0.00	3.30	50.00	
TOTAL						

Submitted by: Date:

Save and print the worksheet.

5. You work for COMPUTERS R US, a wholesale distributor for several makes of microcomputers. You have decided to computerize your inventory report using an electronic spreadsheet. Develop a worksheet using the following data (model, item number, quantity on hand, and unit cost):

   Macintosh, 4213, 21, 774.21

   IBM PC, 1246, 12, 1632.44

   IBM PS/2, 4403, 18, 1251.10

   COMPAQ 386, 7213, 9, 1118.33

   AST 286, 5012, 12, 343.22

   In addition to the above data, include a total inventory amount (quantity times cost) for each model and a total amount for all models.

   Save the worksheet.

4 Putting Quattro Pro to Work

Now that you have mastered the basics of electronic spreadsheets, you are prepared to learn the additional features that allow you to design sophisticated reports, develop graphs, and turn your worksheet into a database. These features are presented in this chapter.

APPLICATION 1

Designing a Report Format

In this section you learn how to use the Print command options within Quattro Pro to design a report format. These options allow you to specify headings and footers on each page of a report, insert page breaks, and change margins. You can also use the Print options to specify how characters are printed (such as boldface, italics, compressed type, and so on). Print options change the appearance of a worksheet when printed; they do not change the contents of a worksheet. Designing a report format is especially important for multiple-page worksheets.

Figures 4-1 and 4-2 show the same worksheet printed two ways, one using the default settings, which are built in to the Quattro Pro program, and the other after changes made with the Print options. The process is to complete a worksheet, select the Print command from the main menu, and change the Print options as desired. Below is a brief description of how each Print option is used.

Block Specifies the area of the spreadsheet to be printed.

Headings Chooses between Left Heading, specifying one or more columns to be printed as headings on the left side of each page, and Top Heading, specifying one or more rows to be printed as headings on the top of each page.

Destination Sends the worksheet data to a printer or to a disk file for use in the future. (***NOTE:*** Usually you will send the data to a printer. However, you can save the worksheet as a print file in ASCII format. If you save a worksheet as a print file, Quattro Pro appends the extension .PRN, and you can use the file with other programs such as word processing.)

Page Layout Changes margins or page lengths and specifies headings, footers, and page breaks. Also used to cause special character printing such as boldface or compressed type.

Format Specifies that the worksheet be printed as displayed on the screen or that a list of the contents of each cell, along with the cell address and cell format, be printed.

Adjust Printer Moves the paper in the printer to the top of the next page and resets Quattro Pro's line counter, which determines the placement of page breaks, headings, footers, and margins.

FIGURE 4-1

Large worksheet printed using default settings

STATEMENT OF INCOME
The Arizona Water Power Company

	For the years Ended Thousands of Dollars		Dec. 31
	1988	1987	1986
OPERATING REVENUES:			
Electric................................	$228,438	$203,841	$230,406
Gas and other...........................	43,238	53,881	103,002
Total operating revenues..........	271,676	257,722	333,408
OPERATING EXPENSES:			
Operations:			
Gas purchased.........................	25,496	37,293	61,832
Power purchased.......................	30,288	28,343	37,926
Fuel cost.............................	24,852	16,930	22,840
Other.................................	43,807	40,556	42,849
Maintenance.............................	11,284	8,447	12,993
Depreciation and amortization...........	24,384	20,488	17,489
Federal and state income tax............	22,994	19,985	23,994
Total operating expenses..........	183,105	172,042	219,923
NET OPERATING INCOME......................	88,571	85,680	113,485
OTHER INCOME (DEDUCTIONS):			
Earnings of subsidiaries................	2,544	2,299	4,076
Allowance for equity funds during const..	429	9,932	15,398
Investment tax credit amortization......	16,884	20	20
Other...................................	739	(388)	172
Total other income - net..........	20,596	11,863	19,666
INTEREST CHARGES (CREDITS):			
Interest on long-term debt..............	38,664	40,233	45,002
Allowance for borrowed funds for const....	(548)	(5,933)	(9,320)
Other...................................	10,390	684	11,003
Net interest charges..............	48,506	34,984	46,685
INCOME before cummulative effect of changes in accounting practices......	60,661	62,559	86,466
CUMMULATIVE EFFECT OF CHANGES IN ACCOUNTING PRINCIPLES:			
Accrual of unbilled revenues...........		17,388	
Provision for abandonments.............		(37,444)	
NET INCOME................................	60,661	42,503	86,466
DEDUCT - Preferred stock dividend..........	12,944	13,229	12,738
INCOME AVAILABLE FOR COMMON STOCK..........	47,717	29,274	73,728
Average common shares outstanding (000s)....	17,343	16,888	16,733
EARNINGS (LOSS) PER SHARE OF COMMON STOCK:			
Before cummulative effect of changes in accounting principles...............	2.75	2.92	4.41
Cummulative effect of changes in accounting principles...............		(1.19)	
	$2.75	$1.73	$4.41

FIGURE 4-2

Large worksheet printed with changes in default settings

STATEMENT OF INCOME
The Arizona Water Power Company

For the years Ended Dec. 31
Thousands of Dollars

	1988	1987	1986
OPERATING REVENUES:			
Electric	$228,438	$203,841	$230,406
Gas and other	43,238	53,881	103,002
Total operating revenues	271,676	257,722	333,408
OPERATING EXPENSES:			
Operations:			
Gas purchased	25,496	37,293	61,832
Power purchased	30,288	28,343	37,926
Fuel cost	24,852	16,930	22,840
Other	43,807	40,556	42,849
Maintenance	11,284	8,447	12,993
Depreciation and amortization	24,384	20,488	17,489
Federal and state income tax	22,994	19,985	23,994
Total operating expenses	183,105	172,042	219,923
NET OPERATING INCOME	88,571	85,680	113,485
OTHER INCOME (DEDUCTIONS):			
Earnings of subsidiaries	2,544	2,299	4,076
Allowance for equity funds during const..	429	9,932	15,398
Investment tax credit amortization	16,884	20	20
Other	739	(388)	172
Total other income - net	20,596	11,863	19,666
INTEREST CHARGES (CREDITS):			
Interest on long-term debt	38,664	40,233	45,002
Allowance for borrowed funds for const.	(548)	(5,933)	(9,320)
Other	10,390	684	11,003
Net interest charges	48,506	34,984	46,685
INCOME before cummulative effect of changes in accounting practices	60,661	62,559	86,466

Page 1

STATEMENT OF INCOME
The Arizona Water Power Company

For the years Ended Dec. 31
Thousands of Dollars

	1988	1987	1986
CUMMULATIVE EFFECT OF CHANGES IN ACCOUNTING PRINCIPLES:			
Accrual of unbilled revenues		17,388	
Provision for abandonments		(37,444)	
NET INCOME	60,661	42,503	86,466
DEDUCT - Preferred stock dividend	12,944	13,229	12,738
INCOME AVAILABLE FOR COMMON STOCK	47,717	29,274	73,728
Average common shares outstanding (000s)	17,343	16,888	16,733
EARNINGS (LOSS) PER SHARE OF COMMON STOCK:			
Before cummulative effect of changes in accounting principles	2.75	2.92	4.41
Cummulative effect of changes in accounting principles		(1.19)	
	$2.75	$1.73	$4.41

Page 2

Spreadsheet Print	Sends specified block to the printer or to a file.
Graph Print	Used to print graphs.
Quit	Returns to spreadsheet. ESC will also return you to the spreadsheet.

If you make changes in the Print options, they are saved when you save the worksheet. The changes also remain in effect when you use the /File|Erase command. However, if you exit Quattro Pro and re-enter, the default settings will be in effect again.

Before working with Print options, you need to understand Quattro Pro's default settings. If your printer uses standard 8.5 × 11 inch paper and the standard print size of 10 CPI (characters per inch), then the maximum amount of data you can print is 80 characters across and 66 rows down (Figure 4-3). However, Quattro Pro has built-in margins of 4 characters left and right and 2 lines (rows) top and bottom. An additional 3 lines at the top and bottom are reserved for headings and footers. Thus, with these default settings the maximums are reduced to 72 characters across and 56 rows down, as shown in Figure 4-4.

If a worksheet is too long to fit on one page, the top and bottom margins could be changed to allow more rows, or a page break could be inserted to cause the printer to skip to another page at any point in the worksheet.

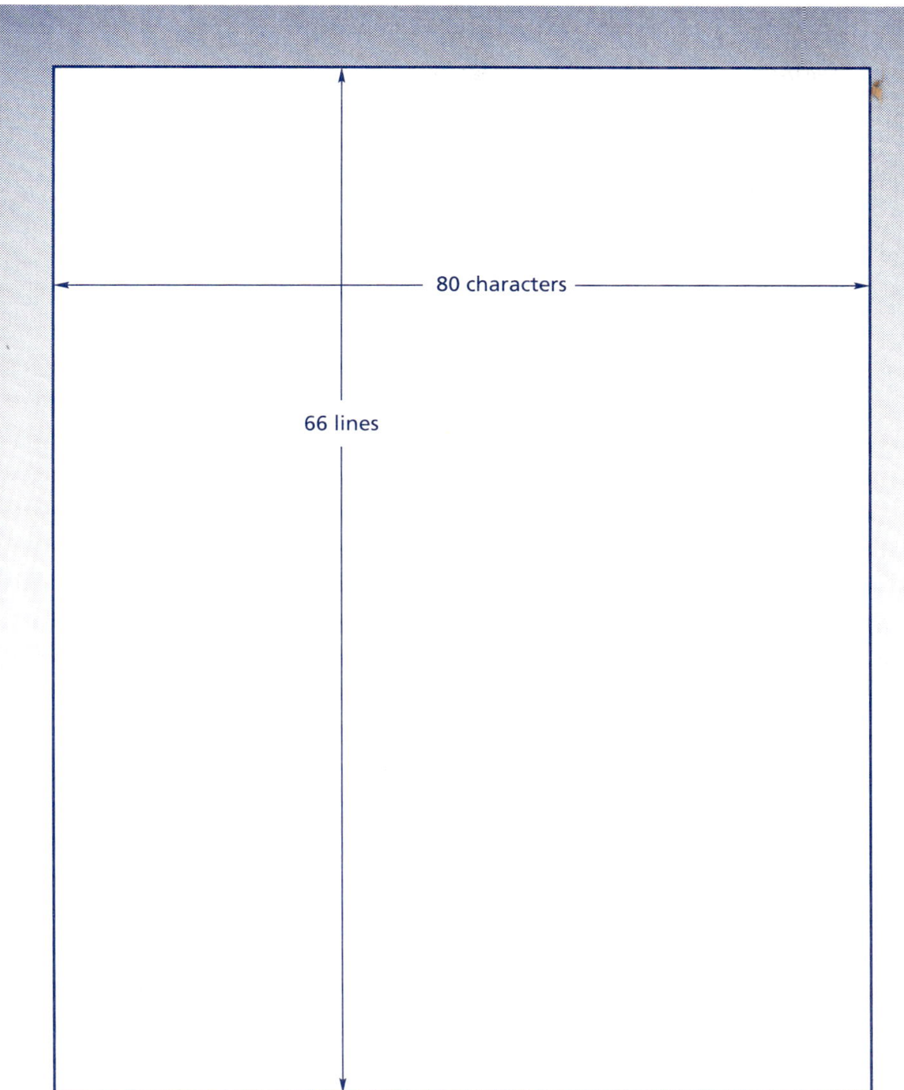

FIGURE 4-3

Standard 8.5 × 11 inch paper

If a worksheet is wider than 72 characters, the first page contains as many columns as will fit across the page, and another page is printed with the rest of the columns. If this occurs, you could paste the two pages together to create one wide printout, as shown in Figure 4-5. Another option for wide worksheets is to change the margins and fonts and use setup strings to cause the printer to print characters in small (compressed) type, allowing more characters to be printed across the page. These options are explained in the following section.

The student data disk contains a file called REPORT. If you were to print this file using the default settings, the output would resemble Figure 4-1. There are some problems with this printout. First, because the worksheet is too wide to fit across the paper, column H is printed on the third and fourth pages. Second, there is no title on the second page to indicate what the worksheet values represent. Third, the page break for the second page falls in the middle of

FIGURE 4-4

Quattro Pro default margin settings

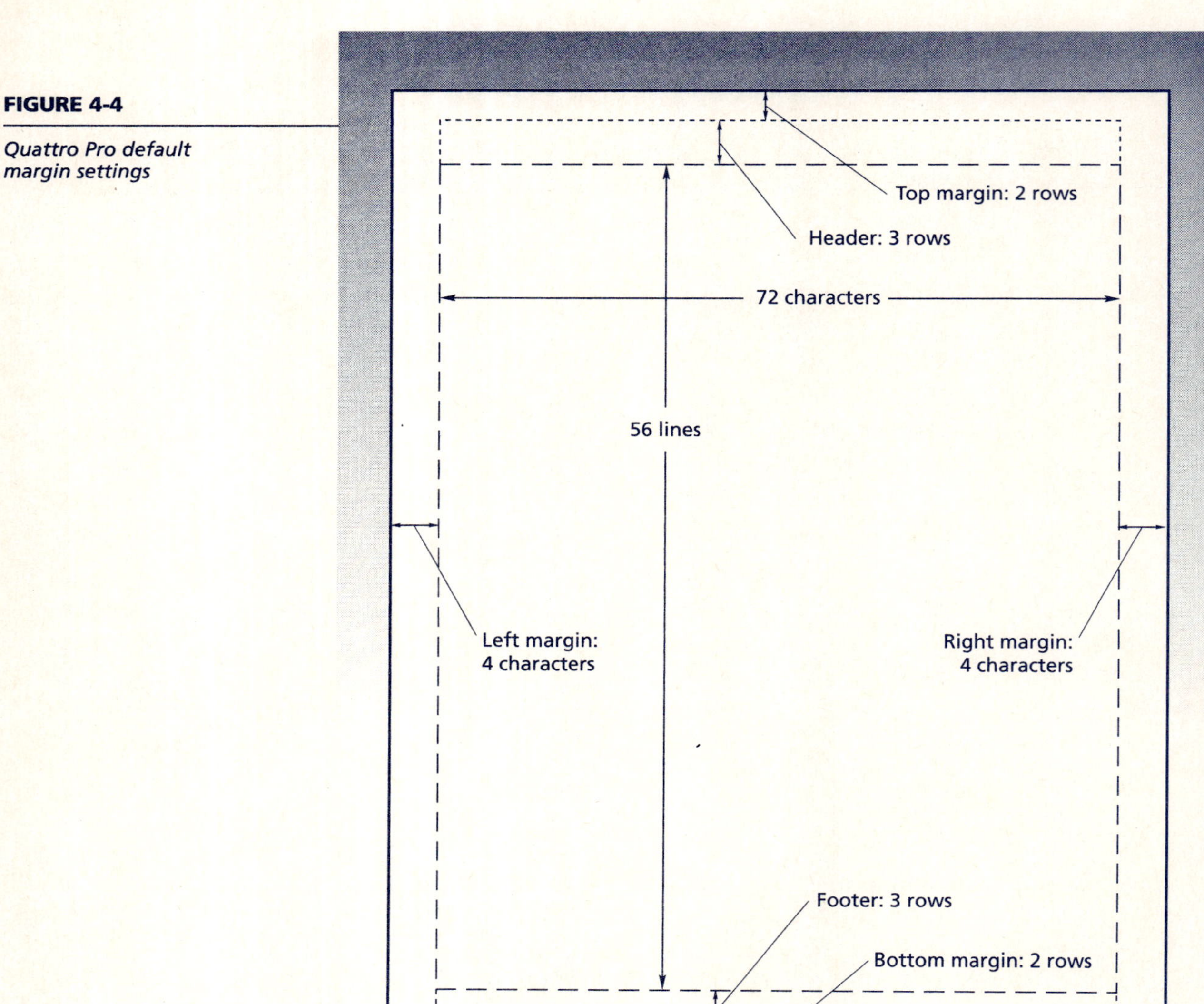

a group of items that should not be separated. You are going to retrieve this file and change the default settings so that when the worksheet is printed it resembles Figure 4-2, which has the following differences.

- It's printed on two pages.
- Headings are printed at the top of each page.
- Page numbers are printed at the bottom of each page.
- The left margin is larger.
- Characters are printed in smaller (compressed) type so all the columns fit across the paper.

FIGURE 4-5

Pasting two pages together, side by side

STATEMENT OF INCOME The Arizona Water Power Company	For the years Ended Thousands of Dollars		Dec. 31
	1988	1987	1986
OPERATING REVENUES:			
Electric..................................	$228,438	$203,841	$230,406
Gas and other.............................	43,238	53,881	103,002
Total operating revenues...........	271,676	257,722	333,408
OPERATING EXPENSES:			
Operations:			
Gas purchased...........................	25,496	37,293	61,832
Power purchased.........................	30,288	28,343	37,926
Fuel cost...............................	24,852	16,930	22,840
Other...................................	43,807	40,556	42,849
Maintenance.............................	11,284	8,447	12,993
Depreciation and amortization............	24,384	20,488	17,489
Federal and state income tax.............	22,994	19,985	23,994
Total operating expenses...........	183,105	172,042	219,923
NET OPERATING INCOME.......................	88,571	85,680	113,485
OTHER INCOME (DEDUCTIONS):			
Earnings of subsidiaries..................	2,544	2,299	4,076
Allowance for equity funds during const..	429	9,932	15,398
Investment tax credit amortization........	16,884	20	20
Other.....................................	739	(388)	172
Total other income - net...........	20,596	11,863	19,666
INTEREST CHARGES (CREDITS):			
Interest on long-term debt................	38,664	40,233	45,002
Allowance for borrowed funds for const....	(548)	(5,933)	(9,320)
Other.....................................	10,390	684	11,003
Net interest charges...............	48,506	34,984	46,685
INCOME before cummulative effect of changes in accounting practices......	60,661	62,559	86,466
CUMMULATIVE EFFECT OF CHANGES IN ACCOUNTING PRINCIPLES:			
Accrual of unbilled revenues...........		17,388	
Provision for abandonments.............		(37,444)	
NET INCOME.................................	60,661	42,503	86,466
DEDUCT - Preferred stock dividend..........	12,944	13,229	12,738
INCOME AVAILABLE FOR COMMON STOCK..........	47,717	29,274	73,728
Average common shares outstanding (000s)....	17,343	16,888	16,733

Load the REPORT worksheet and complete the following steps to change the Print options.

Retrieve REPORT

Creating a Page Break If you are printing a multiple-page worksheet, a page break will occur after 56 lines; however, this may not be the ideal place to split a page. You can specify a page break in three ways. First, you could change the page length from 66 to some other number. This might be useful if the paper you are using is not 11 inches long. Second, you could type page-break characters into the worksheet. When Quattro Pro encounters these characters during printing, the program instructs the printer to skip to the next page. The characters are a split bar (¦) followed by two colons (Figure 4-6). These characters must be entered in the first column of a blank row. Third, and easiest, the /Style¦Insert Break command can be used to automatically insert page-break characters in a blank row. Complete the following to use the Insert Break command to insert a page break at row 43.

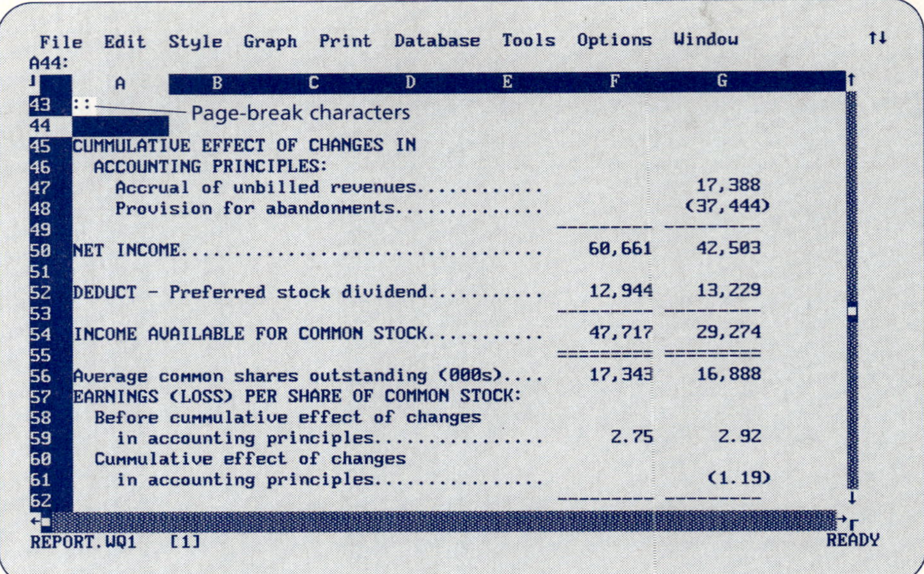

FIGURE 4-6

Page-break characters inserted into worksheet

ACTION	*RESULT*
Press (F5) **and type** A43 (↵)	Moves cell selector to cell A43
Press / S	Brings up Style menu
Press I	Selects Insert Break and inserts page-break characters (Figure 4-7)

Specifying Page Headings Now that the worksheet will be printed on more than one page, you need to consider page headings and footers. Figure 4-2 shows the column headings that normally would be printed only on the first page. By using the /Print¦Headings¦Top Heading option, the data in these rows can be printed on the top of each page of the report.

Press / P	Brings up Print menu
Press H	Selects Headings
Press T	Selects Top Heading

The prompt is:

```
Column headings to print across the top of each page: A44
```

Enter A1.H5 (↵)	Specifies the rows to be used as heading

You can have more than one row as a top heading and you can also specify left (column) headings. ***NOTE:*** If you specify a row heading, do not include that row in the block to be printed. Otherwise, that row will print twice on the first page.

Numbering Pages Figure 4-2 shows a page number printed at the center of the bottom of each page. The /Print¦Layout¦Footer option is used to

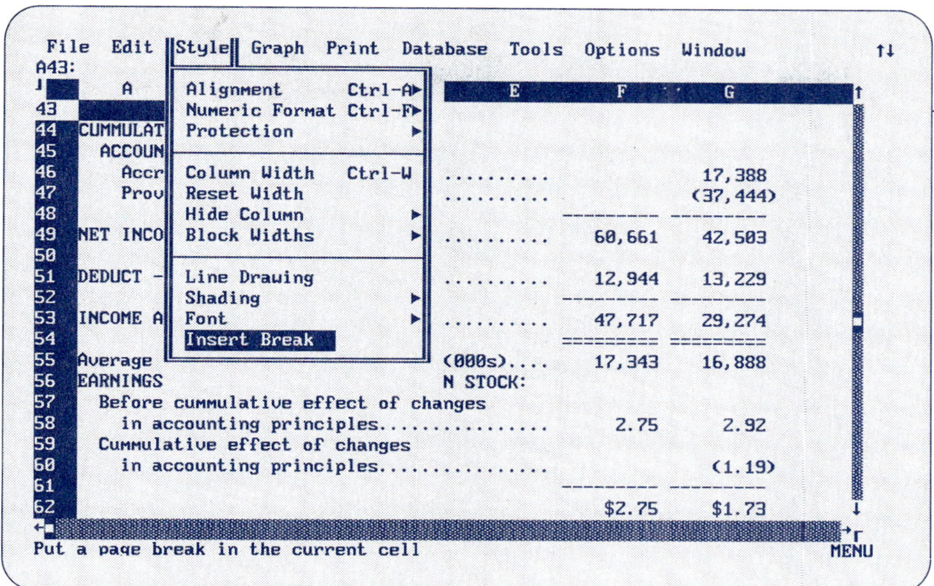

FIGURE 4-7

Inserting page breaks into a worksheet

indicate page numbers, as well as other text you want printed at the bottom of each page. Any text can be used as a footer, as well as the following three special symbols.

- \# Wherever this symbol appears, the current page number is printed.
- @ Wherever this symbol appears, the current date is printed.
- ¦ This symbol determines the position of the text: left, center, or right.

The ¦ symbol works as a tab, with the first one centering the text and the second one aligning it to the right, as shown in the examples that follow.

When you type:	**The footer prints:**
Page #	Page 1
¦ Page #	Page 1 (centered)
¦¦ Page #	Page 1 (right)

Complete the following steps to have page numbers printed. From the Print menu:

Press L	Selects Layout
Press F	Selects Footer option

The message is:

`A line of text to be printed at the bottom of each page:`

Type ¦ Page # ↵	Specifies the footer as the page number printed in the bottom center of every page

NOTE: To place text at the top of every page, you would choose the /Print¦Layout¦Headings option and follow the same procedure. This is useful if you wish page numbers to appear at the top of each page or if you wish to include a heading in the report that does not appear on the spreadsheet.

Changing Margins Figure 4-2 shows a left margin of 10 characters. Use the /Print¦Layout¦Margins menu to change the margin setting. From the /Print¦Layout menu:

Press M	Selects Margins menu
Press L	Selects Left Margin

The prompt is:

`Left margin (number of characters from the left edge) (0..254): 4`

Type 10 ↵	Changes the left margin to 10
Press ESC	Returns to /Print¦Layout menu

Setup Strings You could also have the characters printed in small (compressed) type. Figure 4-2 shows a printout in which the characters are printed in compressed type rather than the standard type size. You can do this by adding instructions, called setup codes, to the spreadsheet, which are carried out when the spreadsheet is printed. The printer codes vary with different makes of printers; therefore, it is necessary to check your printer manual for the correct codes. The Quattro Pro manual also includes setup codes for many printers. The following example uses codes for an Epson or compatible dot-matrix printer.

The codes you specify are typed as a sequence of characters called a string; the command used in Quattro Pro is /Printer¦Layout¦Setup String. There are two ways to specify a setup string. One is to embed the string directly into the worksheet by entering it in the first cell of a blank row. Embedded strings have more flexibility because you can have different codes for different parts of the worksheet. ***NOTE:*** You must precede an embedded setup string with two split bars (¦¦).

If you are using an Epson-compatible printer, you could also complete the following to cause the printout to be in compressed type. (If you are using a different printer, refer to the printer manual or the Quattro Pro manual for the correct codes.) From the /Print¦Layout menu:

Press S	Selects Setup String option

The prompt is:

`Specify printer code to be sent to the printer:`

Type \015 ↵	Enters the code for compressed type (Figure 4-8)

Whenever you use compressed type, you also need to change the right margin so more than 80 characters can be printed across the page. From the /Print¦Layout menu:

Press M R	Selects Right Margin option

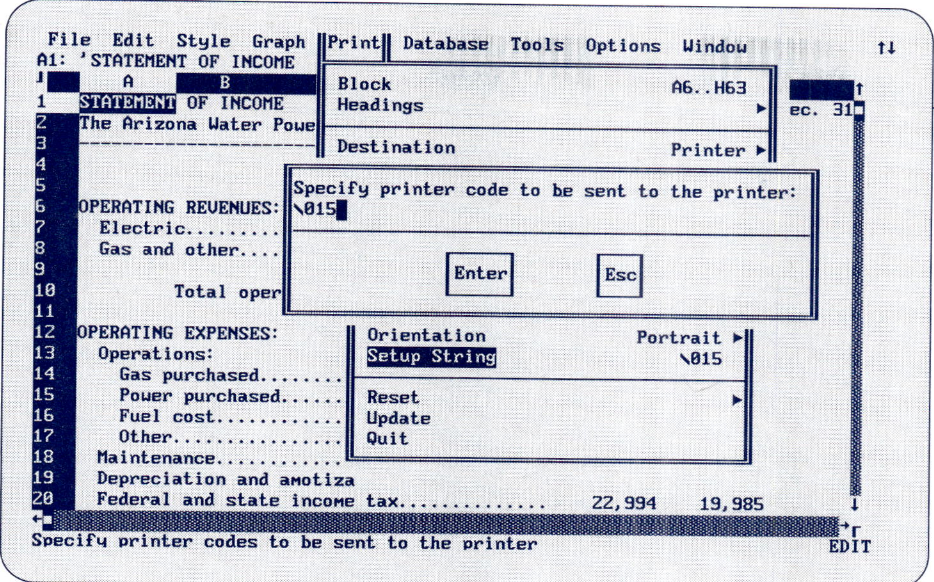

FIGURE 4-8

Specifying printer codes

Type 132 ↵	Changes right margin to 132
Press ESC **twice**	Returns to Print menu
Press B	Selects Block command
Enter A6.H63 ↵	Specifies the block to print

Screen Preview It is often useful to be able to see what a report will look like before it is printed out, because this allows you to make any necessary adjustments. This feature is especially valuable if you have used special codes or if you wish to check that the headings, footers, and page breaks are properly set up. To see what will print, first use the /Print¦Destination¦Screen Preview option, and then press S. From the Print menu:

Press D	Brings up the Destination menu
Press S	Chooses Screen Preview

Screen Preview appears to the right of Destination on the main Print menu. At this point, proceed as if you were going to print the spreadsheet.

Press S	In a few seconds, the report appears on the screen

Use + to "zoom in" to check each section (Figure 4-9) and N to preview the second page. When you are finished examining the report, press Q.

Press +	"Zooms in" to the report
Press N	Previews the next page
Press Q	Returns to Print menu

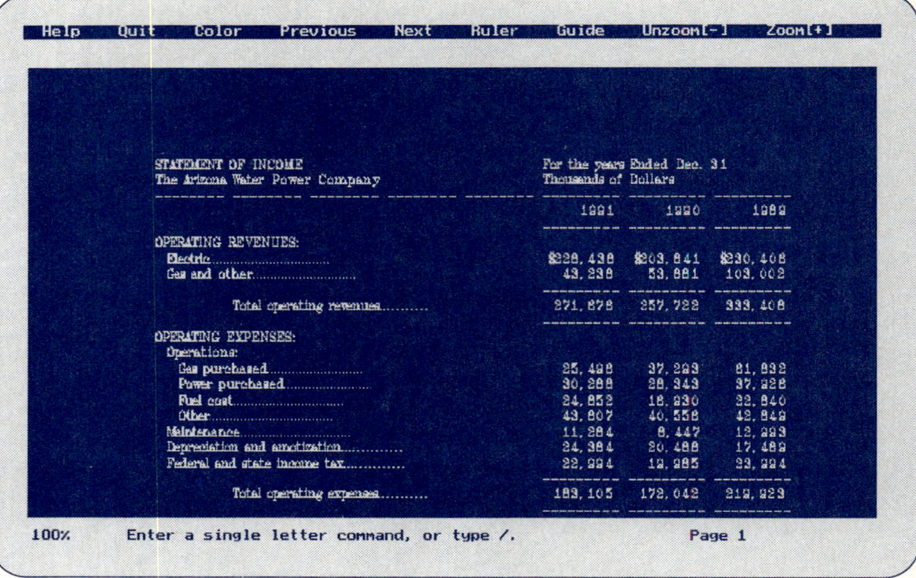

FIGURE 4-9

Screen preview

Before printing, you must change the destination to Printer. From the Print menu:

Press D P	Printer should appear to the right of Destination on the main Print menu

If you are using a dot-matrix printer, make sure the top of the paper in the printer is aligned with the print head, as shown in Figure 4-10. If you are using a laser printer, make sure there is paper in the feeder. Then select the /Print¦Adjust Printer option and press A for Align. This resets Quattro Pro's line counter to ensure correct placement of page breaks, headings, footers, and margins. When printing is finished, you can use the /Print¦Adjust Printer¦Form Feed option to move the paper forward one page, if necessary. From the Print menu:

Press A A	Selects Align option
Press S	Prints the worksheet
Press A F	Selects Form Feed option
Press Q	Returns to the worksheet

This completes the report design. All page layout, headings, and block settings are saved when you save a worksheet. If you want to reset these to the default settings, use the /Print¦Layout¦Reset¦All option.

Presentation-Quality Spreadsheets If you have a printer that can print graphics characters, you can enhance the appearance of your spreadsheets by drawing solid lines and changing typefaces. To draw lines, you would use the /Style¦Line Drawing command. You can also use Quattro Pro commands to cause the characters to be printed in special ways. For instance, you could have

FIGURE 4-10

Paper alignment in printer

characters printed in italics or extra-large type. To do this, you would change the **font**. The procedure for changing fonts involves using the /Style¦Font menu to change to one of Quattro Pro's built-in fonts. The kinds of typefaces each printer can print vary, so check with your instructor about which fonts to use. To practice these features, you will use the student budget worksheet you developed in the last chapter. You will replace the dashed lines with solid lines and have the title displayed in large type.

Retrieve STUBUDGT

Drawing Solid Lines: For this application, you will draw two single lines, from A4 to L4 and from A17 to L17. First, you must erase the existing dashed lines. For the first line, from A4 to L4:

Press (F5) **and type** A4 (↵)	Brings up the GoTo prompt and moves the cell selector to A4
Press (SHIFT)-(F7)	Enters Extended mode
Press (→)	Extends the block from A4 through L4
Press / E E (or (CTRL)-E)	Erases block with dashed lines
Press (F5) **and type** A4 (↵)	Moves the cell selector to A4
Press (SHIFT)-(F7)	Enters Extended mode
Press (→)	Extends the block from A4 through L4
Press / S L	Brings up /Style¦Line Drawing command

A menu is displayed, with choices for placement of the line.

Type T	Indicates that the line should be placed at the top of the block (in this case, at the top of the row)

Next, you are prompted to choose line types: none, single, double, or thick.

Type S	Selects Single line and returns you to the Placement menu

Type Q	Exits from Placement menu

To draw a line from A17 to L17, you can copy the previously drawn line.

Press (F5) **and type** A4 (↵)	Moves the cell selector to A4
Press (SHIFT)-(F7)	Enters Extended mode
Press (→)	Extends the block from A4 through L4
Press / E C (or (CTRL)-C)	Brings up the Copy command
Type A17	Specifies A17 as the start of the destination block
Press (↵)	Copies line to A17.L17

NOTE: To erase a previously drawn line, first use (SHIFT)-(F7) to highlight the block, and then choose /Style¦Line Drawing. At the Placement menu, choose the same position as the line you wish to erase (Top, in this case), and in the Line Types menu, choose None.

Changing Fonts: Quattro Pro comes with eight fonts you can use to change the appearance of text. Because too many fonts, like too many lines, can make a spreadsheet more difficult to read instead of easier, you should use italics, boldface, and different type sizes with caution. To change fonts, first select the font you wish to use, and then specify the block to be printed with that font. To change the title of the worksheet to 18-point (18 pt) type:

Press / S	Selects Style menu
Press F	Brings up menu of available fonts

You can use (↑) or (↓) to highlight the font you wish to use. By default, text is printed with font 1; therefore, to change the appearance of the text, place the highlight on another font. ***NOTE:*** The following instructions assume that font 1 is set to Bitstream Dutch 12-point Black and that font 2 is set to Bitstream Dutch 18-point Black.

Press (↓)	Selects font 2
Press (↵)	Prompts you for block of text to be printed with that font
Enter E1.H1 (↵)	Specifies that the title, STUDENT BUDGET ANALYSIS, is to be printed in large type

You may not see any difference in the appearance of the spreadsheet on the screen. In order to see the change in the way it will print, choose /Print¦Destination¦Screen Preview.

Press / P D S	Selects Screen Preview as destination for file
Press B	Displays prompt for block
Enter A1.L19 (↵)	Enters block to print
Press S	Displays spreadsheet on the screen
Press +	Zooms in on the spreadsheet

For solid lines and fonts to print properly, the computer must be connected to a printer capable of graphics, and the destination on the Print menu must be set to Graphics Printer.

Press (ESC) **twice**	Returns to Print menu
Press D G	Changes destination for file to Graphics Printer
Press S	Prints the worksheet
Erase the worksheet	

Developing Graphs

APPLICATION 2

Quattro Pro allows you to develop graphs from data within a worksheet. Graphs aid in analyzing past or current data and in visualizing future situations. They also can help in discovering trouble spots and pinpointing new trends. Note that the graphs shown in this section may appear slightly differently on your computer, due to difference in the types of monitors. The difference will be especially marked if your computer has a color monitor.

A graph is a visual representation of relationships among values. The most common formats are line, bar, and pie graphs. Line graphs (Figure 4-11) are useful in describing and comparing numerical data that deals with trends or changes over time. For example, you could show sales figures, by year, for the past five years. Bar graphs (Figure 4-12) are most useful for showing comparisons among groups of data. For example, you could show actual sales figures along with forecasted sales figures. Pie graphs (Figure 4-13) are best used to show percentages or parts in relation to the whole. For example, you could show the part of total sales represented by each product.

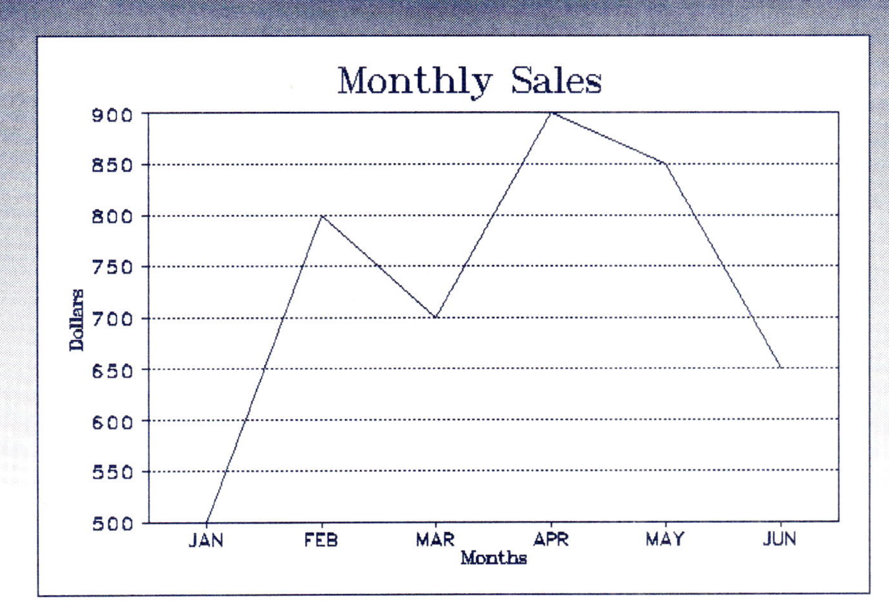

FIGURE 4-11

Line graph

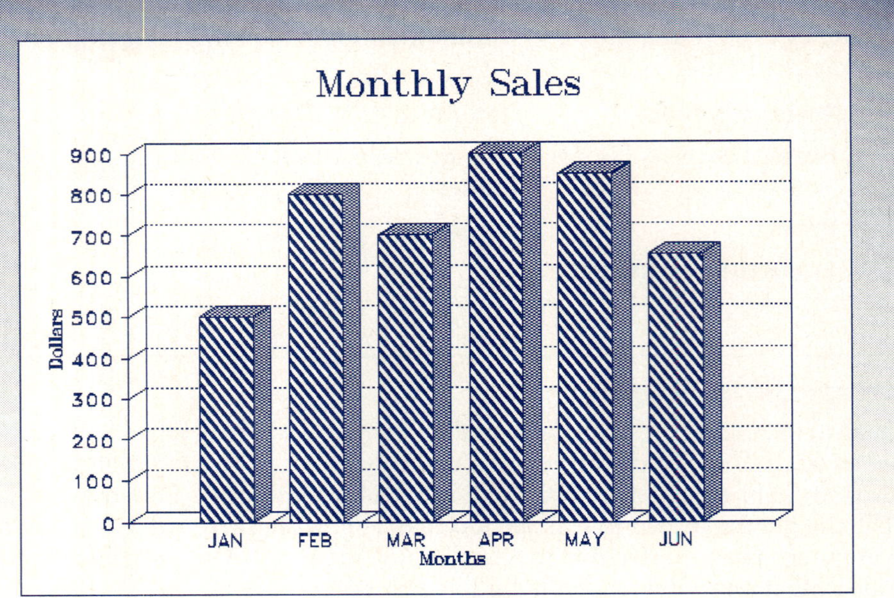

FIGURE 4-12

Bar graph

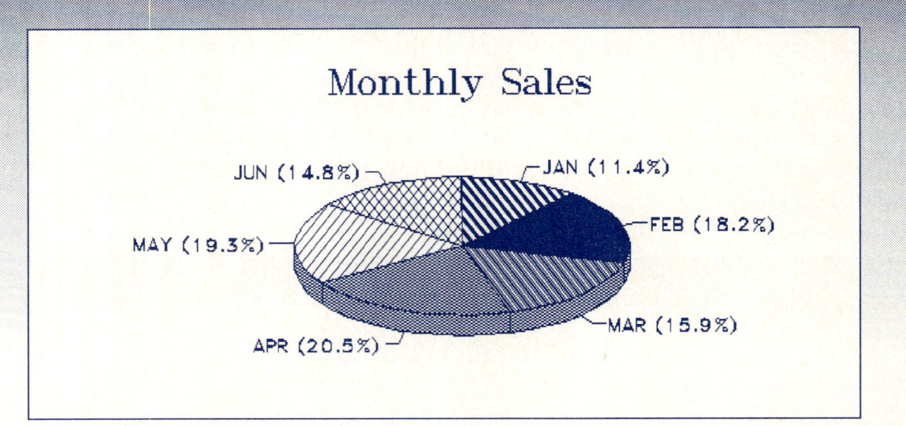

FIGURE 4-13

Pie graph

Line and bar graphs use horizontal and vertical axes for their basic format. The horizontal line is called the **x-axis**, and the vertical line is called the **y-axis**. The x-axis usually shows the data classifications (such as months, years, or words used to identify items or groups). The y-axis is a scale showing the unit of measurement (such as dollars).

To develop a graph, you must first complete a worksheet and specify the data to be used for each part of the graph. For line and bar graphs, this would be the data that goes on the x- and y-axes. The data comes from blocks of cells that you specify. To practice the Graph options, you will use a worksheet named MO_SALES to develop various graphs. This worksheet contains a company's monthly sales. After developing a graph, you can view, customize, and save it. Retrieve MO_SALES. The cell selector should be at A1.

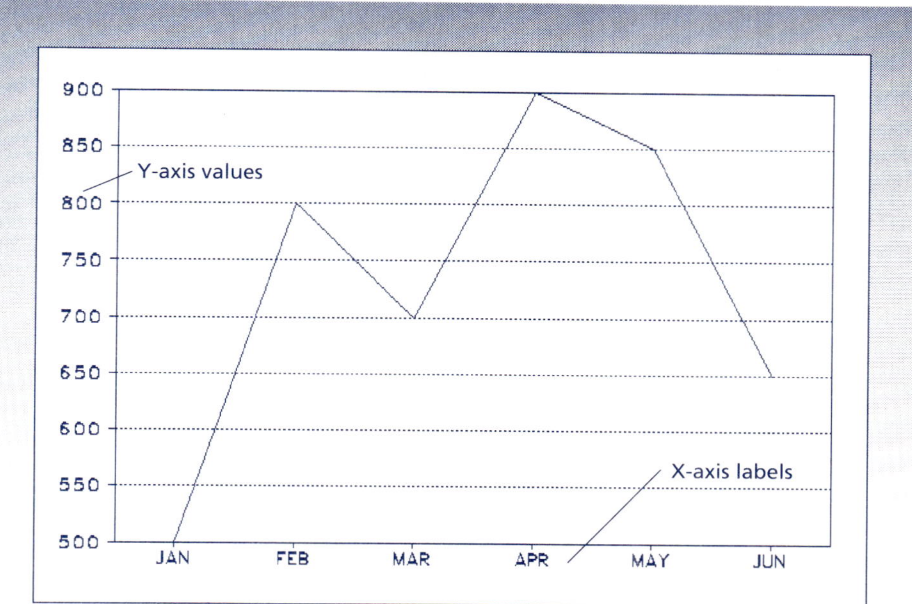

FIGURE 4-14

Line graph using MO_SALES

Notice that the month labels (JAN,FEB...) are in row 4 and that the values are in row 6. Figure 4-14 shows a line graph developed using the data in this worksheet. The labels on the x-axis represent a timeline, and the sales figures on the y-axis represent units of measurement. The Quattro Pro program needs to know the location of the labels and the location of the values to develop the graph. The x-axis labels come from block B4.G4, and the y-axis values come from block B6.G6.

The process for developing a graph is:

- Have a worksheet displayed that has the data you want to graph.
- Select the Graph menu from the main menu.
- Select the Graph Type option and specify the type of graph.
- Indicate the block that contains the x-axis labels.
- Indicate the block that contains the y-axis values.
- Specify titles for the graph and the x- and y-axes.
- View the graph.

You can view the graph at any time after specifying the x-axis labels and the y-axis values.

Line, Bar, and Pie Graphs Complete the following to develop the graph shown in Figure 4-11.

Press / G	Brings up Graph menu
Press G	Selects Graph Type menu

Quattro Pro provides 11 graph types. Start with Line.

Press L	Selects Line graph and returns to Graph menu
Press S	Brings up Series menu

A **series** is a set of values.

Press X	Selects x-axis labels

The prompt is:

```
Enter X-axis labels block: A1
```

Here you need to specify the block of cells that contains the labels (JAN, FEB,...) to be placed on the x-axis.

Enter B4.G4	Specifies the block containing the x-axis labels
Press ↵	Returns to /Graph¦Series menu

Next, you must specify the block for the y-axis. Quattro Pro allows you to plot up to six different series of values on the y-axis. For example, if the company had two sales regions, you would plot the first region as 1st Series and the second as 2nd Series. As this worksheet has just one set of values (Region 1), only the 1st Series is needed.

Press 1	Selects 1st Series

The prompt is:

```
Enter 1st Series block: A1
```

Enter B6.G6 ↵	Specifies the block containing the y-axis values
Press Q	Returns to Graph menu

At this point you have specified all the information necessary to create the graph. You can now view it.

Press V	Displays the line graph

Figure 4-14 shows the graph as you have developed it. The sales values have been plotted correctly, but there is no indication of what they represent. Use the /Graph¦Text menu to place titles on the x- and y-axes and at the top of the graph.

Press ESC	Returns to Graph menu
Press T	Brings up Text menu

The Text menu gives you the following options.

1st Line	Places a title at the top of the graph.
2nd Line	Places a second title line at the top of the graph.
X-Title	Specifies a title for the x-axis, at the bottom of the graph.

Y-Title	Specifies a title for the y-axis, at the left of the graph.
Secondary Y-Axis	Specifies a title for an optional secondary y-axis, at the right of the graph.
Legends	Specifies labels, called **legends**, for each item in the y series.
Font	Changes the typeface for text used in the graph.
Quit	Returns to main Graph menu.

ACTION	*RESULT*
Press 1	Selects 1st Line

The prompt is:

```
1st Title line:
```

Type Monthly Sales ⏎	Enters a title for the graph
Press X	Selects X-Title
Type Months ⏎	Enters the title for the x-axis
Press Y	Selects Y-Title
Type Dollars ⏎	Enters the title for the y-axis
Press Q	Returns to Graph menu
Press V	Displays the graph

The line graph is complete with titles. Now, with a few keystrokes, you can change the graph type to Bar and then to Pie.

Press (ESC)	Returns to Graph menu
Press G	Selects Graph Type
Press B	Specifies Bar graph
Press V	Displays the bar graph
Press (ESC)	Returns to Graph menu
Press G	Selects Graph Type
Press P	Specifies Pie graph
Press V	Displays the pie graph

Notice, in the pie graph, that the sales amounts are converted to percentages. This is because a pie graph shows each item of the pie as a part of the whole. In this case, each month's sales is presented as a percentage of the sales for the full six-month period.

Press (ESC)	Returns to Graph menu

Rotated Bar Graphs A variation of the bar graph is the **rotated bar graph**. It displays the bars horizontally rather than vertically.

Press G	Selects Graph Type

Press R V	Specifies Rotated Bar and displays the graph
Press (ESC)	Returns to Graph menu

You now have the skills to develop the basic types of graphs. The next section shows how you can enhance the appearance of graphs using the Customize function. You will also learn about saving and printing graphs.

Customizing a Graph

You can make several enhancements to the basic graph design. Enhancements can aid in readability of a graph and draw attention to important parts of the graph. Some of the most useful options are explained here.

Graph Key While customizing graphs, you will use specialized menus, and you will find it helpful to be able to view the graphs without returning to the View command on the main Graph menu. For that reason, Quattro Pro provides a Graph function key, (F10), that can be used to view the latest graph developed. No matter which section of the worksheet or what menu you are in, you can press this key to display the graph. If no graph has been developed, the screen will go blank. To return to the worksheet you can press any key. This function key can be extremely useful when you are using many of Quattro Pro's customizing features.

Press (F10)	Displays the current graph
Press (ESC)	Returns to the worksheet

Enhancing a Line Graph To enhance a line graph, you can use symbols, called **markers**, that are plotted on the graph. Figure 4-15 shows a graph with markers plotted where the sales amounts and months come together (where JAN and 500 intersect, FEB and 800 intersect, and so on). Graphs with markers can be used to show sales amounts more precisely. In this section, you will first change the graph to marker type and then to marker and line type. Start by changing the Graph Type to Line, and then use the Customize menu to make the necessary adjustments.

Press G	Selects Graph Type
Press L	Specifies Line graph
Press C	Brings up Customize Series menu
Press M	Brings up Markers & Lines menu
Press F	Brings up Format menu
Press G	Changes the format of the entire graph
Press S	Changes the format to marker symbols only
Press (F10)	Displays graph
Press (ESC)	Returns to /Graph¦Customize Series¦Markers & Lines¦Format menu
Press G B	Changes format to markers and lines
Press (F10)	Displays graph

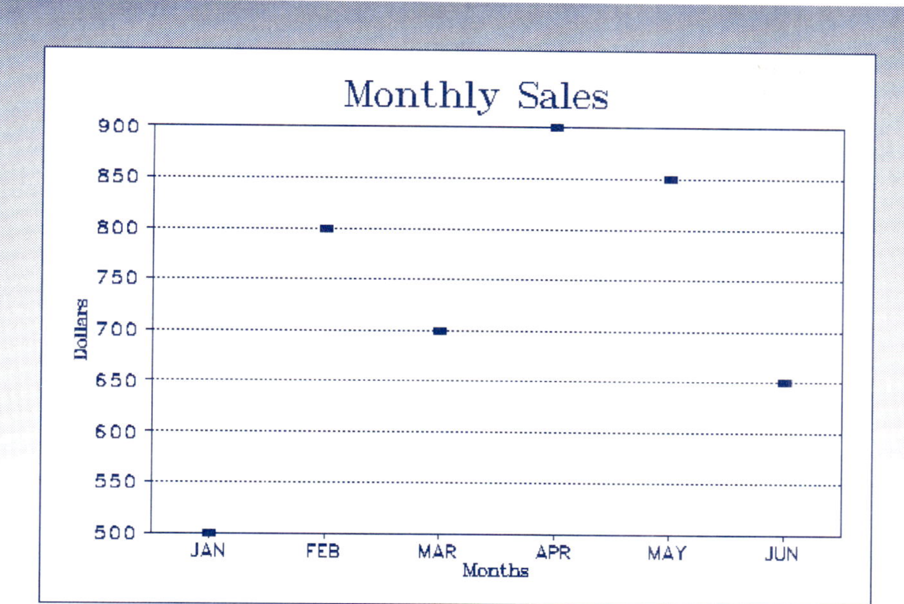

FIGURE 4-15

Markers graph

Press (ESC) Returns to menu

You can also use the /Graph¦Customize Series¦Markers & Lines menu to change the styles of markers and lines used in graphs, as you will see later in this chapter.

Enhancing a Bar Graph Compare the graph in Figure 4-16 with the graph displayed on your monitor. Figure 4-16 shows a bar graph with several customized features. There are no grid lines, a legend has been added, the fill pattern is changed, and the values are displayed. The steps below allow you to make the changes to duplicate Figure 4-16.

First, notice the grid lines at each increment (100, 200, ...). These can be changed to a different type, such as an unbroken line, or removed from the graph altogether. Complete the following to remove the grid lines.

Press (ESC) Returns to Graph menu

Press O Selects Overall menu

Press G Selects Grid

Press C Clears the graph of grid lines

Press (F10) Displays the graph with no grid lines

Second, you can attach a label, called a legend, to the series.

Press (ESC) Q Returns to Graph menu

Press T Selects Text menu

Press L Selects Legends menu

Press 1 Selects 1st Series

FIGURE 4-16

Enhanced bar graph

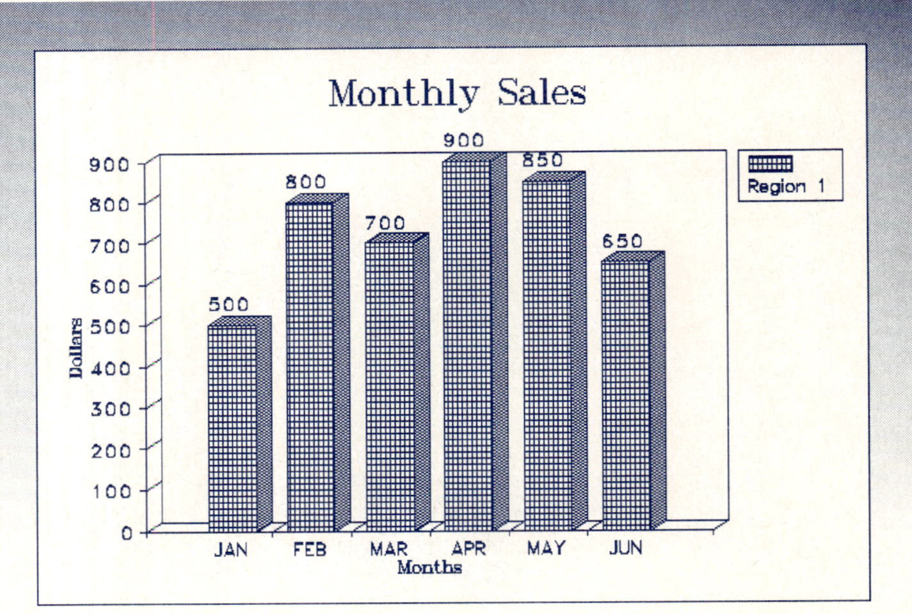

The prompt is:

```
1st Series legend Entry:
```

Type Region 1 (↵)	Specifies a title for the 1st Series
Press (F10)	Displays the graph

Third, notice that the symbol used to fill in the bars is a \. Use the Customize Series menu to change this fill pattern to a +.

Press (ESC) Q Q	Returns to Graph menu
Press C	Selects Customize Series menu
Press F	Selects Fill Patterns option
Press 1	Selects 1st Series

A list of patterns appears, each with a corresponding letter. The letter H corresponds to the + symbol.

Press H	Selects + symbol as the fill pattern
Press (F10)	Displays the graph

A final customizing feature for this graph is called Interior Labels. This option lets you place the exact series values within the graph.

Press (ESC) Q	Returns to Customize Series menu
Press I	Selects Interior Labels
Press 1	Selects 1st Series

The prompt is:

```
Spreadsheet data to label this series: A1
```

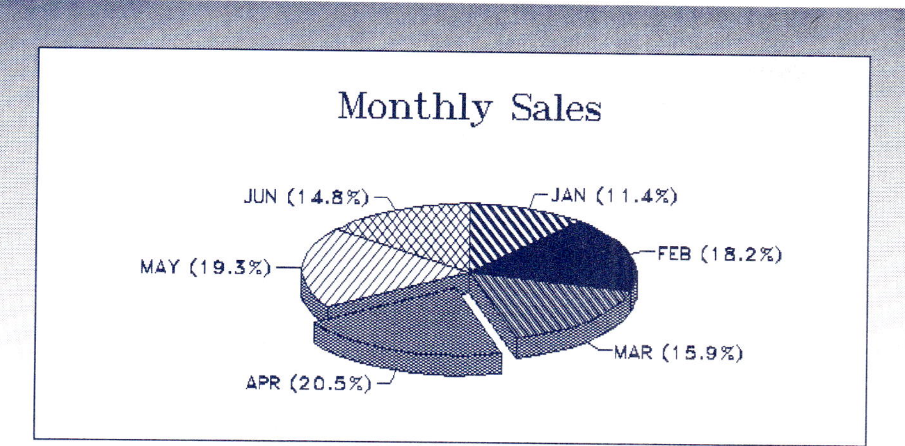

FIGURE 4-17

Pie graph with exploded slice

You need to specify the block of cells in the worksheet that contains the labels you want displayed in the graph.

Enter B6.G6 (↵)	Specifies the block of values

A menu appears with a list of locations for the values. You want to put them above each bar.

Press A	Specifies Above
Press (F10)	Displays the graph

Before continuing, quit the Graph menu and return to the worksheet.

Press (ESC) Q Q Q	Returns to the worksheet

Enhancing a Pie Graph To enhance a pie graph, you will use the Explode option to separate a slice of a pie from the rest of the pie (see Figure 4-17). This is used to focus attention on one or more slices. First change the graph to a pie type; then select the Customize Series menu.

Press Q Q Q	Returns to main Graph menu
Press G P	Changes the graph type to Pie
Press C	Selects Customize Series menu
Press P	Selects Pies menu
Press E	Selects Explode

A list of slices appears. You need to indicate the slice to explode. April has the highest sales, so explode it. Because April is the fourth value in the series, it will be the fourth slice.

Press 4	Selects 4th Slice

The choices are:

```
Don't Explode
Explode
```

Press E	Specifies Explode
Press (F10)	Displays graph

You can explode more than one slice at a time by repeating these steps. Before continuing, change the graph type to Bar.

Press (ESC) Q Q Q	Returns to Graph menu
Press G B V	Changes Graph Type to Bar and displays the graph

Working with More than One Series

Until now you have been developing graphs with one series of data (Region 1). With Quattro Pro you can develop graphs with up to six series. On your data disk is a file called MO_SALS2. This is a worksheet using the same company's sales for Region 2 as well as Region 1. Figure 4-18 shows a line graph with two data series that was developed using MO_SALS2. Load this file and complete the steps below to duplicate this graph.

Retrieve MO_SALS2	
Press / G G L	Specifies line graph
Press S X	Selects X-Title
Enter B4.G4 (↵)	Specifies x-axis labels
Press 1	Selects 1st Series
Enter B6.G6 (↵)	Specifies the block containing the values for the 1st Series
Press 2	Selects 2nd Series
Type B7.G7 (↵)	Specifies the block containing the values for the 2nd Series
Press (F10)	Displays the graph
Press (ESC) Q	Returns to Graph menu
Press T	Selects Text menu
Press 1	Selects 1st Line
Type Monthly Sales (↵)	Enters first line of graph title
Press 2	Selects 2nd Line
Type By Region (↵)	Enters second line of title
Press X	Selects X-Title
Type Months (↵)	Enters x-axis title
Press Y	Selects Y-Title
Type Dollars (↵)	Enters y-axis title
Press (F10)	Displays the graph

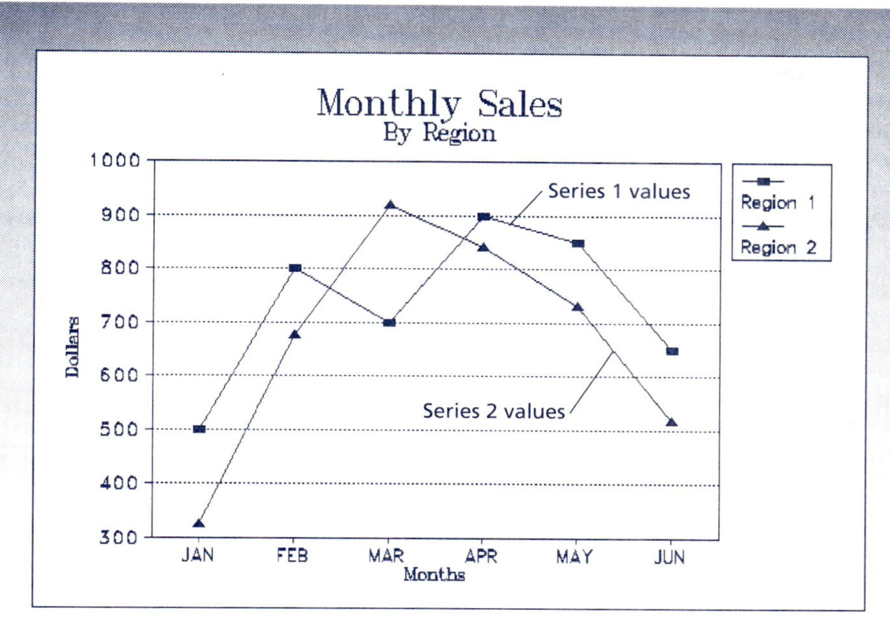

FIGURE 4-18

Line graph with two data series

The titles are complete, but it is difficult to determine which line is Region 1 and which is Region 2. To show this distinction, first use the Legends feature to label each series, and second, specify different markers for each.

Press (ESC)	Returns to /Graph¦Text menu
Press L	Selects Legend menu
Press 1	Specifies 1st Series
Type Region 1 (↵)	Enters the legend for the 1st Series
Press 2	Selects 2nd Series
Type Region 2 (↵)	Enters the legend for the 2nd Series
Press (F10)	Displays the graph

Next, use the Marker & Lines feature to have the regions displayed with different markers.

Press (ESC) Q Q	Returns to Graph menu
Press C M F G B	Specifies markers and lines for both series
Press Q	Returns to Markers & Lines menu

Now the marker on series 2 can be changed to distinguish it from series 1. Change the series 2 symbol to a filled triangle. From the /Graph¦Customize Series¦Markers & Lines menu:

Press M	Selects Markers
Press 2	Selects 2nd Series

A menu appears with several choices of markers. Select F for the Filled Triangle symbol.

Press F	Selects Filled Triangle
Press (F10)	Displays the graph

Area, Stacked Bar, and Multiple Graph Types A variation of the line graph is the area graph, which stacks the series values. This is shown in Figure 4-19.

Press (ESC) Q Q Q	Returns to Graph menu
Press G A	Specifies Area graph
Press (F10)	Displays the graph

This is useful in plotting total sales, as well as for the two region sales amounts. A similar effect can be achieved by using a stacked bar graph.

Press (ESC)	Returns to Graph menu
Press G S (F10)	Specifies Stacked Bar and displays the graph

When using more than one series of values, you can have a different graph type for each series. Figure 4-20 shows a graph in which the series 1 values are a bar type and the series 2 values are a line type of graph. To do this, you set the Graph Type for Bar. Then, use the Override option from the Customize Series menu to set the series 2 values to Line.

Press (ESC)	Returns to Graph menu
Press G B	Specifies Bar graph
Press C	Selects Customize Series menu

FIGURE 4-19

Area graph

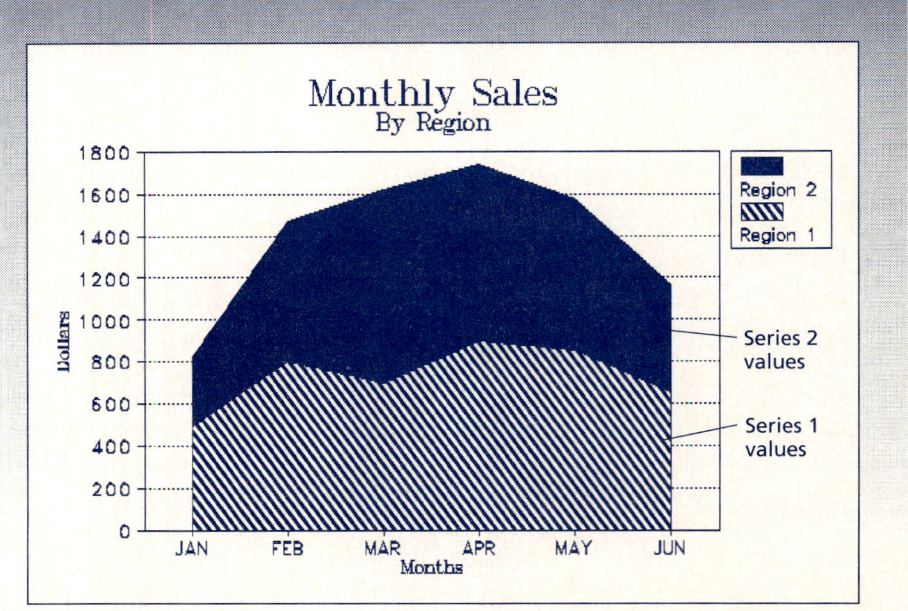

Press O	Selects Override option and brings up Series menu
Press 2	Selects 2nd Series

A menu appears with the graph types that can be specified for the second series.

Press L	Specifies Line graph for 2nd Series
Press (F10)	Displays the graph

Three-Dimensional Graph Types Another way to present more than one series is the three-dimensional (3-D) graph type. This graph places the second series behind the first, which gives the graph depth as well as height and width. Though this type of graph can be a very dramatic way to present data, caution should be exercised in using it, because data in the first series may block data in the second. To illustrate this, you will first create a 3-D bar graph and then a 3-D ribbon graph.

Press (ESC) Q Q	Returns to Graph menu
Press G 3	Selects 3-D Graphs

A menu appears with different types of 3-D graphs.

Press B	Selects Bar and returns to Graph menu
Press V	Displays the graph

Notice that though the bars look solid and impressive, much of the data in the first series is hidden behind the second series. To display the data more clearly, change the 3-D graph type to a ribbon graph.

Press (ESC)	Returns to Graph menu

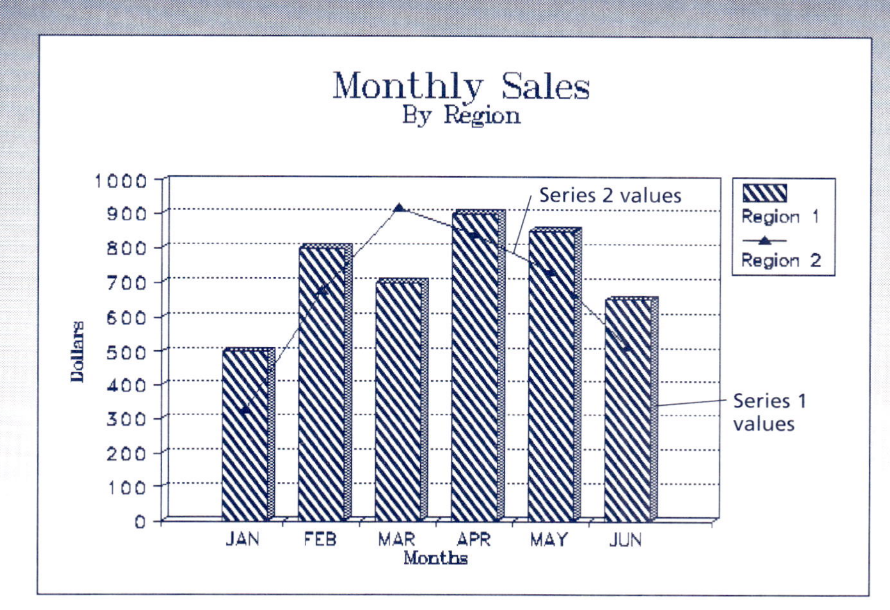

FIGURE 4-20

Multiple graph types

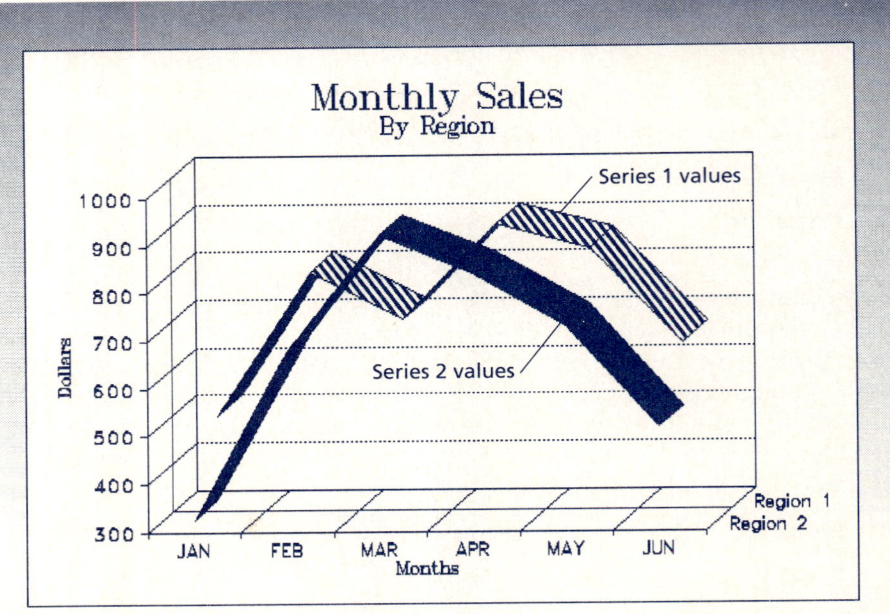

FIGURE 4-21

Three-dimensional ribbon graph

Press G 3	Selects 3-D Graphs
Press R	Selects Ribbon
Press V	Displays the graph (Figure 4-21)

XY Graph Type

The XY graph is different from the others, because both the x- and y-axes represent values. This graph plots the relationship between two sets of values and does not involve a timeline. Figure 4-22 shows an XY graph that plots the relationship between employee age and the number of sick-leave days taken per year. The x-axis represents the employee age and is referred to as the **independent variable**. The y-axis represents the number of days and is referred to as the **dependent variable**: This graph illustrates how the number of sick-leave days taken *depends* on the employee's age. Develop this graph as follows.

Press (ESC) Q	Returns to worksheet
Retrieve SICKLEVE	
Press / G G	Selects Graph Type menu
Press X	Specifies XY graph type
Press S	Selects Series menu
Press X	Selects x-axis values
Enter B3.B9 ↵	Specifies block of values for x-axis
Press 1	Specifies 1st Series
Enter C3.C9 ↵	Specifies block of values for the first y-axis series
Press (ESC)	Returns to Graph menu

FIGURE 4-22

XY graph

Press T	Selects Text
Press 1	Selects 1st Line
Type Employee Age/Sick Leave ↵	Enters graph title
Press X	Selects X-Title
Type Age ↵	Enters title for x-axis
Press Y	Selects Y-Title
Type Sick Leave (days) ↵	Enters title for y-axis
Press Q V	Displays the graph

The graph appears with a line representing the plotted values.

Press ESC	Returns to Graph menu

Saving and Retrieving a Graph

When you save a worksheet, the last graph developed with it is also saved. Then when you retrieve the worksheet, that graph also is retrieved. If you want to save more than one graph with a worksheet, you can use the /Graph¦Name command, as illustrated in the following.

Press N	Brings up the Name menu

The choices are:

Display	Displays a previously saved graph. (***NOTE:*** The worksheet must be retrieved first.)
Create	Saves the current graph with a specified name.

Autosave Edits	Automatically saves changes made to a graph before carrying out a command that would replace that graph. When working with more than one graph in a spreadsheet, Autosave Edits should be turned on. This feature is available only in Quattro Pro version 3.0.
Erase	Deletes a named graph.
Reset	Deletes all named graphs associated with the worksheet.
Slide	Displays a named graph for a specified period, as though it were part of a slide show.
Graph Copy	Copies a named graph from one worksheet to another.

ACTION	*RESULT*
Press C	Selects Create

The prompt is:

`Enter graph name:`

Type AG_GRAPH (↵)	Specifies a name for the graph

NOTE: You still must save the worksheet in order to save the graph. Later, when you want to retrieve this graph, you would load the worksheet and use the Display option described above.

Printing a Graph

To print a graph, first display it. Then, use the /Print¦Graph Print command. Make sure your computer is linked to a printer, the printer is on, and the paper is aligned.

Press (ESC) / P	Brings up the Print menu
Press G	Displays the Graph Print menu

The choices are:

Destination	Sends graph to a print file for use later, to a graphics printer, or to a screen preview.
Layout	Specifies the size and placement of the graph on the page.
Go	Begins printing.
Write Graph File	Stores the graph in a file to be used with word processing, desktop publishing, or Lotus files.
Name	Selects a named graph to print.
Quit	Returns to the worksheet.

Previewing the Graph Quattro Pro provides default settings for graphs, as well as for reports. Figure 4-23a shows the current graph with the default settings. Notice that the graph is printed in the middle of the page. To see what

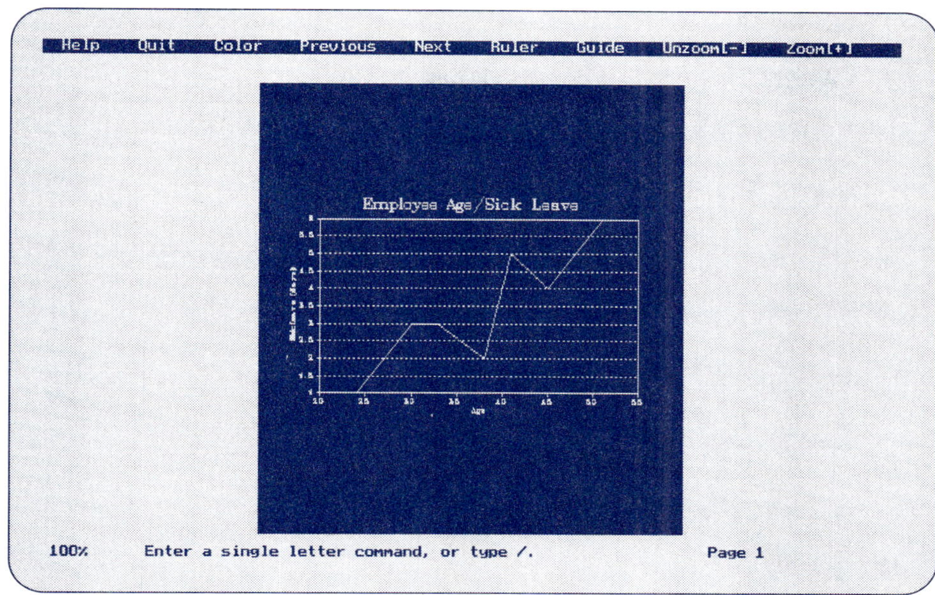

FIGURE 4-23a

Screen preview of a graph with default layout settings

the graph will look like before printing it out, you can use /Print¦Graph Print¦Destination¦Screen Preview. From the /Print¦Graph Print menu:

Press D S	Selects Screen Preview from the Destination menu

Screen Preview appears to the right of Destination on the Graph Print menu.

Press G	Selects Go

In a few seconds, the graph is displayed on the screen as it will be printed.

Press Q	Returns to the /Print¦Graph Print menu

Before printing, you must change the destination to Graphics Printer.

Press D G	Selects Graphics Printer from the Destination menu

Graphics Printer appears to the right of Destination on the Graph Print menu.

Laying Out the Graph The Layout menu is important because it allows you to specify the size of your graph and its location on the page. You can also have the graph printed vertically (Portrait) or horizontally (Landscape). The Layout menu choices are:

Left Edge	Specifies the number of inches from the left edge of the paper.
Top Edge	Specifies the number of inches from the top of the paper.
Height	Specifies how tall the graph will be.
Width	Specifies how wide the graph will be.

Dimensions	Specifies whether inches or centimeters are used in measuring margins, height, and width. The default is inches.
Orientation	Prints the graph vertically (Portrait) or horizontally (Landscape).
4:3 Aspect	Default is set to preserve ratio of width and height in the graph. If you wish the graph to appear as a square, rather than a rectangle, 4:3 Aspect should be set to No.
Reset	Reinstates layout settings of the last saved graph.
Update	Saves the new graph settings as defaults.
Quit	Returns to the worksheet.

Figure 4-23b shows the current graph previewed with the following changes:

```
Left Edge: 1.5
Top Edge: 3
Height: 5
Width: 5
4:3 Aspect: No
```

To make these changes, from the /Print¦Graph Print menu:

Press L	Selects Layout
Press L	Selects Left Edge
Type 1.5 ↵	Enters 1.5 as the left measurement
Press T	Selects Top Edge
Type 3 ↵	Enters 3 as the top measurement
Press H	Selects Height

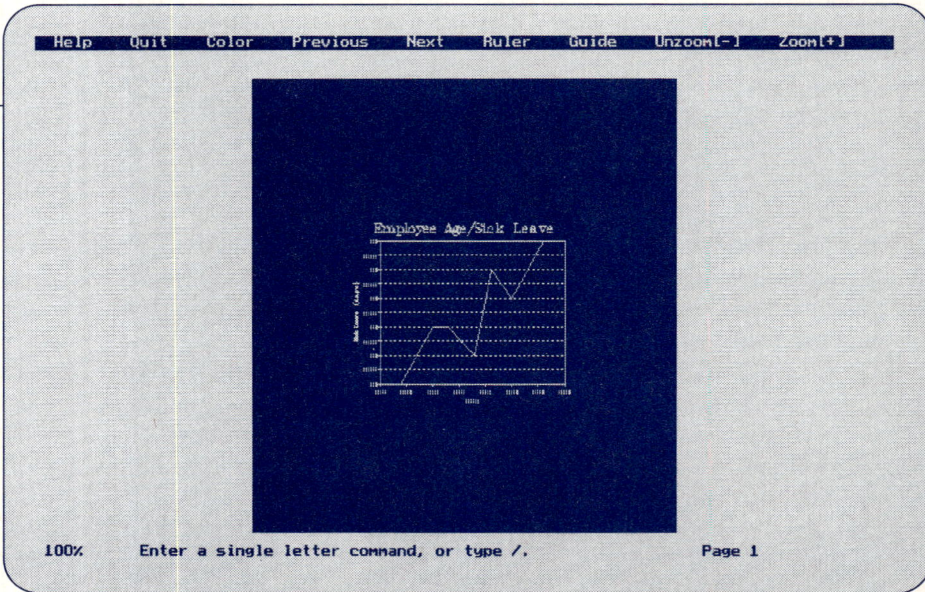

FIGURE 4-23b

Screen preview with changes in layout settings

Type 5 (↵)	Enters 5 as the height
Press W	Selects Width
Type 5 (↵)	Enters 5 as the width
Press 4	Selects 4:3 Aspect
Press N	Specifies No

Notice that the default settings have been changed in the Layout menu.

Press (ESC)	Returns to the Print menu
Press G	Begins printing the graph

Depending on your printer, the printing process may take several minutes. If for some reason you want to stop the printing, press (CTRL)-(BREAK). When the printing is completed:

Press Q Q	Returns to the worksheet

Quick Graph

When working with spreadsheets, you may sometimes wish to quickly view data quickly in graphical form without having to set up a complete, presentation-quality graph. Quattro Pro provides a Quick Graph feature, (CTRL)-G, to allow you to do that. First, make sure that Graph Type on the Graph main menu is set to the type of graph you wish to create. Next, use (SHIFT)-(F7) to specify the block that contains the data. Finally, press (CTRL)-G, and the graph is displayed. *Do not do this now.*

This completes the section on developing graphs. The following exercise will help you practice the skills you have learned.

CHALLENGE EXERCISE

Retrieve a file called STORE1 from your data disk and develop a set of graphs that plot the total sales by month. Then develop a set of graphs that plot the men's- and women's-wear figures by month. Be sure to use the /Graph¦Customize Series features to specify titles and other enhancements.

DATABASE MANAGEMENT USING QUATTRO PRO

In this section you learn how to use Quattro Pro to create and manage a database. A database management program aids companies in organizing data and developing reports that provide information for decision making. With Quattro Pro you can take an ordinary worksheet and, with the proper structure, use it as a database.

What Is a Database?

A database is a collection of related data. A telephone directory, a library's book collection, a lawyer's client list, a company's employee or customer list, and a college's collection of student grades are all examples of databases. The data is facts and figures. The telephone directory contains data—names, addresses, and phone numbers—that is related. One name, address, and phone number relates to one person; all of the names are related in that they are contained in a particular directory. Each book in a library's collection has a title, author, and subject—pieces of data that relate to the particular book. The books are related to each other because they belong to a certain library. A company's data on its employees—including name, salary, and job title—is related because one name, salary, and job title relates to one employee; the data for one employee relates to the data for the other employees in that all of the employees work for the same company (see Figure 4-24a).

How Is a Database Used?

A database can be used in three important ways. First, a database allows you to "keep track" of data. For example, a college must maintain records of former and current students, including facts on courses taken, grades received, and grade-point average (GPA) accumulated. A car dealership would keep track of a customer's service record, because facts such as the mileage at the last oil change, automobile purchase date, and name and address of the registered owner are useful to the service department.

Second, a database can be used to provide information for decision making. A list of facts and figures is of limited use. But a database management program can convert raw data into information that is useful for making decisions. For example, it may be a fact that a certain student applicant has a cumulative high school GPA of 3.15. But it is only when this figure is compared with the 3.00 GPA needed to be accepted at the college that this becomes useful information for the registrar. It may be a fact that a company has received an order for 250 widgets. This becomes information for decision making only when this number is compared with the inventory on hand of only 175 widgets. A company has a database that includes each salesperson, his or her territory, and total sales. From these facts, a report can be developed showing the top salesperson in each

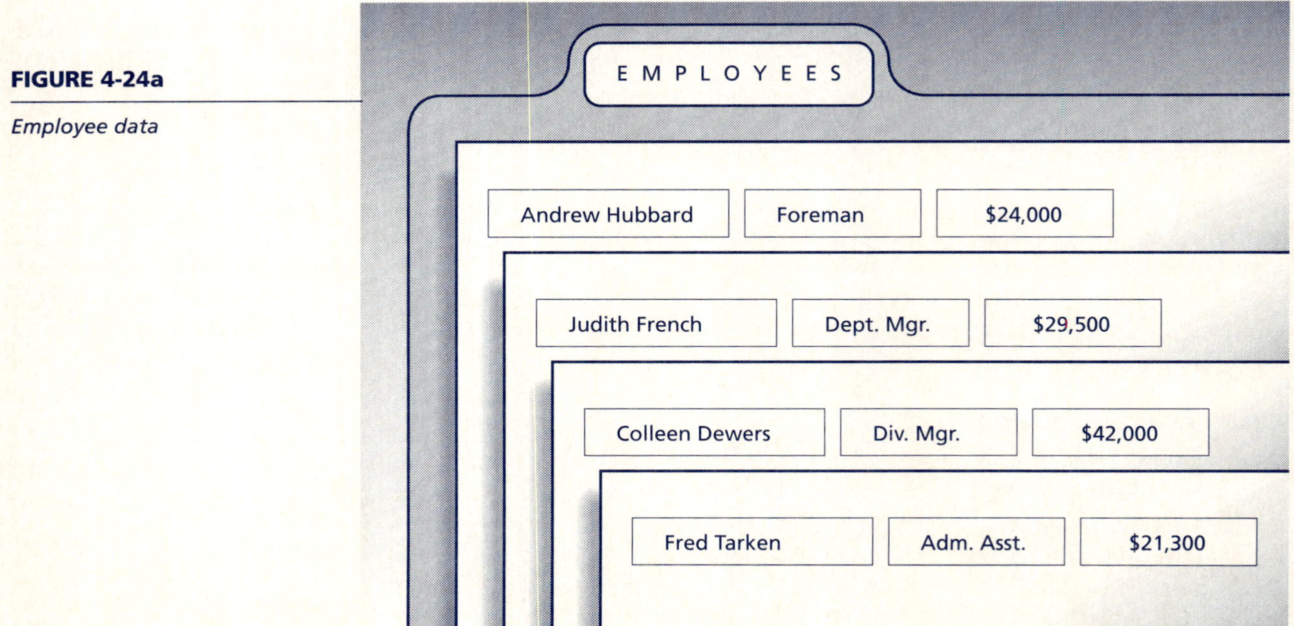

FIGURE 4-24a

Employee data

region. This is useful information for the sales manager who must make a decision on how to distribute bonuses. Using a database, a company may be able to answer such questions as:

- Which customers have purchased over $10,000 worth of merchandise in the past year?
- What is the average age of our workforce?
- Who are the top ten salespersons?
- How do our total sales break down by geographical region?
- Which customers take more than 60 days to pay their bills?

Third, by developing and managing a database, a company may be able to discover some valuable correlations. For example, assume a company maintains an employee database that includes, among other things, facts on employee sick leave and whether or not the employee smokes. By analyzing this data, the personnel director discovers that those employees who smoke take an average of 50 percent more sick-leave days than those who do not smoke. Because of this correlation, the personnel director decides to develop programs and provide incentives to help employees stop smoking. (To avoid antagonizing the workforce unnecessarily, the personnel director might first wish to examine other data to investigate whether smokers make up for the additional sick leave by being especially productive when they are at work.) For another example, if a sales manager determines that 8 of the top 10 salespersons have master's degrees, he or she might, based on this correlation, decide to reimburse the tuition cost for a salesperson pursuing a master's degree.

These are some other examples of correlations one could discover by analyzing the data in a database:

- Number of years a person has been employed and amount of absenteeism.
- Geographical region and size of customer order.
- Participation in extracurricular activities in college and salary offered for first job after graduation.

Thus, a database may allow you to keep track of data, change facts and figures into information for decision making, and determine correlations among the data.

How to Implement a Database Management Program

A database can be created by listing facts and figures on pieces of paper or index cards and storing them in a filing cabinet or card file. This manual process is used frequently. A company could keep an index card for each employee and record on it such facts as the employee's name, address, Social Security number, salary, job title, department, and phone extension. If there were only a few employees, the process for searching through the database for a particular employee's salary might not be too difficult (the cards would probably be organized alphabetically by last name). But what if you wanted a report of the employees listed by department with their phone extensions, or the highest paid employees in each department and their salaries, or employees' names sorted by zip code? Each of these reports would be difficult to develop manually, especially if there were hundreds of employees.

A database management program allows you to computerize this manual process. You can develop and maintain a database and generate reports using a computer and a database management program. The process used in managing any computerized database involves six steps.

1. Define the database. To establish the initial design for the database you must determine:
    - What facts do you want to keep track of? A simple mailing list would have name and address data items.
    - What names will be used to identify the data items? A mailing list might use the following data-item names: CUSTOMER, STREET, CITY, STATE, and ZIP.
    - Are any of the data items numeric? If so, they must be identified as such, so the computer can distinguish them from nonnumeric data. This is important because you may want to perform calculations (such as totaling) that can be done only with numeric data. For example, a zip code could be entered as a nonnumeric data item, but a salary, to be used to establish correlations, would have to be entered as a numeric data item.
    - What is the maximum length of each data item? This will help determine the column width. A zip code would need at least five characters and a state abbreviation would need at least two.
2. Enter the data. Once a database has been designed, the facts and figures can be entered.
3. Sort the database. Rearrange the order in which the data is displayed (for example, alphabetically by last name).
4. Search the database. After data has been entered, specific information can be located, such as what percentage of a company's employees have advanced degrees.
5. Update the data. Whenever the status of one of the data items changes, the database also must be changed. If a company hires a new employee, a customer moves, or a salesperson quits, the database would need updating.
6. Develop reports. The value of a database is in taking the facts and figures and changing them into information, in the form of reports, that can be used for decision making.

Each of these steps is part of developing and managing a database.

Before beginning Application 3, in which you learn how to carry out these steps using Quattro Pro, you need to understand how a database is organized. This will help you when you define the database.

Structure of a Database

Fields To understand how a database is organized, consider a company that wants to keep track of customers' names, addresses, and amount of their last purchase. Each of these data items needs to be entered separately into the database, but they are related (one name, address, and purchase amount relates to one customer). Thus, in designing the database, the company might use the following data-item names:

NAME	STATE
STREET	ZIPCODE
CITY	PURCHASE

There are six data items, each with a title (name). These data items are called **fields**. A field is a discrete piece of data that would be meaningless to break down any further. For example, a customer's street address might be 1242 81st Ave. To break up this data (to put 1242 in one field and 81st Ave. in another field) would not be useful. Among the six data items, the only one that might be broken down further is the NAME field, into FIRST NAME and LAST NAME fields.

Records Together the data items in fields make up a **record**. A record is a collection of related fields. In the example above, one customer's NAME, STREET, CITY, STATE, ZIPCODE, and PURCHASE are all related because each item deals with that one customer. If a company had 500 customers, there would be 500 records, one for each customer.

Files All the records (customers, in this case) taken together make up a **file**. A file is a collection of related records: All of them have something in common. In the example, each record relates to the others because they are all customers of the company. A database can have more than one file. For example, a company may have a customer file, an employee file, an inventory file, and so forth. Figure 4-24b illustrates the concepts of fields, records, and files using the employee data example.

There are many different types of database programs. Some are separate from spreadsheet programs, whereas others, such as Quattro Pro, are part of an electronic spreadsheet. The latter makes the setting up of the database easy because it can be developed once the worksheet is completed.

When you develop a database using a spreadsheet program, the fields are placed in columns, the records are placed in rows, and the file is the entire worksheet. Study Figure 4-25, a typical worksheet. Notice that it contains information about employees including name, title, and salary. Each of these categories (fields) is placed in a separate column, and each person's information (record) is on a different row. All that is needed to change this worksheet into a database is to place headings on each category. Figure 4-26 shows the same worksheet with category headings: NAME, TITLE, and SALARY. These are field names that identify each column as a unique field with similar data. Also, notice that the database is in a rectangular shape and that there is no empty

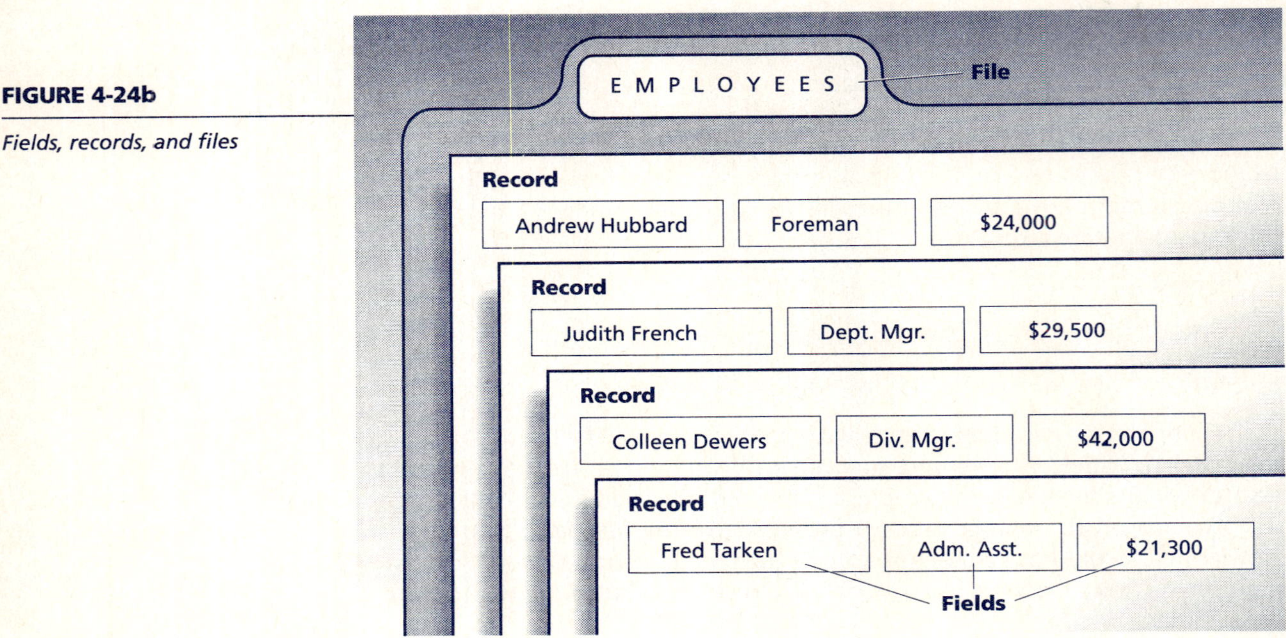

FIGURE 4-24b

Fields, records, and files

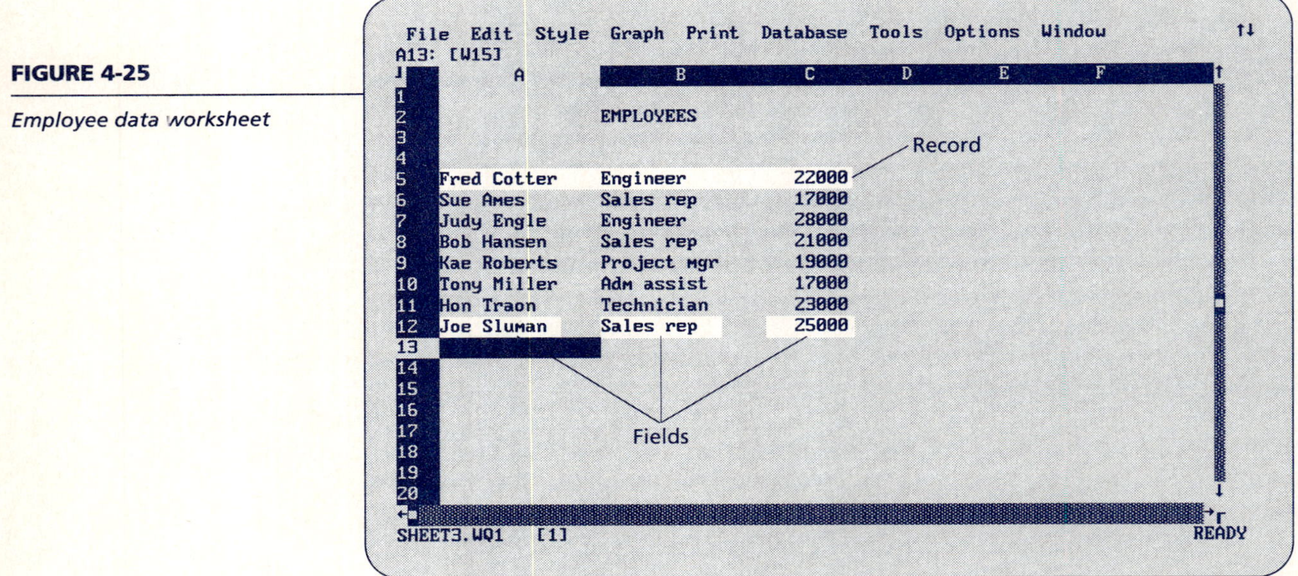

FIGURE 4-25

Employee data worksheet

row between the field names and the field data. Thus, to change a worksheet into a database, you must:

- Group similar data into columns (such as names, titles, and salaries).
- Specify a field name for each column of data (such as NAME, TITLE, and SALARY). These field names must be in the row immediately above the data.

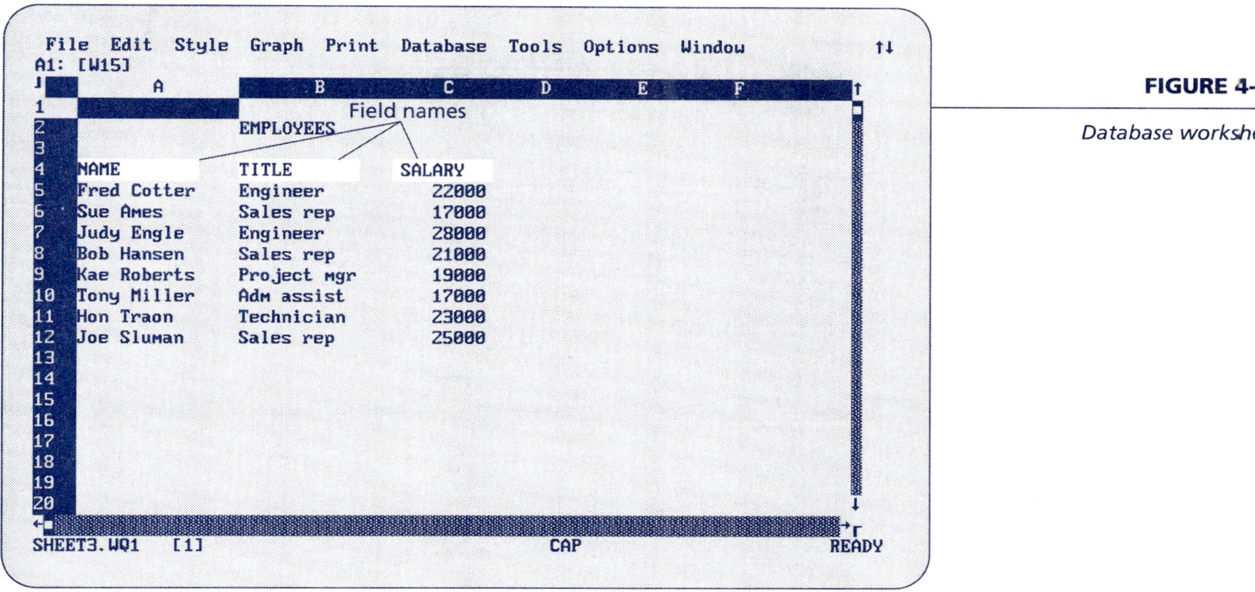

FIGURE 4-26

Database worksheet

With these guidelines in mind, you can develop the database in Application 3.

APPLICATION 3

In this application, you will define a computerized database, add and sort records, and search the database for specific information. The example used is a newly formed college ski club that needs a way to keep track of membership. The club officers have to mail announcements concerning meetings and ski trips to each member and generate reports on dues collections. Therefore, each member's name, address, and dues paid must be included in the database file.

Defining the Database

As mentioned earlier, a database is comprised of fields. When defining a database, you need to determine the field name, field type (alphanumeric or numeric), and field length (in characters). The following are needed for the ski club database:

Field	**Length**	**Type**
LASTNAME	10	Alphanumeric (can have letters and numbers)
FIRSTNAME	10	Alphanumeric
STREET	20	Alphanumeric
CITY	10	Alphanumeric
STATE	6	Alphanumeric
ZIP	6	Alphanumeric
DUES	6	Numeric (can have numbers, decimal points, and minus signs only)

NOTE: Even though only two characters are needed for a state field and only five for a zip field, these have been made larger to prevent the data from running together on the screen.

On your data disk is a file called MEMBERS. This worksheet contains all the record information, except field names, for the ski club database. By specifying field names you can turn the worksheet into a database. Load this file and enter the field names as specified below.

Retrieve MEMBERS

The cell selector should be at A1.

Press ⓥ	Moves cell selector to A2
Type LASTNAME →	Enters LASTNAME as the field name for column A and moves cell selector to B2
Type FIRSTNAME →	Enters FIRSTNAME as field name and moves cell selector to C2
Type STREET →	Enters STREET as field name and moves cell selector to D2
Type CITY →	Enters CITY as field name and moves cell selector to E2
Type STATE →	Enters STATE as field name and moves cell selector to F2
Type ZIP →	Enters ZIP as field name and moves cell selector to G2
Type DUES ↵	Enters DUES as field name

With the database defined and the record data entered, you can perform various operations on the data, such as sorting and searching. These database operations are located in the Database menu. Start by using the /Database¦Sort command.

Sorting the Database

Quattro Pro allows you to rearrange the order of the records (rows) in your database according to the entries in one or more fields. Thus, you could use the LASTNAME field to sort the records alphabetically by last name. If you have two people with the same last name, you could use the FIRSTNAME field as a second sort field. The process for sorting a database is to select the Sort command from the Database menu, specify the block of cells that has the data, indicate the field to sort, and specify whether the records are to be arranged in ascending or descending order. If necessary, specify whether a second sort field is to be used. Finally, press G for Go.

Complete the following to sort the records alphabetically by last name.

Press / D — Brings up the Database menu

The choices are:

Sort	Rearranges the record order.
Query	Searches the database.

Restrict Input	Develops a form used for data input.
Data Entry	Designates the type of data that can be entered into each field.
Paradox Access	Accesses a database management program called Paradox. (***NOTE:*** This program may not be available to you.)

ACTION	*RESULT*
Press S	Selects Sort

A menu appears with:

Block	Specifies the database cells to be sorted.
1st-5th Key	Specifies the fields to sort.
Go	Begins the sort.
Reset	Clears the sort settings.
Sort Rules	Changes the default settings for the sort.
Quit	Returns to the worksheet.

Press B	Selects Block

The prompt is:

`Block of data to be sorted: G2`

NOTE: It is important that you include all the data fields (columns) that you want to sort. However, do not include the field names when specifying the block.

Enter A3.G8	Specifies the block to sort (Figure 4-27)
Press ↵	Returns to Sort menu
Press 1	Selects 1st sort key

The prompt is:

`Column to be used as first sort key: G2`

Type A2 ↵	Specifies LASTNAME column as the field to sort

The prompt is:

`Sort Order (A or D):`

Press A ↵	Specifies Ascending order
Press G	Sorts the records (Figure 4-28)

Now sort the records using two fields (columns), zip and last name. Use the same block you specified in the previous example.

Press / D S	Selects /Database¦Sort command
Press 1	Selects 1st sort key

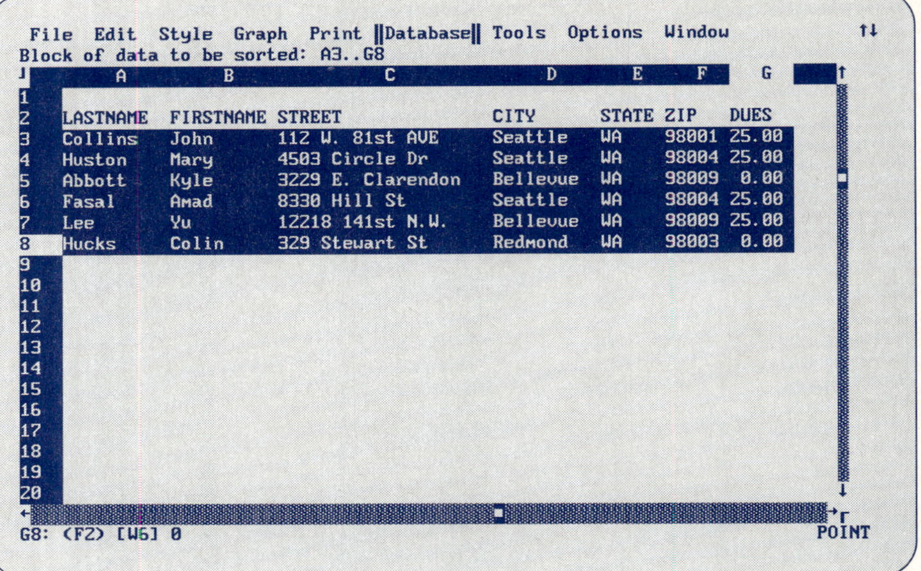

FIGURE 4-27

Block of cells to sort

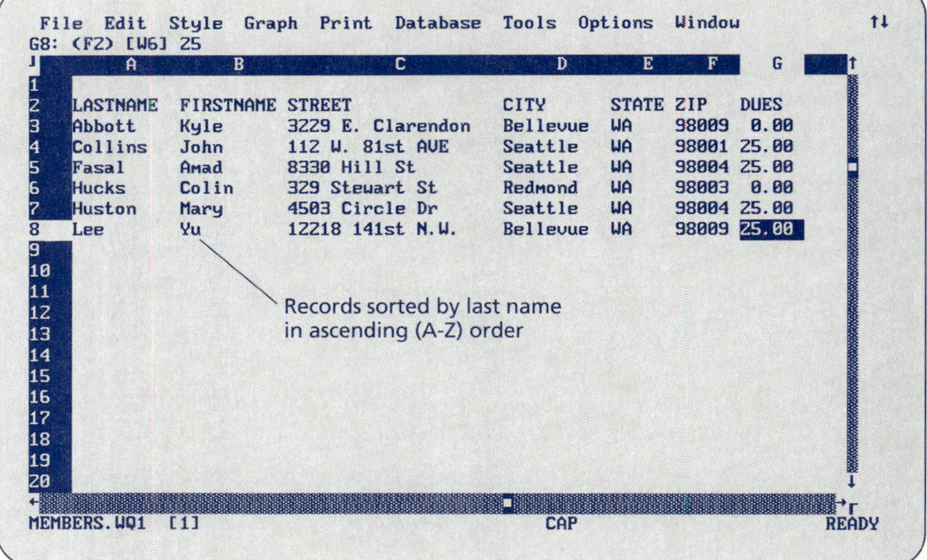

FIGURE 4-28

Database sorted by last name

Type F2 ↵	Specifies F column (zip) as first sort field
Press A ↵	Specifies Ascending
Press 2	Selects 2nd sort key
Type A2 ↵	Specifies column A (last name) as the second sort field
Press A ↵	Specifies Ascending
Press G	Sorts the records

The records are rearranged with the lowest zip code first. Wherever two records have the same zip code (e.g., 98009), the last name determines which record comes first.

Searching the Database

In this section, you will search through a database and locate specific records. For instance, you can locate all members who live in Seattle or all members who have not paid their dues. The process is to select the Query command from the Database menu and specify the criterion you want to look for, such as CITY="Seattle" or DUES=0. After the criterion is set up, you can have Quattro Pro highlight all records that meet the criterion and then copy these records to a different location in the spreadsheet or delete them.

Formula Criteria To implement a database search, you must specify which field to search and what data in the field to search for. This is done using a formula criterion. For example, if you wanted to locate all the members who live in Seattle, the formula criterion would be CITY="Seattle". This statement says, "Find any record in which Seattle is in the CITY field." To use a field name such as CITY in a formula, you must first use the Assign Names command, as you will see in the next section.

Another way to write this criterion is +D3="Seattle". This says, "Search the D column, starting at row 3, for Seattle." Both of these criteria are called formulas, because they use one or more of the following operators.

=	equals
<	less than
>	greater than
<=	less than or equal to
>=	greater than or equal to
<>	not equal to

Using Criteria Tables To have Quattro Pro use formula criteria to search through a database, the criteria must be entered into **criteria tables**. The simplest form of criteria table contains only one search criterion. Criteria tables are especially useful if you are performing several searches in a database. They are set up within a worksheet and saved with it. A criteria table lists the data to search for beneath the field names you want to search through. If more than one criterion is listed in a *single row,* Quattro Pro searches for records that match *all* of the conditions. If, however, criteria are listed in *separate rows,* Quattro Pro searches for records that match *either* of the conditions.

Figure 4-29 shows three different criteria tables. The first one searches for records that have Seattle in the CITY field. The second one searches for records that have Seattle in the CITY field and 25.00 in the DUES field. The third one searches for records that have Redmond in the CITY field or zip codes greater than 98004.

To set up a criteria table, select an area in the spreadsheet and enter the field names in the first row of the table. Then, beneath the appropriate field

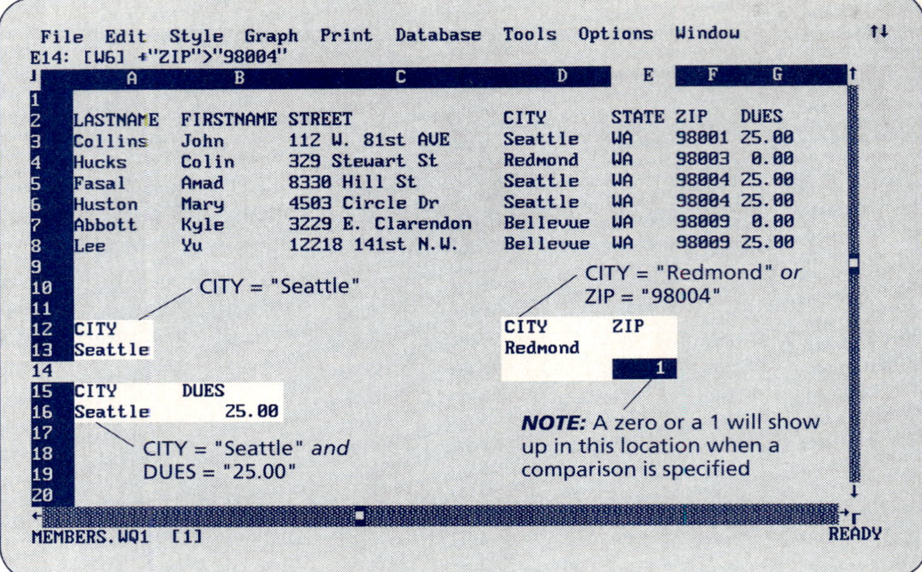

FIGURE 4-29

Examples of criteria tables

name, enter the data you want to search for, either as an exact match or as a condition. An example of an exact match is:

CITY

Seattle

An example of a condition is:

DUES

+DUES>0

You can combine conditions with #AND#, #OR#, or #NOT#. ***NOTE:*** When specifying conditions, use a plus sign (+) before the field name. After entering the criteria table into the spreadsheet, use the Criteria Table option on the /Database|Query menu to indicate where the table is located. You follow that procedure in the next example.

Query Command To search a database, select the Query command from the Database menu, specify the block of cells making up the database, specify the criteria table, and indicate what to do with the records that are found—highlight, copy, or delete.

Press / D	Selects the Database menu
Press Q	Selects the Query option

The Query menu appears with the following choices.

Block	Specifies cells in the database.
Criteria Table	Specifies the block containing the search criteria. This is a table you set up to indicate which field to search and what to search for.

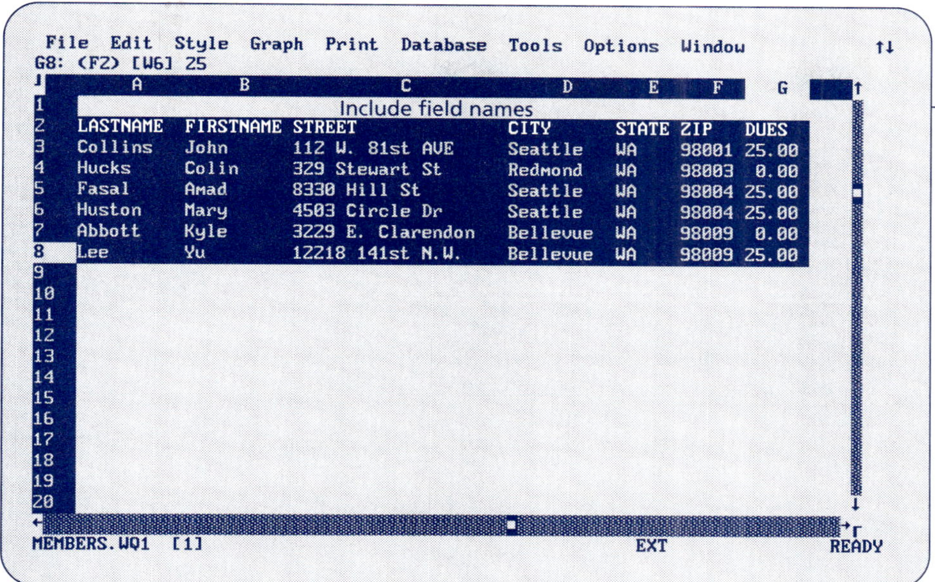

FIGURE 4-30

Specifying the block of cells in the database

Output Block	Specifies the location in the spreadsheet where records are copied to with the Extract and Unique options.
Assign Names	Assigns names to each column using the field names.
Locate	Highlights each record that meets the search criterion.
Extract	Copies records that match the criterion to another part of the spreadsheet.
Unique	Same as Extract, except that it does not copy duplicate records.
Delete	Erases all records meeting the search criterion.
Reset	Erases all query settings.
Quit	Returns to the worksheet.

The first step is to specify the block. ***IMPORTANT:*** Be sure to include the field names as part of the block (refer to Figure 4-30), because the Query command, unlike the Sort command, has to include them.

Press B	Selects Block option
Enter A2.G8 ↵	Specifies the block

The next step is to use the Assign Names option to automatically assign the field names to the first data entry in each column (thus, LASTNAME would be assigned to A3, FIRSTNAME to B3, and so forth). This allows the field names to be used in the formula criterion instead of the cell locations.

Press A	Automatically assigns field names

Next, you must enter a search criterion and tell Quattro Pro where it is located.

Press Q	Returns to the worksheet
Press (F5) **and type** A11 (↵)	Moves cell selector to A11
Type CITY (↓)	Enters field name to search into A11
Type Seattle (↵)	Enters city to search for into A12
Press / D Q	Brings up /Database¦Query menu
Press C	Selects Criteria Table

The prompt is:

Enter criterion block: A12

Type A11.A12 (↵)	Specifies block to use for Criteria Table

At this point you can highlight each record that meets the criterion by using the Locate option, or you can copy or delete the records. Start by highlighting them.

Press L	Selects Locate option

Figure 4-31 shows that the first record, Collins, is highlighted. Use the (↓) and (↑) keys to locate the other matches.

(↓)	Highlights the Fasal record
(↓)	Highlights the Huston record
(↓)	The computer beeps, indicating no more records match the criterion
(ESC)	Returns to Query menu

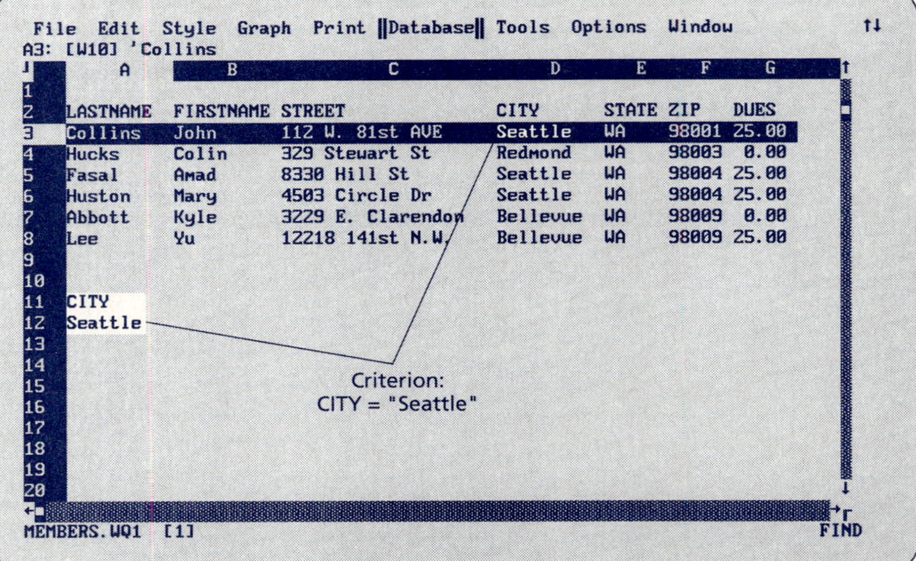

FIGURE 4-31

Locating a record for the criterion CITY="Seattle"

Copying Records The Query command not only allows you to highlight the records that match a search criterion, but it also allows you to copy those records to another part of the spreadsheet. This is useful if you want to print a report that has only selected records (such as those members who have not paid dues). The process is to set aside a block of cells in the spreadsheet to copy the records to. This is called the **output block**. The first row of the output block will have the names of the fields that you specify. You can choose any or all of the fields to include in the output block.

Figure 4-32 shows an output block consisting of the LASTNAME and FIRSTNAME fields. The row these names appear in (15) becomes the first row in the output block. The last row in the block (20) is determined by how many records you think will meet the criterion. After the output block is specified and the criterion is established, the Extract option can be used to display the desired records. Complete the following to set up the search criterion and the output block and extract those members who have not paid their dues.

Press Q	Returns to worksheet
Press (F5) **and type** A11 (↵)	Moves cell selector to A11
Type DUES (↓)	Enters field name to search into A11
Type 0 (↵)	Enters search criterion into A12
Press (F5) **and type** A15 (↵)	Moves cell selector to A15
Type FIRSTNAME (→)	Enters FIRSTNAME and moves cell selector to B15
Type LASTNAME (↵)	Enters LASTNAME
Press / D Q	Brings up the /Database¦Query menu

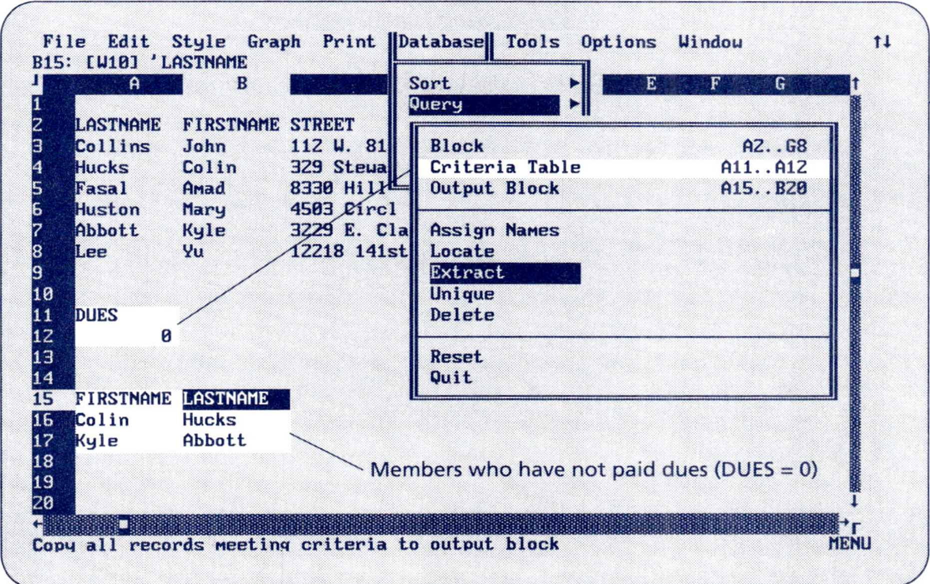

FIGURE 4-32

Extracting records that meet certain criteria

Press O	Selects Output Block option

The prompt is:

```
Enter block to copy to with Extract or Unique: B15
```

Enter A15.B20 (↵)	Indicates output block
Press E	Selects Extract
Press Q	Returns to worksheet

The names of the two members who have not paid their dues are displayed (see Figure 4-32). The /Database¦Query¦Unique option works like the /Database¦Query¦Extract, except that if there are identical records, only one is displayed. The /Database¦Query¦Delete option is used to erase any records that meet the criterion. Because the records are erased from the worksheet, it is a good idea to save the database worksheet *before* using the /Database¦Query¦Delete option.

You can also use a criteria table to find records that meet more than one criterion. Complete the following steps to set up a criteria table to find the records of members who live in Bellevue and have paid their dues (Figure 4-33).

Press (F5) **and** **type** A11 (↵)	Moves cell selector to A11
Type CITY (→)	Enters CITY and moves cell selector to B11
Type DUES (↓) (←)	Enters DUES and moves cell selector to A12
Type Bellevue (→)	Enters Bellevue and moves cell selector to B12
Type 25 (↵)	Enters 25
Press / D Q	Brings up Query menu
Press C	Selects Criteria Table

FIGURE 4-33

Criteria table

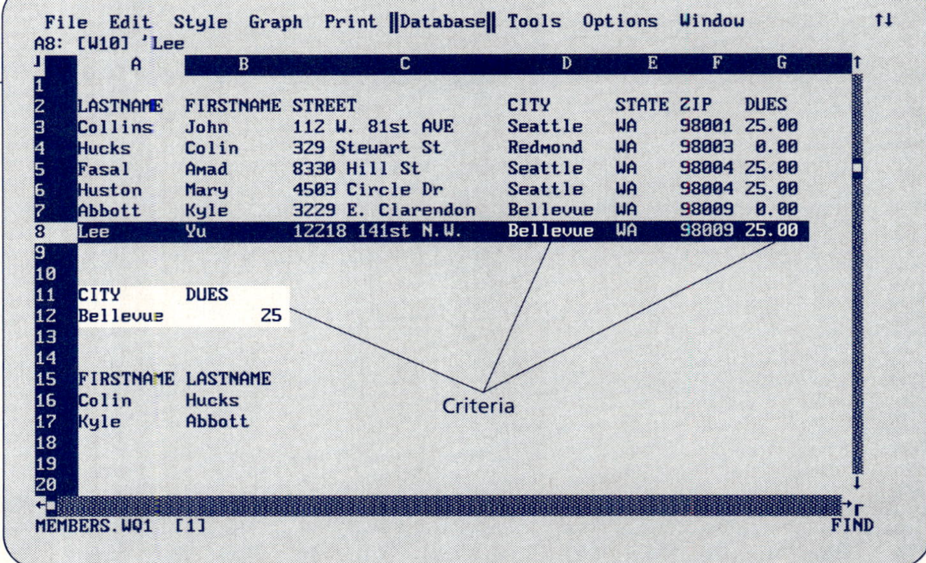

Enter A11.B12 (↵) — Specifies block containing criteria table

Press L — Highlights Yu Lee's record

An added feature of a criteria table is that you can specify wildcards when searching for text. There are three wildcard characters.

? Takes the place of a single character. R?T would find RAT and RUT but not RATE or TROT. Similarly, R??T would find RUST but not RUT.

***** Takes the place of multiple characters at the end of a word. BELL* would find BELLEVUE, BELLINGHAM, and BELLS but not LABELLE.

~ Finds all records that do not match the criteria. ~Seattle would find all records that do not have Seattle in the CITY field, and ~H* in the LASTNAME field would find all those whose last names do not start with H.

You can set up several criteria tables in a worksheet, but you can search with only one at a time.

Query Key Quattro Pro provides a quick way to repeat the last search done. Press (F7), the Query key.

Press (ESC) Q — Returns to the worksheet

Press (F7) — Repeats the last search done and highlights Yu Lee's record

Press (ESC) — Returns to the worksheet

This ends Application 3. This application used only six records, but note that Quattro Pro can handle a database with over 8,000 records. Records can be added by entering them on a row. When records are added, the database block may need to be changed to include them. Practice the skills you have learned by completing the exercises below.

CHALLENGE EXERCISES

1. Add the following people to the MEMBERS file. (***NOTE:*** Type an apostrophe (') before typing the street addresses.)

Michael Porad	June Kesseler
1102 157 Pl	8566 124th St
Bellevue	Kirkland
WA	WA
98007	98019
25.00	25.00

2. Sort the database by last name in ascending order.

3. Extract a list of the names and zip codes for those who live in Kirkland and have paid their dues.

APPLICATION 4

Using Database Functions

Earlier you learned how to use various spreadsheet functions such as Sum and Average to perform calculations within a worksheet. These same types of functions can be used with a database. In addition, you can use search criteria to select a particular part of the database to perform the functions on.

Figure 4-34 shows a database with information on a group of employees. The fields are NAME, DEPT, and SALARY. Using the database functions and a search criterion, you can display the average salary for each department. You begin the process by setting aside two areas in the worksheet. One area is to display the results of the search, and the other area is needed for the criteria table. Figure 4-35 shows these two areas. Cell G3 will be used to display the value (average salary for the sales department). Cells D15 and D16 are used for the criteria table (DEPT=SALES).

A database function can be entered using the following format.

```
@function name(block,column,criteria table)
```

- The function names are the same as used in a regular worksheet, preceded by a D for database (for example, DSUM, DAVG, DCOUNT). They can be entered by pressing (ALT)-(F3) to bring up the function menu, as with all other functions.
- The block is the range of cells that make up the database.
- The column is used to specify the field you want to work with. It is the number of columns to the right of the first column. Thus, in the employee database in Figure 4-34, the column number relating to each field is:

Worksheet column	Field name	Column number
A	NAME	0
B	DEPT	1
C	SALARY	2

- The criteria table is the block of cells that contains the field name and criteria.

In this example, the following database function, which calculates the average salary of the sales department, would be entered in G3.

```
@DAVG(A4.C12,2,D15.D16)
```

The criteria table (D15.D16) will locate all the fields in the database that have SALES in the DEPT field. Then the average will be computed from the SALARY field values (in column 2). Complete the following to practice this function.

Retrieve the worksheet called EMPLOYEE

Press (F5) **and type** D3 (↵)	Moves cell selector to D3
Type AVERAGE SALARY SALES DEPT: (↵)	Enters a heading
Press (F5) **and type** D15 (↵)	Moves cell selector to D15
Type DEPT (↓)	Enters field name and moves cell selector to D16

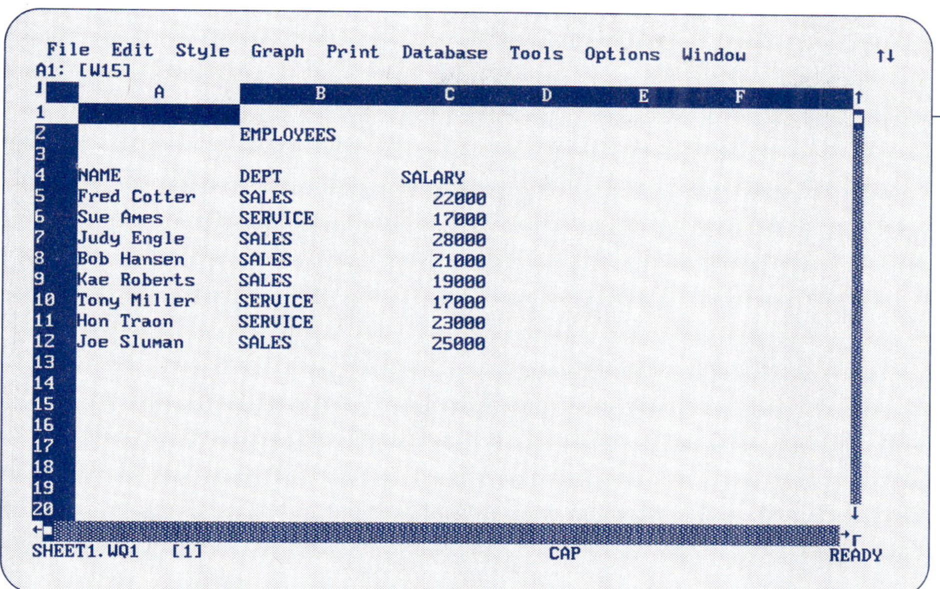

FIGURE 4-34

Employee database

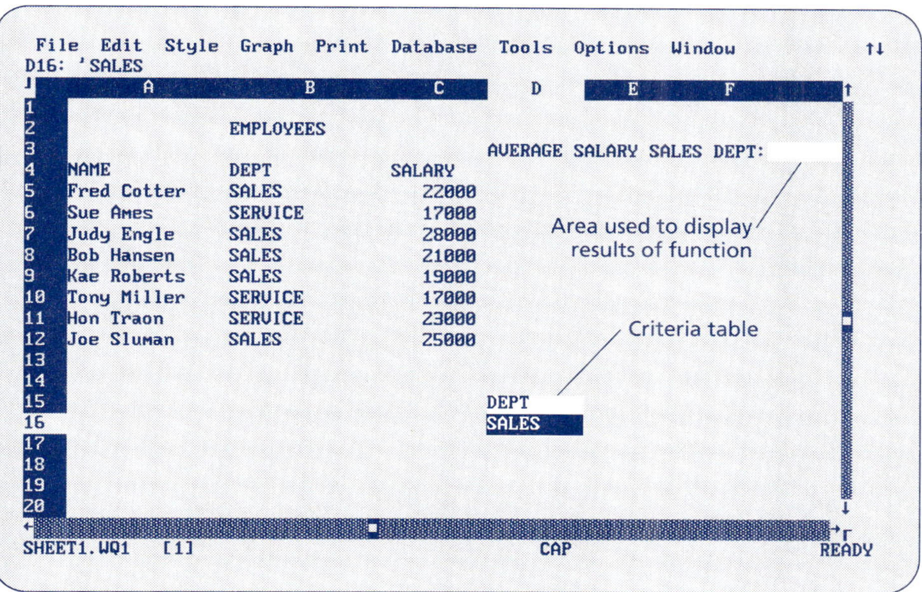

FIGURE 4-35

Areas used for database functions

Type SALES ↵	Enters criteria
Press F5 **and type** G3 ↵	Moves cell selector to G3
Enter @DAVG(A4.C12,2,D15.D16) ↵	Enters database function

In this case, the average salary is computed for the sales department only.

Press F5 **and type** D4 ↵	Moves cell selector to D4
Type AVERAGE SALARY SERVICE DEPT: ↵	Enters heading

Press (F5) **and type** E15 (↵)	Moves cell selector to E15
Type DEPT (↓)	Enters field name
Type SERVICE (↵)	Enters criterion
Press (F5) **and type** G4 (↵)	Moves cell selector to G4
Enter @DAVG(A4.C12,2,E15.E16) (↵)	Enters database function

In this case, the average salary is calculated for the service department only.

CHALLENGE EXERCISE

Using the EMPLOYEE database worksheet, calculate the total amount of salaries for the sales department.

SUMMARY

Having completed this chapter, you should understand some of the most useful features of electronic spreadsheets. You now have the ability to design sophisticated reports, develop graphs, and use your spreadsheet as a database.

WORD LIST

bar graph
criteria table
database
database functions
data series
dependant variable
extract
field name
fields
file
font
graphs
independent variable
legend
line graph
output block markers
pie graph
print options
query
record
rotated bar graph
series
setup strings
sort
typeface
x-axis
y-axis

QUESTIONS

1. List and explain the options available on the /Print|Layout menu.
2. Give an example of when to use a top heading.
3. What are Quattro Pro's default settings for left, right, top, and bottom margins?
4. If a worksheet is wider than a page, what happens during printing?
5. What are fonts? setup strings?
6. Distinguish between the x- and y-axis of a graph.

7. How is a pie graph different from other types of graphs?
8. What problems can arise in using three-dimensional graphs?
9. List and explain four ways a graph can be enhanced.
10. What is a database? Give several examples in your answer.
11. List and explain three uses for a database.
12. Distinguish among fields, records, and files.
13. How is a criteria table used? Give an example.

CHALLENGE EXERCISES

1. On your data disk is a file called LABBUDGT. Retrieve this file and print the worksheet in the following formats.
   - page numbers print out on the right side of the bottom of the page.
   - margins of left: 6; right: 132; top: 4; and bottom: 2.
   - compressed type.
2. On your data disk is a file called DOWJONES. Retrieve this file and develop the following graphs. Include titles, legends, and customizing features that you feel will enhance each graph.
   - bar graph charting the high and low figures for the 10 weeks.
   - line graph charting the high and low figures for the 10 weeks.
   - line graph charting the change for the 10 weeks.
3. On your data disk is a file called CUSTOMER. Retrieve this file and develop a database structure by adding appropriate field names at the top of each column. Then sort the database by company name. Finally, extract the company name and state for all customers that had sales greater than $50,000.

5 Advanced Features

In this chapter, you are introduced to advanced techniques that make it easier to use Quattro Pro in data management and decision making. You will create data entry forms and use macros to help other users input information. You are introduced to Quattro Pro's advanced decision-making features and to graph annotation, used for presenting information more effectively. You will work with more than one spreadsheet at a time, and, finally, use Quattro Pro data with other computer programs.

APPLICATION 1

Advanced Database Features

Creating a Data Entry Form In this application you learn three useful spreadsheet features: lookup functions, protecting cells, and hiding cells. To illustrate these you will create a **data entry form**, which is a spreadsheet template that is used over and over. A data entry form that is developed correctly prevents the user from having to alter the structure and formulas of a worksheet and makes data entry and calculations as automatic as possible.

Figure 5-1 shows a worksheet that could be considered a data entry form. A textbook distributor uses the worksheet to complete and print invoices. The headings and formulas are preset. When a transaction is made, the invoice is loaded and the customer and sales information is entered. The Lookup functions, /Options¦Protection¦Enable, /Style¦Protection, and /Style¦Numeric Format¦Hidden, can be incorporated into the worksheet to make data entry easier and less prone to error. The file is saved on your data disk as INVOICE. Load this worksheet now.

Retrieve INVOICE

The formulas for the template have already been entered. You can use the /Style¦Numeric Format¦Text feature to view them. This is also known as the Show Formulas feature.

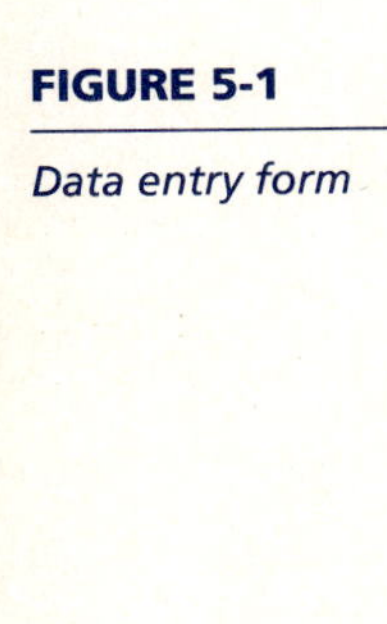

FIGURE 5-1

Data entry form

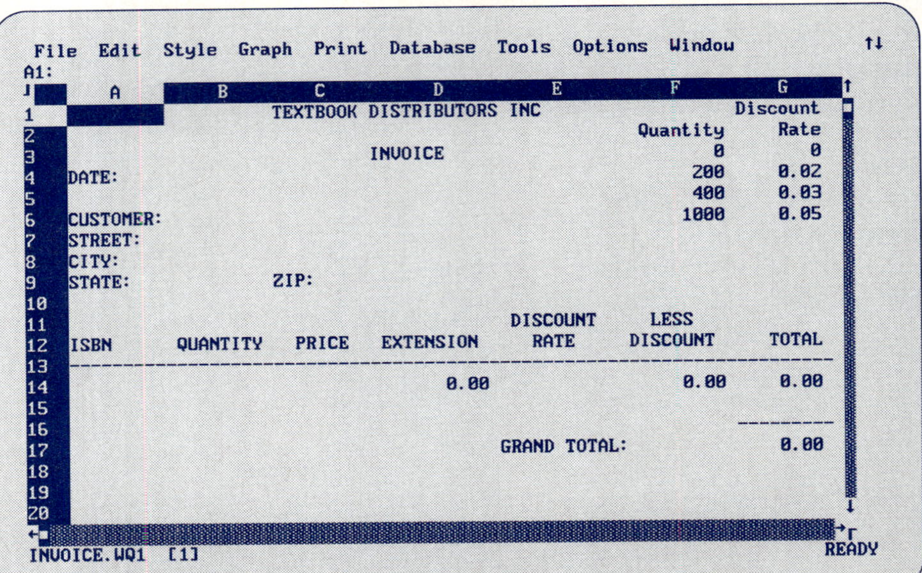

Press / S N (or CTRL-F)	Brings up /Style¦Numeric Format menu
Press T	Selects Text (Show Formulas)
Type A1.G20 ↵	Specifies the block

Figure 5-2 shows the formulas displayed. Quantity is multiplied by price to calculate extension (the total dollar amount), the extension is multiplied by the discount rate to calculate the discount, and the discount is subtracted from the extension to obtain the total. Three values need to be determined to complete this worksheet: quantity, price, and discount rate. The user enters the quantity and price. The discount rate can be determined using the Lookup functions. Before continuing, remove the formulas from the screen.

Press / S N R	Selects /Style¦Numeric Format¦Reset
Enter A1.G20 ↵	Removes the formulas from the screen

Using the Lookup Functions The Lookup functions allow you to search for a value within a range of numbers and insert the value at the cell selector location. @VLOOKUP searches vertically through a specified column for a value, and @HLOOKUP searches horizontally through a specified row. You will use @VLOOKUP to determine the discount percentage listed in the invoice. The company gives discounts from the selling price of a book based on the quantity ordered.

Quantity	Discount rate (%)
200	2
400	3
1000	5

You can use @VLOOKUP to have the computer find the correct discount rate and enter it into the worksheet.

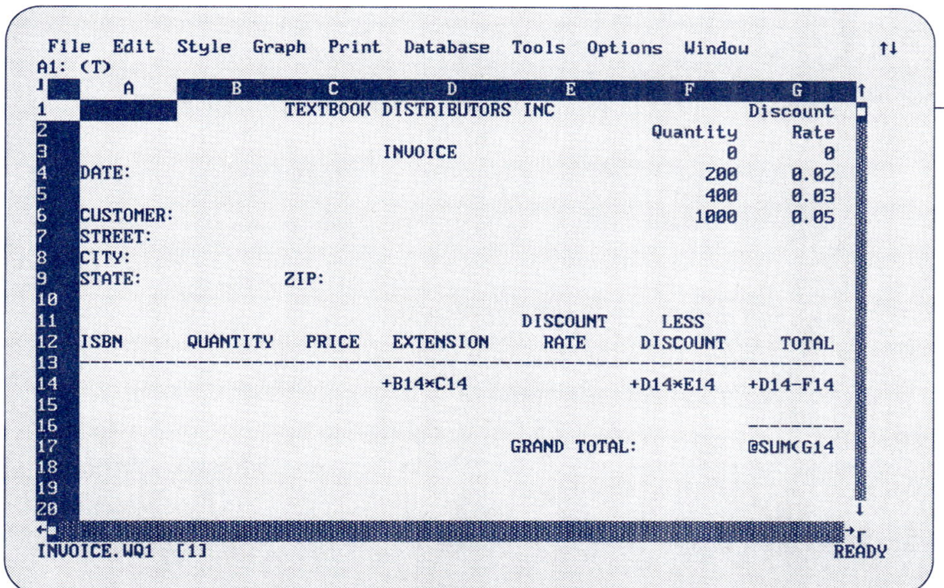

FIGURE 5-2

Displaying formulas

To use @VLOOKUP, you must first set up a table of values in at least two columns. The first column contains the list of values, in ascending order, that the computer is to search through. The second column has a list of corresponding values that the computer will copy to another location in the worksheet. The format for @VLOOKUP is:

```
@VLOOKUP(x,block,column)
```

X is a value or cell reference, block is the location of the table that is to be used for the lookup, and column refers to the number of columns to the right that the "values to be copied" are from the "values to be searched." You can use ALT-F3 to enter the Lookup functions from the function menu.

The quantity and discount figures above represent a table of values. When used with a Lookup function, this is called a **lookup table**. The quantity values, 200, 400, and 1000, can be searched and the corresponding discount rate, .02, .03, and .05, can be located and copied to another cell. The computer searches for the largest number that does not exceed the next value. For example, if the quantity ordered was 700, the computer would search the range until it encountered 1000. Because this value is larger than 700, the computer would stop the search. Then the computer would move as many columns to the right as the function specified and copy the value into the cell where the function is located. Thus, if the column is 1, the computer would move 1 column to the right and select .03 for the discount rate.

The lookup table is already part of the template. Go to the discount rate column (E14) and enter @VLOOKUP.

Press F5 **and type** E14 ↵	Moves the cell selector to E14
Enter @VLOOKUP(B14,F3.G6,1) ↵	Enters the Lookup function

This tells Quattro Pro to take the value in B14 (quantity) and search the block (F3.G6); when it finds the value, to move one column to the right; and to copy the new value into the cell where the cell selector is located (Figure 5-3).

Take a moment to enter the following and see how the discount rate changes.

Press ← **twice**	Moves cell selector to C14
Type 20 ←	Enters 20 as the price and moves the cell selector to B14
Type 700 ↵	Enters 700 as the quantity; the discount rate is .03
Type 300 ↵	Enters 300 as the quantity; the discount rate is .02
Type 1200 ↵	Enters 1200 as the quantity; the discount is .05
Type 100 ↵	Enters 100 as the quantity; the discount rate is 0
Press DEL →	Erases the quantity and moves cell selector to C14
Press DEL	Erases the price

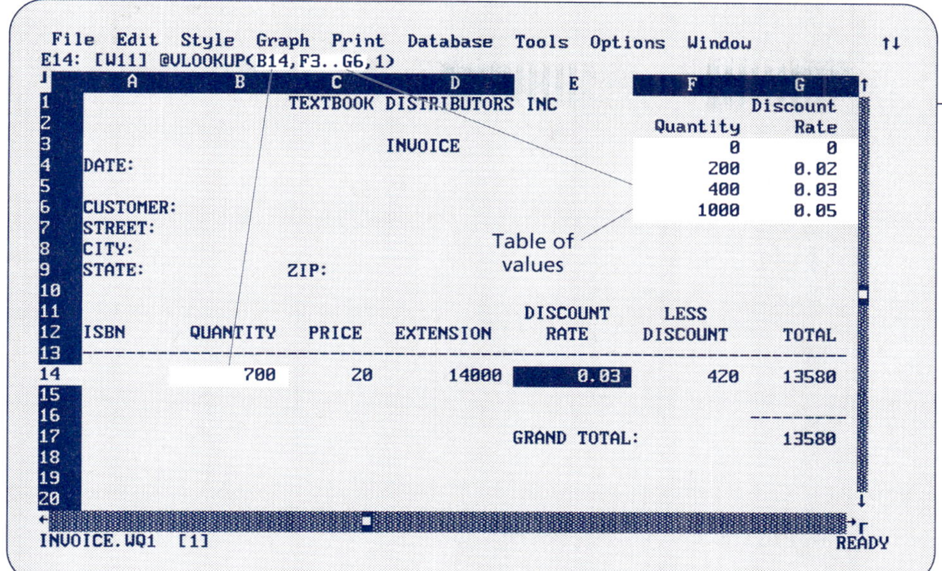

FIGURE 5-3

Lookup function

If the lookup table was arranged horizontally in rows instead of columns, you would use @HLOOKUP.

Protecting the Worksheet Because this worksheet is a data entry form, you want to prevent it, and especially the formulas, from being changed. You can use the Protection features to prevent any of the data from being modified or deleted. The process is to protect the entire worksheet and then, one by one, unprotect those cells that require data to be entered (for example, customer, ISBN, quantity, etc.). To protect the entire spreadsheet, use the /Options|Protection command, and set it to Enable.

Press / O	Selects Options menu

Figure 5-4 shows the Options menu. Protection is turned off (Disable) when the worksheet is first developed. To enable protection:

Press P	Selects Protection feature

The choices are:

```
Enable
Disable
```

Press E	Enables Protection
Press Q	Returns to the worksheet

Now, no entry in the spreadsheet can be changed and nothing can be added. Take a moment to move around the spreadsheet and try to make entries. An error message is displayed each time you try to make an entry. When you are finished, move the cell selector to A1.

Press (HOME)	Moves cell selector to A1

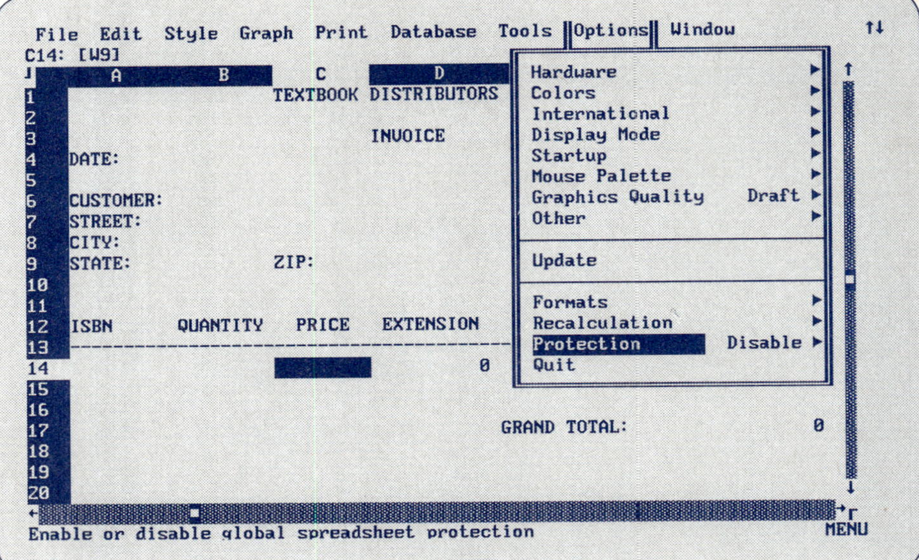

FIGURE 5-4

Protecting a block of cells

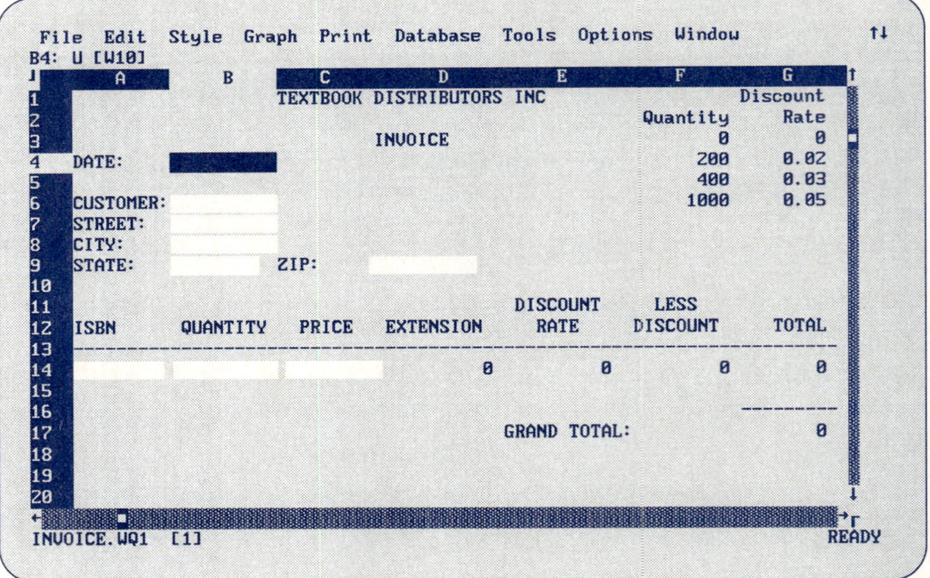

FIGURE 5-5

Cells to be unprotected

Next, you need to unprotect those cells that will be used to input data. Figure 5-5 shows the cells that need to be unprotected. Do this with the Protection feature of the Style menu.

Press / S	Selects the Style menu
Press P	Selects Protection
Press U	Selects Unprotect

The prompt is:

```
Block to be modified: A1..A1
```

Type B4 (↵)	Unprotects cell B4

When the cell selector is placed on the cell, a U will be displayed on the input line.

Press / S P U	Selects Unprotect option
Enter B6.B9 (↵)	Unprotects cells B6 through B9
Press / S P U	Selects Unprotect option
Type D9 (↵)	Unprotects cell D9
Press / S P U	Selects Unprotect option
Enter A14.C14 (↵)	Unprotects cells A14 through C14

Hiding Cells from View The last feature you will add to the INVOICE template is to hide part of the worksheet from view. Quattro Pro allows you to hide the contents of specific cells from view and from being printed. In the template, the lookup table should not be displayed as part of the invoice, because it might be accidentally changed. The process is to select the /Style¦Numeric Format menu and select Hidden. Then specify the block of cells to hide. Hide the lookup table by completing the following.

Press / S N (or (CTRL)-F)	Selects /Style¦Numeric Format
Press H	Selects Hidden option
Enter F1.G6 (↵)	Specifies the block to hide

The lookup table disappears from view, but it is still part of the worksheet. If you move the cell selector to one of these cells the entry will appear on the input line.

With the INVOICE worksheet complete, take a moment to enter data for a customer. (***NOTE:*** Use month, day, year format—May 5, 1992—to enter date.)

Press (F5) **and type** B4 (↵)	Moves cell selector to B4
Type the current date (↓) (↓)	Enters the date into B4 and moves the cell selector to B6
Type University Book Store (↓)	Enters customer name and moves cell selector to B7
Type '4545 Campus Way (↓)	Enters street and moves cell selector to B8
Type Phoenix (↓)	Enters city and moves cell selector to B9
Type AZ (→) (→)	Enters state and moves cell selector to D9
Type '85080 (↵)	Enters zip code
Press (F5) **and type** A14 (↵)	Moves cell selector to A14
Type '0-818483 (→)	Enters ISBN and moves cell selector to B14

Type 750 (→)	Enters quantity and moves cell selector to C14
Type 20 (↵)	Enters price

The values in the worksheet are calculated and it is ready to save and print. Data entry forms can be quite useful for performing repetitive processes. A feature that is often incorporated within data entry forms is macros, which you learn about in the next section.

APPLICATION 2 Using Macros

As you become more proficient in using spreadsheets and as you develop larger and more sophisticated worksheets, two issues become more important: speed and accuracy. These are a function of how well you can move around the spreadsheet, enter data, and perform operations such as saving and printing. Worksheets often involve keystrokes that are repetitive. For example, in the INVOICE worksheet, when a customer purchases books, the user must retrieve the invoice template, move the cell selector to specific cell locations, and enter the data. Then, if desired, the worksheet is saved and printed. The next customer transaction requires the same steps. If there are several customers, the process becomes redundant and time-consuming. Through the use of macros, you can save a series of keystrokes, such as those used to print a worksheet, and quickly execute the whole series at any time. This increases speed and accuracy because the computer carries out the macro instructions without your having to type them each time.

There are two ways to develop a macro. First, you could have Quattro Pro record each keystroke you make while you complete a task such as printing. Second, you could enter (write) the macro as a series of labels in one or more cells. With either method the result is a list of macro instructions, saved in a specified part of your spreadsheet, and executed at your command.

Recording a Macro To illustrate the use of macros, you can use the INVOICE template and create a macro to automatically insert a blank row. Study Figure 5-6. Notice that a limited number of rows (14–15) can be used for listing the books purchased. If a customer buys several different books, more rows must be added. The keystrokes necessary to add one row would be /EIA15 (↵). These seven keystrokes could be repeated for each row required. Using the record method, these keystrokes could be saved as the macro {/ ROW;INSERT}A15~. This macro should be read:

/	Selects the main menu.
Row;Insert	Selects the Insert Row option from the Edit menu.
A15	Specifies A15 as the row to insert.
~	Presses (↵).

Notice that the actual keystrokes (/EIR) are not recorded. Instead, the keystrokes you press are translated into menu-equivalent commands. These make it easier to read the macro. Each menu-equivalent command is made up

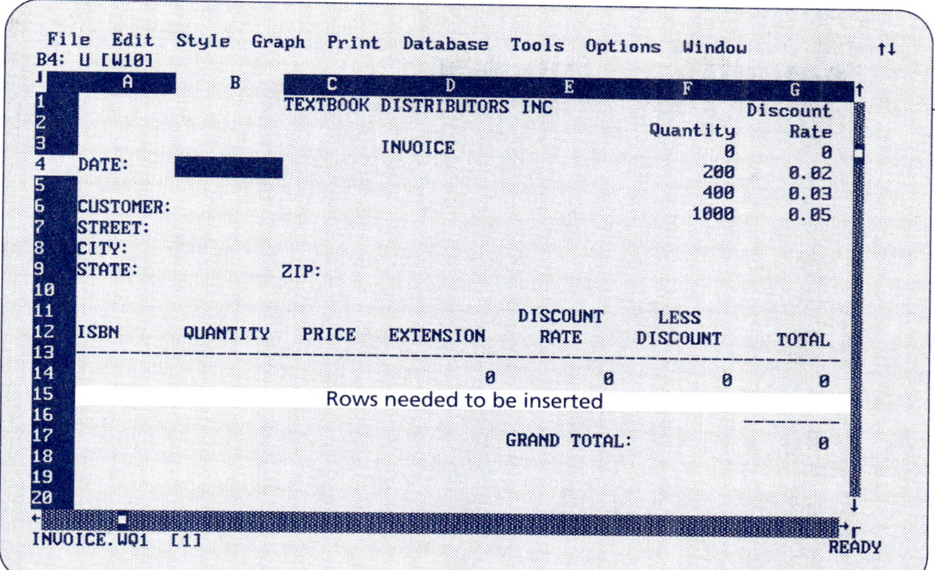

FIGURE 5-6

INVOICE2 template

of two words separated by a semicolon (;). It is surrounded by curly brackets and preceded by a slash and a space. The first word represents the general action and the second word, the specific action of the command. The curly brackets ({}) surround the commands to set them apart from the rest of the macro. The tilde (~) is the symbol used to represent ↵.

The steps used to record a macro are listed below. After studying these steps, you will use them to create a macro within a worksheet called INVOICE2. Do not carry out these steps at this time.

1. Select /Tools|Macro, or hold down the ALT key and press F2. This brings up the Macro menu.
2. Select Record. This begins the macro record process.
3. Carry out the keystrokes you want recorded in the macro.
4. To stop recording, select /Tools|Macro again, and press R.

This process records the macro. To check that it has been recorded properly, you can use the Instant Replay command from the Macro menu. This command, as the name implies, instantly replays the macro you just recorded, so you can make sure it is recorded correctly.

To save the macro in a worksheet (*do not* carry out these steps at this time):

1. Select /Tools|Macro, and choose Paste. When prompted, specify a name for the macro. To make it an instant macro, type a backslash (\) followed by a single letter. For example, you may want to name a macro that is used to insert a row \R, and a macro that prints a worksheet \P.
2. Specify the block of cells that will store the macro. The size of the block depends on the size of the macro. (When Quattro Pro begins recording the macro, it starts with the first cell of the block and continues down.)

This procedure saves the macro with the worksheet. To execute a macro, hold down the ALT key and press the letter you used to name it (for example, R). Figure 5-7 shows the row-insert macro as part of the INVOICE2 template. Complete the following to duplicate this macro. Start with the template called INVOICE2.

Retrieve INVOICE2	
Press F5 **and** **type** A18 ↵	Moves the cell selector to A18
Press / T M (or ALT-F2)	Brings up Macro menu
Press R	Starts the macro record process

Figure 5-8 shows that the RECORD mode is active. Any keystrokes pressed now will become part of the macro.

Press / E I R	Selects /Edit¦Insert¦Row

The prompt is:

`Enter row insert block: A18..A18`

Type A15 ↵	Inserts row above A15

The macro is complete, and you can end the recording process by pressing /Tools¦Macro¦Record.

Press / T M R (or ALT-F2 R)	Ends the record process

To enter the macro with the current worksheet:

Press / T M (or ALT-F2)	Brings up Macro menu
Press P	Selects Paste

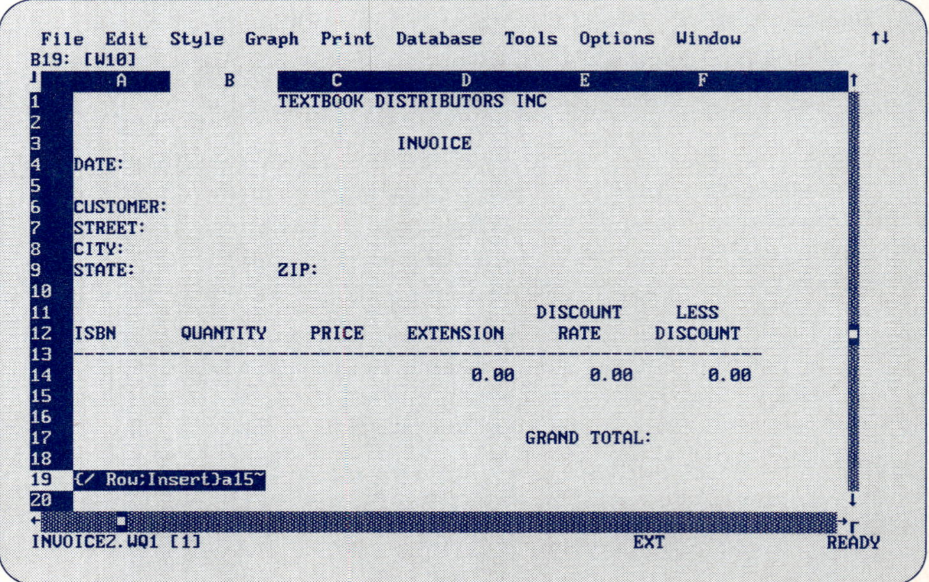

FIGURE 5-7

A macro to insert a row at A15

The prompt is:

Enter name of macro to create/modify:

Type \r ⏎ Specifies a name for the macro

As shown in Figure 5-9, the prompt is:

Enter macro block to paste: A18..A18

Type A19 ⏎ Specifies the block of cells used to store the macro and displays the macro

```
 File  Edit  Style  Graph  Print  Database  Tools  Options  Window
A1:
     A       B       C       D       E       F
1                  TEXTBOOK DISTRIBUTORS INC
2                                  Macro
3                           INVOICE  Record                    On
4  DATE:                             Paste
5                                    Instant Replay
6  CUSTOMER:                         Macro Recording     Logical ▸
7  STREET:
8  CITY:                             Transcript
9  STATE:            ZIP:            Clear Breakpoints
10                                   Debugger               No ▸
11                                   Name                      ▸
12 ISBN      QUANTITY    PRICE   EXTENS Library             No ▸
13 ----------------------------------
14                                   Execute
15                                   Key Reader             No ▸
16
17
18
19
20
Turn the macro recorder On/Off                           REC   MENU
```

FIGURE 5-8

Macro menu

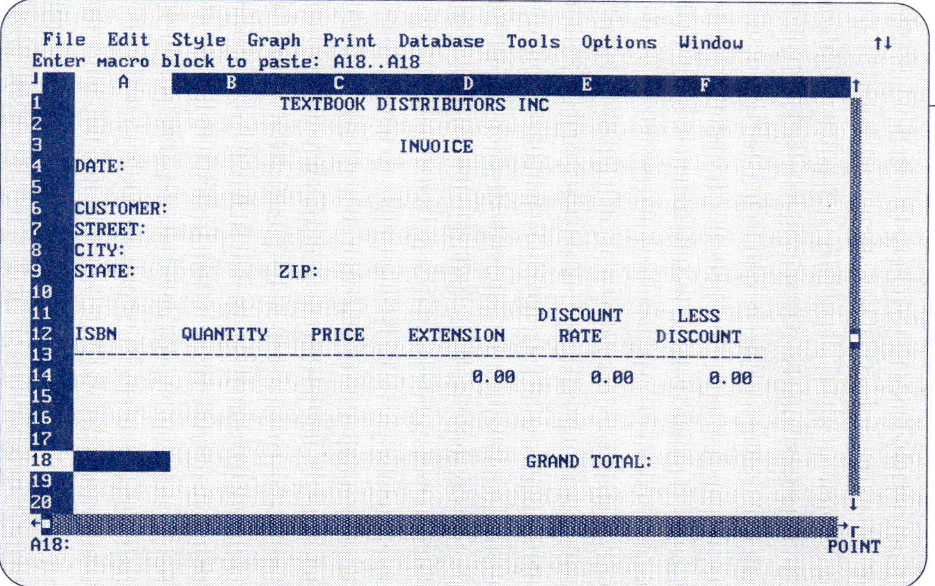

FIGURE 5-9

Creating a macro

Executing a Macro With the macro complete, all you need to do to execute it is use the ALT key and the macro name key.

Hold down ALT **and press** r	Executes the macro and inserts a row above row 15

You can execute the macro as often as needed to accommodate the number of different books each customer orders. This is a simple example; later you will work with longer and more complex macros.

After you begin the execution of a macro, the process continues until either a blank cell or the macro command {Quit} is encountered. If you want to stop the execution of a macro, press CTRL-BREAK. If you try to execute a macro that has an error or that has not been named, Quattro Pro displays a message. You can edit a macro the same way you would edit any label entry, with the F2 key.

Writing a Macro To write a macro, move to a part of the spreadsheet that will be used to store the macro and enter the macro text as you would a label. Then use the Name command from the /Tools¦Macro menu to name and specify the location of the macro. Figure 5-10 shows a macro that will delete a row. Complete the following to write this macro and execute it.

Press F5 **and type** C20 ↵	Moves the cell selector to C20
Type {/ Row;Delete}A15~ ↵	Enters the macro as a label
Press / T M (or ALT-F2)	Brings up the Macro menu
Press N	Selects Name command

The prompt is:

```
Create
Delete
```

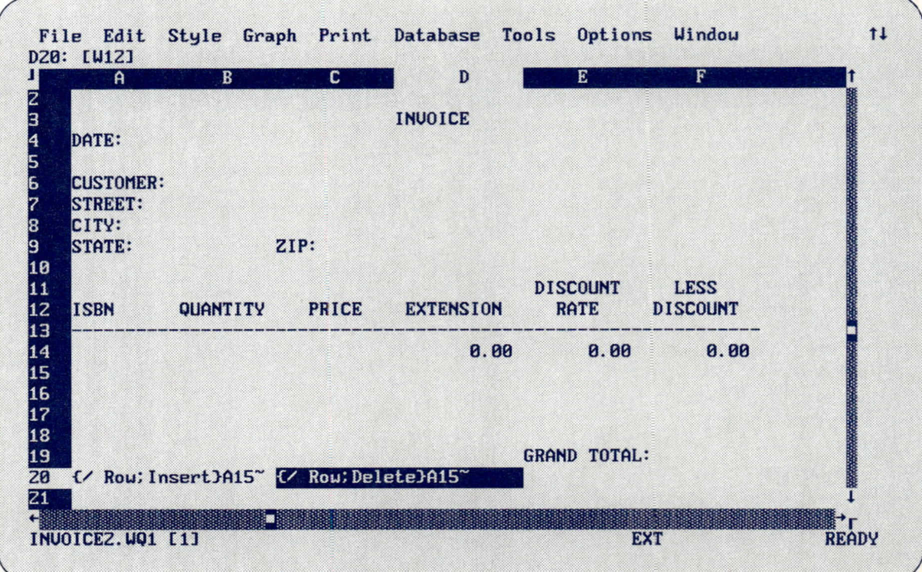

FIGURE 5-10

A macro to delete a row at A15

Type C	Selects Create
Type \D ↵	Enters D as the macro name
Press ↵	Specifies the block that contains the macro
Press ALT-D	Executes the macro and deletes a row

The advantage of the record method to create a macro is that it is quicker and less prone to error. The advantage of the write method is that you can use more complicated macro commands, as explained below.

Using Macro Commands

Quattro Pro provides an extensive array of commands that can be used within macros. These commands go beyond representing keystrokes. For example, you can include a command for the macro to pause, in order to solicit input from the user. You can also include programming commands that allow you to test conditions (similar to the If function) and branch to different parts of a macro. The format for a macro command is:

```
{COMMANDNAME Argument1,Argument2,...}
```

COMMANDNAME is the name of the command, and Argument is information that is needed with the command. For example, the macro statement {Branch B24} includes the command name Branch and the argument B24. This particular macro statement says go to cell B24. Other examples are:

```
{GETLABEL "Enter the Customer name: ",B5}
{GETNUMBER "Enter the Price: ",C15}
{IF H32="Y"}
{QUIT}
```
(This command ends the macro. ***NOTE:*** No argument is needed.)

The format rules for macro commands are:

- They must be enclosed in curly brackets ({ }).
- There must be a space between the command name and the argument.
- Commas must be used to separate the arguments.
- No spaces or other punctuation is allowed within an argument unless there is a string surrounded by quotation marks (for example, {GETLABEL "Enter the Customer name: ",B5}).
- The entire command must be entered into one cell.
- The command can mix upper- and lowercase.

Arguments can include:

- Numbers: actual numbers, formulas, or references to a cell that contains a number or formula.
- Strings: a text entry or a reference to a cell that has a text entry.
- Location: reference to a cell, a cell block, or a cell name.

- Condition: a logical expression that can be evaluated as true or false, such as H32="Y".

With these rules in mind, you can carry out the next application.

APPLICATION 3 Using Interactive Macros

Figure 5-11 shows an **interactive macro**, which is a macro that pauses during execution for input from the user. This is a common feature that increases both speed and accuracy when completing a worksheet such as the INVOICE template. The purpose of this macro is to make it easy for the user to complete the invoice by automatically moving the cell selector to each cell that requires input, such as date and customer name. After the cell selector is moved, the macro pauses to allow data input and then moves again when ↵ is pressed. To represent the cell selector movement keys within a macro you use {Down}, {Up}, {Right}, and {Left}. When a user retrieves the INVOICE worksheet, the cell selector is located at A1. The first step is to move the cell selector to B4 so the date can be entered. Thus, the first macro statement is: {Down}{Down}{Down}{Right}. Then the macro command {?} is used to pause the macro and allow input of the date. This process continues until all data is entered and the {Quit} command is encountered. Complete the following to create the macro shown in Figure 5-11. Start by retrieving another copy of the INVOICE2 template.

Retrieve INVOICE2

Press (F5) **and type** B21 ↵ — Moves the cell selector to B21, where the macro will be stored

Type {Down}{Down}{Down}{Right} — Enters first statement of macro

Press ↓ — Moves cell selector to B22

Type {?}~ — Enters next statement of macro (pause)

Press ↓ — Moves cell selector to B23

Type {Down}{Down} ↓ — Enters macro statement and moves cell selector to B24

Type {?}~ ↓ — Enters pause and moves cell selector to B25

Type {Down} ↓ — Enters macro statement and moves cell selector to B26

Type {?}~ ↓ — Enters pause and moves cell selector to B27

Type {Down} ↓ — Enters macro statement and moves cell selector to B28

Type {?}~ ↓ — Enters pause and moves cell selector to B29

Type {Down} ↓ — Enters macro statement and moves cell selector to B30

Type {?}~ ↓ — Enters pause and moves cell selector to B31

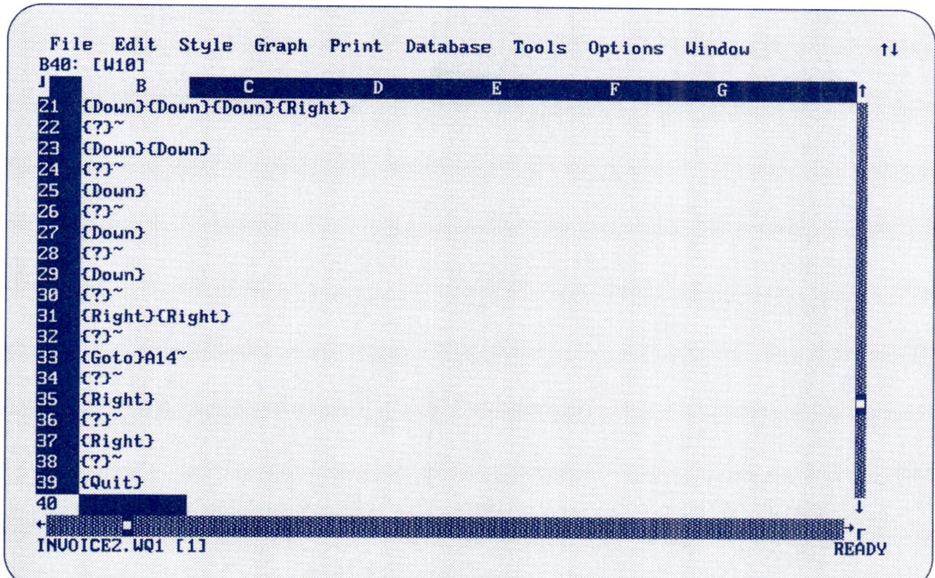

FIGURE 5-11

Interactive macro

Type {Right}{Right} (↓)	Enters macro statement and moves cell selector to B32
Type {?}~ (↓)	Enters pause and moves cell selector to B33

At this point in the invoice, the cell selector needs to be moved to cell A13 so that the ISBN can be entered. Instead of using the arrow keys to do this, you can add a command for the GoTo key, (F5). To represent the GoTo key, use the macro statement {Goto}.

Type {Goto}A14~ (↓)	Enters the macro statement and moves the cell selector to B34
Type {?}~ (↓)	Enters pause and moves cell selector to B35
Type {Right} (↓)	Enters macro statement and moves cell selector to B36
Type {?}~ (↓)	Enters pause and moves cell selector to B37
Type {Right} (↓)	Enters macro statement and moves cell selector to B38
Type {?}~ (↓)	Enters pause and moves cell selector to B39
Type {Quit} (↵)	Ends the macro

Now that the macro has been written into the spreadsheet, you can give it a name and specify the location where it is to be stored.

Press / T M (or (ALT)-(F2))	Brings up the Macro menu
Press N C	Selects the Create option
Type \I (↵)	Names the macro I
Enter B21.B39 (↵)	Specifies the block of cells used to store the macro

Now you will move the cell selector to A1 and execute the macro using the following customer information.

Date: (current) (***NOTE:*** Use month, day, year format, as in May 5, 1992.)

Customer: University Book Store

Street: 4545 Campus Way

City: Phoenix

State: AZ

Zip code: 85080

ISBN: 0-818483

Quantity: 750

Price: 20

NOTE: When you begin the execution of a macro, the word MACRO appears at the bottom of the screen. If you want to stop the execution of an interactive macro, press CTRL-BREAK. Then press the ESC key.

Press HOME	Moves cell selector to A1
Press ALT-i	Begins the execution of the macro

As shown in Figure 5-12, the cell selector moves to B4 and the macro pauses to accept input from the user.

Type the current date ↵	Enters the date into B4 and moves the cell selector to B6
Type University Book Store ↵	Enters customer name and moves cell selector to B7

FIGURE 5-12

Executing the interactive macro

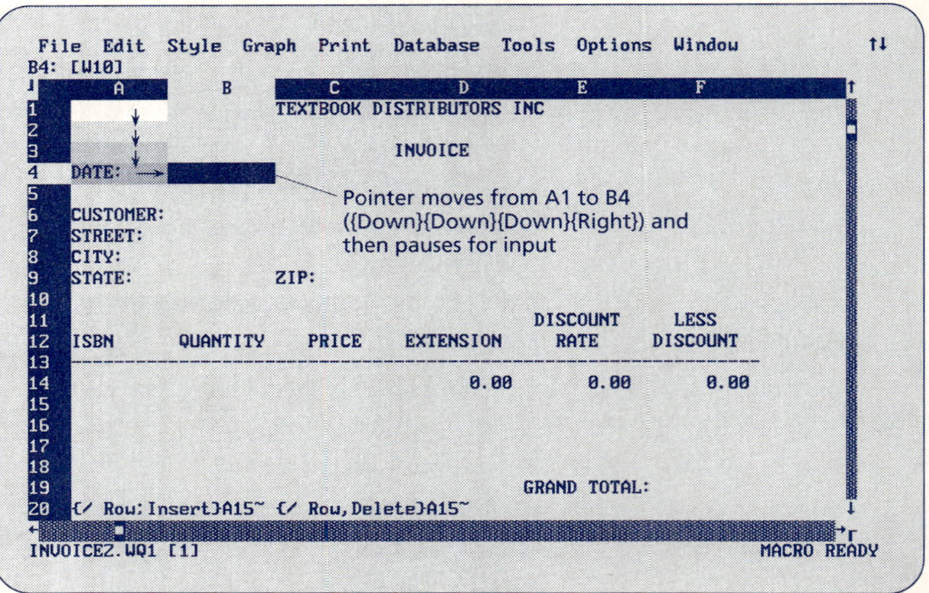

Type '4545 Campus Way ⏎	Enters street and moves cell selector to B8
Type Phoenix ⏎	Enters city and moves cell selector to B9
Type AZ ⏎	Enters state and moves cell selector to D9
Type '85080 ⏎	Enters zip code and moves cell selector to A14
Type '0-818483 ⏎	Enters ISBN and moves cell selector to B14
Type 750 ⏎	Enters quantity and moves cell selector to C14
Type 20 ⏎	Enters price and ends macro

This interactive macro helps to prevent errors and to speed up the data entry process by automatically moving the cell selector to the desired cells.

APPLICATION 4

In this application, you learn another type of interactive macro. You also learn to use the If command, used to test for conditions, and the Branch command, used to move to a different location in the macro.

GETLABEL and GETNUMBER Commands

The macro you created in the previous example moved the cell selector to a cell, paused for data entry, and then continued. With the GETLABEL and the GETNUMBER commands, you can have Quattro Pro display a prompt at the top of the spreadsheet and pause for user input. Then whatever is typed is placed in the specified cell. For example, the macro command {GETLABEL "Enter the Customer name: ",B6} causes the message "Enter the Customer name: " to be displayed at the top of the spreadsheet. When the user types the data, it is placed in cell B6. GETLABEL is used for text entries and GETNUMBER is used for value entries.

Figure 5-13 shows a macro that uses a series of GETLABEL and GETNUMBER commands. Retrieve another copy of the INVOICE2 template, enter this macro into cells B21 to B29, and name it \G.

Retrieve INVOICE2

Press F5 **and type** B21 ⏎	Moves cell selector to B21
Type {GETLABEL "Enter the date: ",B4}	Enters the first macro statement
Press ↓	Moves cell selector to B22
Type {GETLABEL "Enter the Customer Name: ",B6}	Enters next macro statement
Press ↓	Moves cell selector to B23

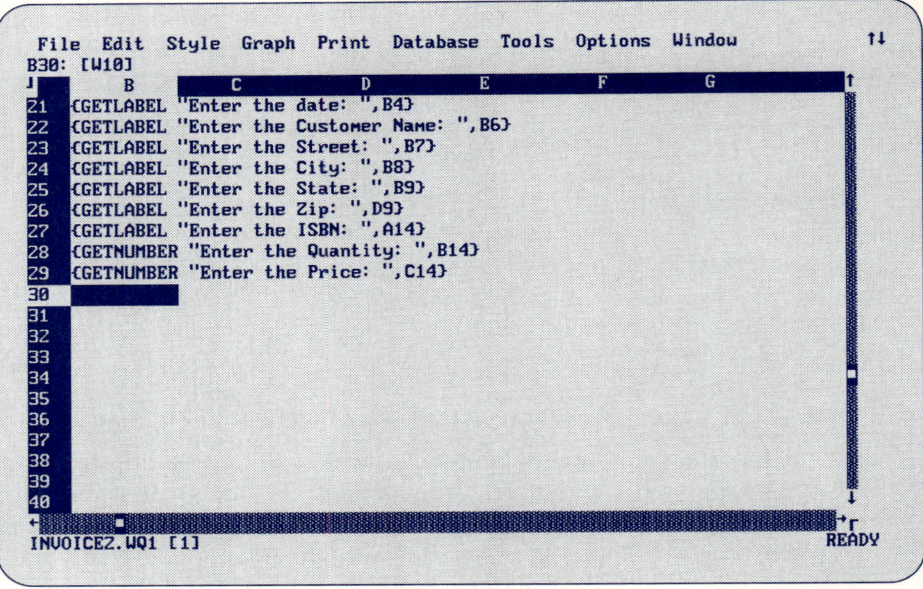

FIGURE 5-13

Macro commands

Type {GETLABEL "Enter the Street: ",B7}
Enters next macro statement

Press ⓓ — Moves cell selector to B24

Type {GETLABEL "Enter the City: ",B8}
Enters next macro statement

Press ⓓ — Moves cell selector to B25

Type {GETLABEL "Enter the State: ",B9}
Enters next macro statement

Press ⓓ — Moves cell selector to B26

Type {GETLABEL "Enter the Zip: ",D9}
Enters next macro statement

Press ⓓ — Moves cell selector to B27

Type {GETLABEL "Enter the ISBN: ",A14}
Enters next macro statement

Press ⓓ — Moves cell selector to B28

Type {GETNUMBER "Enter the Quantity: ",B14}
Enters next macro statement

Press ⓓ — Moves cell selector to B29

Type {GETNUMBER "Enter the Price: ",C14}
Enters next macro statement

Press ↵ — Ends the macro

Now give this macro a name and specify the block it is to be stored in. Then go to A1 and execute the macro.

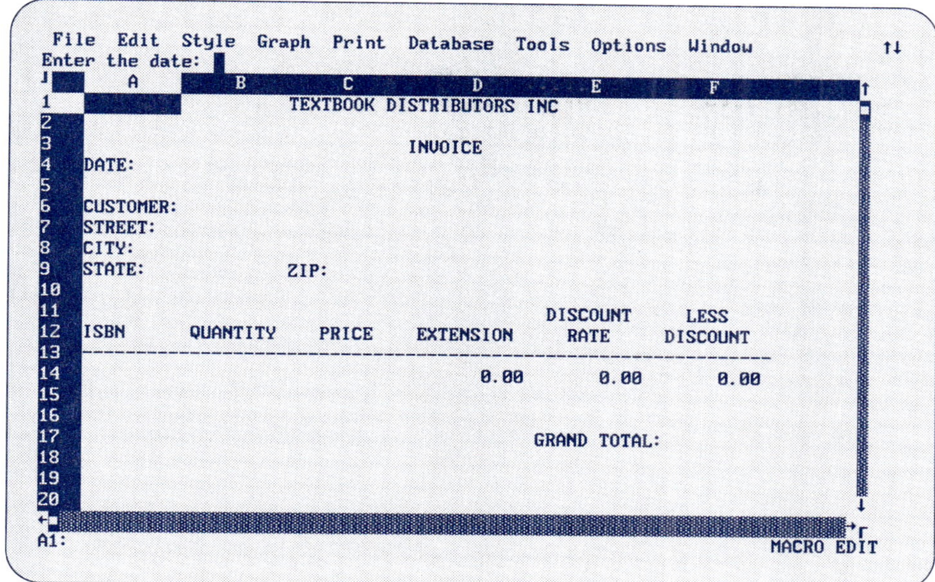

FIGURE 5-14

Executing an interactive macro

Press / T M N C	Selects Create from the /Tools¦Macro¦Name menu
Type \G ↵	Names the macro \G
Enter B21.B29 ↵	Specifies the block the macro is stored in
Press (HOME)	Moves cell selector to A1
Press (ALT)-g	Executes the macro

Figure 5-14 shows the prompt that appears at the top of the screen.

Type the current date ↵	Enters the date into B4, and the next prompt appears
Type University Book Store ↵	Enters the customer name, and the next prompt appears

Continue to complete this invoice using the same data as before. ***NOTE:*** On numeric entries, such as 4545 Campus Way, you do not need an apostrophe, because using GETLABEL in the macro informs Quattro Pro that you are entering text, not numbers.

If and Branch Commands

In the earlier example, each customer requires a separate invoice. Thus, if you wished to complete more than one invoice in a session you would have to repeat the macro. That is, after completing the macro you would need to move back to the beginning (B21). This can be done using the If and Branch commands. The macro If command, like the If function, can be used to test a condition. The Branch command can be used to move to any location in the macro.

Study the macro in Figure 5-13. The last entry asks for the price. After the price is entered, the process is completed. This macro can be modified by adding statements to ask the user whether there is another invoice to complete. If the answer is yes, the macro can be repeated by moving to cell B21. Figure 5-15 shows the modified macro. In cell B30 is: {GETLABEL "Do you want to complete another invoice Y/N? ",H32}. The user responds by typing a Y or an N; the response is placed in cell H32. The next macro statement is: {If H32 ="Y"}{Branch B21}. This says that if the contents of cell H32 is Y, continue on with the rest of the macro statement, {Branch B21}, which branches the execution of the macro to cell B21; if the contents of cell H32 is not Y, then continue the execution of the macro down the column to cell B32, the {Quit} command.

Add these three statements to the current macro and execute it as follows.

Press (PGDN) — Moves cell selector down one screen

Press (F5) **and type** B30 (↵) — Moves cell selector to B30

Type {GETLABEL "Do you want to complete another invoice Y/N? ",H32}

Press (↓) — Enters the macro statement and moves the cell selector to B31

Type {If H32="Y"}{Branch B21} — Enters the macro statement

Press (↓) — Moves cell selector to B32

Type {Quit} (↵) — Ends the macro

Press / T M N C — Selects Create from the /Tools¦Macro¦Name menu

Type \g (↵) — Names the macro \g

```
 File  Edit  Style  Graph  Print  Database  Tools  Options  Window        ↑↓
G32:
     B        C          D          E         F        G
21 {GETLABEL "Enter the date: ",B4}
22 {GETLABEL "Enter the Customer Name: ",B6}
23 {GETLABEL "Enter the Street: ",B7}
24 {GETLABEL "Enter the City: ",B8}
25 {GETLABEL "Enter the State: ",B9}
26 {GETLABEL "Enter the Zip: ",D9}
27 {GETLABEL "Enter the ISBN: ",A14}
28 {GETNUMBER "Enter the Quantity: ",B14}
29 {GETNUMBER "Enter the Price: ",C14}
30 {GETLABEL "Do you want to complete another invoice Y/N? ",H32}
31 {If H32="Y"}{Branch B21}
32 {Quit}
33
34
35
36
37
38
39
40
INVOICE2.WQ1 [1]                                     EXT          READY
```

FIGURE 5-15

If and Branch statements

Enter B21.B32 (↵) Specifies the block to store the macro

Press (HOME) Moves cell selector to A1

Press (ALT)-g Executes the macro

Type in the following data (use (↵)) and stop after entering the price.

Date: (current)
Customer: Campus Book Store
Street: 101 45th Ave
City: Berkeley
State: CA
Zip code: 94710
ISBN: 0-349283
Quantity: 500
Price: 32

After you enter the price and press (↵), the prompt "Do you want to complete another invoice Y/N?" appears at the top of the spreadsheet.

Type Y (↵) Causes the macro to branch to cell B21 and begin the process again

If you had entered N the macro would have quit. As you can see, the process could continue indefinitely. The If and Branch commands are often used together to provide a way to repeat a part of the macro or to move to another macro. For instance, there could be a separate macro that prints the worksheet. The user could be asked whether the worksheet is to be printed. If so, the macro could branch to the print macro. A list of macro commands and keystroke equivalents is located in the appendix. Before continuing, stop the execution of the macro as follows.

Press (CTRL)-(BREAK) Stops the macro

Press (ESC) Returns to worksheet

Automatically Executing a Macro — *APPLICATION 5*

The macro you have just completed speeds the entry of data. However, the user must still start the macro after the invoice is loaded. Because the user may be unfamiliar with macros or even spreadsheets, there are several ways to make the execution of the macro easier. First, each macro in a spreadsheet can be labeled with the macro name. Figure 5-16 shows a spreadsheet with several macros. The column to the left of each macro lists the macro name. Second, a message can be placed at the top of the spreadsheet to indicate to the user what to do to start the data entry process. This is shown in Figure 5-17. Third, a macro will automatically execute immediately after the spreadsheet is loaded if you name the macro \0 (zero).

On your data disk is a file called AUTOMAC. A macro has been created and saved with the name \0. Retrieve this worksheet and you will notice that the macro begins automatically.

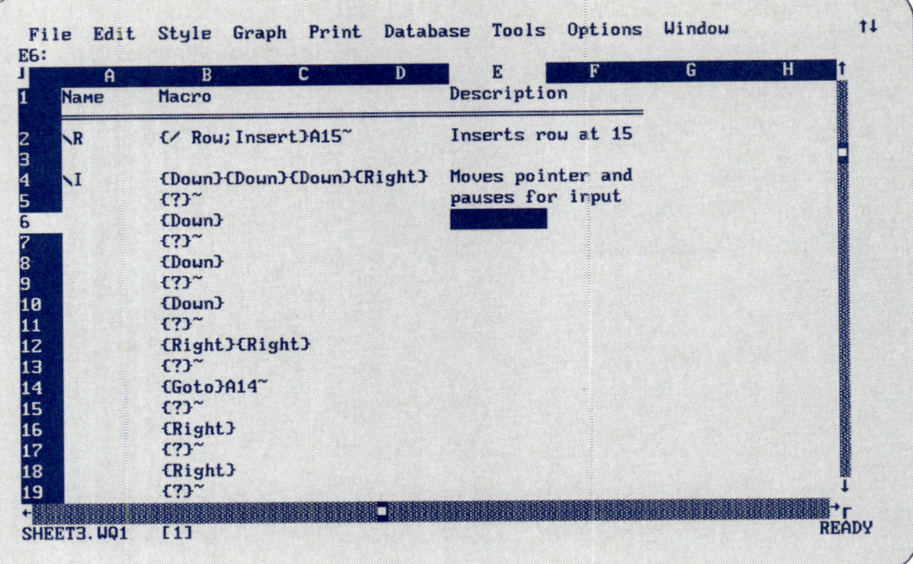

FIGURE 5-16

Labeling macros

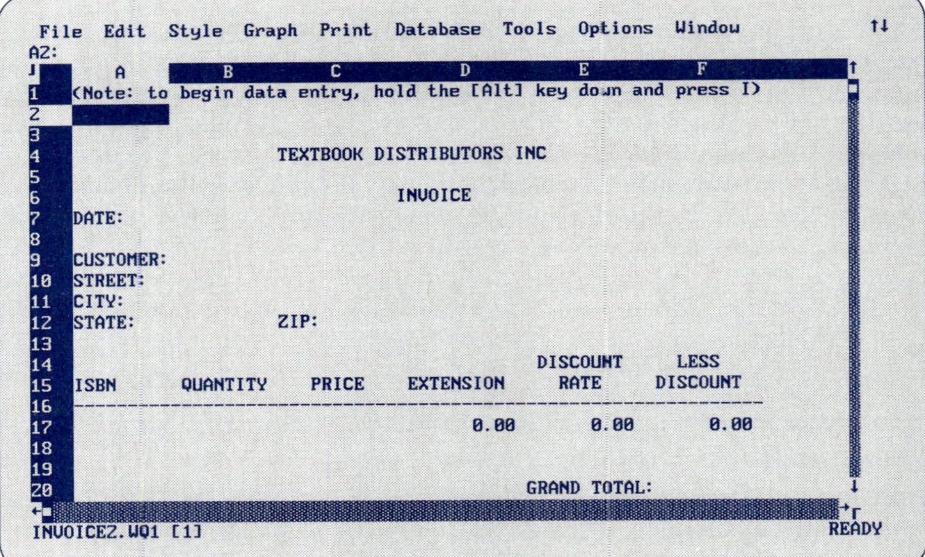

FIGURE 5-17

Including a message to the user

Retrieve AUTOMAC

Notice that the "Enter the date: " prompt appears automatically. There can be only one auto-execute macro per spreadsheet. If you no longer want a macro to automatically execute, then you can use the /Tools¦Macro¦Name¦Delete option from the Macro menu to delete the macro name (\0) and give it another name. Before continuing, stop the execution of the macro.

Press (CTRL)-(BREAK)	Stops the macro
Press (ESC)	Returns to worksheet

Deleting, Editing, and Saving a Macro

There are two steps to deleting a macro. First, delete the macro name using the Delete option from the /Tools¦Macro¦Name menu (/TMND). Then erase the macro commands from the spreadsheet using the /Edit¦Erase Block command.

Macros are label entries and can be edited using the F2 key. Macros also are saved with the worksheet.

As you become more familiar with macros, you will find it helpful to use two additional features, a macro library and the list of macro commands.

Macro Library

If you use a set of macros with more than one spreadsheet, you may find it useful to create a special spreadsheet that contains those macros. That spreadsheet is called a **macro library**. To create a macro library, begin with a blank spreadsheet, and enter the macros you wish to save. Either record the macros and then paste them into the worksheet or enter them using macro commands and then name them. To let Quattro Pro know that the spreadsheet is a macro library, select /Tools¦Macro¦Library¦Yes. Then save the spreadsheet with a name you will remember, such as LIBRARY.

To use your macro library with another spreadsheet, you must have both files open at the same time. To do this, use the /File¦Open command to display both files on the screen, rather than the /File¦Retrieve command. To use a macro library, first select /File¦Open. You are prompted for the name of the file to open. Type the name of the macro library file (don't forget to include A: if it is on drive A). Then, select /File¦Open again to open the spreadsheet file you wish to use the macros with. The spreadsheet file will cover the macro library file, but the macros will be available for you to work with. For more examples of /File¦Open, consult "Working with More than One Spreadsheet" later in this chapter, or the Quattro Pro manual.

List of Macro Commands

Quattro Pro provides a pop-up list of macro commands from which macros can be entered, similar to the pop-up function menu. To see the list of macro commands, press SHIFT-F3. Because there are so many, they are organized in categories according to function. The macro command categories are:

- Keyboard commands, including cell selector movement keys and function keys.
- Screen commands.
- Interactive commands, such as ?, GETLABEL, and GETNUMBER.
- Program commands, such as If and Branch.
- Cell commands, which affect the way data is stored in cells.
- File commands.
- / commands, the menu-equivalent commands. There are so many of these that they are further divided into general headings.

Refer to the Quattro Pro manual or Quick Reference for macro commands listed under each category. To remove the pop-up list from the screen, press (ESC).

APPLICATION 6 Advanced Features for Decision Making

Quattro Pro provides a number of useful techniques to aid in decision making. You can find out how many values fall within a given range by using a **frequency distribution**, and you can use the Solve For command to work backwards from the result of a formula, to find out what the formula's components should be. These techniques are illustrated in this section.

Determining a Frequency Distribution

The /Tools¦Frequency command allows you to determine the number of values that fall within given ranges. This useful command can be used with a worksheet database or an ordinary worksheet. An example is an instructor with a list of test scores who wants to determine how many students scored in the 90s, how many scored in the 80s, and so forth. Figure 5-18 shows a worksheet that has the students' names and scores. Column D has a list of ranges called a bin block. Column E has the number of scores in each range, called a **frequency distribution**.

To create a frequency distribution, first decide on the ranges and enter them in ascending order within a single column of the worksheet. This becomes the bin block. Then select the Frequency command from the Tools menu and specify the block of values (scores in this case) that you want to analyze. Then specify the block of cells that contains the bin block. Complete the following to practice this command.

Retrieve SCORES

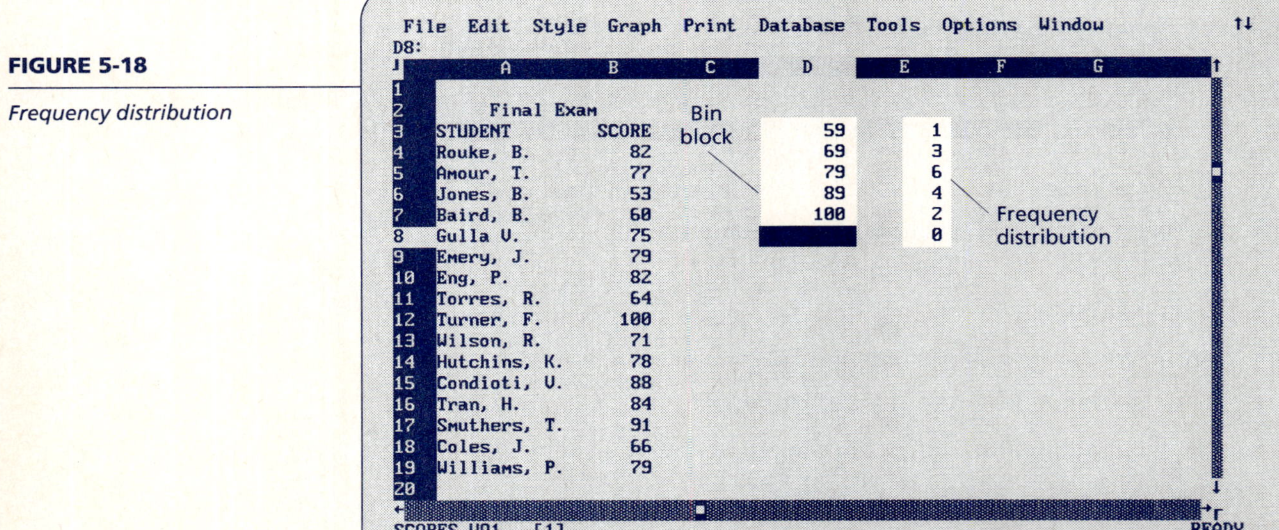

FIGURE 5-18

Frequency distribution

Press (F5) **and type** D3 ↵ Moves cell selector to D3

Type 59 ↓ Enters the bin block values

Type 69 ↓

Type 79 ↓

Type 89 ↓

Type 100 ↵

Press / T Selects Tools menu

Press F Selects Frequency command

The prompt is:

```
Specify values block: D7
```

Type B4.B19 ↵ Enters the block

The prompt is:

```
Specify Bin block: D7
```

Type D3.D7 ↵ Enters the block

The frequency distribution table is created in column E. The way to read this table is: one score is 59 or below, three scores are 60–69, six scores are 70–79, four scores are 80–89, two scores are 90–100, and no scores are above 100. Quattro Pro does not automatically recalculate the frequency distribution when you make changes in the worksheet values, so you would need to complete the step again.

After a frequency distribution table has been developed, an XY graph could be created to display the relationship between the ranges and the number of scores within each range.

Entering Sequential Values

To enter the values for the bin block, you could have used the /Edit¦Fill command instead of typing each value. This command fills the specified block with numbers separated by a specified interval, or **step**. The procedure is to select /Edit¦Fill; you are prompted for, first, the block to fill; second, a beginning value; third, a step value; and fourth, an ending value. Practice this command using SCORES.

Press / E F Selects /Edit¦Fill, and you are prompted for a block to fill

Type D11.D14 ↵ You are prompted for a starting value

Type 59 ↵ You are prompted for a step value

Type 10 ↵ You are prompted for an ending value

Type 89 ↵ Fills the block with values 59–89, separated by 10

Cells D11 through D14 now contain the values 59, 69, 79, and 89. If you wished to add the value 100, you would have to type it in yourself.

This can be a very useful command in entering a long series of sequential values without typing. For example, if you wished to analyze stock market data over a 20-year period from 1970 through 1990, you could use /Edit¦Fill to enter the years. The starting data would be 1970, the step value would be 1, and the ending value would be 1990.

APPLICATION 7

Solve For Option

One of Quattro Pro's most useful features is the Solve For option. In Chapter 3 of this book, you learned how to use Quattro Pro to carry out what-if analyses by setting up a template and entering different variables. Although this is a useful technique, it is sometimes easier to start off with the desired result of a formula and then work backwards. For example, instead of inserting different loan amounts into a worksheet to see what the monthly payments of each will be, you can start by estimating the desired monthly payments, and use Solve For to work backwards to find out how big the loan principal can be.

This is illustrated in the following example. The CARPAYMT worksheet contains a list of cars and prices. Assume that you can get financing at 8 percent annual interest, payable over four years. The prices of the cars range from $6,488 to $21,500, and you are not sure which would fit within your monthly budget. One way to find out would be to use the PMT function, which allows you to calculate monthly payments, given the loan principal, interest rate, and term of the loan. You could then calculate the monthly payments for each car individually. However, that would be time-consuming. A more efficient process would be to first figure out what monthly payments would fit your budget and then use /Tools¦Solve For to calculate what the loan principal could be. The process is to select /Tools¦Solve For; specify the formula cell, target value, and variable cell; and select Go.

Retrieve CARPAYMT

Press (F5) **and type** G9 (↵) — Moves cell selector to G9

This cell contains the formula you will use (Figure 5-19).

Press / T S — Selects /Tools¦Solve For menu

The /Tools¦Solve For menu has several options:

Formula Cell	The cell containing the formula you wish to work with.
Target Value	The desired result of the calculation. In this case, it is the monthly payment that fits your budget.
Variable Cell	The cell Quattro Pro can modify to get the target value.
Parameters	Specifies certain procedures for Quattro Pro to use when solving the formula.
Go	Starts the calculation.
Reset	Clears all settings and returns them to their default value.
Quit	Returns to spreadsheet.

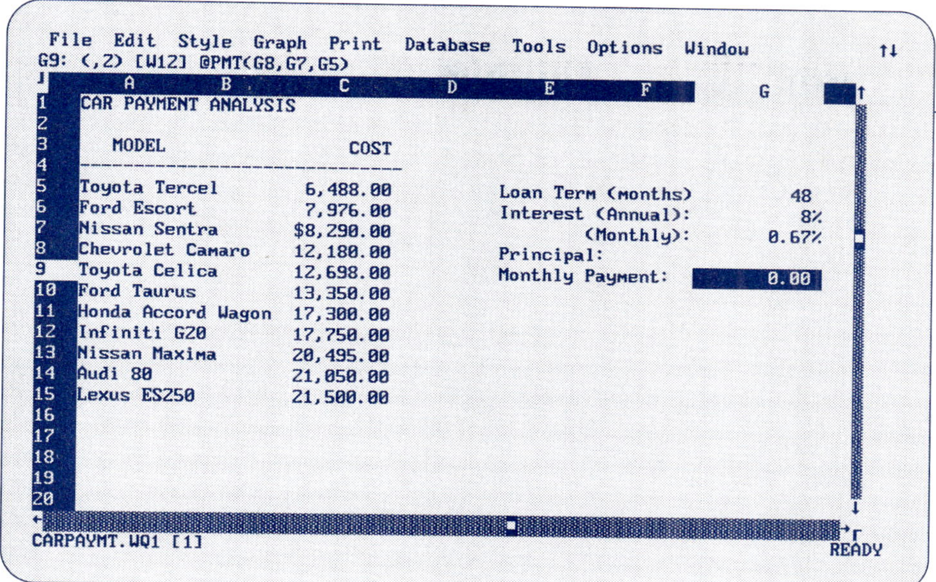

FIGURE 5-19

CARPAYMT worksheet

Press F	Selects Formula Cell
Type G9 ↵	Enters G9 as the formula cell
Press T	Selects Target Value
Type 400 ↵	Enters 400 as the target value (in this case, the monthly payments)
Press V	Selects Variable Cell
Type G8 ↵	Enters G8 as the variable cell

NOTE: In a more complicated formula, it speeds up calculations to place a "best guess" value in the variable cell.

Press G	Selects Go

The principal is calculated, based on a desired monthly payment of $400.

Press Q	Returns to worksheet and displays the result

With a monthly payment of $400, you could afford a loan up to $16,384.77. To calculate the principal with a new monthly payment, select /Tools¦Solve For and choose a new target value.

Press / T S	Selects /Tools¦Solve For menu
Press T	Selects Target Value
Type 450 ↵	Enters 450 as target value
Press G Q	Calculates and displays results

Notice that you need not change the formula cell or the variable cell on the Solve For menu, because they stay the same for this calculation. To clear all settings, you would select /Tools¦Solve For and choose Reset. It is a good idea to use Reset before beginning a completely new calculation.

APPLICATION 8

Annotating Graphs

In most cases, the graph features discussed in Chapter 4 are enough to design clear and effective graphs. Sometimes, though, additions such as text boxes and arrows can present information even more effectively. For that reason, Quattro Pro provides an **annotator** to add those features to a graph. The procedure is to first create a graph and then use the special annotator screen to enhance its appearance. This is illustrated using the file SALESFIG, which includes the named graph SALES.

Retrieve SALESFIG

This worksheet consists of sales figures for two products in 1991. The information is presented in the graph SALES. Use /Graph¦Name¦Display to display the graph (Figure 5-20).

Press / G N D — Selects /Graph¦Name¦Display

A window appears prompting you for the graph to display.

Press (↵) — Selects SALES

The graph clearly shows the two series. Let's assume, though, that one of the most important aspects of this set of figures is that product 2 has sold over 1,000 for the first time ever. That important fact would not be apparent to anyone viewing the graph.

To include that information, you can annotate the graph. Quattro Pro's annotating features are very powerful. This section introduces them through a simple example: adding a text box. You will add a text box that says First Time Above 1000!, with an arrow pointing to the product 2 series.

Press (ESC) — Returns to Graph menu

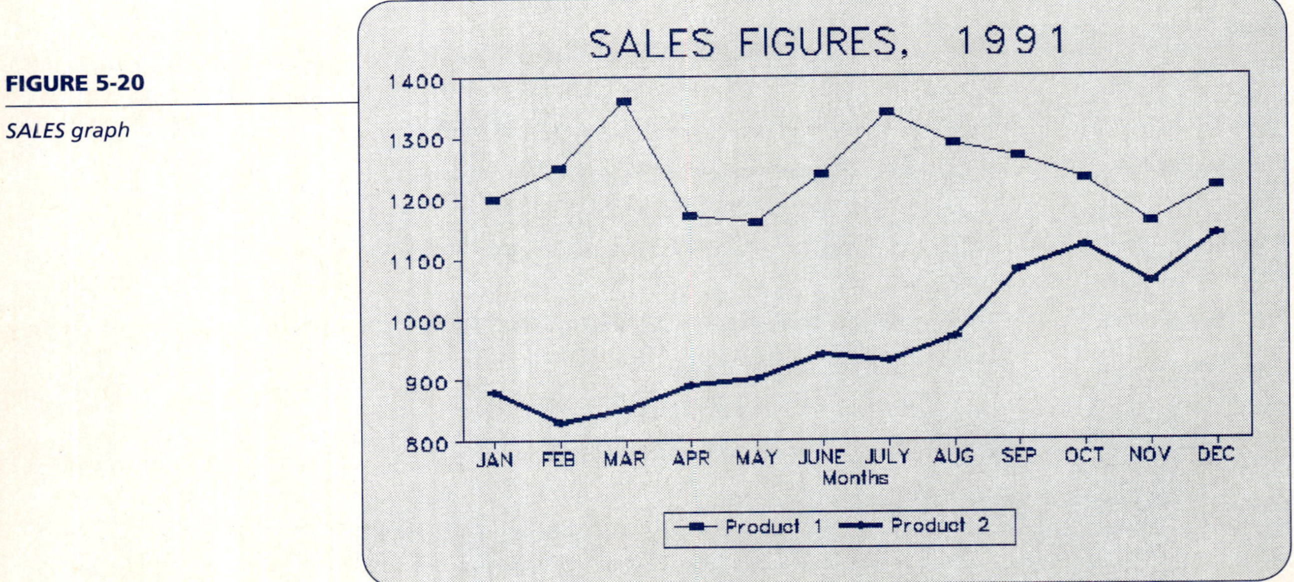

FIGURE 5-20

SALES graph

Press A   Selects Annotate

The annotator screen appears (Figure 5-21). The SALES graph is displayed in a section called the **draw area**. It is surrounded by the following sections.

- **Toolbox** (top row): contains pictures, called **icons**, each of which represents a particular feature of the annotator. You can use the icons to create parts of your graph, called **elements**, to enter Edit mode, or to exit the annotator. The toolbox is the annotator equivalent of the menu bar on the spreadsheet screen. To activate it, press /.
- **Property sheet** (top right box): lists adjustable properties of the chosen elements. When you first enter the annotator, the element listed is the background. If you have a color monitor, it can be adjusted by changing the color.
- **Gallery** (bottom right box): lists available options for the property sheet. When you first enter the annotator, it lists possible colors for the background.
- **Status Box** (below draw area): displays messages to guide you through the annotator.

You will first choose the text box icon from the toolbox and create a text box in the lower right corner of the graph. Then, you will choose the arrow icon to point from the text box to the product 2 series line.

Press /   Activates the toolbox

Press T   Selects text box icon

Note that the property sheet has changed to list different properties of boxed text and that a cursor has appeared in the middle of the graph. Use (→) and (↓) to

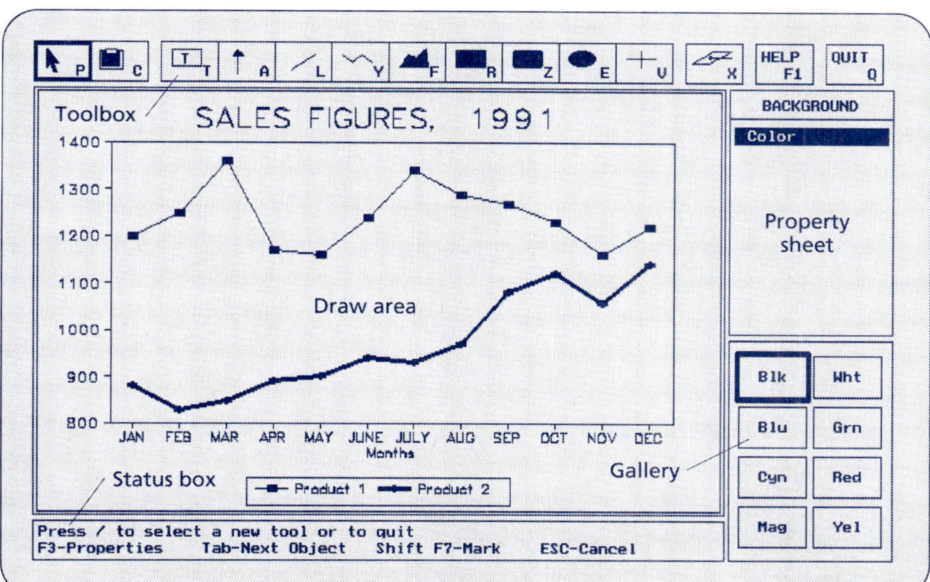

FIGURE 5-21

Graph annotator screen

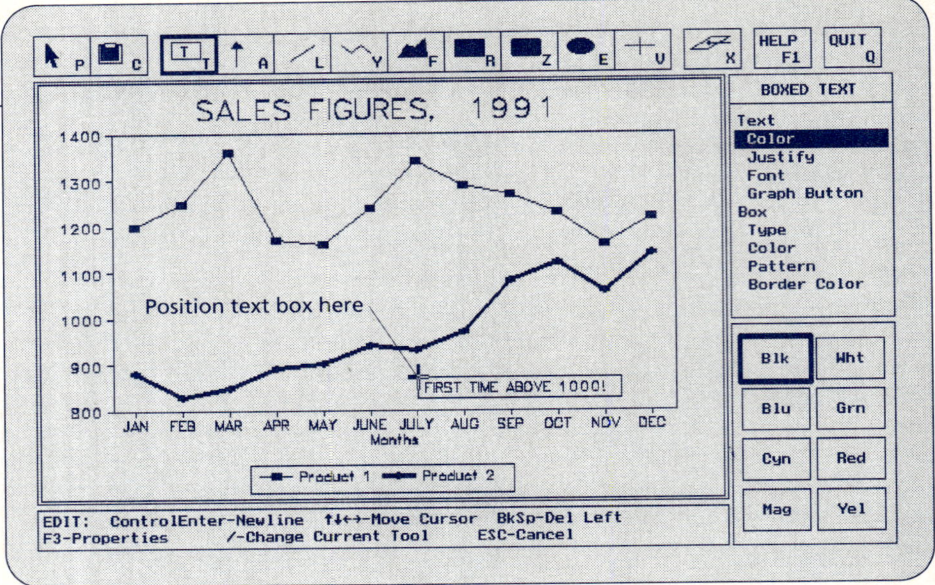

FIGURE 5-22

Text boxes

position the cursor in the lower right of the graph (refer to Figure 5-22). When the cursor is properly positioned:

Type a period	Indicates beginning position of text box
Type FIRST TIME ABOVE 1000!	Inserts text

Notice, as you start to type, that a box surrounds the words. As you type, the box extends to accommodate the entire text.

Press ↵	The graph is redrawn, and the cursor is positioned at the top right corner of the text box

You will next draw an arrow to connect the text box to the product 2 line.

Press /	Activates the toolbox
Press A	Selects arrow icon

Use → and ↓ to move the cursor until it is in the middle of the text box, over the A in ABOVE.

Type a period	Indicates the start of the arrow

Use ← and ↑ to draw a line from the text box to the marker at SEP (refer to Figure 5-23).

Press ↵	The arrow is fixed in place

You have now successfully completed the annotation of the graph. To leave the annotator, select Quit from the toolbox.

Press / Q	Selects Quit and returns to the Graph menu

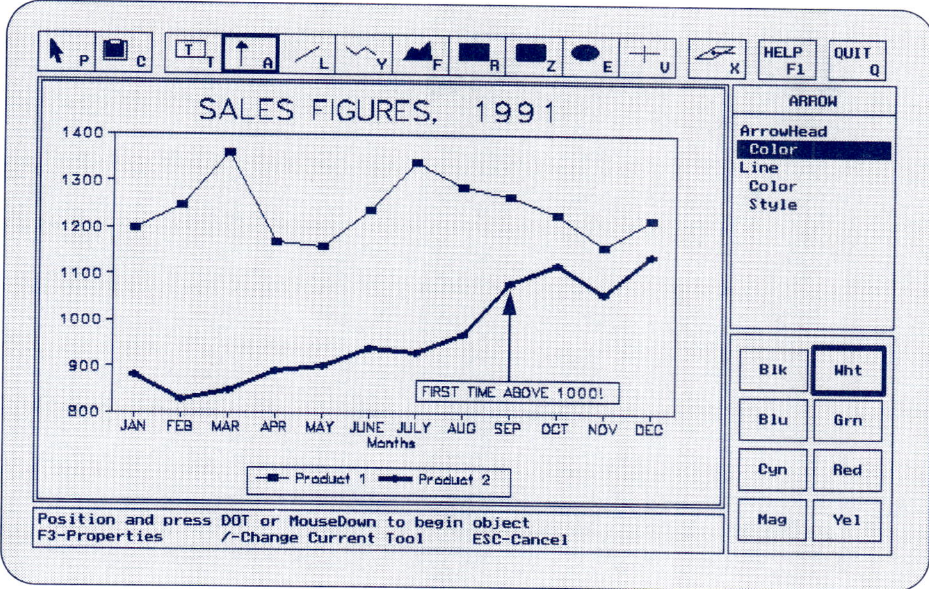

FIGURE 5-23

Adding an arrow

Press (F10) Displays the graph

Press (ESC) Returns to Graph menu

To save the graph with the new changes, choose /Graph¦Name¦Create, and press (↵) when prompted for a graph name. (***NOTE:*** In Quattro Pro 3.0, if /Graph¦Name¦Autosave Edits is on, the changes are automatically saved.)

Press N C Selects /Graph¦Name¦Create

Press (↵) Saves changes to graph SALES

This ends the section on annotating graphs.

Working with More than One Spreadsheet

APPLICATION 9

This section presents two different ways to work with more than one spreadsheet. The first is to use commands to combine data from several worksheets or to extract data from one worksheet and save it to another. The second is to **link** worksheets, so that changes to one are automatically reflected in the other.

Combining and Extracting Worksheet Data

Combining Worksheets Quattro Pro allows you to merge two or more worksheets together. By using the /Tools¦Combine command you can add, subtract, or replace (copy over) data in a worksheet. To illustrate, you will add the sales data from three stores to obtain overall company sales. Sales data for each store is broken down into five departments: men's and women's wear, men's and women's accessories, and other (Figure 5-24). The file names for the worksheets are STORE1, STORE2, and STORE3. The worksheets for the stores are

FIGURE 5-24

STORE1 worksheet

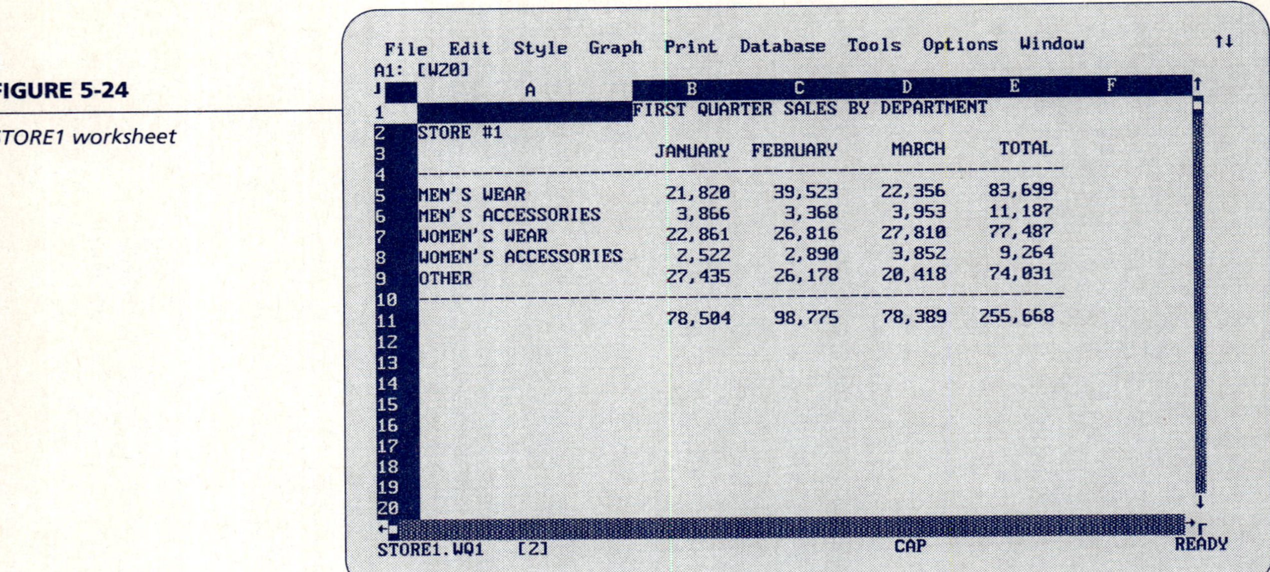

identical except for the sales amounts. You will start by loading STORE1 and then combining the STORE2 and STORE3 worksheets.

Retrieve STORE1

Press / T	Brings up the Tools menu
Press C	Selects Combine command

The Combine window appears, listing several options. If you choose Copy, the second worksheet replaces the first one. If you choose Add, the values in the two worksheets are added. The latter is the option you want.

Press A	Selects Add

The options are:

```
File
Block
```

File combines all the data in the worksheets, and Block allows you to select specific cells to combine.

Press F	Selects File
Press (ESC) **twice**	Clears the C:\ directory
Type A:STORE2 (↵)	Specifies STORE2 as the file to combine

The two files are combined and the values are added. Repeat these steps for STORE3. Then change the heading to TOTAL SALES — ALL STORES and save the worksheet as TOTSTORE.

Extracting Data The /Tools|Xtract command allows you to save a portion of a spreadsheet to a separate file. This is useful if you want to break down a

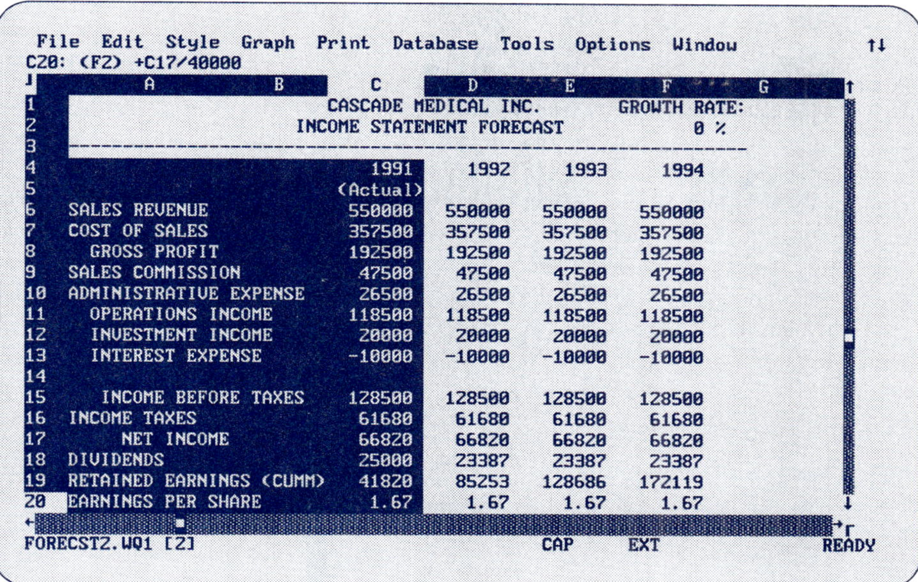

File Edit Style Graph Print Database Tools Options Window

C20: (F2) +C17/40000

	A	B	C	D	E	F	G
1			CASCADE MEDICAL INC.		GROWTH RATE:		
2			INCOME STATEMENT FORECAST			0 %	
3							
4			1991	1992	1993	1994	
5			(Actual)				
6	SALES REVENUE		550000	550000	550000	550000	
7	COST OF SALES		357500	357500	357500	357500	
8	GROSS PROFIT		192500	192500	192500	192500	
9	SALES COMMISSION		47500	47500	47500	47500	
10	ADMINISTRATIVE EXPENSE		26500	26500	26500	26500	
11	OPERATIONS INCOME		118500	118500	118500	118500	
12	INVESTMENT INCOME		20000	20000	20000	20000	
13	INTEREST EXPENSE		-10000	-10000	-10000	-10000	
14							
15	INCOME BEFORE TAXES		128500	128500	128500	128500	
16	INCOME TAXES		61680	61680	61680	61680	
17	NET INCOME		66820	66820	66820	66820	
18	DIVIDENDS		25000	23387	23387	23387	
19	RETAINED EARNINGS (CUMM)		41820	85253	128686	172119	
20	EARNINGS PER SHARE		1.67	1.67	1.67	1.67	

FORECST2.WQ1 [2] CAP EXT READY

FIGURE 5-25

Extract feature

large worksheet into smaller parts. The process is to choose the Xtract command from the Tools menu and then specify whether to save the file with formulas left as is or to convert the formulas to their values. Usually you will want to extract the formulas so that the new worksheet can be updated. However, if the block of cells you plan to extract has formulas or functions that may be affected by cells outside the block, then you should choose to convert them to values.

Figure 5-25 shows a spreadsheet. You will retrieve it and then save a portion (the highlighted block) to a new file.

Retrieve FORECST2

Press / T X — Selects the /Tools | Xtract command

The choices are:

Formulas
Values

Press F — Selects Formulas

The prompt is:

Enter xtract file name:

Press (ESC) **twice** — Clears the file name, path, and drive

Type A:ACTUAL91 (↵) — Names the new file

The prompt is:

Enter xtract block: F4..F4

Type A4.C20 (↵) — Specifies block to extract and saves the data

Now retrieve the new file.

Retrieve ACTUAL91

That part of FORECST2 (A4.C20) that you extracted is displayed as the ACTUAL91 worksheet. The FORECST2 worksheet is not affected by this operation.

Open File Command A useful technique in working with more than one spreadsheet is to use the Open File command, /File¦Open, rather than Retrieve, to display worksheets. /File¦Open is very similar to the /File¦Retrieve command. The one difference is that /File¦Retrieve automatically removes any previously displayed spreadsheets from the computer's memory, allowing you to work with only one spreadsheet at a time. The /File¦Open command, in contrast, allows you to work with several spreadsheets at once. This command is illustrated in the following section on linking spreadsheets. To display all open worksheets on the screen, select /Window¦Tile.

Linking Worksheets

The problem with combining and extracting data from worksheets is that once the data is combined or extracted, it cannot be affected by changes to the initial worksheet. For example, once you have combined the data from STORE1, STORE2, and STORE3 into TOTAL SALES, you would have to make changes to both the individual and combined worksheets to update the information. If you had many worksheets to combine, this could become very complicated. For that reason, Quattro Pro allows you to link worksheets, so changes in one are automatically reflected in the other. This is illustrated in a worksheet called LINKSALE. This worksheet contains links to STORE1, STORE2, and STORE3, so changes made to any of those files automatically update the totals in LINKSALE.

Retrieve LINKSALE

When you retrieve a linked spreadsheet, a menu is displayed on the screen prompting you for link options. The choices are:

```
Load Supporting
Update Refs
None
```

Load Supporting also opens all the files to which the spreadsheet is linked. Update Refs displays the file without loading the linked files. None temporarily replaces the link references with "NA" (not available).

Press L — Selects Load Supporting

In a few moments, the spreadsheet LINKSALE is displayed. Quattro Pro has also loaded STORE1, STORE2, and STORE3, but they are temporarily hidden behind LINKSALE.

The values in LINKSALE may look identical to the ones in TOTSTORE after using /Tools¦Combine to combine values from STORE1, STORE2, and STORE3. However, instead of numbers, cells B6 through D10 contain formulas referencing the other three spreadsheets. To see these formulas, move to cell B6.

Press (F5) **and type** B6 (↵) — Moves cell selector to B6 (Figure 5-26)

The input line displays the formula:

```
(,0) [W10] +[STORE1]B5+[STORE2]B5+[STORE3]B5
```

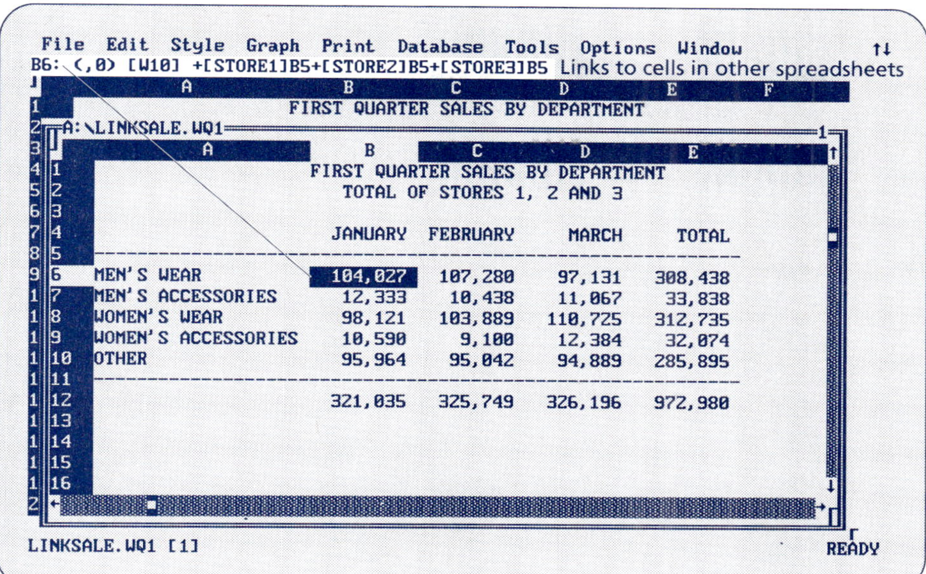

FIGURE 5-26

Linking worksheets

(,0) refers to the numeric format, [W10] refers to the width, and +[STORE1]B5+[STORE2]B5+[STORE3]B5 is the formula referencing cells in the other spreadsheets. The only difference between a spreadsheet link and an ordinary formula is the name of the spreadsheet to link to, which must be enclosed in square brackets ([ ]). A linked formula using the Sum function, for example, would follow the same form as an ordinary Sum function, except that the cell addresses would be preceded by the name of the spreadsheet. Instead of @SUM(D6.D12), the formula would read @SUM([STORE1]D6.D12). The disk drive and directory are not needed if all the linked spreadsheets are on the same disk and in the same directory.

The advantage of linking spreadsheets in this way is that if values in STORE1, STORE2, or STORE3 are changed, LINKSALE will change accordingly. To demonstrate, first select /Window¦Tile to display sections of all four spreadsheets on the screen.

Press / W T	Selects /Window¦Tile

Sections of all four spreadsheets are displayed (Figure 5-27). Each is in a separate window. You cannot move from one to another by pressing the arrow keys. Instead, to move the cell selector from one to the other, hold down (ALT) and type the number of the window to move to. The window number is displayed in the upper right corner of the window. To make it easier to see changes, position all four spreadsheets so that JANUARY appears in the upper left corner of each window. In LINKSALE:

Press (→) and then (↓) 4 times	Positions LINKSALE so JANUARY is in the upper left corner
Press (ALT)-3	Moves cell selector to STORE1
Press (→) twice and (↓) 8 times	Positions STORE1 so JANUARY is in the upper left corner

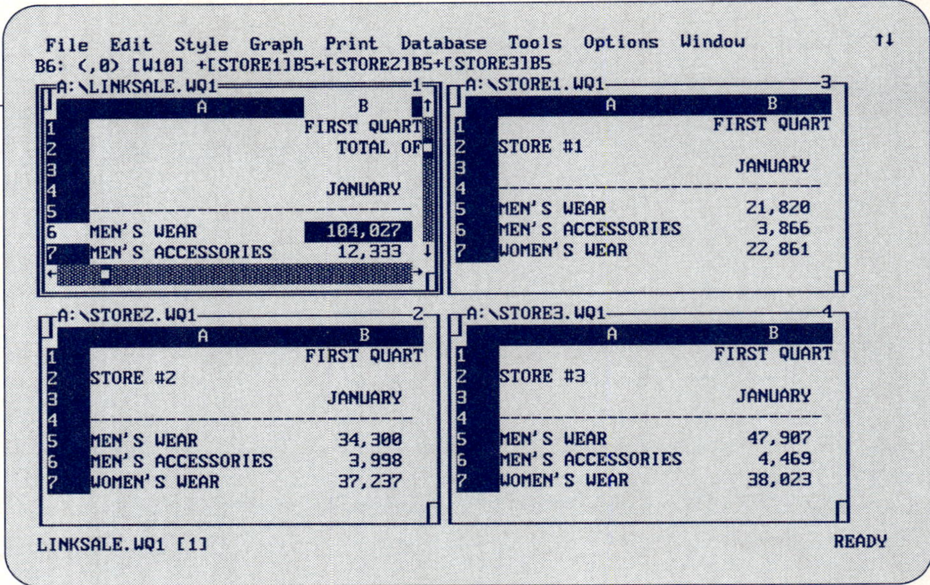

FIGURE 5-27

Using the Tile command to display worksheets side by side

Press (ALT)-2	Moves cell selector to STORE2
Press (→) **twice and** (↓) **8 times**	Positions STORE2 so JANUARY is in the upper left corner
Press (ALT)-4	Moves cell selector to STORE3
Press (→) **twice and** (↓) **8 times**	Positions STORE3 so JANUARY is in the upper left corner

Next, move back to STORE1 to see how changes affect the totals in LINKSALE.

Press (ALT)-3	Moves cell selector to STORE1
Press (F5) **and type** B5 (↵)	Moves cell selector to B5

As you change the value in B5 of STORE1, watch the corresponding changes in B6 of LINKSALE.

Type 121800 (↵)	The corresponding value in LINKSALE changes to 204,007

Now move to STORE3 and change the value for MARCH.

Press (ALT)-4	Moves cell selector to STORE3
Press (F5) **and type** D5 (↵)	Moves cell selector to D5
Type 56 (↵)	Changes value in LINKSALE, D6, to 60,393

It is not necessary to open LINKSALE in order to make changes in STORE1, STORE2, or STORE3. You can use /File¦Open or /File¦Retrieve to display each file separately, make changes, and save the file. The next time you load LINKSALE, the totals will be automatically updated. If you wish to see the totals without opening the linked files, select Update Refs from the pop-up menu when you first load LINKSALE.

This concludes the section on linked spreadsheets. Before continuing, select /File¦Close All to close all the worksheets.

Press / F L	Selects /File¦Close All
Press Y	Selects Yes

Because all worksheets have been closed, the usual blank worksheet is not displayed. Choose /File¦Exit to exit Quattro Pro or /File¦Open to open a new file.

USING QUATTRO PRO WITH OTHER PROGRAMS

An important feature of any application program is the ability to interchange data with other programs. For example, you are using Quattro Pro to develop worksheets, but a friend might be using Lotus 1-2-3. Fortunately, Quattro Pro can exchange files created with other popular programs as shown on the list below. To save a Quattro Pro worksheet so it can be used by one of these programs, append the appropriate extension to the file name when you save the worksheet. To have Quattro Pro retrieve a file created by one of these programs, use the appropriate file extension when loading the worksheet.

Program	**Extension**
dBASE III, III+, IV	.DBF
dBASE II	.DB2
Lotus 1-2-3, version 2.01 or 2.2	.WK1
Lotus 1-2-3, version 1A	.WKS
Lotus 1-2-3, Educational	.WKE
Multiplan	.SLK
Paradox	.DB
Quattro (earlier versions)	.WKQ
Reflex, version 2	.R2D
Reflex, version 1	.RXD
Symphony, version 2.0	.WR1
Symphony, version 1.2	.WRK
VisiCalc	.DIF

NOTE: To save files in dBASE II format, use the .DB2 extension and then change the extension to .DBF before loading the file in dBASE II. To retrieve dBASE II files, use .DBF as the extension.

Importing and Exporting Text Files

Files created by programs other than those mentioned above can also be copied into a Quattro Pro spreadsheet by using the /Tools¦Import command. This command works with three standard formats: ASCII text files, Comma & " " delimited files, and Only Comma files.

ASCII text files are most commonly developed with word processors. In many word processing programs, saving a document as an ASCII text file is an optional feature. When you import an ASCII file, Quattro Pro enters each line

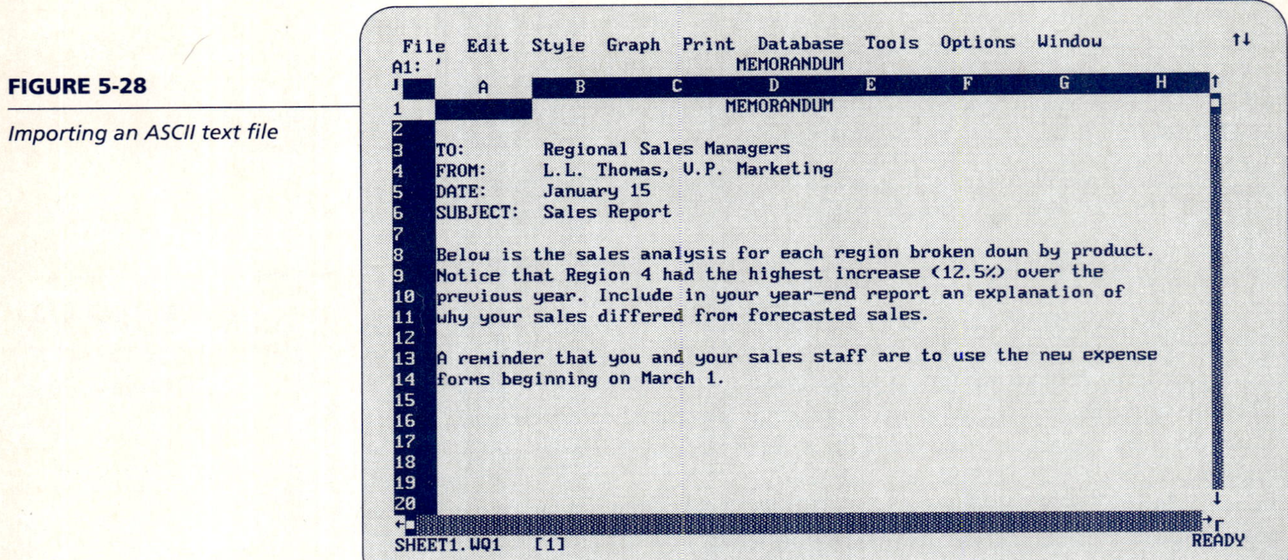

FIGURE 5-28

Importing an ASCII text file

of the file as a label in the first column of a designated block. Only one cell is used per line. Figure 5-28 shows an ASCII file that has been imported into Quattro Pro. ASCII text files often have the extension .TXT or .PRN.

Comma delimited and " " files are text files that separate data using commas and quotation marks. Each line of the file is imported to a row in the spreadsheet. Data items that are separated by commas are placed in different columns. In addition, data items that are surrounded by quotation marks are imported as labels; items without quotation marks are imported as values. Saving a file as a comma and " " delimited file is an optional feature of many database programs.

Only Comma files are text files that separate data using commas only. Each line of the file is imported to a row in the spreadsheet, and the data items are separated by commas.

Exporting Quattro Pro as a Text File

If you want to use a Quattro Pro worksheet with another program that is not directly compatible, you can save the worksheet as an ASCII file. A file saved in the ASCII format is basically the raw data in the worksheet as it appears when you print it. None of the formulas or formatting is saved. Therefore, this process is most often used when you want to export your worksheet to a word processing program.

To save a worksheet in the ASCII format, you print it to disk. The process is to select the Print menu, specify the block to be saved, set the margins (top: 0; bottom: 0; left: 0; right: 80), and specify the destination as File. Enter a file name and press ↵. Then press S to print the spreadsheet to the file. The file extension .PRN is automatically appended to the file name you specified.

SUMMARY

This chapter introduced you to advanced features in Quattro Pro. These features include creating data entry forms, writing macros, using frequency distributions, and using the Solve For option. You were also introduced to graph annotation and working with more than one spreadsheet at a time. The final feature you covered is using Quattro Pro with other programs.

WORD LIST

annotator
bin block
Combine command
data entry form
draw area
exporting
frequency distribution
gallery
Hidden cells command
importing
interactive macro
Lookup functions
lookup table
macro
Macro commands
macro library
property sheet
Protection command
sequential values
Solve For option
spreadsheet links
status box
toolbox

QUESTIONS

1. What is a data entry form?
2. Give an example of how the Lookup functions work.
3. What is a macro, and what is the purpose of creating one?
4. List and explain three Macro commands.
5. Describe the process for filling a block with sequential values.
6. What is the value of the Solve For option?
7. Describe the process for annotating graphs.
8. Explain the difference between the /File¦Open command and the /File¦Retrieve command.
9. Explain the difference between the Combine command and spreadsheet links in obtaining totals from several spreadsheets.
10. Under what circumstances would you use Combine? Under what circumstances would you link spreadsheets?
11. Why might you want to import or export data?

6 Customizing Quattro Pro

In this chapter you will fine-tune, or customize, Quattro Pro so it will suit your needs better. You will change default settings, such as the number of decimal places for spreadsheet values and the directory for Quattro Pro to search for files. If you have the hardware capabilities, you can choose to use a mouse to enter data and WYSIWYG mode to display data. You will undo mistakes with Undo and Transcript, use Debug mode to find errors in macros, and change the menu structure and command names. ***NOTE:*** You should have mastered the first five chapters before beginning this one.

Every spreadsheet program comes with built-in settings called default values. An example would be the default setting for decimal places. Also, every spreadsheet comes with a particular menu structure and command names. For instance, to copy data you use the /Edit¦Copy command. As you become more experienced with spreadsheets you may want to change specific default settings, the menu structure, or command names to make the program easier and quicker to operate. For example, you may decide that you want values to always display two decimal places or that the /File¦Copy command should be renamed the Range command. In this section you will change the default settings within Quattro Pro; in later sections you will use the /Options¦Startup¦Edit Menus command to change command names and the menu structure.

CHANGING DEFAULT SETTINGS

The process for changing the default settings is to choose the Options menu from the main menu and select the desired option. Then make the desired changes. After changes are made, you can save them so that each time you load Quattro Pro the new default settings are used. To illustrate the process, you will first change the default setting for number of decimal places to 2 and the default directory to A:. Then you will save the settings so that when Quattro Pro is loaded again the new settings are used. Start by loading Quattro Pro and entering the value 100.

Changing Display of Decimal Places

Load Quattro Pro if you have not already done so.

Type 100 (↓)	Enters 100 into A1 and moves cell selector to A2
Type 100.00 (↵)	Enters 100 into A2

Notice that no decimal places are displayed. This is because the default setting is General, which displays decimal places only if they contain a value. You will change this setting to 2.

Press (DEL)	Erases contents of cell A2
Press (↑) (DEL)	Erases contents of cell A1
Press / O	Brings up Options menu

The Options menu (Figure 6-1) appears with the following options.

Hardware	Specifies information about your computer screen and printer.
Colors	Changes the colors displayed on the screen.

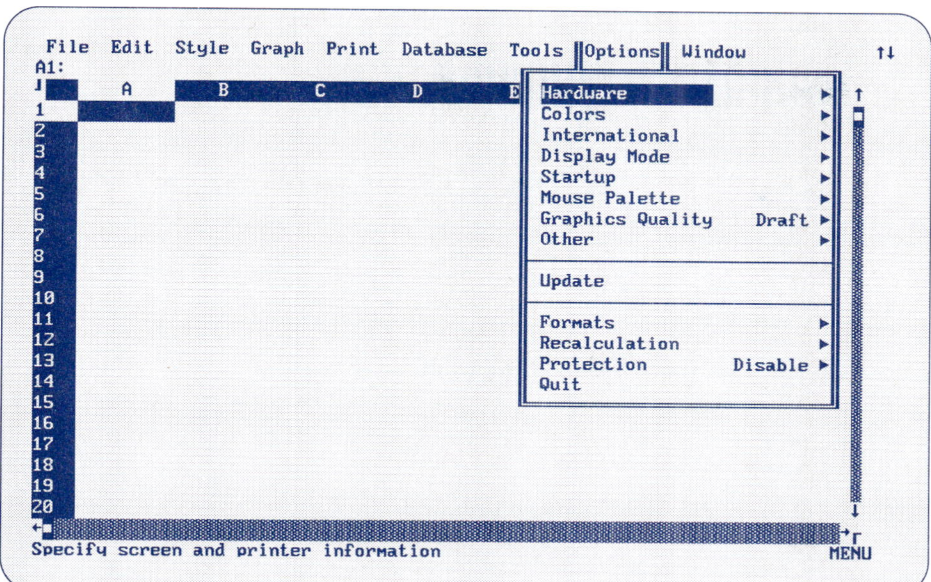

FIGURE 6-1

Menu for default options

International	Specifies standards used to display currency, date, and time.
Display Mode	Specifies the type of monitor you have and how spreadsheets should be displayed.
Startup	Specifies information Quattro Pro uses when the program is started.
Mouse Palette	Changes settings for using the mouse palette.
Graphics Quality	Specifies how fonts should be displayed.
Other	Specifies a number of settings, including Undo.
Update	Saves the default setting changes so they are automatically used when the program is loaded thereafter.
Formats	Changes settings that affect the display of data in the worksheet.
Recalculation	Specifies the sequence in which formulas are calculated and whether the recalculation is manual or automatic.
Protection	Protects the spreadsheet from changes.
Quit	Returns to worksheet.

Select /Options|Formats to change the number of decimal places.

Press F	Selects Formats command
Press N	Selects Numeric Format
Press F	Selects Fixed

The prompt is:

```
Fixed number of decimal places [0...15]: 2
```

Press ↵	Specifies 2 as the default setting for decimal places
Press Q Q	Returns to worksheet
Type 100 ↵	Enters 100.00 into A1

Notice that two decimal places are now displayed, even though no decimal places were typed.

Changing the Default Directory

When Quattro Pro is loaded, the program assumes that worksheet files are in the same directory of the hard disk that the program is in. If your data files are in another directory or on a floppy disk, you may wish to change the default directory so Quattro Pro will look for the worksheet files in the right place. The procedure for this is to select /Options¦Startup¦Directory and specify the new default directory. To change the default directory to drive A, follow these steps:

Place your data disk in drive A

Press / O	Brings up the Options menu
Press S	Selects Startup
Press D	Selects Directory

You are prompted for a path name.

Type A: ↵	Specifies drive A
Press Q Q	Returns to worksheet

Saving New Default Settings

When changes are made in a default setting, the changes must be saved before they become effective. This is done with the /Options¦Update command. When you choose this command, all changes made to default settings are saved to a file called RSC.RF. When Quattro Pro is being loaded, it reads this file and loads the default settings. The /Options¦Update command alters the program, so be sure this is what you want to do before proceeding.

CAUTION: Check with your instructor or lab assistant to determine whether you should save the changes to your hard drive.

Press / O	Selects Options menu
Press U	Selects Update and saves the new settings
Press Q	Returns to worksheet

To load the new default directory settings, quit and then reload Quattro Pro.

Press / F X (or CTRL-X)	Exits Quattro Pro

Load Quattro Pro (with the data disk in drive A)

Press / F R	Selects Retrieve

Quattro Pro will search the A drive for files to retrieve.

The new default setting is in effect. If you want to restore the program to the original settings, you can use the same process and save the changes. As you can see, changing the default settings can save you time by allowing you to configure the program to your needs.

Press (ESC) **until you return to the worksheet**

CHANGING THE MENU STRUCTURE AND COMMAND NAMES

Another customizing feature of Quattro Pro allows you to change the menu structure and alter menu command names. For instance, you may want to change the name of the Copy command to Duplicate, or add a menu item to the main menu. These can be accomplished by first using /Options¦Startup¦Edit Menus to create a customized menu and then selecting the customized menu with /Options¦Startup¦Menu Tree. If you wished to load the new menu structure each time you start Quattro Pro, your final step would be to select /Options¦Update to make the new menu Quattro Pro's default menu. The next section illustrates the first two steps, creating and selecting a new menu structure and command names. Check with your instructor or lab assistant *before* selecting /Options¦Update to make the changes part of Quattro Pro's default startup settings.

The first step is to use the Edit Menus screen to change the menu structure by adding a Save/Get option to the main menu.

Press / O	Selects Options menu
Press S	Selects Startup options
Press E	Selects Edit Menus

A message is displayed on the screen:

```
Loading the Menu Tree
```

After a few moments, the Edit Menus screen appears (Figure 6-2). The screen has pull-down menu commands across the top and a window with three panes. The middle pane displays the current menu tree. The top section is the Current Item section. It presents information about the current menu selection. The bottom pane is the Clipboard Menu. The clipboard stores any menu items you have deleted from the current menu tree, so you can paste them into another section.

When you load the Edit Menus screen, the File command in the current Menu Tree section is highlighted. You can use the (↓) and (↑) keys to move the highlight to any command. Note that the description in the Current Item pane at the top of the screen changes accordingly.

Press (↓)	Moves highlight to Edit command and the Current Item description changes
Press (↑)	Moves highlight back to File command

To display the submenus (also called **child menus**) associated with each of the main menu choices (its **parent**), position the highlight on that choice and press the plus key (+) on the numeric keypad. To move from a main menu choice to its submenu, use the (→) key. Use (↑) and (↓) to move among submenu choices and (←) to move from the top submenu choice back to the parent menu. To hide the submenu again, press the minus key (–) on the numeric keypad.

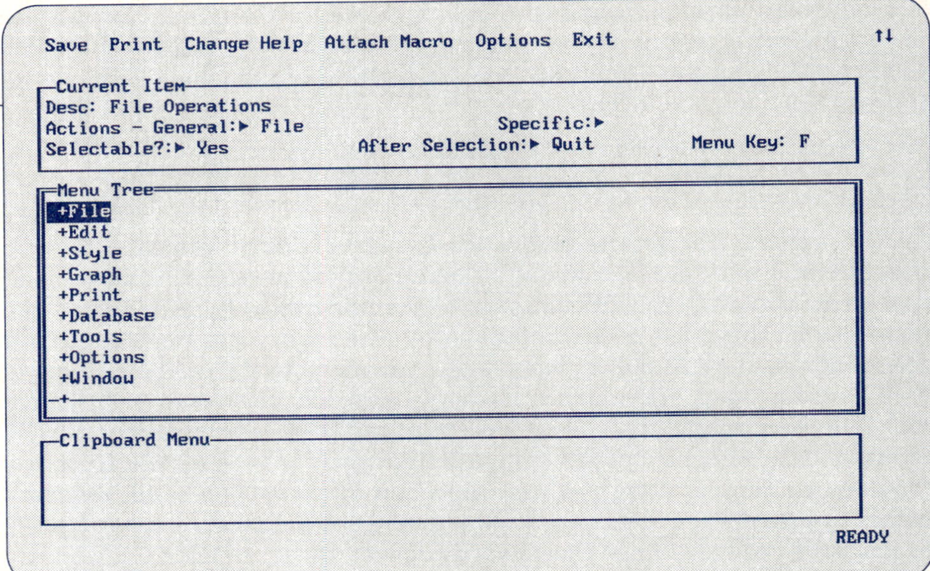

FIGURE 6-2

Modifying the current menu

Start with the highlight on the File command:

Press + (on numeric keypad)	Displays the File submenu
Press (→)	Moves highlight to New
Press (↓)	Moves highlight to Open
Press (↓)	Moves highlight to Retrieve
Press (↑) twice	Moves highlight back to New
Press (←)	Moves highlight back to File
Press – (on numeric keypad)	Hides submenu again

You can also edit the menu.

- To insert a new command below the current (highlighted) command, press (↵) to create a blank line and type the name of the new command on that line. You can then define its characteristics using the Current Item pane.
- To insert a new command in a submenu, press (↵) to create a blank line and (TAB) to indent the item before typing the name and defining its characteristics.
- To delete a command, position the highlight on it and press (DEL). This places the command in the clipboard.
- To insert the most recently deleted command from the clipboard above the current (highlighted) command, press (INS).

Combining the last two editing techniques makes it possible to "cut-and-paste" to create a new menu structure, as you will see later in this section.

The (F6) key is used to move the highlight among the three panes. If nothing is in the clipboard, (F6) moves between the top two panes only.

Press (F6)	Moves the highlight to the top pane

The top pane is used to describe and change the name and function of commands. For instance, if you are creating a new menu command such as Save/Get, you would use the top part of the screen to explain how this command works. Following is a description of the items in the top part of the screen. Note that all of these items can be altered.

Desc	Description of what the command does.
Actions – General	General type of action that takes place when the command is chosen.
Specific	Specific action that takes place when this command is chosen.
Selectable?	Specifies whether or not the item can be selected from the menu. A few items are for display only.
After Selection	Tells Quattro Pro what to do when the command is selected. The three options are: **Stay** (on the current item); **Go to Parent** (menu); and **Quit** (the menus).
Menu Key	Key to press to choose the command.

You can change any of these items by locating the highlight on the item and editing the entry.

Adding a New Command

In this section you will create a menu command called Save/Get. This command will be displayed as an option on the main menu and will allow you to save and retrieve worksheets in the same way as the File command. When you change the menu structure, you can work only with existing commands. Thus, this new menu item (Save/Get) is just a more convenient way of organizing the /File¦Save and the /File¦Retrieve commands.

Press (F6)	Moves the highlight to the Menu Tree pane

Move to the top of the menu if you are not there already.

Press (↵)	Inserts a blank line beneath File
Type Save/Get (↵)	Inserts Save/Get into current menu

An error message appears, warning that the first letter of this menu item, S, is already in use on the main menu. You will have to choose another letter to select this command, by editing the Current Item pane.

Press (ESC)	Removes error message
Press (F6)	Moves the highlight to the Desc section of the Current Item pane

Type Save and Retrieve Spreadsheet ↵ — Enters description of menu item

Press ↓ **4 times**	Moves highlight to After Selection?
Press ↵	Selects After Selection?

This brings up a window with three choices:

```
Stay
Quit
Go to Parent
```

Press Q	Specifies Quit
Press →	Moves highlight to Menu Key
Type A	Selects A as menu key
Press F6	Moves back to Current Menu pane

Having defined the main menu item, you will cut-and-paste to move the Save and Retrieve commands from the File menu to the Save/Get menu and change the name of the Retrieve command to Get.

Press ↑	Highlights File
Type + (numeric keypad)	Displays child menu
Press → **and then** ↓ **4 times**	Highlights Save
Press DEL	Deletes Save from File menu and places it in the clipboard
Press ↑ **4 times, then** ← ↓	Highlights Save/Get
Press ↵ TAB	Positions highlight to insert a submenu item

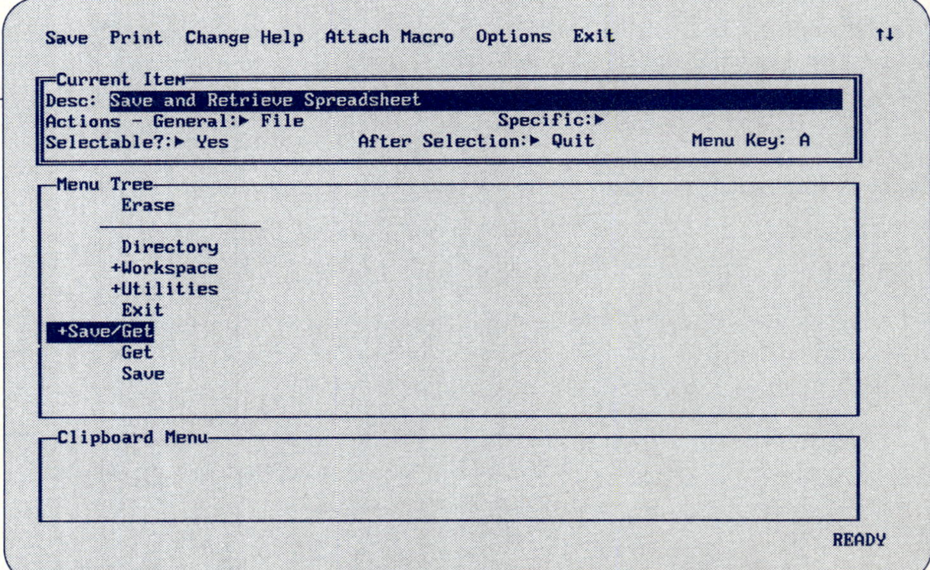

FIGURE 6-3

Creating a new menu item

Press (INS)	Inserts Save into the child menu of Save/Get
Press (←) (↑) (→) (↓) (↓)	Highlights Retrieve
Press (DEL)	Deletes Retrieve from File menu and places it in the clipboard
Press (↑) (↑) (←) (↓) (→)	Highlights Save
Press (INS)	Inserts Retrieve above Save
Press (F2)	Enters Edit mode
Press (BACKSPACE) **8 times**	Deletes Retrieve
Type Get (↵)	Changes name of item to Get
Press (↓) **twice**	Places highlight on blank line
Press (F6)	Moves highlight to top pane
Press (←)	Highlights After Selection?
Press (↵) Q	Selects Quit
Press (←) **4 times**	Highlights Desc
Type Return to Spreadsheet (↵)	Enters description

The new current menu and submenu are completed (Figure 6-3).

Saving a New Menu

When a change is made in the menu structure, it must be saved before it becomes effective. The new menu is saved in a file with the extension .MU and can be chosen using the /Options¦Startup¦Menu Tree command. To save the menu, use the pull-down menu items at the top of the screen. These menu items are activated by pressing /. The choices are:

Save	Stores changes in a new menu tree file with the extension .MU.
Print	Prints the menu tree file.
Change Help	Changes the Help message for an item.
Attach Macro	Attaches a macro to a menu item.
Options	Changes how menus are displayed.
Exit	Returns to spreadsheet.

To save the new menu you just created:

Press / S	Selects Save
Press (ESC)	Moves cursor to C:\QPRO\ prompt
Type SAVEGET (↵)	Saves the menu tree in a file called SAVEGET.MU (Quattro Pro automatically adds the .MU extension)

This may take a few minutes. When the process is complete:

Press / X	Selects Exit

In a few moments, you are returned to the worksheet.

Using a New Menu

To select the new menu, you must use /Options¦Startup¦Menu Tree.

Press / O S M — Selects Menu Tree from the /Options¦Startup menu

A window appears with the Menu Tree options. Save/Get should be one of the options (the number of menu options may vary).

Move the highlight to SAVEGET and press ↵ — Selects Save/Get as the menu tree

After a few minutes, the new menu is loaded. Notice the new command—Save/Get—with the *a* highlighted.

Press / a — Selects Save/Get

Try out the new submenu

By choosing either command you can save or retrieve a worksheet. Notice, though, that the new menu will not be set up to accept CTRL key shortcuts. To return to the original menu, use /Options¦Startup¦Menu Tree and choose QUATTRO as the menu tree option.

Press ESC **until you return to the worksheet**

Press / O S M — Brings up choice of menu trees

Move highlight to QUATTRO and press ↵ — Loads the QUATTRO menu

In a few moments, the original menu tree is displayed. To save the new menu so it is automatically loaded whenever you start Quattro Pro, first use /Options¦Startup¦Menu Tree and choose SAVEGET, then use /Options¦Update to make it the default menu. Be sure to check with your instructor or lab assistant *before* doing this in a computer lab.

Using the Lotus 1-2-3 Menu Tree

Lotus 1-2-3 is a well-known and widely used spreadsheet. If you are familiar with Lotus, you can take advantage of the Lotus alternative menu available in Quattro Pro. To load this menu, select /Options¦Startup¦Menu Tree, and choose 123 by placing the highlight on it and pressing ↵. In a few minutes, the Lotus menu tree is loaded. To reset the Quattro Pro menu structure, you have to exit and then reload the program. This completes the section on changing the menu structure.

UNDO

The Undo feature, on the /Options¦Other menu, allows you to undo any action you have just performed in Quattro Pro by pressing /Edit¦Undo, or ALT-F5. Before you can use this feature, Quattro Pro must be customized so Undo is enabled. To do this, choose /Options¦Other¦Undo and select Enable.

Press / O O — Brings up /Options¦Other menu

Press U — Selects Undo

A window appears with the choices:

```
Enable
Disable
```

Press E — Selects Enable

To see how this works, you will delete a row containing data and use (ALT)-(F5) to get it back. First, enter the following data (start at A1):

Type PRINTER (→)	Enters PRINTER and moves cell selector to B1
Type COST (↓) (←)	Enters COST and moves cell selector to A2
Type Canon (→)	Enters Canon and moves cell selector to B2
Type 349 (↓) (←)	Enters 349 and moves cell selector to A3
Type Diconix (→)	Enters Diconix and moves cell selector to B3
Type 369 (↓) (←)	Enters 369 and moves cell selector to A4
Type Panasonic (→)	Enters Panasonic and moves cell selector to B4
Type 335 (↓) (←)	Enters 335 and moves cell selector to A5
Type TOTAL: (→)	Enters TOTAL: and moves cell selector to B5
Enter @SUM(B1.B3) (↵)	Enters formula

Imagine that you now decide to erase this data.

Press / E E (or (CTRL)-E)	Selects /Edit¦Erase
Enter A1.B5 (↵)	Enters block to erase

Oops! You have just realized that was your only copy of those prices. Fortunately, you can select /Edit¦Undo, or press (ALT)-(F5), to undo that last erase.

Press / E U (or (ALT)-(F5)) — Selects /Edit¦Undo and retrieves the erased data

/Edit¦Undo only undoes your most recent action. To undo a more complicated series of steps, choose /Tools¦Macro¦Transcript.

TRANSCRIPT

As you spend more and more time using computers, you run the risk of accidentally losing your work. A power failure can shut down your computer in the middle of a session, or you can inadvertently erase your spreadsheet or quit the program without saving your work. Whatever the cause, time and effort have been wasted, and you must begin again from scratch. Also, in complicated worksheets, you may not realize right away that you have made a mistake or erased essential data. Once you have realized it, you may not be able to correct the problem without losing all the work you did subsequently.

For these reasons, Quattro Pro provides a feature called Transcript on the /Tools¦Macro menu. Transcript records every keystroke you make. Using Transcript makes it possible for you to re-create a worksheet that you lost through a power failure or a mistake. You can even re-create it up to a certain point, leave out or correct the mistaken command, and continue to rebuild the worksheet. Transcript can also be used to record keystrokes, sections of which can be used to create macros. In fact, Transcript records keystrokes in the same way as the /Tools¦Macro¦Record command does.

The steps for using Transcript are to choose it from the /Tools¦Macro menu and then run it to view, edit, or replay keystrokes. In the following example, you will use Transcript to record a sequence of keystrokes used to develop a worksheet. Then you will exit Quattro Pro without saving the spreadsheet and use Transcript to re-create it.

Before continuing, quit and reload Quattro Pro.

Press / F X (or CTRL-X)	Selects /File¦Exit
Press Y	Exits Quattro Pro

NOTE: Transcript saves keystrokes in a file called QUATTRO.LOG. Depending on how your computer is set up, you may find it helpful to use the DOS Del command to delete QUATTRO.LOG before beginning the next section.

Load Quattro Pro

Complete the following steps very carefully. Because Transcript keeps track of each of your keystrokes, if your keystrokes differ from those listed in the following section, Transcript's record will differ accordingly.

Press CAPS LOCK (if needed)	Turns on uppercase mode
Type NAME ↓	Enters NAME in A1 and moves cell selector to A2
Type JUDY ↓	Enters JUDY in A2 and moves cell selector to A3
Type BOB ↓	Enters BOB in A3 and moves cell selector to A4
Type LIU ↓	Enters LIU in A4 and moves cell selector to A5
Type BROCK → **and then** ↑ **4 times**	Enters BROCK in A5 and moves cell selector to B1
Type SALARY ↓	Enters SALARY in B1 and moves cell selector to B2
Type 2311 ↓	Enters 2311 in B2 and moves cell selector to B3
Type 2314 ↓	Enters 2314 in B3 and moves cell selector to B4
Type 2482 ↓	Enters 2482 in B4 and moves cell selector to B5
Type 2434 ↓	Enters 2434 in B5 and moves cell selector to B6

At this point, assume the user exits Quattro Pro without saving the spreadsheet (a power failure would have the same effect).

Press / F X (or CTRL-X)	Selects /File¦Exit
Press Y	Exits Quattro Pro and erases spreadsheet

Without Transcript, the data in the spreadsheet would now be lost. First, reload Quattro Pro.

Load Quattro Pro

To use Transcript to recover the spreadsheet, select it from the /Tools¦Macro menu.

Press / T M T	Selects /Tools¦Macro¦Transcript

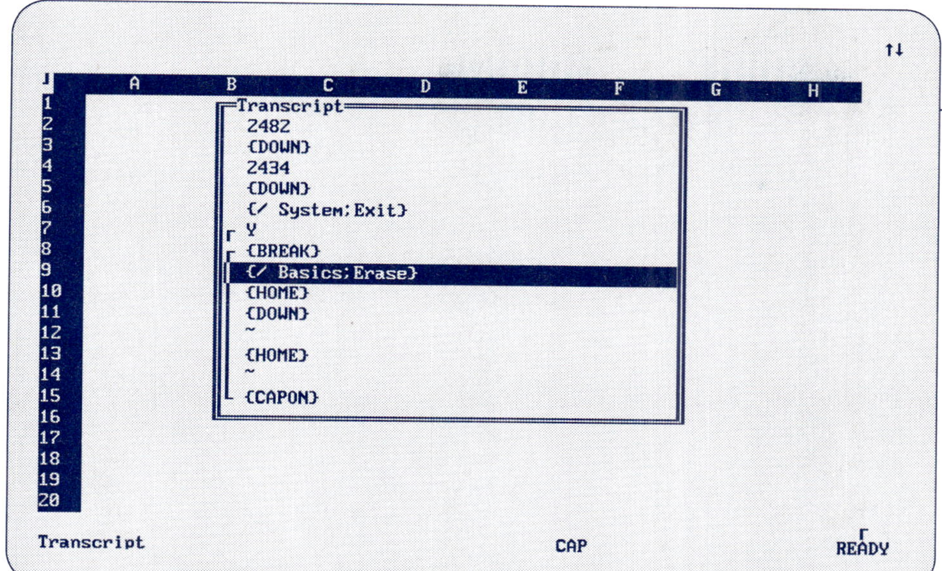

FIGURE 6-4

Transcript—command history

Figure 6-4 shows the window that displays the command history of the worksheet. This window displays the keystroke sequence and allows you to view each step. The lines

```
{/ Basics;Erase}
{HOME}
```

are automatically placed in the command history whenever you begin a worksheet. These lines clear the worksheet and place the cell selector at A1. They also signify the starting point of the keystrokes that created the worksheet. To edit or re-create the worksheet, use the Edit History menu.

Press / Brings up the Edit History menu

Figure 6-5 shows the Edit History menu. It contains the following options:

Undo Last Command Plays back the command history from the last time a worksheet was saved, retrieved, or erased to the command immediately preceding the last command. This is useful if your last command was a major mistake that you want to undo.

Restore To Here Plays back the command history from the last time a worksheet was saved, retrieved, or erased to the end of the line highlighted in the command history window. This allows you to re-create the first part of a worksheet.

Playback Block Plays back the block of actions marked off in the command history window. This allows you to re-create selected parts of a worksheet.

Copy Block Copies a block of the command history into a worksheet for use as a macro.

FIGURE 6-5

Pop-up Transcript menu

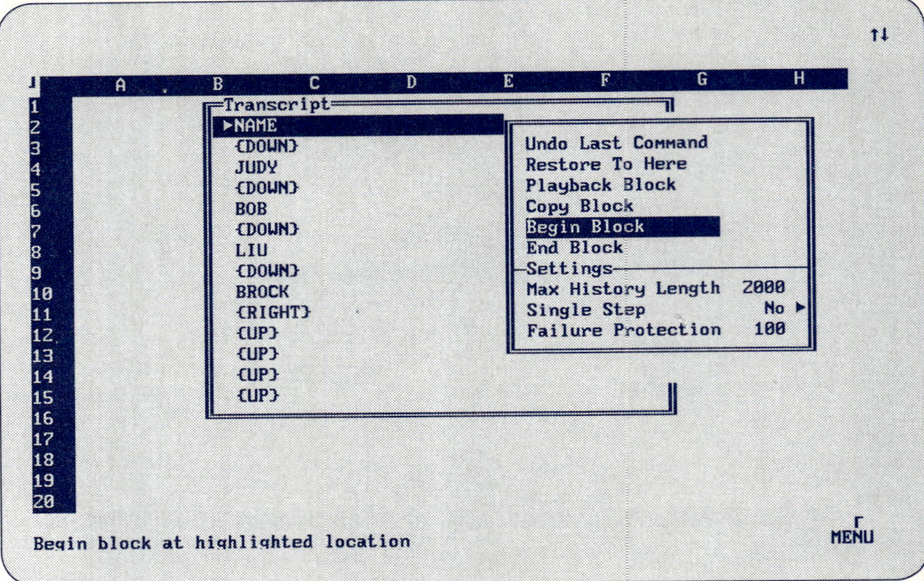

Begin Block	Marks the beginning of a block of actions to be played back or copied to a worksheet.
End Block	Marks the end of a block of actions.
Max History Length	Specifies how large the Transcript file can be before it is saved in a backup file.
Single Step	Replays actions one keystroke or command at a time. This is useful for finding errors in a worksheet.
Failure Protection	Specifies how often your actions are saved. The default is 100 (that is, actions are saved 100 at a time). If you enter 1, each action is saved immediately. However, this would severely slow the process of creating a worksheet.

Use Begin Block, End Block, and Playback Block to re-create the worksheet. First, move the highlight to the NAME line and bring up the Edit History menu to specify Begin Block. Then move the highlight to the line containing the last keystroke ({Down} after 2434), bring up the Edit History menu again, and specify End Block. Finally, select Playback Block to execute the lines within the designated block.

Press (ESC)	Returns to Command History
Press (PGUP) **twice and then** (↑) **5 times**	Moves highlight to NAME line
Press /	Brings up Edit History menu
Press B	Selects Begin Block

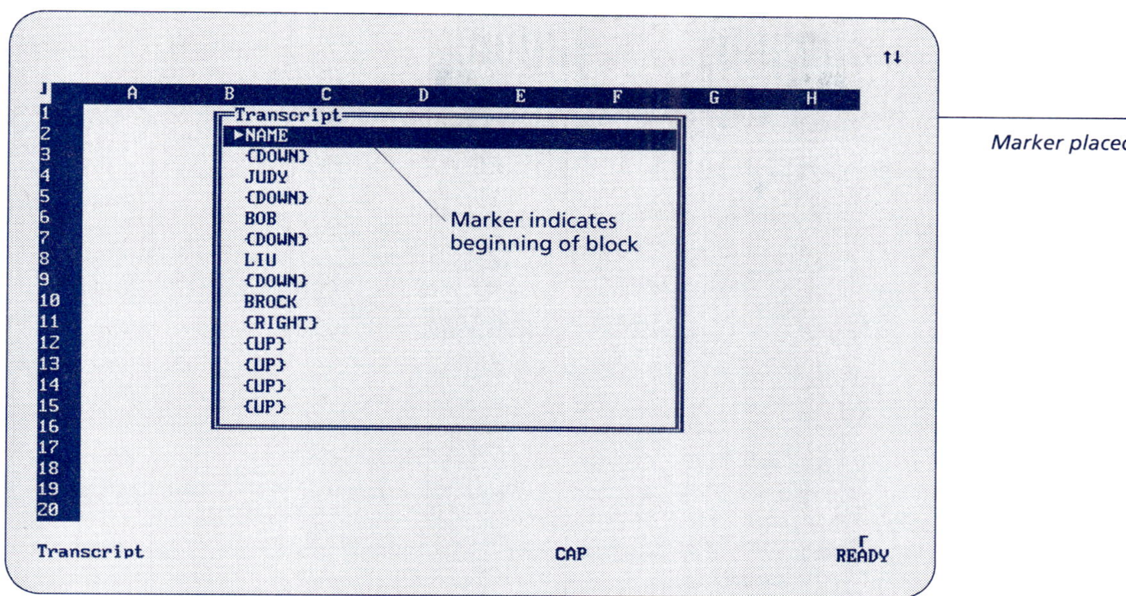

FIGURE 6-6

Marker placed by NAME entry

Figure 6-6 shows how a marker has been placed at the NAME line.

Press (PGDN) **and then** ⓓ **9 times**	Highlights {Down} below 2434 line
Press / E	Specifies End Block

All of the lines within the block are now marked.

Press / P	Specifies Playback Block

Transcript executes the blocked area of the command history and rebuilds the spreadsheet.

Although these steps are useful in re-creating part or all of a worksheet, the other options are helpful in finding and correcting mistakes. For instance, if you accidentally used the /Graph¦Customize Series¦Reset command and lost all graph settings, you could use the Undo Last Command option to re-create the graph except for the last action (/Graph¦Customize Series¦Reset). Or you could use the Single Step feature to execute one action at a time in order to locate a mistake in the spreadsheet. The Copy Block option is useful if you want to insert part or all of the Transcript record into a worksheet as a macro. Do this now by selecting the names only as a macro.

Press / T M T	Brings up command history
Press (PGUP) **twice and then** ⓤ **5 times**	Moves highlight to NAME
Press / B	Selects Begin Block
Press ⓓ **9 times**	Moves highlight to {Right} after BROCK
Press / E	Selects End Block
Press / C	Selects Copy Block

The prompt is:

Enter name of macro to create/modify:

Type NAMES (↵) Enters macro name

The prompt is:

Enter macro block to paste: B6..B6

Type G1 (↵) Specifies G1 as the location to paste the macro, and the macro is inserted in the worksheet

You can execute this macro at any time. This ends the section on Transcript.

DEBUG MODE

Quattro Pro provides a feature, Debug, that allows you to find and correct errors in macros. This feature is especially useful when working with long and complex macros. To enter Debug mode, press (SHIFT)-(F2), or select /Tools¦Macro¦Debugger¦Yes. Then select Execute from the /Tools¦Macro menu and enter the block where the macro is located. A window appears on the screen that shows each macro command as it is executed. You can step through the macro one command at a time, and you can also have trace cells displayed that show how each macro command affects the contents of a specified cell.

In addition, Debug lets you set breakpoints within macros. When the macro encounters a breakpoint, it stops execution. When you press the spacebar or (↵), execution begins again. Breakpoints allow you to quickly execute a macro to a point where a problem may exist, correct the problem, and then quickly execute the rest of the macro.

To illustrate, you will retrieve a file called PRODSALE; using Debug, you will then find and correct the error in the macro used with this worksheet. The PRODSALE worksheet has a sales report template (Figure 6-7a) and a data entry macro (Figure 6-7b). The macro prompts the user for input, using GetLabel and GetNumber commands, and repeats the process if more than one product is to be listed. Let's assume that after setting up this template and executing the macro, you notice that the grand total amount is incorrect. You will then use Debug to locate and correct the error in the macro. Before starting, notice that the macro, \R, is in cells I1 through I12 and that the grand total is in F16. You will designate F16 as the **trace cell**: As you use Debug, this cell will be constantly displayed to show changes as they occur after each data item is entered. After each week's sales are entered, the grand total will be updated. Start by retrieving the PRODSALE worksheet from your data disk.

Retrieve PRODSALE

Press (SHIFT)-(F2) Begins Debug mode, and the word DEBUG appears in the status line

You could also have pressed /Tools¦Macro¦Debugger¦Yes.

Press (ALT)-(F2) E Selects Execute from the Macro menu

You could also have pressed /Tools¦Macro¦Execute. The prompt is:

Enter block of macros to execute:

Enter I1.I12 ↵ Enters block with macros

A window appears, divided into two panes (Figure 6-8). The top pane is the Debug Window, which shows the macro commands line by line. The highlighted line will be executed when the spacebar is pressed. The bottom

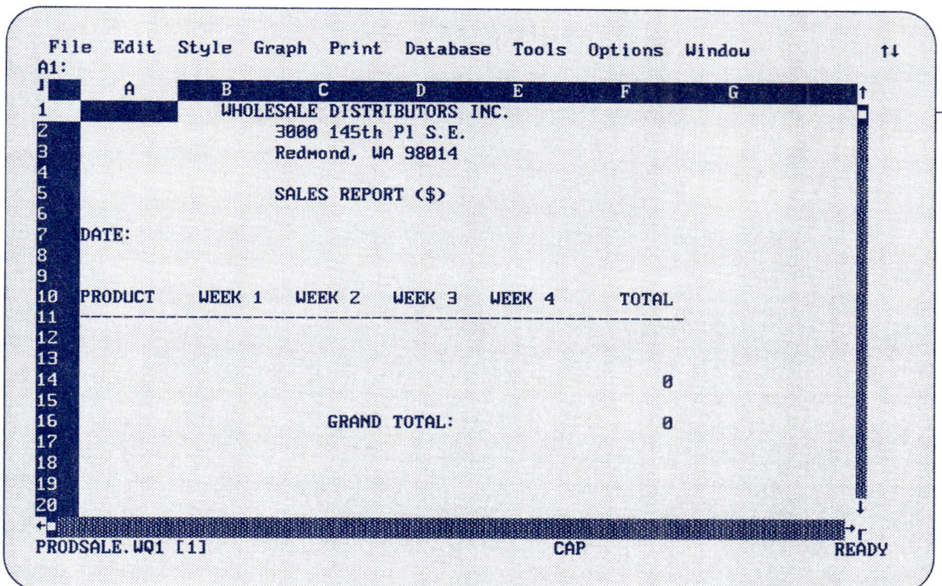

FIGURE 6-7a

PRODSALE worksheet

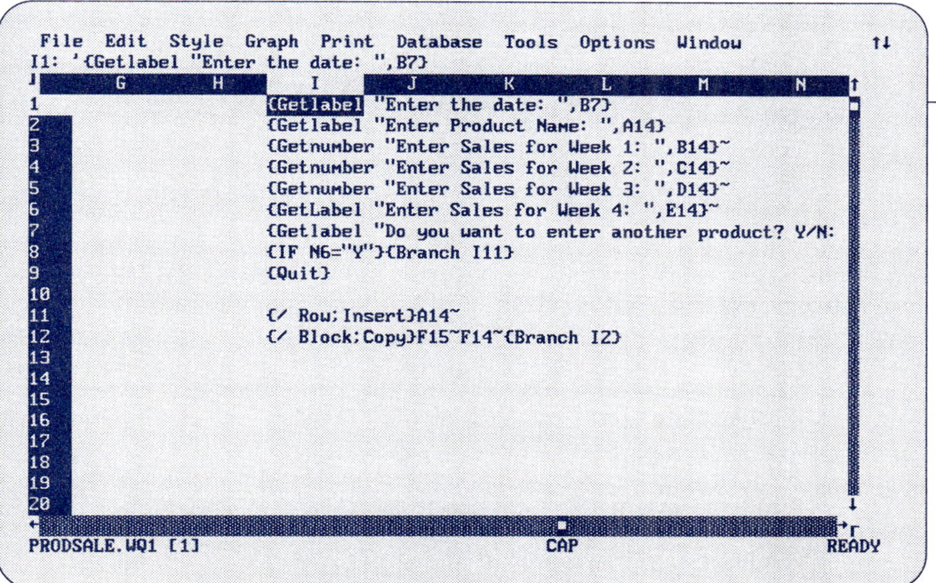

FIGURE 6-7b

Macro commands in PRODSALE worksheet

pane is the Trace Window. It contains trace cells, the cells you wish to view while the macro is executed. To set a trace cell, press / to bring up the Debug menu.

Press /	Brings up Debug menu

The Debug menu appears with the following options.

Breakpoints	Allows you to specify a point at which the execution of the macro will be suspended.
Conditional	Allows you to specify a condition that, if true, suspends the operation of the macro.
Trace Cells	Allows you to monitor the contents of a cell or cells as a macro is being executed.
Abort	Stops the execution of the macro and returns you to the spreadsheet.
Edit a Cell	Allows you to make changes to the macro being debugged.
Reset	Removes Breakpoints, Conditional, and Trace Cells commands.
Quit	Exits the Debug menu and completes the execution of the macro.

Press T	Selects Trace Cells
Press 1	Selects 1st trace cell
Type F16 ↵	Specifies F16 as the trace cell
Press Q Q	Exits Debug menu

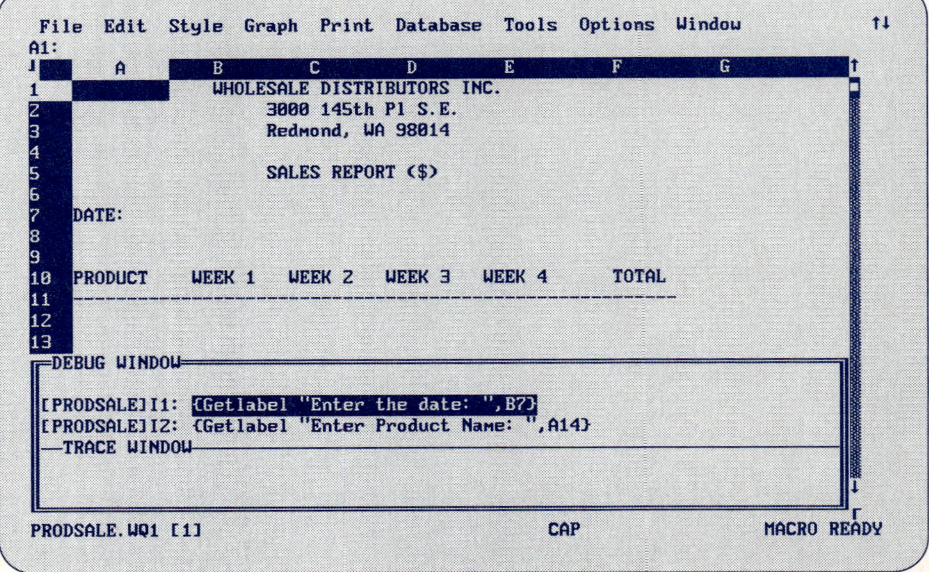

FIGURE 6-8

Debug and Trace windows

Now start the debugging process by using the spacebar to step through the macro one command at a time.

Press spacebar	Executes the first macro command

Figure 6-9 shows the execution of the first macro command. The command is located in cell I1 and reads:

```
{Getlabel "Enter the date: ",B7}
```

The prompt at the top of the screen is "Enter the date:".

Type the current date ↵	The next macro line is highlighted
Press spacebar	Enters the current date into cell B7 and highlights the next macro line

The prompt is:

```
Enter Product Name:
```

Type NEC5200 ↵	The next macro line is highlighted
Press spacebar	Enters product name and executes next macro line

The prompt is:

```
Enter Sales for Week 1:
```

Type 200 ↵	Enters 200 as sales for week 1
Press spacebar	The trace cell reflects the sales entry of 200

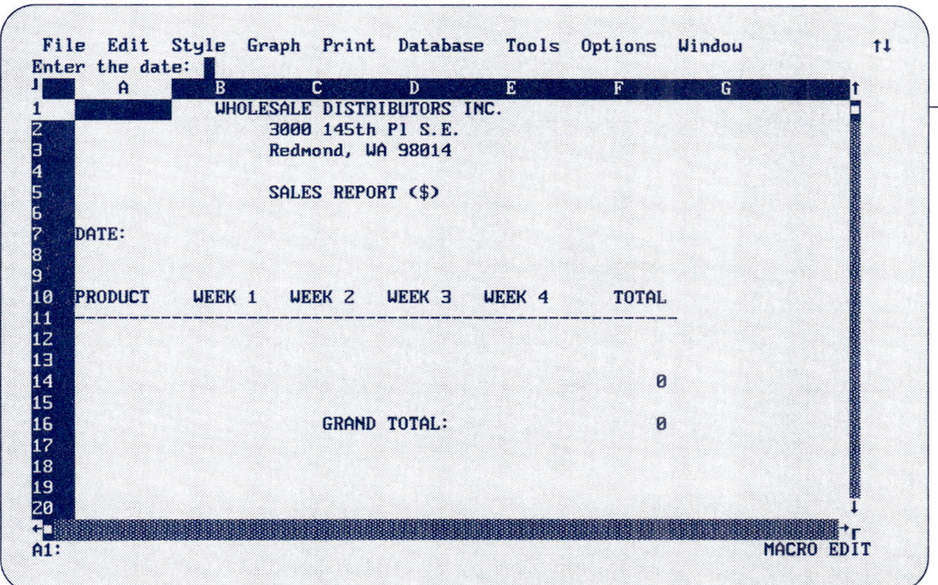

FIGURE 6-9

Debugging a macro

Press spacebar	Executes next macro command

The prompt is:

`Enter Sales for Week 2:`

Type 150 (↵)	Enters 150 as sales for week 2
Press spacebar	The trace cell now shows 350, the cumulative sales total
Press spacebar	Executes next macro command

The prompt is:

`Enter Sales for Week 3:`

Type 100 (↵)	Enters 100 as sales for week 3
Press spacebar	Again, the trace cell is updated to reflect the correct total (450)
Press spacebar	Executes next macro command

The prompt is:

`Enter Sales for Week 4:`

Type 200 (↵)	Enters 200 as sales for week 4
Press spacebar	

Notice that the amount in the trace cell has not changed. It should be 650 but remains at 450. Look at the Debug Window and notice that the macro command for week 4 sales is:

```
{Getlabel "Enter Sales for Week 4: ",E14}~
```

The wrong command (GetLabel) was used. The sales amount, 200, was entered as a label, not as a value, and therefore was not included in the total. Use the Edit a Cell option of the Debug menu to correct this macro command.

Press /	Brings up the Debug menu
Press E	Selects Edit a Cell
Type I6 (↵)	Displays the contents of cell I6 at the top of the screen

The cell contents are already in Edit mode on the input line, so you can use arrow keys, (DEL), and (BACKSPACE) to change the word Getlabel to Getnumber. When you are finished:

Press (↵)	Enters the corrected macro command
Press (ESC)	Returns to debug process
Press spacebar	Executes the next macro command

The prompt is:

`Do you want to enter another product? Y/N:`

Type N (↵)	Specifies no

Press spacebar twice Returns to worksheet

The incorrect worksheet appears in full view. Now you can repeat the process with the edited macro. Before continuing, turn off Debug:

Press SHIFT-F2 Turns off Debug. You could also have selected /Tools¦Macro¦Debugger¦No

Press ALT-R Begins the execution of the macro

Continue by entering the date and sales amounts as specified earlier.

This completes the section on Debug mode. This feature is especially useful in finding and correcting errors in long and complex macros.

WYSIWYG (WHAT YOU SEE IS WHAT YOU GET)

If you have Quattro Pro 3.0 and an EGA or VGA board capable of 640×350 resolution, you can display spreadsheets in WYSIWYG mode. What-you-see-is-what-you-get (WYSIWYG) mode gets its name from the fact that any changes you make that affect the way a spreadsheet is printed appear on the screen without your having to use /Print¦Destination¦Screen Preview. Any font changes, for example, are shown on the actual spreadsheet. To choose WYSIWYG mode, select /Options¦Display Mode¦WYSIWYG.

USING A MOUSE

If you have a mouse, you can use it to choose Quattro Pro commands and define blocks more quickly than by using just the keyboard. Quattro Pro automatically detects whether or not you have a mouse. If you do, a pointer appears on the screen, and on the right side of the screen you will see the **mouse palette**. By positioning the pointer on items in the mouse palette and clicking (quickly pressing and releasing the left mouse button), you can duplicate many keyboard features. Refer to Figure 6-10 when going through the following list (starting from the top):

?	Click on this for Help instead of pressing F1.
▲◀▶▼	Click on these arrows instead of pressing END plus arrow keys to move to the end of an area in the given direction.
Esc	Click on this instead of pressing ESC.
↵	Click on this instead of pressing ↵.
Del	Click on this instead of pressing DEL.
@	Click on this instead of pressing ALT-F3 to bring up the function menu.

You can also use a mouse to choose menu commands by simply positioning the pointer on the command and clicking. For any command that presents you with a box with both Enter and Cancel, you can use the mouse to click on the proper choice. Finally, you can use the mouse to point out blocks. To point out a single cell, position the pointer on that cell and click. To point out a multiple-cell block, first position the pointer on the first cell in that block. Then, hold down the mouse button while moving the pointer to the last cell in the block. When the pointer reaches the last cell, release the mouse button. (Moving the

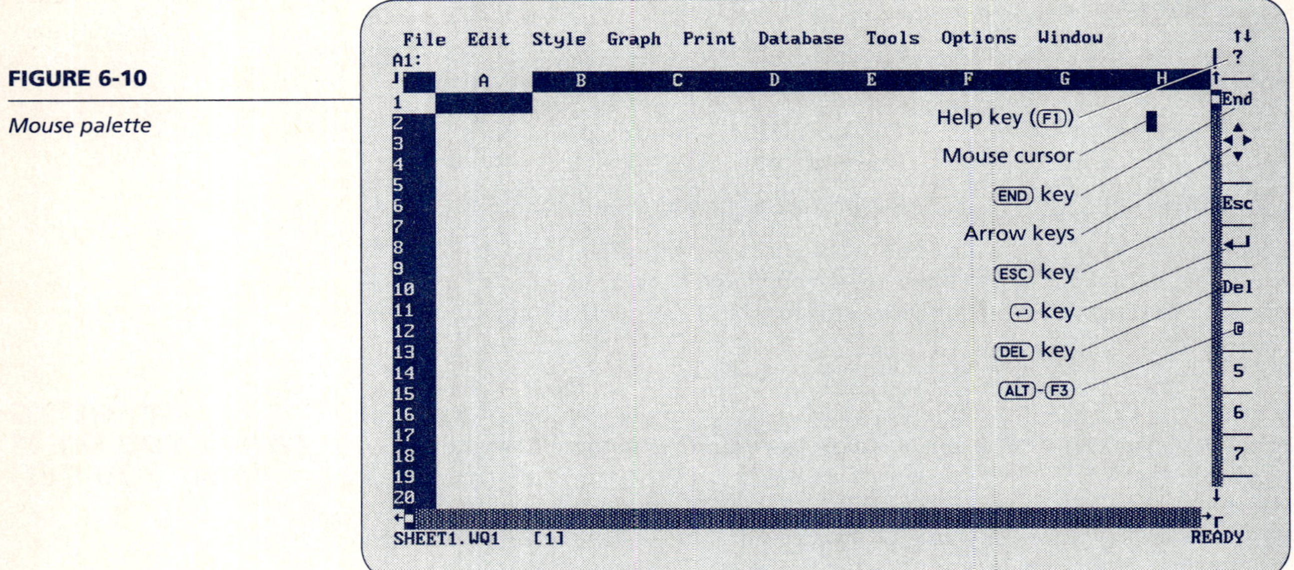

FIGURE 6-10

Mouse palette

pointer while holding down the mouse button in this way is called **dragging**.) If the block includes more than one row or column, point it out by dragging the mouse from the cell in one corner diagonally across to the other corner.

You will also find it easier to use a mouse with the Annotating Graph screen. You can select a tool to work with by clicking on it with the mouse. You can also move elements by dragging them with the mouse, instead of using the arrow keys on the keyboard.

SUMMARY

Having completed this chapter, you know how to customize Quattro Pro. You can change default values, menu commands, and the menu structure to tailor the program to your individual needs. You are also able to use Undo, Transcript, and Debug to help find and correct errors in worksheets and macros and to prevent the accidental loss of your work.

WORD LIST

breakpoint
child menu
Clipboard menu
Debug mode
default values
dragging
Lotus 1-2-3 menu
Menu Tree
mouse palette
trace cell
Transcript
Undo
WYSIWYG

QUESTIONS

1. What is a default value (specify three examples in your answer)?
2. Why would you want to change a default value?
3. What is the advantage of a mouse?
4. What is the value of Undo? When would it be especially useful?
5. What is the value of Transcript? When would it be especially useful?
6. Why is Debug useful?
7. How is the Edit Menus screen organized?
8. Why would you change the menu structure?
9. What is Lotus 1-2-3, and why would Quattro Pro provide a menu tree for it?

Appendix

CELL SELECTOR MOVEMENT KEYS

Keys	Movement
(↑) (←) (↓) (→)	On the right side of the keyboard are the arrow keys that move the cell selector up or down one row at a time and left or right one column at a time. Thus, if the cell selector is located at cell B8, pressing (↓) once moves the cell selector to B9. Then pressing (→) once moves the pointer to cell C9.
(HOME)	Moves the cell selector to A1.
(END)	Always used with another direction key as described below.
(END) (HOME)	Moves to the lower right of the nonblank part of the spreadsheet.
(END)-(↑)	If current cell has an entry, moves up to the next nonblank cell beneath an empty one. If current cell is empty, moves up to the next nonblank cell.
(END)-(↓)	If current cell has an entry, moves down to the next nonblank cell beneath an empty one. If current cell is empty, moves down to the next nonblank cell.
(END)-(→)	If current cell has an entry, moves right to the next nonblank cell followed by an empty one. If current cell is blank, moves right to the next nonblank cell.
(END)-(←)	If current cell has an entry, moves left to the next nonblank cell followed by an empty one. If current cell is blank, moves left to the next nonblank cell.
(CTRL)-(←) or (SHIFT)-(TAB)	Moves the cell selector left one screen.
(CTRL)-(→) or (TAB)	Moves the cell selector right one screen.
(PGUP) (PGDN)	These two keys move the cell selector up or down one screen (20 rows).
(F5)	This function key allows you to go to any cell in the worksheet. When you press (F5), a prompt appears at the top of the screen asking you to specify a cell address. When you type the cell address and press (↵), the cell selector quickly moves to that cell. This is referred to as the GoTo key.

DOS COMMAND SUMMARY

This Command Summary lists the DOS commands discussed in the book. For additional commands and functions, refer to the DOS manual.

Command	Description
CD	Change to a new directory
COPY	Copy a file from one disk or directory to another
DATE	Change or confirm the date in the computer's main memory
DEL	Delete a file from a disk or directory
DIR	List files on a disk or in a directory
DISKCOPY	Copy the entire contents of a disk to another disk
FORMAT	Prepare a disk for use
PROMPT PG	Display the current directory at the prompt
TIME	Change or confirm the time in the computer's main memory

QUATTRO PRO COMMAND SUMMARY

This Command Summary lists the commands discussed in the book. Functions are listed separately. Commands available only in Quattro Pro version 3.0 are designated ***(v. 3.0)***. For additional commands, refer to the Quattro Pro manual.

File Commands

Command	Description
/File¦Open	Opens an existing spreadsheet without replacing the currently displayed spreadsheet
/File¦Retrieve	Opens an existing spreadsheet and replaces the currently displayed spreadsheet
/File¦Save	Saves the current spreadsheet
/File¦Close	Closes the current spreadsheet
/File¦Close All	Closes all open spreadsheets
/File¦Erase	Removes the current spreadsheet from the computer's main memory
/File¦Exit	Exits Quattro Pro

Edit Commands

Command	Description
/Edit¦Copy	Copies the contents of a cell block to another part of the spreadsheet
/Edit¦Move	Moves the contents of a cell block to another part of the spreadsheet
/Edit¦Erase Block	Erases the contents of a cell block
/Edit¦Undo	Reverses the most recent command ***NOTE:*** /Options¦Other¦Undo must be set to Enable
/Edit¦Insert	Inserts a specified row or column
/Edit¦Delete	Deletes a specified row or column
/Edit¦Names¦Create	Gives a block a specific name, which can be used instead of cell addresses in commands and functions
/Edit¦Fill	Fills a cell block with a specified sequence of numbers

Style Commands

Command	Description
/Style¦Alignment	Sets the alignment of the contents of a block
/Style¦Numeric Format	Sets the numeric format of the content of a block
/Style¦Protection	Disables/enables protection of a block of cells; usually used to remove protection from specific cells if the /Options¦Protection command has been set to protect the spreadsheet
/Style¦Column Width	Sets the width of columns
/Style¦Reset Width	Returns column to its default width
/Style¦Hide Column	Hides columns from view; also restores hidden columns to view
/Style¦Block Width	Sets the width of each column in a block
/Style¦Line Drawing	Draws single and double lines and boxes around blocks
/Style¦Font	Sets the font for the contents of cells
/Style¦Insert Break	Inserts a page-break symbol above the current row; used to divide spreadsheets into pages during printing

Graph Commands

Command	Description
/Graph¦Type	Chooses the type of graph to display; types include bar, pie, rotated pie, x-y, and three-dimensional
/Graph¦Series	Specifies blocks to use for x and y series
/Graph¦Text	Adds text to graphs in the form of titles and legends
/Graph¦Customize Series	Customizes series in a variety of ways: changes marker symbols and fill patterns, designates legend titles and position, explodes pie slices, and resets series
/Graph¦Overall¦Grid	Removes grid lines from the graph
/Graph¦Name¦Create	Saves a graph with a name
/Graph¦Name¦Autosave Edits¦On *(v. 3.0)*	Automatically saves changes to a named graph
/Graph¦View	Displays current graph on the monitor
/Graph¦Fast Graph	Displays graph created from the selected block of data
/Graph¦Annotate	Enters Graph Annotator
/Graph¦Quit	Returns to spreadsheet

Print Commands

Command	Description
/Print¦Block	Specifies block to print
/Print¦Headings	Specifies block to use as top heading or left heading
/Print¦Destination	Specifies whether to print spreadsheet on a printer, save it to a disk file, or preview it before printing
/Print¦Layout	Sets layout features, such as margins, page length, headings, footers, orientation, and printer setup commands
/Print¦Adjust Printer	Adjusts paper in printer
/Print¦Spreadsheet Print	Starts print process; the spreadsheet will be printed to whatever destination has been specified with /Print¦Destination
/Print¦Graph Print	Sets destination and layout for graphs
/Print¦Quit	Returns to spreadsheet

Database Commands

Command	Description
/Database ¦ Sort	Sorts the database according to one or more key fields
/Database ¦ Query	Sets up queries to search for or extract data according to specified criteria

Tools Commands

Command	Description
/Tools ¦ Import	Imports a text file from another program
/Tools ¦ Combine	Combines two blocks or spreadsheet files
/Tools ¦ Xtract	Extracts part of a spreadsheet and saves it as a separate file
/Tools ¦ Frequency	Sets up a frequency table for specified values
/Tools ¦ Solve For	Calculates a formula backwards, starting from the desired result and solving for a value that will produce that result

Macro Command	Description
/Tools ¦ Macro ¦ Record	Records keystrokes as a macro
/Tools ¦ Macro ¦ Paste	Saves the macro as part of a spreadsheet
/Tools ¦ Macro ¦ Transcript	Saves all keystrokes entered while in Quattro Pro; they can then be played back or copied as a macro
/Tools ¦ Macro ¦ Debugger	Debugs macros
/Tools ¦ Macro ¦ Name	Names and deletes macros
/Tools ¦ Macro ¦ Library	Designates spreadsheet as a macro library
/Tools ¦ Macro ¦ Execute	Executes a macro

Options Commands

Command	Description
/Options¦Display Mode¦WYSIWYG *(v. 3.0)*	Sets the monitor to display spreadsheets exactly as they will appear when they are printed out
/Options¦Startup	Sets the default directory and menu tree
/Options¦Startup¦Edit Menus	Enters Edit Menu screen, used to modify the menu tree
/Options¦Other¦Undo	Enable or disable /Edit¦Undo, which allows the most recent operation to be reversed
/Options¦Update	Stores changes as defaults
/Options¦Formats	Specifies format defaults for spreadsheets
/Options¦Recalculation¦Mode	Specifies whether recalculation of values should be automatic or manual
/Options¦Recalculation¦Circular Cell	Searches for circular cell references
/Options¦Protection	Enables or disables spreadsheet protection
/Options¦Quit	Returns to spreadsheet

Window Commands

Command	Description
/Window¦Tile	Displays all open windows on the screen
/Window¦Options	Specifies whether windows are to be horizontal or vertical, synchronized or not
/Window¦Options¦Locked Titles	Specifies rows and columns to lock into place while scrolling through spreadsheet

This is a *partial* list—see the Quattro Pro manual for complete list.

FUNCTIONS

Aggregation and Counting

Command	Description
@AVG(*block* **)**	Average of the block
@COUNT(*block* **)**	Number of nonblank cells in the block
@MAX(*block* **)**	Maximum value in the block
@MIN(*block* **)**	Minimum value in the block
@STD(*block* **)**	Standard deviation of all nonblank cells in the block
@SUM(*block* **)**	Sum of values in the block
@VAR(*block* **)**	Variance of all nonblank cells in the block

Financial

Command	Description
@CTERM(*int,fv,pv* **)**	Number of compounding periods
@DDB(*cost,salvage,life,period* **)**	Double declining depreciation allowance
@FV(*pmt,int,term* **)**	Future value of an annuity
@IRR(*guess,block* **)**	Internal rate of return
@NPV(*int,block* **)**	Present value of future cash flow
@PMT(*prin,int,term* **)**	Payment amount for a loan
@PV(*pmt,int,term* **)**	Present value of an annuity
@RATE(*fv,pv,term* **)**	Periodic interest rate
@SLN(*cost,salvage,life* **)**	Straight-line depreciation allowance
@SYD(*cost,salvage,life* **)**	Sum-of-the-year's-digits' depreciation allowance of an asset
@TERM(*pmt,int,fv* **)**	Number of payment periods of an investment

Miscellaneous

Command	Description
@HLOOKUP(*x,block,row* **)**	Horizontal lookup
@IF(*cond,x,y* **)**	*x* if condition is true, *y* if condition is false
@ROUND(*x,n* **)**	*x* rounded to the number of digits (*n*) specified
@TODAY	Current date
@VLOOKUP(*x,block,column* **)**	Vertical lookup

Database Functions

Command	Description
@DAVG(*block,column,criteria* **)**	Average values in column of block that meet criteria
@DCOUNT(*block,column,criteria* **)**	Number of values in column of block that meet criteria
@DMAX(*block,column,criteria* **)**	Maximum value in column of block that meets criteria
@DMIN(*block,column,criteria* **)**	Minimum value in column of block that meets criteria
@DSTD(*block,column,criteria* **)**	Standard deviation of values in column of block that meet criteria
@DSUM(*block,column,criteria* **)**	Sum of values in column of block that meet criteria
@DVAR(*block,column,criteria* **)**	Variance of values in column of block that meet criteria

MACRO COMMANDS

This is a *partial* list—see the Quattro Pro manual for complete list.

Command	Description
{?}	Pauses the macro and accepts input from the keyboard until ↵ is pressed
{Branch *location* **}**	Passes the execution to another macro at location
{GETLABEL *prompt, location* **}**	Pauses the macro, displays the prompt, and stores the keystrokes as a label in location
{GETNUMBER *prompt, location* **}**	Pauses the macro, displays the prompt, and stores the keystrokes as a value in location
{Quit}	Ends macro execution

Macro Key-Equivalent Commands

Keys	Macro Command
↵	{cr} or ~ (tilde)
BACKSPACE	{BACKSPACE} OR {BS}
ESC	{ESCAPE} or {ESC}
DEL	{DELETE} or {DEL}
INS	{INSERT} or {INS}
HOME	{HOME}
END	{END}
PGUP	{PGUP}
PGDN	{PGDN}
CTRL-→ or TAB	{BIGRIGHT}
CTRL-← or SHIFT-TAB	{BIGLEFT}
↑	{UP} or {U}
↓	{DOWN} or {D}
→	{RIGHT} or {R}
←	{LEFT} or {L}
CTRL-BACKSPACE	{CLEAR}
CTRL-D	{DATE}
F2	{EDIT}
F3	{NAMES}
ALT-F3	{FUNCTIONS}
SHIFT-F3	{MACROS}
F4	{ABS}
F5	{GOTO}
ALT-F5	{UNDO}
F6	{WINDOW}
F7	{QUERY}
SHIFT-F7	{MARK}
F9	{CALC}
F10	{GRAPH}

SHORTCUT KEYS

Keys	Function
ALT-O	/Window ¦ Pick
ALT-*number*	Switches to window with that number
CTRL-A	/Style ¦ Alignment
CTRL-C	/Edit ¦ Copy
CTRL-D	Enters a date
CTRL-E	/Edit ¦ Erase Block
CTRL-F	/Style ¦ Numeric Format
CTRL-G	/Graph ¦ Fast Graph
CTRL-I	/Edit ¦ Insert
CTRL-M	/Edit ¦ Move
CTRL-N	/Edit ¦ Search & Replace ¦ Next
CTRL-P	/Edit ¦ Search & Replace ¦ Previous
CTRL-R	/Window ¦ Move ¦ Size
CTRL-S	/File ¦ Save
CTRL-T	/Window ¦ Tile
CTRL-W	/Style ¦ Column Width
CTRL-X	/File ¦ Exit

FUNCTION KEYS

Keys	Function
F1	Help
F2	Edit
F3	Choices (displays block names)
F4	Abs (adds $ to absolute cell references)
F5	GoTo
F6	Pane (moves between panes of a window)
F7	Query
F8	Table
F9	Calc (recalculates manually)
F10	Graph
ALT-F2	Macro menu
ALT-F3	Function menu
SHIFT-F2	Debug
SHIFT-F3	Macro commands
SHIFT-F7	Select (mark blocks)

ERROR MESSAGES

This is a *partial* list—see the Quattro Pro manual for complete list.

Message	Meaning
Cannot open: *file*	Quattro Pro cannot find a file by the name you specified. Check the file name and the drive or directory specification.
Directory does not exist	You specified a directory that does not exist. Check to see that you have the correct path name.
Drive not ready	The disk drive is not ready to read or write. Check to make sure a disk is in the drive and the door is closed.
File not found	Quattro Pro cannot find the file you specified. Make sure the file name and drive specification (path) are correct. If using a floppy disk, make sure the correct disk is in the drive.
Incomplete formula	The formula as it is entered is incomplete. Re-enter the formula, checking that all parts are entered properly.
Invalid cell or block address	The block you specified is not valid. Re-enter the cell locations for the block, separated by a period.
Invalid spreadsheet file	You tried to retrieve a file that Quattro Pro cannot read.
No block defined	The command requires a block of cells, but no block is specified. Specify a block, and then select the command again.
Printer I/O errors	The printer is not ready to print. Make sure the printer is turned on, is connected to the computer, and has paper. Then try printing again.
Syntax error	The format of the formula is incorrect. Change the format.

Index